JOURNAL FOR THE STUDY OF THE NEW TESTAMENT
SUPPLEMENT SERIES
197

Sheffield Academic Press

Making Sense in (and of) the First Christian Century

F. Gerald Downing

Journal for the Study of the New Testament
Supplement Series 197

Copyright © 2000 Sheffield Academic Press

Published by
Sheffield Academic Press Ltd
Mansion House
19 Kingfield Road
Sheffield S11 9AS
England

Typeset by Sheffield Academic Press
and
Printed on acid-free paper in Great Britain
by Bookcraft Ltd
Midsomer Norton, Bath

British Library Cataloguing in Publication Data

A catalogue record for this book is available
from the British Library

ISBN 1-84127-124-1

CONTENTS

ACKNOWLEDGMENTS

Nine of these linked studies have appeared in other publications, mostly in the last decade; one will appear at around the same time as this volume. The three most recently prepared appear here for the first time.

I wish to express my thanks to editors and presses for their kind permission to reprint the following:

' "Honor" among Exegetes', *CBQ* 61.1 (1999), pp. 53-73.

'The Ambiguity of "The Pharisee and the Toll-Collector", Luke 18:9-14 in the Greco-Roman World of Late Antiquity', *CBQ* 54.1 (1992), pp. 80-99.

'The Woman from Syro-Phoenicia and her Doggedness', in G.J. Brooke (ed.), *Women in the Biblical Tradition*, (Lewiston: Edwin Mellen Press, 1992), pp. 130-49.

'Cynics and Christians, Oedipus and Thyestes', *JEH* 44.1 (1993), pp. 1-10.

'Deeper Reflections on the Jewish Cynic Jesus', *JBL* 117.1 (1998), pp. 97-104.

'Common Strands in Pagan, Jewish and Christian Eschatologies', *ThZ* 51.3 (1995), pp. 197-211.

'Magic and Scepticism in and around the First Christian Century', in T. Klutz (ed.), *Magic* (Sheffield: Sheffield Academic Press, forthcoming).

'Ontological Asymmetry in Philo and Christological Realism in Paul, Hebrews and John', *JTS* (NS) 41.2 (1990), pp. 423-40.

'Interpretation and the 'Culture Gap', *SJT* 40 (1987), pp. 161-71.

'Reflecting the First Century', *ExpT* 95 (1982), pp. 176-77.

Most of these studies have been shared early on in their time with the Ehrhardt Biblical Seminar in the Department of Religions and Theology in the University of Manchester, the kindness and help of whose members I also acknowledge. I gratefully acknowledge the honorary research fellowship which I currently enjoy.

Some small revisions have been made (in style of punctuation, bibliographical details, etc.) and in some of the introductions and conclusions.

ABBREVIATIONS

AB	Anchor Bible
ABD	David Noel Freedman (ed), *The Anchor Bible Dictionary* (New York: Doubleday, 1992)
AC	*L'antiquité classique*
AGJU	Arbeiten zur Geschichte des antike Judentums und des Ur-christentums
AHES	*Archive for History of Exact Sciences*
ANF	Ante Nicene Fathers
AJP	*American Journal of Philology*
ANRW	Hildegard Temporini and Wolfgang Haase (eds), *Aufstieg und Niedergang der römischen Welt: Geschichte und Kultur Roms im Spiegel der neueren Forschung* (Berlin: W de Gruyter, 1972–)
ASNS	*Annali della Scuole Normale Superiore*
BBET	Beiträge zur biblischen Exegese und Theologie
BETL	Bibliotheca ephemeridum theologicarum lovaniensum
BHT	Beiträge zur historischen Theologie
Bib	*Biblica*
BibInt	*Biblical Interpretation: A Journal of Contemporary Approaches*
BIS	Biblical Interpretation Series
BNTC	Black's New Testament Commentaries
BR	*Bible Review*
BS	The Biblical Seminar
BSP	Bochumer Studien zur Philosophie
BTB	*Biblical Theology Bulletin*
BZ	*Biblische Zeitschrift*
CBQ	*Catholic Biblical Quarterly*
CCWJC	Cambridge Commentaries on Writings of the Jewish and Christian World 200 BC to AD 200
CH	*Church History*
CNT	Commentaire du Nouveau Testament
CQ	*Church Quarterly*
CS	Classical Studies
CurTM	*Currents in Theology and Mission*
EKKNT	Evangelisch-Katholischer Kommentar zum Neuen Testament

EKL	E. Faldbusch *et al.* (eds.) *Evangelisches Kirchenlexikon: Internationale theologische Kirchenlexikon* (5 vols.; Gottingen: Vandenhoeck & Ruprecht, 1986)
EPRO	Études préliminaires aux religions orientales dans l'empire romain
ESHM	European Seminar in Historical Methodology
EvT	*Evangelische Theologie*
ExpTim	*Expository Times*
FRLANT	Forschungen zur Religion und Literatur des Alten und Neuen Testaments
FB	Forschung zur Bibel
GR	*Greece and Rome*
GRR	*Graeco-Roman Religion*
GTA	Göttingen theologische Arbeiten
HCS	Hellenistic Culture and Society
HeyJ	*Heythrop Journal*
HTK	Herders Theologischer Kommentar zum Neuen Testament (Freiburg: Herder, 1976–)
HTR	*Harvard Theological Review*
HTS	Harvard Theological Studies
IBS	*Irish Biblical Studies*
ICC	International Critical Commentary
IDB	George Arthur Buttrick (ed.), *The Interpreter's Dictionary of the Bible* (4 vols.; Nashville: Abingdon Press, 1962)
Int	*Interpretation*
JAC	*Jahrbuch für Antike und Christentum*
JAP	*Journal of Applied Philosophy*
JBL	*Journal of Biblical Literature*
JEH	*Journal of Ecclesiastical History*
JfSJ	*Journal for the Study of Judaism*
JHC	*Journal of Higher Criticism*
JHS	*Journal of Hellenic Studies*
JJS	*Journal of Jewish Studies*
JQR	*Jewish Quarterly Review*
JR	*Journal of Religion*
JRS	*Journal of Roman Studies*
JSJ	*Journal for the Study of Judaism in the Persian, Hellenistic and Roman Period*
JSNT	*Journal for the Study of the New Testament*
JSNTSup	*Journal for the Study of the New Testament*, Supplement Series
JSOT	*Journal for the Study of the Old Testament*
JSOTSup	*Journal for the Study of the Old Testament*, Supplement Series
JTS	*Journal of Theological Studies*
KEK	Kritische-exegetische Kommentar

LCL	Loeb Classical Library
LCM	*Liverpool Classical Monthly*
Mod C	*Modern Churchman* (now *Modern Believing*)
NCB	New Century Bible
Neot	*Neotestamentica*
NIGTC	New International Greek Testament Commentary
NPNF	Nicene and Post-Nicene Fathers
NovT	*Novum Testamentum*
NovTSup	*Novum Testamentum*, Supplements
NTS	*New Testament Studies*
NTT	*Nederlands Theologisch Tijdschrift*
NTD	Das Neue Testament Deutsch
NTOA	Novum Testamentum et orbis antiquus
OTP	James Charlesworth (ed.), *Old Testament Pseudepigrapha*
PA	Philosophia Antiqua
PG	J.-P. Migne (ed.), *Patrologia cursus completa…* *Series graeca* (166 vols.; Paris: Petit-Montrouge, 1857–83)
PL	J.-P. Migne (ed.), *Patrologia cursus completus…* *Series prima [latina]* (221 vols.; Paris: J.-P. Migne, 1844–65)
PRE	G. Wissowa (ed.), *Paulys Realencyclopädie der classischen Altentumwissenschaft* (Stuttgart: Metzlerscher, 1893–)
PRE Supp.	*Paulys Realencyclopädie*, Supplementband; from 1951, Stuttgart: Druckenmüller
RAC	*Reallexikon für Antike und Christentum*
RelS	*Religious Studies*
RNT	Regensburger Neues Testament
RPA	*Revue de philosophie ancienne*
RQ	*Restoration Quarterly*
RTL	*Revue théologique de Louvain*
RTP	*Revue de théologie et de philosophie*
SBB	Stuttgarter biblische Beiträge
SBLDS	Society of Biblical Literature Dissertation Series
SBLSBS	Society of Biblical Literature Sources for Biblical Study
SBLTT	Society of Biblical Literature Texts and Translations
SBS	Stuttgarter Bibelstudien
SBT	Studies in Biblical Theology
SHTC	*Studies in the History of Christian Thought*
SJT	*Scottish Journal of Theology*
SNTS	Society for New Testament Studies/Studiorum Novi Testamenti Societas
SNTSMS	Society of Biblical Studies Monograph Series
SJP	*Southern Journal of Philosophy*
SWR	Studies in Women and Religion
TAPA	*Transactions of the American Philological Association*

TDNT	Gerhard Kittel and Gerhard Friedrich (eds.), *Theological Dictionary of the New Testament* (trans. Geoffrey W. Bromiley; 10 vols.; Grand Rapids: Eerdmans, 1964–)
TJT	*Toronto Journal of Theology*
TWNT	Gerhard Kittel and Gerhard Friedrich (eds.), *Theologisches Wörterbuch zum Neuen Testament* (11 vols.; Stuttgart, Kohlhammer, 1932–79)
TU	Texte und Untersuchungen zur Geschichte der altchristlichen Literatur, ed. O. von Gebhurdt and A. von Harnack (Leipzig; J.C. Heinrichs, 1891–; from 1952, Berlin: Akademie Verlag).
TynBul	*Tyndale Bulletin*
TZ	*Theologische Zeitschrift*
VC	*Vigiliae christianae*
WBC	Word Biblical Commentary
WMANT	Wissenschaftliche Monographien zum Alten und Neuen Testament
WUNT	Wissenschaftliche Untersuchungen zum Neuen Testament
YCS	Yale Classical Studies
ZNW	*Zeitschrift für die neutestamentliche Wissenschaft*
ZTK	*Zeitschrift für Theologie und Kirche*

INTRODUCTION

It has been very refreshing and illuminating for many of us to find more and more colleagues taking a careful interest in the wider social world of the early Christians. Too often in the past exegetes have treated these early followers of Jesus as though they comprised a theological club, with no other concerns, no other context and no other pressures (with the possible exception of imagined Roman thought-police). Among the insights gained of late have been not a few from social anthropology. Yet disappointment may swiftly follow. It has been all too easy (despite disclaimers) for social anthropologists' models to be imposed on the ancient sources, rather than deployed heuristically, as research tools.

This collection begins with an essay which has appeared quite recently in one of the journals: ' "Honour" among Exegetes'. Some scholars would assure us emphatically that a uniform sense of honour and shame was dominant over all other concerns in the ancient Mediterranean world, though quite alien to 'us north-westerners'. Yet, on the contrary, and on the basis of readily available ancient and modern evidence, it can readily be shown that neither generalization is valid.

The scholars who risk imposing models from social anthropology also tell us that people in the ancient Mediterranean world had a very different implicit sense of being a person, 'dyadic' and dependent on others' attitudes and reactions, not 'monadic' and individualist as most of 'us' are taken to be. Again such assertions need to be checked more carefully against both modern and ancient evidence. 'Persons in Relation' (Ch. 2) aims to show that at least some modern philosophy of social psychology and quite a wide range of ancient texts contradict both sides of the comparison. 'We' are often as 'dyadic' as were any in the past; and people in the past can evince as much individual self-awareness as any we are likely to discover among ourselves.

On the other hand we can often in other contexts far too easily assume that our own unreflective ways of articulating common concerns are universal. Exegetes note that our New Testament texts talk of releasing people from their faults or debts; but because we prefer the shorter expressions, 'forgive' and 'forgiveness', they and we use just these words, and then take it for granted that the older authors are saying what we intend in our common usage of them. 'Forgivingness? Or Forgiveness? Or the Remission of Offences?' (Ch. 3) argues that there is a noteworthy difference, it is not a mere matter of convenient abbreviation. (Which sets of these words, if any, we then use remains, of course, in our hands.)

Sweeping generalizations about the ancient world (whether explicit as in talk of 'honour', or implicit as in talk of 'forgiveness') warrant grave suspicion (as does the immediately foregoing itself until it has been given some backing!). Chapter 4, 'The Ambiguity of "The Pharisee and the Toll Collector"' attempts to show something of the diversity of opinions recorded among ancient Graeco-Roman authors on the issues of repentance, self-humiliation and the forgiveness of offences that seem to be touched on in the parable. There is often no simple clarity available. The ancient world was very varied, as were many of its religious and other groups. But this chapter also attempts to offer a model for the first stage of an investigation of New Testament material in context, focusing in turn on various conventionally distinguished cultural settings. (A full investigation demands something like the approach of Vernon K. Robbins, in his analysis of 'inner texture', 'intertexture', 'social and cultural texture' and 'ideological texture', once spade-work as thorough as this or better still has been done.)[1]

A similar approach is exemplified in Chapter 5, 'The Woman from Syrophoenicia, and her Doggedness'. It is still the case that many investigations of early Christian life end abruptly with a particular writer's date for the completion of the New Testament canon of writings. Interpretations of the earliest texts offered by authors who lived much nearer to the first Christian century demand attention, and here it is noted that John Chrysostom and others pick up the Cynic resonances in the story that more nearly contemporary parallels would anyway indicate.

---

1.   V.K. Robbins, *The Tapestry of Early Christian Discourse: Rhetoric, Society and Ideology* (London: Routledge, 1996); and *idem*, *Exploring the Texture of Texts* (Valley Forge, PA: Trinity Press International, 1996); and cf. the appraisal in F.G. Downing, 'Le problème du choix de l'intertexte: Paul, s'oppose-t-il radicalement ou superficiellement à la culture de son temps?', in D. Marguerat and A. Curtis (eds.), *Intertextualités: La Bible en échos* (La Monde de la Bible, 40; Geneva: Labor et Fides, 2000), pp. 238-50.

'Deeper Reflections on the Jewish Cynic Jesus' (Ch. 6) places the Cynic issues on a wider stage, and responds to various repeated but poorly evidenced responses to my *Cynics and Christian Origins*, and other writing on the theme.[2]

Cynicism, with its outrageous 'naturalism', needs also to be considered as part of the setting for the 'reception' of early Christianity, charged with indulging in incest and cannibalism. This is investigated in 'Cynics and Christians, Oedipus and Thyestes' (Ch. 7). Cynic philosophy is a more likely context for the accusations, rather than the mystery cults standardly proposed but never in fact in our ancient texts faced with these combined accusations.

(I address the question of when Christians were first publicly charged on these and other counts—perhaps as early as the late first century CE —in my 'Pliny's Prosecutions of Christians: Revelation and 1 Peter'. This has already been reprinted once, so does not appear here. Pliny can find no records of such action in the sources to which he has regular access on other issues, sources including provinces where Christians are thought first to have been arraigned. There were no precedents; Pliny's own cases (around 110–12 CE) constitute the 'fiery trial' which the hearers of 1 Peter and Revelation were facing.)[3]

One criticism advanced against various proposals of a Christian Cynicism is that they do not give sufficient weight to eschatology in the teaching attributed to Jesus. In actual fact I myself insist on retaining such material in my own reconstructions of Jesus' message—I try to portray him as taking strands from various sources (as many other Jewish teachers did, of course). One of the alternative reconstructions much canvassed of late focuses on a posited belief supposedly current among all or at least most of Jesus' Jewish predecessors and contemporaries and then also held by Jesus himself, a belief to the effect that all Jews were still in a state of punitive 'exile' since the sixth-century fall of Jerusalem; an exile for whose ending Jesus—and various others—thought themselves the divinely appointed agents. Chapter 8, 'Exile in Formative Judaism', argues that positive evidence for such an idea is confined

---

2.   In particular, F.G. Downing, *Christ and the Cynics* (JSOT Manuals, 4; Sheffield: JSOT Press, 1988) and *Cynics and Christian Origins* (Edinburgh: T. & T. Clark, 1992).

3.   F.G. Downing, 'Pliny's Prosecutions of Christians: Revelation and 1 Peter', *JSNT* 34 (1988), pp. 105-23; repr. in S.E. Porter and C.A. Evans (eds.), *The Johannine Writings* (BS, 32; Sheffield: Sheffield Academic Press, 1995), pp. 232-49.

to one strand in the Dead Sea Scrolls. For the rest a great variety of expectations emerge.

It is also often still taken for granted that 'eschatology' is a concern restricted to Jewish people, only they thought in a linear, essentially 'historical' mode, while 'Greek thought' was essentially cyclical (yet another sweeping generalization). 'Common Strands in Pagan, Jewish and Christian Eschatologies' (Ch. 9) attempts to correct this conclusion. There is variety in all strands, and overlap among the strands. (A companion piece, detailing Epicurean motifs in Jewish and Christian eschatologies, is not reprinted here.)[4]

The foregoing studies deploy (neo-)Platonic, Stoic, Peripatetic, Cynic and Epicurean sources, 'highbrow' and more popular.[5] There is—quite properly—less of an inclination these days than once there was to imagine any immediate influence of Platonism (through Philo of Alexandria, or other assimilators) in our New Testament authors. However, Philo is still often used as a foil: 'If even Philo didn't think that way, then simpler, more traditional folk cannot be supposed to have done so.' In Chapter 10, 'Ontological Asymmetry in Philo and Christological Realism in Paul, Hebrews and John', there are countered arguments of J.D.G. Dunn and others to the effect that figures such as 'the Logos' are for Philo (and so, for other contemporaries) 'only' ideas in God's mind. On more careful examination, some 'ideas in God's mind' turn out to be 'more real' (!) for Philo than humans are. That for Christians Christ as Word of God, Son of God, could have been 'real' ('really alive') before his birth as Jesus of Nazareth was certainly thinkable: a relevant conceptual apparatus was available. (Whether any early Christians used it is another question.)[6]

Some—including the present author—nonetheless find it difficult to use for themselves concepts such as 'imminent eschatology' or 'onto-

---

4.   F.G. Downing, 'Cosmic Eschatology in the First Century: "Pagan", Jewish and Christian', *AC* 64 (1995), pp. 99-109.

5.   For a defence of this procedure, F.G. Downing, 'A bas les aristos: The Relevance of Higher Literature for the Understanding of Early Christianity', *NovT* 30.3 (1988), pp. 212-30; to be reprinted as ch. 1 of *idem, Doing Things with Words in the First Christian Century* (JSNTSup, 200; Sheffield: Sheffield Academic Press, 2000).

6.   A shorter piece of mine on Philo and the New Testament has been reprinted elsewhere already: 'The Resurrection of the Dead: Jesus and Philo', *JSNT* 15 (1982), pp. 42-50; repr. in S.E. Porter and C.A. Evans, *The Historical Jesus* (BS, 33; Sheffield: Sheffield Academic Press, 1995), pp. 167-75.

logical asymmetry' (of Jesus or any other figure). In the same way, the ancient practice of magic (Ch. 11) might seem to put us out of reach of the first Christian century. Is the past not a completely 'foreign country', where 'they do things differently', to such an extent that we cannot hope to understand them? Is there not a 'culture gap' which we cannot hope to bridge, making all these efforts of which this volume is an example somewhat pointless? I have tried to answer this question in detail in much of the foregoing: on honour and shame, on dyadic personality, and much else. In Chapter 12, 'Interpretation and the Culture Gap', I have tried to argue both theoretically and with the help of detailed examples that it is always a matter of 'more or less', not 'all or nothing', and our best approach to making sense of others making sense is through considering their attitudes to one another, to 'the divine', and to the world around (rather than through technicalities and technologies).[7] People back then often tried to 'make sense' in ways that it is very difficult to differentiate from our own.

In the discussion of Philo's ontology in Chapter 10 there is noted the readiness of modern divines to assert that in the figure of Jesus God is 'revealed', and this is contrasted with the much greater reticence of older theologians. To ground this point the collection ends with a brief study of 1 Cor. 13.12, 'now we see in a glass, darkly', in its contemporary context. (I discussed the whole issue at much greater length in my *Has Christianity a Revelation?* and responded to some criticisms of that volume in 'Revelation, Disagreement and Obscurity'.)[8]

In his *Exploring the Texture of Texts*, Vernon Robbins argues persuasively the need for authors or readers to come clean about themselves.[9] I do not readily deploy the typology he adopts from Bryan Wilson, but I do accept that readers have a right to have some indication of where or how a study may be driven by more than the surface arguments. My family of origin was middle class, comfortable by being careful, never hungry; we were practising Anglicans, my parents conservative. I attended state 'grammar' schools, and read theology at Oxford in the

---

7. See in particular, F.G. Downing, *Strangely Familiar: An Introductory Reader to the First Century, to the Life and Loves, the Hopes and Fears, the Doubts and Certainties, of Pagans Jews and Christians* (Manchester: Downing, 1985; current address if wanted in SNTS or SBL lists.)

8. F.G. Downing, *Has Christianity a Revelation?* (London: SCM Press, 1964); 'Revelation, Disagreement and Obscurity', *RelS* 21 (1986), pp. 219-30.

9. Robbins, *The Tapestry*, pp. 24-25; *Exploring the Texture of Texts*, pp. 96-99.

mid-1950s, convinced of a call to ordination. Diana, my wife, with her faith, liveliness, insights, cultural interests and environmental concerns, sustains and enriches me. I have served 25 years as an Anglican parish priest, and 14 helping others train for ordained ministry. I have been a member of the Labour party since 1962, a middling socialist to the left of Tony Blair. The world-affirming ascetic Jesus I find in the synoptic tradition continues to draw me and disturb my more settled convictions even if he often has regrettably scant effect on my attitudes and actions. On the other hand, I do not think I adapt my sketch of him to suit my politics, my concern for the two-thirds world, our global environment, and so forth. I would have liked to find him a socialist, but know that the evidence does not support the wish. I do not expect him to have said or stimulated the saying of all that needs to be said.

My main theological project in retirement is an exploration of resources for incarnational and trinitarian, and other Christologies. I remain 'catholic' and critical, retaining the catholic agnosticism of my first major publication (1964), which rebutted modernist claims that God is 'revealed' to us in or through Jesus.[10] However, I find explicit 'post-modernism' too dogmatic to be convincing.

In various writings I have joined with those who insist it is more important to try to change the world for the better than to interpret it. But we still need some understanding of what we seek to change, and struggling to make sense of people in the first century trying to make sense of their world—and even to change it, or aspects of it, for the better—may drive us to try to understand our own a little more clearly, and even a mite more humbly. Christians of various sorts among us may have particularly precious reasons to make the effort.

---

10. Downing, *Has Christianity a Revelation?*; for the aspirations, see *idem, A Man for Us and a God for Us* (London: Epworth Press, 1968); and *Jesus and the Threat of Freedom* (London: SCM Press, 1987).

Chapter 1

'HONOUR' AMONG EXEGETES*

Included in a passage in Luke devoted to mealtimes is a pericope whose overriding concerns are quite clearly 'honour' and 'shame':

> When you are invited by anyone to a marriage feast, do not sit down in the most prominent place, lest a more honourable man (ἐντιμότερός) than you be invited by him, and the one who invited both of you comes and says to you, 'Give place to this man', and then you begin with shame (μετὰ αἰσχύνης) to take the lowest place. But when you are invited, go and sit in the lowest place, so that when your host comes he may say to you, 'Friend, go up higher'. Then you will be honoured (ἔσται σοι δόξα) in the presence of all who sit at table with you (Lk. 14.8-10).

1. *Honour to whom Honour is Due*

This Lucan 'parable' concentrates on honour and shame to the exclusion of all else. There is no reference to the couple being wedded, to the food or drink, to hunger or thirst, to the quality of the conversation or other entertainment, to the wealth or poverty of the host and his guests, to the size of his family, to the setting in city, town or village... It is all *about* shame and honour, your relative place in the respect of others around you and your own awareness of it. And this is a matter of unargued and overwhelming importance.

These sensitivities of guests at a meal are also commonplace in the ancient world, as the commentators have noted. Luke's concern is just rather more blatant than that expressed for instance by Plutarch:

*   Reprinted from *CBQ* 61.1 (1999), pp. 53-73, by kind permission. Biblical quotations in English are basically from the Revised Standard Version, with minimal further revisions by the present author. The American spelling of 'honour', etc., is retained in some quotations. There are a small number of other minor revisions.

> When we have taken our places...we ought not to try to discover who
> has been placed above us, but rather how we may be thoroughly agree-
> able to those placed with us, by trying at once to discover in them
> something that may serve to initiate and maintain friendship...For, in
> every case, a man who objects to his place at table is objecting to his
> neighbour rather than his host, and makes himself objectionable to both.[1]

By glancing at a concordance one will see how often the vocabulary
of respect, of honour and shame is deployed in the New Testament writings. Roman Christians are to 'pay all their dues: taxes...revenue, respect to whom respect is due, honour to whom honour is due' (Rom.
13.7).[2] Those who persevere in well-doing are obviously seeking 'glory
and honour' (Rom. 2.7), which is what Jesus has already won (Heb. 2.9;
2 Pet. 1.17).[3] It is obvious to Paul that for men and women conformity
with conventional hair styles will be a matter of pride or shame (1 Cor.
11.13-15). He hopes the Corinthians will have completed their promised collection for Jerusalem before his arrival, lest he—and they—be
put to shame (2 Cor. 9.4); and so on.

According to some recent social historians of the New Testament
honour and shame are the 'pivotal social values', the 'core values' for
the Mediterranean world of which Jesus and the first Christians were a
part.[4] The impression conveyed is that this concern for respect is more

---

1.   Plutarch, *The Dinner of the Seven Wise Men* 149AB, in F.C. Babbit (trans.),
Plutarch's Moralia, II (LCL; 16 vols.; London: Heinemann; Cambridge, MA: Har-
vard University Press, 1928), pp. 363-65; cited by W. Braun, *Feasting and Social
Rhetoric in Luke 14* (SNTSMS, 85; Cambridge: Cambridge University Press, 1995)
p. 46, along with many other references. With Braun I would take Lk. 14.8-10 as a
Lucan construction.

2.   See especially H. Moxnes, 'Honour and Righteousness in Romans', *JSNT*
32 (1988), pp. 61-77.

3.   On Hebrews, see D.A. deSilva, 'Despising Shame: A Cultural-Anthropological Investigation of the Epistle to the Hebrews', *JBL* 113.3 (1994), pp. 439-61.

4.   'Pivotal social values' according to B.J. Malina and J.H. Neyrey, 'Honor
and Shame in Luke–Acts: Pivotal Values of the Mediterranean World', in J.H.
Neyrey (ed.), *The Social World of Luke–Acts: Models for Interpretation* (Peabody,
MA: Hendrickson, 1991), pp. 24-46; B.J. Malina, *The New Testament World: Insights from Cultural Anthropology* (Louisville: Westminster/John Knox Press, rev.
edn, 1993), pp. 28-62; P.F. Esler, *The First Christians in their Social Worlds:
Social-Scientific Approaches to New Testament Interpretation* (London: Routledge,
1994), p. 25. 'Core': J. Plevnik, 'Honor/Shame' in J.J. Pilch and B.J. Malina (eds.),
Biblical Social Values and their Meaning (Peabody, MA: Hendrickson, 1993), pp.

1. 'Honour' among Exegetes

than an occasional significant feature, it is both pervasive and dominant; but it is also alien to those of us brought up in Western Europe or
North America, we are unlikely to understand it or discern it, or even be
willing to perceive it in the texts, although it really (often? always?)
constitutes *the* clue to their understanding. A deciphering of this alien
code by the anthropologically initiated becomes indispensable.

Honour to whom honour is due. If we are concerned at all with the
New Testament world, we must be grateful to those who attempt to en-
large and enrich and refine the insights available to us. So I intend here
to argue that 'respect' ('honour and shame') is *an* issue of which we
need to be aware, but that it is only dominant, ('pivotal'), central ('the
core') when and where it is clearly shown to be (as in our first example). But then, as such it is by no means foreign to us westerners. Further, if the issues are to afford us a useful heuristic or hermeneutical
tool, they need to be much more carefully analysed and argued than
they seem to have been in much recent writing that has come my way.
In what follows I shall first attempt an appraisal of the model as it is
deployed by some leading exponents, and then, second, sketch some
typical examples where 'honour and shame' are clearly far from dominant concerns, where they are secondary, or are accorded no attention at
all.

2. *'Honour and Shame' as a Heuristic or Hermeneutical Tool*

a. *Just how Alien to us are Concerns for Honour and Shame?*
Perhaps we may start with the supposed strangeness of such ideas to
West Europeans and North Americans. 'In Western culture, it is not
honor and shame so much as guilt that drives human behavior.'[5] Two of
the cultural anthropologists most quoted by New Testament social historians in this connection are J.G. Peristiany and J. Pitt-Rivers. With

---

95-104 (95) (as my original essay appeared in *CBQ* this article was mis-ascribed to
J.J. Pilch, whom I thank for kindly pointing out the mistake); see also the brief
introductory remarks in D.A. deSilva, 'The Wisdom of Ben Sira: Honor, Shame
and the Maintenance of the Values of a Minority Culture', *CBQ* 58 (1996), pp. 433-
35. The (older) dictionaries of the Bible are not very helpful. In *TDNT* only R. Bultmann, 'αἰδώς' (I, pp. 169-71) and 'αἰσχύνη' (I, pp. 189-91) indicates the possible
importance of the themes; G. Kittel and G. von Rad', δοκέω, δόξα' (II, pp. 232-55)
and J. Schneider, 'τιμή' (8, pp. 169-80) are too tied to the occurrences of the particular words.
  5.   Plevnik, 'Honor/Shame', p. 103.

reference to an earlier and formative collection of essays, they write that
some readers concluded, wrongly,

> that the use of the word 'shame' in the title implied that we considered
> the culture of the Mediterranean...a 'shame culture' rather than a 'guilt
> culture', a distinction that had been launched originally by Margaret
> Mead, but that had convinced us of its utility no more than it had Alfred
> Kroeber...It appears to us that the distinction had been lifted from the
> popular philosophy of the anglophone countries and applied in fields
> where its relevance was dubious, for the sentiment of shame seems to be
> universal and guilt is simply internalised shame...[6]

Whether or not we are driven by guilt, is a concern for 'honour and
shame' really 'alien to most North Europeans'?[7] In the earlier collection Peristiany wrote already that 'all societies have their own forms of
honour and shame', that among various societies there are 'significant
analogies' and 'equally significant differences';[8] and Pitt-Rivers in-
stanced concepts of honour in contemporary Anglo-Saxon countries,
where honour is acquired 'through the fact of possession' rather than
'through the act of beneficence'.[9] From the kind of shoe to the size of
desk to the model of company car; from the 'statement' made by the
kind of lager one drinks to the fate of the town football team, from the
motorist 'cut up' at the traffic lights to the teacher rebuked before his or
her pupils, today's Western society has its own formulas for respect
maintained, lost, or gained.

---

6.   The editors' introduction in J.G. Peristiany and J. Pitt-Rivers (eds.), *Honor
and Grace in Anthropology* (Cambridge Studies in Social Anthropology, 76; Cambridge: Cambridge University Press, 1992), p. 6. The earlier collection to which
they refer is J.G. Peristiany (ed.), *Honour and Shame: The Values of Mediterranean
Society* (London: Weidenfeld & Nicolson, 1965). In mentioning Alfred Kroeber,
they have in mind his *Anthropology: Race, Language, Culture, Psychology, Prehistory* (New York: Harcourt, Brace & World, rev. edn, 1948).

7.   The claim that it is alien to most North Europeans has been made by Esler,
First Christians, p. 27; cf. Malina and Neyrey, 'Honor and Shame in Luke–Acts',
p. 26; J.H. Neyrey, 'Despising the Shame of the Cross: Honor and Shame in the
Johannine Passion Narrative', in V.H. Matthews and D.C. Benjamin (eds.), *Honor
and Shame in the World of the Bible* (Semeia, 68; Atlanta: Scholars Press, 1996),
pp. 113-37 (115).

8.   The editor's introduction in Peristiany (ed.), *Honour and Shame*, pp. 9-10.

9.   J. Pitt-Rivers, 'Honour and Social Status', in J.G. Peristiany (ed.), *Honour
and Shame: The Values of Mediterranean Society* (London: Weidenfeld & Nicolson,
1965), pp. 19-77 (60).

For sure, the term 'honour' (as a personal possession or property) is little used in current British and perhaps also American English, but then, it appears, is applied either to some public award or to an internalized sense of (or insistence on) one's own integrity. A person 'of honour' is one who would act honourably whether doing so gained them respect or not. When 'honour' (and 'shame') are then used as technical, anthropological terms for public social phenomena, which, we are assured, are foreign to us, we seem to be encouraged to rely without further question on those experts who claim to understand this alien ancient ubiquitous concept. If, instead, we use terms like 'respect', 'embarrassment', 'disgrace', and so forth, and in ways we are more used to, it may be easier to avoid being mystified. We clearly have more in common with the ancient Mediterranean world than the technical terminology might indicate.

b. *Just how Uniform is Concern for Honour and Shame?*
When Pitt-Rivers and Peristiany wrote their seminal essays about 'Mediterranean society', they were trying to describe and analyse similarities *and differences* in societies they had themselves investigated in person in the middle of the twentieth century. They insisted that there were still considerable differences in fact between countries and epochs, so that honour is 'never a matter of homogeneous abstract principles', and in some instances the origins of such a feature of a given culture are importantly traced to non-Mediterranean sources.[10] Peristiany commented later,

> Our aim in treating the Mediterranean as a whole was epistemological only, and we never attempted to define it geographically. Thus when mention is made of 'the Mediterranean concept of honor' we recognise that it

---

10. Pitt-Rivers, 'Honour and Social Status', pp. 38-39. On this see, importantly, J.K. Chance, 'The Anthropology of Honor and Shame: Culture, Values and Practice', in V.H. Matthews and D.C. Benjamin (eds.), *Honor and Shame in the World of the Bible* (Semeia, 68; Atlanta: Scholars Press, 1966), pp. 139-51 (144-45), who appreciates the intentions of Neyrey and others but criticizes their performance; he quotes in particular M. Herzfeld, ('Honor and Shame: Problems in the Comparative Analysis of Moral Systems', *Man* 15 [1980] pp. 339-51 [349]): 'Massive generalizations of "honour" and "shame" have become counterproductive'. See also D.A. deSilva, *Despising Shame: Honor Discourse and Community Maintenance in the Epistle to the Hebrew* (SBLDS, 152; Atlanta: Scholars Press, 1995), p. 15.

> indicates a tendency to associate masculine honor with female purity only
> rather vaguely, for there are areas near the Mediterranean where this
> connection is not made at all, for example certain areas of northern Spain
> or the Mzab or Ouled Naïl of Algeria, and that in any case there is
> considerable variation within what is loosely termed...the Mediterranean
> concept of honor.[11]

Yet without further argument (so far as I can detect), scholars such as
Malina, Neyrey, Pilch, Plevnik and Esler generalize a simplified form
of the observations of Peristiany and Pitt-Rivers and their associates to
cover 'the Mediterranean world...in general'[12] without differentiation,
and at a time two thousand years before our own. To assume that questions about 'honour', 'respect', and 'shame' are worth asking is one
thing; to assume that these issues are pervasive, dominant, and largely
uniform, is quite another. In fact the authors here criticized do at times
allow for the possibility that what 'counts as' honourable in one setting
may not in another.[13] But this seems to have little effect on their exegesis of particular passages. In particular, we meet generalizations about
women in the supposed system without any allowance for the possible
variations noted for recent times by Pitt-Rivers and Peristiany, no attention, for instance, to the differences linked with class and locality Pitt-
Rivers found in mid-twentieth century Spain. No, 'honour is *always*
male and shame is *always* female.'[14] We are not told how this affects
'honouring' mother as well as father, or the 'honourable women' Luke
finds in Pisidian Antioch and Beroea (Acts 13.50; 17.12); nor how this
relates to Plutarch's discussion of womanly excellence, γυναικῶν
ἀρετῆς:

11. The editors' introduction in Peristiany and Pitt-Rivers (eds.), *Honor and
Grace*, p. 6. The quotation, condensed by the editors in *CBQ*, is here given in full.
12. Malina, *New Testament World*, ch. 2, *passim*; Malina and Neyrey, 'Honor
and Shame', p. 26; Plevnik, 'Honor/Shame', p. 95; Esler, *First Christians*, p. 25.
13. Malina and Neyrey, 'Honor and Shame', pp. 26-27; cf. Plevnik, 'Honor/
Shame', p. 97; deSilva, 'Wisdom of Ben Sira', p. 434.
14. Malina, *New Testament World*, pp. 49-51; Malina and Neyrey, 'Honor and
Shame in Luke–Acts', p. 44; Plevnik, 'Honor/Shame', p. 96. Compare, again,
Chance, 'Anthropology of Honor and Shame', p. 141 and pp. 143-44, on objections
to generalizations about female 'shame'; G.M. Kressel, 'An Anthropologist's Response to the Use of Social Science Models in Biblical Studies', in V.H. Matthews
and D.C. Benjamin, *Honor and Shame in the World of the Bible* (Semeia, 68;
Atlanta: Scholars Press, 1966), pp. 153-59.

Regarding the virtue [excellence] of women, Clea, I do not hold the same opinion as Thucydides. For he declares that the best of women is she about whom there is the least talk among people outside regarding either censure or commendation, feeling that the name of the good woman, like her person, ought to be shut up indoors and never go out. But to my mind Gorgias appears to display better taste in advising that not the form but the fame (δόξα) of a woman should be known to many. Best of all seems the Roman custom which publicly renders to woman as to men a fitting commemoration at the end of their life.[15]

Plutarch then recounts a series of traditional stories of women admired —and honoured—for their political courage and good sense. In just one (11) of the many assembled is a womanly sense of shame at stake. Now, it may be that the opinion ascribed to Thucydides could be shown to be 'normal'; but the issue is disputed, and the unsupported generalization about women and honour over the whole first-century Mediterranean world is obviously unjustified.

Further evidence for this conclusion, if it is needed, is provided by recent studies of women as office-holders in Graeco-Roman pagan, Jewish and Christian society in late antiquity. The available data may suggest that there are more instances in some areas than in others of women who are honoured in their own right, but examples can be adduced from Italy, the Balkans, and Egypt, as well as from Asia Minor in particular.[16]

The New Testament social historians under discussion seem quite often to be in conflict with the mentors they claim, and at times among themselves as well. Bruce Malina tells us that disagreement among his disciples dishonours the teacher; but a few pages later assures us that in an elective group the leader's honour is guaranteed.[17] Questions remain unasked and unanswered: where in all this is Mark, for instance? Why does he have Jesus so constantly 'dishonoured' by disciples at odds

15. Plutarch, *Bravery of Women* 242EF, in F.C. Babbitt (trans.), *Plutarch's Moralia*, III (LCL; London, Heinemann; Cambridge, MA: Harvard University Press, 1931), pp. 475-81 (475). γυναικῶν ἀρεταί is perhaps better rendered 'Excellences' or even 'Honour of Women'.

16. See the powerful recent study by Ute E. Eisen, *Amtsträgerinnen in frühen Christentum: Epigraphische und literarische Studien* (Forschungen zur Kirchen- und Dogmengeschichte, 61; Göttingen: Vandenhoeck & Ruprecht, 1996), noting the survey of recent research findings, pp. 34-40.

17. Malina, *New Testament World*, pp. 32 and 48.

with him? (Mk 8.32; 9.18, 34; 10.13-14, 37). Mark even allows a woman to win a point against Jesus (Mk 7.28-29).[18] Commenting on Mark 10.18, 'Why do you call me "good"?' Malina tells us, 'Jesus repudiates the compliment, as any honorable man would.'[19] We can only wonder, then, why Matthew repudiates this honourable repudiation of the compliment (Mt. 19.17).

Malina, arguing against 'some [who] have stated that Jesus acted without concern for honor because he advocated the worth of serving and forgiveness [when] in fact he acted quite in line with honor by claiming the worth of such "female" behavior, which he urged on his followers', states in conclusion that 'honor and shame patterns do not determine what is honorable or shameful'.[20] It begins to look as though everything somehow *must* support the thesis; it is not just that everything *can* be interpreted in accord with it, rather, that nothing could possibly count against it. To value anything is to honour it, and so every system of values becomes an honour system; and then, of course, the thesis becomes vacuous.[21] 'Honour' becomes a concept so polymorphous as to have little or no explanatory value (just as Ptolemaic astronomy or the 'phlogiston' theory could be endlessly harmonized with apparently discrepant findings). A concept which explains everything explains nothing. If claims to honour and refusal of honour are being made to look 'really' or 'fundamentally' the same, then at least we need a fresh terminology that allows us to appreciate the difference in the agents' responses in some other way. The divergent honour systems are then what should concern us, for, as Peristiany insists, 'some societies make much more constant reference than others to these forms of social

18. Cf. F.G. Downing, 'The Syro-Phoenician Woman and her Doggedness', in G.J. Brooke (ed.), *Women in the Biblical Tradition* (Studies in Women and Religion, 31; Lewiston: Edwin Mellen Press, 1992), pp. 129-49, repr. here, ch. 5.

19. Malina, *New Testament World*, p. 99.

20. Malina, *New Testament World*, pp. 53-54.

21. Or, as deSilva ('Wisdom of Ben Sira', p. 435) puts it, 'Honor itself is vacuous apart from culture-specific content.' Plevnik, 'Honor/Shame', p. 93, seems to admit as much: 'the terms "honor" and "shame" are vacant...they are really high context words whose content must be deduced from actual social behavior'. No one is to be allowed to escape entirely; cf. again Chance, 'Anthropology of Honor and Shame', p. 146 (with reference to J.H. Neyrey), 'is the author...perhaps unwittingly projecting his analytical model onto the data?' If we put 'honour' outside every bracket in the equation, we might as well divide through and eliminate it: it adds nothing to our understanding of what lies within.

evaluation',[22] to respect from peers and others. Some rather more care-fully nuanced use of the 'honour and shame' model will be worth con-sidering.

c. *Significant Exceptions*
The example quoted from Luke at the outset could hardly be read in any other way. 'Honour' and 'shame' are the prime concerns at issue.[23] Richard Rohrbaugh (followed with further detailed argument by Willi Braun) has argued, however, that in Luke's following story of the re-fused invitations (Lk. 14.16-24) this same desire for respect, for 'hon-our', continues to be relevant.[24] Those invited may well be supposed to have calculated not only the cost of returning the invitation (a factor alluded to at Lk. 14.12), but also (implicitly) the question whether ac-cepting it would enhance, maintain or diminish their own respective reputations. 'None will risk cutting himself off from his peers.' This latter concern is not stated, but there is enough illustrative material available from the world around to make this reading plausible. The invitees are snubbing the host, dishonouring him with their concocted excuses. It is not the possible waste of food that then seems to anger him. He wants a house full of guests, but now he has to accept a quite different reference group drawn from the poor of the city and even those outside the city. Significantly, both Rohrbaugh and Braun insist explicitly that this is to refuse "the system" of the elite': 'the host appears to turn his back not only against the expected vengeance [of those he had seen as his honorific peers], but against the entire system that governed his original invitation itself'.[25]

We could, of course, still follow Malina's lead and insist that the ple-beian townsfolk and the outsiders from 'the highways and hedges' are now to 'do him the honour' of accepting the host's offer, and so retain the semblance of a dominant honour system—the word, at least. But even then it would still surely be much more significant to register the

22. The editor's introduction in Peristiany (ed.), *Honour and Shame*, p. 10.
23. Braun (*Feasting and Social Rhetoric*, p. 44) notes some strained attempts to read it as other than prudential concern for respect.
24. R. Rohrbaugh, 'The Pre-Industrial City in Luke–Acts', in J.H. Neyrey (ed.), *Social World of Luke–Acts: Models for Interpretation* (Peabody, MA: Hendrickson, 1991), pp. 140-46; cf. Braun, *Feasting and Social Rhetoric*, pp. 96-131.
25. Rohrbaugh, 'Pre-Industrial City', p. 146; Braun, *Feasting and Social Rhet-oric*, pp. 113 and 115.

fact that in terms of the only recognized honour system such guests could win him no honour at all—no honour worth the name. Much better are Rohrbaugh's and Braun's carefully qualified suggestions, making full use of the interpretative insights afforded by this model in the social context for which we have evidence (Lk. 14.8-10 included), and they also allow Luke to have his say both in the story and in his preface to it (Lk. 14.12-14). From the initial prudential advice Luke seems very clearly to move on to exclude the ethic of reciprocity, so central to the working of the honour system. And then, as we have just seen, the climax is this tale where the search for worthwhile honour is entirely abandoned.

Braun and Rohrbaugh impose the honour–shame grid illuminatingly but lightly, so we may discern elements of it that could very well be implicit (though we must repeat, they are still only conjectural, however indicative we find Luke 14.8-10). At the same time, what actually appears to be being said explicitly in rejection of related aspects of the contemporary value system can still be heard. Luke (or Luke and Jesus before him) are allowed to reject any recognizable form of the system; the model does not determine what they are permitted to have said.

If we turn from a discussion of formal meals to accounts of apparently less formal eating, we may again very properly ask questions about respect—honour—sought, accorded, lost, maintained or gained. But we have to *ask* whether these questions represent the 'core', the 'pivotal' concern; or whether they are secondary, or even quite irrelevant. When we take feeding stories in the Gospels as our examples, it is obvious that satisfying the hunger of thousands in the desert would be likely to enhance the reputation of a healer and teacher. Only John (6.14) suggests this response. Should we take it that the other evangelists nonetheless expect us to see Jesus' prime motive as the enhancing of his reputation? We are told that in this 'agonistic' culture almost every social interaction is seen as an opportunity to gain honour, at others' expense.[26] Certainly we could read these stories in this light. In the Feeding of the Five Thousand, the disciples' question 'challenges' Jesus with ignoring the plight of his audience, he 'ripostes' with, 'You give them something to eat', they admit their defeat, and he satisfies the need.[27] But this does not really work. Challenges are accepted only

---

26. Malina, *New Testament World*, p. 37; Esler, *First Christians*, p. 27.

27. 'A request for help is a challenge to honor', say Malina and Neyrey, 'Honor and Shame', p. 51. 'Challenge' and 'riposte' are seen as important moves in an

among equals, we are told. If a teacher met a challenge from his pupils, and accepted, he would (*ex hypothesi*) lose honour, not gain it—whatever the physical outcome might be. In the Feeding of the Five Thousand Mark and Matthew agree that Jesus takes the initiative, from an express motive of compassion. In the former story the disciples evince a simple concern for the crowd's well-being. Does our model oblige us—and warrant us—simply to disallow any priority to these apparently commonplace and readily comprehensible motives, for respect (honour) *must* always be pivotal?[28]

Life in the east Mediterranean world of late antiquity was far more complex, our sources suggest, as we can see from just one example provided by Lucian. His shoe-maker, Micyllus, encountering a wealthy acquaintance, Eucrates, wants to move onwards, lest he shame Eucrates, he says, 'by joining his company in my poor workaday cloak'. Nonetheless, Eucrates nonetheless invites him to a festive dinner in place of a philosopher who is ill. The sick man, in fact, turns up, as a matter of duty, he says, so as not to insult his host. Eucrates responds that he would have had the food sent to the sick philosopher anyway. The disappointed Micyllus turns away, but Eucrates, noticing that he is very downcast, says, 'You come in, too, Micyllus, and dine with us. I'll make my son dine with his mother in the women's quarters.' Micyllus continues, 'I went in, therefore, after coming within an ace of licking my lips for nothing...I was ashamed, however, because I seemed to have driven Eucrates' lad out of the dining room.' The philosopher then spoils the cabaret acts by jawing on about vice and virtue.[29] Eucrates risked shame by inviting the poor and shabby workman in the first place, and compassion ruled in the event. Food itself was a prime motive, and entertainment was worth more than being honoured by a

'agonistic' (competitive, combative) culture by Plevnik, 'Honor/Shame', p. 100; Malina, *New Testament World*, p. 34; Esler, *First Christians*, pp. 27-28.

28. On concurrent value systems, see deSilva, *Despising Shame*, pp. 15-16. Chance ('Anthropology of Honor and Shame', p. 148), remarks that 'there is more to Mediterranean culture than honor and shame.' Kressel ('Anthropologist's Response', p. 159) is unduly dismissive, however, of Neyrey's essay, 'Despising the Shame of the Cross': the theme of honour-and-shame does surely constitute one strand—if only one—in John.

29. Lucian, *The Dream or, The Cock* 8–11, in A.M. Harmon (trans.), *Lucian*, II (LCL; 8 vols.; London: Heinemann; Cambridge, MA: Harvard University Press, 1915), pp. 189-93. A little more detail is included here than appeared in the version in *CBQ*.

philosophical discourse. 'Honour', respect, is only one issue, and a subordinate one at that (and one readily internalized; there is not a hint that Micyllus's shame at displacing his host's son was in any way public).[30]

In his *Euboean Discourse* Dio of Prusa introduces a peasant who, when challenged, says, 'Many is the time I have pitied shipwrecked travellers who have come to my door, taken them into my hut, given them to eat and drink, helped them in any way I could, and accompanied them until they got out of the wilderness...I never did that to win a testimonial or gratitude, why I never knew where the men came from even.'[31] Now of course this is a romantic view of peasant life, though Dio elsewhere claims himself to have been well received as a penniless Cynic foot-traveller. But he clearly expects it to make sense, that people can act in a 'non-agonistic' way, with no concern for increasing their own honour, still less at the expense of others' honour. Of course Dio himself accepts that civic honour (respect, and self-respect, sensitivity to shame) is an important motive. When the beneficiary of the good Euboean's kindness later finds him arraigned in town, he insists that the man is entitled to a recompense that honours him.[32] Yet if honour were pivotal, if everything turned on it, it should not be possible for Dio even to suggest an action driven by some other prime let alone exclusive motive. This is to say that on the hypothesis of 'pivotal honour' it ought not to be possible for Dio to say what he says here.

d. *Ancient Critiques of Honour*: κενοδοξία
First-century Mediterranean documents show an awareness of the possibility of κενοδοξία, empty or false honour, fame, respect. κενοδοξία comes from too obviously seeking honour, from pretending not to care when in reality you obviously do, in fact precisely from making honour pivotal. J.K. Campbell has described a twentieth-century Greek pastoral

---

30. For such a mixture of motives in very varing proportions, see many of the other accounts of meals collected by Braun, *Feasting and Social Rhetoric*, or by K.E. Corley, *Private Women, Public Meals* (Peabody, MA: Hendrickson, 1993).

31. Dio Chrysostom, *Discourses* 7.52-53, in J.W. Cohoon (trans.), *Dio Chrysostom*, I (LCL; 5 vols.; London: Heinemann; Cambridge, MA: Harvard University Press, 1932), p. 317.

32. Dio Chrysostom, *Discourses* 7.60, p. 321; cf. 7.83, p. 333, for the judgment that such a peasant would be ashamed not to offer help. (Cohoon, *Dio Chrysostom*, I, p. 333, renders αἰσχύνοντο ἄν as 'a sense of self-respect would compel them'.)

group, the Sarakatsani, for whom competition for honour (*timê*) was paramount.[33] The Sarakatsani as described also have an alternative 'somewhat tenuous' ethos, that of the Greek Orthodox Church. As Campbell notes, 'contradictions and inconsistencies exist in the values and beliefs of many societies'.[34] The 'honour' code of values predominates on most but not all occasions. It does not have to be constantly pivotal; there are other options, adopted on other occasions.

We do well to allow that for the first-century Mediterranean world, too, 'honour and shame' were important options, which could predominate. But there were other options; and we have to ask which values and which combinations of available values were actually chosen, and not re-translate everything in terms of one set. Granted, Malina, Neyrey Plevnik and others explain that 'what counts as honourable' can vary within a given culture, even while, however constituted, it remains everyone's aim.[35] Yet it is not enough simply to allow that there are alternative 'courts of honour', sub-communities where respect may be accorded even if withheld in the wider world. Food, wealth, health, compassion, friendship, physical pleasure can all be prime aims, with only minor components of honour or none at all.[36] (We consider this further in the final section.)

The most frequent and trenchant critique of the concern for respect, fame, 'honour' and 'shame' came from the Cynics, including plebeians. Pseudo-Crates tells the wealthy, 'You really have nothing because of your rivalry, jealousy, fear and κενοδοξία, vainglory.' But he also admits to 'Diogenes', 'fame (δόξα) has so far not yet released us from bondage to her'.[37] The aim was to care not a whit about others' respect.

---

33. J.K. Campbell, 'Honour and the Devil', in J.G. Peristiany, *Honour and Shame: The Values of Mediterranean Society* (London: Weidenfeld & Nicolson, 1965), pp. 141-70. He notes that 'the critical moment in the development of a young shepherd's reputation is his first quarrel', p. 148.

34. Campbell, 'Honour and the Devil', p. 167.

35. Malina, *New Testament World*, pp. 52-54; Plevnik, 'Honor/Shame', p. 97; Malina and Neyrey, 'Honor and Shame', pp. 26-27.

36. deSilva, *Despising Shame*, pp. 25, 81. On 'counter values' over against status and patronage, cf. T. Engberg-Pedersen, 'Plutarch to Prince Philoppapus on How to Tell a Flatterer from a Friend', in J.T. Fitzgerald (ed.), *Friendship, Flattery and Frankness of Speech* (NovTSup, 82; Leiden: E.J. Brill, 1995), pp. 61-79 (76 and 79).

37. Pseudo-Crates 7 and 8, trans. R.F. Hock, in A.J. Malherbe (ed.), *The Cynic Epistles: A Study Edition* (SBLSBS, 12; Missoula, MT: Scholars Press, 1977), p. 59.

'To be enslaved to others' opinion, good or bad, is terrible.'[38] The Cynics set out to be 'shameless'.[39] Nor is it just the case that Cynics have 'internalized' the system. Stoics such as Epictetus (and his idealized Cynic) may have, but Stoics still respect the social system; Cynics repudiate it.[40] Stoics cope with incidental shame, Cynics court it. That, of course, laid the Cynics wide open to the counter-charge that they were as concerned for others' opinions as anyone else, but were just seeking a different kind of respect, or respect for unconventional reasons. When 'Antisthenes' folds his cloak so that its 'shameful' shabbiness is obvious, 'Socrates' says, 'I can see your desire for respect peeping through.'[41] This is not the place to debate the integrity or otherwise of individual Cynics or Cynics as a whole. The point is that if honour were universally 'pivotal', if everything turned on it for everyone, there would be no possibility of articulating a critique of it, no way in which people could mount accusations and counter-accusations of hypocrisy among those seeking it. If everything were done and meant to be done to gain respect, no one could be criticized for making that their aim. But that is precisely what the Cynic critique does; and the Cynics were not alone.

Understanding of the problems inherent in any concern for honour and sensitivity to shame were widespread.[42] We find explicit discussions of all sorts of false moves that may trip up even those whose concern for respect and self-respect is approved, as well as disdain for empty boasting, over-weening pride, unsustained pretensions. But more than that, writers such as Cicero, Seneca, Epictetus, Plutarch, can all

---

38. Pseudo-Crates 16, trans. Hock, in Malherbe (ed.), *The Cynic Epistles*, p. 67; cf. 29. In the same volume see Pseudo-Diogenes 5; 7.1; 9; 10; etc., trans. B. Fiore. See also Dio Chrysostom, *Discourses* 4.116-24.

39. This is quite contrary, of course, to Plevnik's generalization, 'all human beings seek to have shame', 'Honor/Shame', p. 96. On this see Lucian, *Philosophies for Sale* 10-11; *idem*, *Peregrinus* 17; Diogenes Laertius, *Lives of Eminent Philosophers* 6. 32, 46, 58, 61, 69, 97.

40. deSilva (*Despising Shame*, p. 96) too readily takes Epictetus's idealized portrait as true for Cynics as such.

41. Diogenes Laertius, *Lives* 6.8, in R.D. Hicks (trans.), *Diogenes Laertius*, II (LCL; 2 vols.; London: W. Heinemann; Cambridge, MA: Harvard University Press, 1925), p. 9; cf. 6.26; and Lucian, *Passing of Peregrinus*, *passim*.

42. Useful reflection on this, with a survey of sources, are provided by S.M. Pogoloff, *Logos and Sophia: The Rhetorical Situation of 1 Corinthians* (SBLDS, 134; Atlanta: Scholars Press, 1992), pp. 197-235.

castigate any person who is ambitious for honour.[43] The φιλότιμος can be criticized in Plutarch's circle, admired among Campbell's twentieth-century Sarakatsani.

d. Hypocrisy, and the Early Christian Critique, in Context

If public honour were everyone's overt and recognised aim, no one could be accused of 'hypocrisy' in making reputation their goal. To pray, give, fast ostentatiously in public would be understood by all as natural and right. There could be no disparity between overt and real prime aim, because there would only ever be one real (and overt) prime aim in everything: honour. One might be criticised for aiming badly, with the wrong criteria, or for aiming at the wrong audience, the wrong 'court of honour',[44] but one could never be accused in so doing of pretence, hypocrisy in making honour one's aim.

Among early Christian sources, the charge of 'hypocrisy' occurs frequently only in Matthew; but it is found in Q (the source Matthew and Luke seem to share), in Luke's own matter, in Mark and in Paul.[45] In common usage of the first century 'hypocrisy' (ὑποκρισία, ὑπόκρισις) may have become a dead metaphor, simply indicating (dis) simulation, pretence;[46] but the image of the play-actor could still be used in a much more lively way. The term could be deployed positively, as in the *Letter of Aristeas* much earlier, and by Teles and Epictetus: you should play your genuine 'role' well.[47] It can also, of course, and importantly, be used negatively; for instance by Lucian of Samosata in criticizing some plebeian Cynics, 'play-actors' in everything but their failure to change their costumes: they were apes putting on a show.[48] He could direct the same criticism against philosophers in general, 'cloaking themselves in the high-sounding name of Virtue, elevating their eyebrows, wrinkling

---

43. Cicero, *De officiis* 2.43, and 88; Seneca, *Epistulae morales* 94.64-66; Epictetus, *Dissertations* 3.26.34; 4.3.10; Plutarch, *Moralia: On Praising Oneself Inoffensively* 546F; and 555EF, 558D; see the whole closely related discussion in Plutarch *Moralia: On How to Tell a Flatterer*, *passim*, but in particular 48D-49F, 70D-72B; and also deSilva, 'Despising Shame', pp. 456-57.

44. On the 'court of honor' see, e.g., deSilva, 'Wisdom of Ben Sira', pp. 446-49.

45. Mt. 6.2, 5, 16, etc. In Q the charge is found in Mt. 7.5, Lk. 6.42; cf. Lk. 13.14. It is also found at Mk 7.6; 12.15; Gal. 2.13; and 1 Tim. 4.2, 1 Pet. 2.1.

46. As in Philo, *Quis haeres* 43; 4 Macc. 6.15; Josephus, *War* 1.26.2 §520

47. *Ep. Arist.* 219; Teles, *Discourses* 2 (5H); Epictetus, *Dissertations* 4.7.13; *Encheiridion* 17.

48. Lucian, *Nigrinus* 24; see also Lucian, *The Dead Come to Life* 32, 36.

up their foreheads and letting their beards grow...like actors in trag-edy'.[49] Epictetus could also deploy the metaphor in this way, of the philosopher without integrity, as well as of the make-believe Jew.[50] Philo complains that 'everyone sets money [*sic*] or reputation (δόξα) as his aim', adding the caustic comment, 'his benevolence is hypocrisy'.[51] Whether it is still a live metaphor in the New Testament may be de-bated.[52] Mostly, it is used negatively of persons who perform some act or series of actions not for their own value, but for the respect that may be gained in society, 'that they may be honoured (δοξασθῶσιν) by peo-ple...seen by people'; or 'outwardly appear righteous to people' (Mt. 6.2, 5, 16; 23.28). Such behaviour has only to be pointed out to be seen as the reprehensible folly of a minority.

So, too, Mark's Pharisee 'play-actors' maintain public ritual and re-mark its absence in others, but neglect less noticeable compliance with encoded law (Mk 7.6; cf. Lk. 13.15). With every show of respect they ask what seems to be a serious and important question, although they have no intention of acting on the response. Malina sees here a chal-lenge and response in the battle for honour at another's expense,[53] but if honour were inevitably their aim, there could be no 'pretence' in their making it so. Mark says it was a trap, his Jesus says they are playing a charade in which he refuses to join. Though indeed honour may still be a lesser, simply implicit issue, in no way is it 'pivotal', the 'core' of the conflict.

If we began by taking the 'Q' 'mote and beam' saying (Lk. 6.41-42) to be concerned with honour, we would expect some such prudential advice as, 'with that beam in your eye, you'll be laughed to shame'. Instead we are told to be self-critical and reformed so as to be helpful,

49. Lucian, *Icaromenippus* 29, in A.M. Harmon (trans.), *Lucian*, II (LCL; Lon-don: Heinemann; Cambridge, MA: Harvard University Press, 1915), pp. 269-323 (317).

50. Epictetus, *Dissertations* 1.29.41-24 (the tragic actor [τραγῳδός] and the buf-foon have in common everything but their lines); and 2.9.19-20; cf. Dio Chrysos-tom, *Discourses* 4.47-48, on role-playing.

51. Philo, *Conf. Ling.* 48, in F.H. Colson and G.H. Whitaker (trans.), *Philo*, IV (LCL; 10 vols., 2 supplements; London: Heinemann; Cambridge, MA: Harvard University Press, 1932), pp. 9-119 (35).

52. On ὑποκρίτης as a live metaphor in the Jesus tradition, see R.A. Batey, 'Jesus and the Theatre', *NTS* 30.4 (1984), pp. 563-73.

53. Malina, *New Testament World*, p. 59.

rather than pretend to moral superiority. But perhaps honour is so little relevant anyway that it is not even in view here.

What Kephas 'feared' from 'the circumcision party' in Antioch is not stated (Gal. 2.12);[54] but suppose it were loss of respect: Paul would then be dismissing this concern as irrelevant. In fact Paul sounds much closer to Epictetus: Kephas, Barnabas and the rest were play-acting (Gal 2.14-15) as observant Jews to make an impression, when their observance was in practice quite minimal. Making an impression, gaining respect, is not a universally acceptable aim.

It is clear from the foregoing not only that honour and shame were at times—yet only at times—important issues; but also that there was even then a ready awareness of the ease with which the aim could be corrupting or self-defeating, or both, whether one remained sensitive to shame or sought to be free of it. It was not the kind of unreflective and monochrome 'system' that seems to be outlined by Malina and others, where everyone shares the same attitude to honour (however constituted) in every social interaction. As already insisted, it is not simply a matter of alternative 'courts of honour', different 'significant others'. Pogoloff, for instance, shows how readily someone like Paul can pick up elements of this critical appraisal of respect, of honour and shame, and expect his hearers to understand: 'Paul employs this rhetoric to criticize those who are boasting on the typical grounds of culture, power and birth (1 Cor. 1.26, 29; 3.18)'.[55]

So, as we noted at the outset, the language of honour and shame comes naturally to the lips of early Christians, but so, too, does the conventional critique, itself reinforced by the centrality of the crucifixion of Jesus. Yes, he came to glory and honour—yet precisely by despising the shame (Phil. 2.5-11; Heb. 12.2; cf. 1 Cor. 1.18-21). 'Power in weakness, confidence of honor while apparently put to shame—that was the paradox of Christian existence in a Jewish and Graeco-Roman environment.' So Halvor Moxnes concludes a careful discussion of the tensions in Romans between the acceptance of the honour code of the wider world in 13.7 (and compare 12.17, 'what is respectable—καλά—in the

54. H.D. Betz, *Galatians* (Hermeneia; Philadelphia: Fortress Press, 1979), p. 109) says there is 'much speculation' about this.

55. Pogoloff, *Logos and Sophia*, p. 229. (I shall argue elsewhere that Pogoloff, like many others, has missed here important Cynic resonances in Paul's argument.)

sight of all') on the one hand, and the opposition to this world's corrupt ways denounced in chapters 1–3.[56] The overt concern for honour, and at times in quite conventional terms, is much more extensive and pervasive in Romans than it is in the Thessalonian, Corinthian and Galatian letters. As I hope to have shown elsewhere, this is part of a move away from a more radical, even Cynic-like opposition to majority values on Paul's part.[57]

David deSilva's treatment of the themes of shame and honour in Hebrews is also well worth noting. It is quite clear that the terms are retained, Jesus already enjoys the highest honour, and the Christian will share it. But this means for now 'despising shame' as that is defined by most contemporaries, it is to give up looking for any of the respect desired in the wider community around.[58]

e. *Interim Conclusion*

Both deSilva and Moxnes quote Malina and Neyrey approvingly, though deSilva at times also critically. Perhaps the difference of approach illustrated above is simply a matter of emphasis. Malina could be taken to be insisting on the prevalence of the abstract 'system'; deSilva and Moxnes could just be contrasting the different *contents* that Paul and Hebrews honour. What is honoured, and what counts as respect differ vastly; but 'respect', or 'honour' of some kind or other is still everyone's primary aim. But in that case we have reached a very high level of abstraction indeed, for, as we have now shown, 'honour' *can no longer entail public recognition, can no longer be necessarily agonistic (gained at someone else's expense), and cannot entail a difference of gender.* All that is then left is a handful of rhetorical commonplaces which are so general as to have minimal interpretative value. One might as well say that everyone in the ancient world had a value system. What is left is, yes, 'honour—in a sense', but in a sense so different from that painstakingly constructed by the social anthropologists that the common rhetoric risks becoming Pickwickian.

---

56. Moxnes, 'Honour and Righteousness', *JSNT* 32 (1988), p. 73.

57. F.G. Downing, *Cynics, Paul and the Pauline Churches: Cynics and Christian Origins*, II (London: Routledge, 1998) and compare, again, T. Engberg-Pedersen, 'Plutarch to Prince Philopappus', p. 76, on divergent value systems.

58. deSilva, 'Despising Shame', p. 459 especially.

3. There were Other and Often Prior Concerns
in the Ancient Mediterranean World

I have not at all been arguing that respect, 'honour', is in fact at issue in every passage where ὑποκριτής occurs (only in Matthew is it clearly at issue). I am actually trying to show that 'honour' is only occasionally pivotal and is often negligible if present at all. The authors of the passages cited insist that domination by *any* ulterior motive is to be rejected as a sham; and, *a fortiori*, that honour acquired with such a motive would be entirely unacceptable (not even 'unrespectable', 'dishonourable', 'shameful'; simply unacceptable). If honour and shame were as universally dominant, pivotal, everyone's prime and acknowledged motive, as Malina and others have been suggesting, then it could by definition never be thought hypocritical to act with gaining or with retaining the respect of others as one's prime motive; whereas clearly when that aim is detected, for Christians and others, such a motive for any otherwise commendable deed is a prime example of hypocrisy as such, and certainly objectionable. Honour may indeed on stated occasions be pivotal; but even where it is it may be suspect, especially among Christians (and Cynics).

We have happily noted, and with agreement, some studies whose authors argue cogently that honour and shame are more or less important elements in a particular ancient Christian narrative or disquisition. Not every study is as persuasive, as coherent, or as well evidenced.

a. *Life before Honour*
In his essay on the four Lucan beatitudes, Jerome Neyrey tells us that 'loss of honour is more serious to ancient peasants than the mere loss of wealth'; the peasant followers of Luke's Jesus are ostracized by their families as 'rebellious sons', are frightfully dishonoured, and as a consequence, are also dispossessed. All's well, however, for they have Jesus' respect.[59] When we are presented with such a broad generalization about first century Mediterranean peasants it is hard to know quite where to begin our response. We do not have ancient peasant sources to tell us in their own words one way or the other about their respective

---

59. J.H. Neyrey, 'Loss of Wealth, Family and Honour', in P.F. Esler (ed.), *Modelling Early Christianity: Social-scientific Studies of the New Testament in its Context* (London: Routledge, 1995), pp. 139-58 (154).

concerns for honour or sustenance, health, physical injury, friendship, pleasure, property. Ancient peasants cannot tell us whether what might be true of some mid-twentieth century peasants investigated by Peristiany and Pitt-Rivers and their associates was, or was not, true of all, some or any first century east Mediterranean subsistence farmers.

If we understand factors in first-century east Mediterranean assessments of honour at all, we know that slavery was widely held to be intensely dishonourable.[60] Yet people paid taxes in Roman provinces or in client kingdoms, though that was itself a sign of servitude (the Galilaeans paid up in the end, according to Josephus, despite their initial rebellion led by Judas).[61] Faced with the choice, most people allowed themselves and their children to be sold into slavery as prisoners of war or for debt, rather than run off and die of starvation (not all turned to banditry); debtors may well have sold themselves into slavery, rather than commit suicide.[62] Some Judaeans and Galilaeans rebelled, peasants included, in the middle of the first century, for a range of reasons; many previous generations and later ones did not rebel, Jews in Palestine and other peoples elsewhere; again, it seems, for a range of reasons.[63]

Neyrey, however, insists, Jesus' ostracized and dispossessed followers still have what they seek, 'honour'—but from Jesus. Again, the

60. Dio Chrysostom, *Discourses* 14.1, (citied by deSilva, *Despising Shame*, p. 176); Josephus *War* 2.16.4 §349. The slippage between our expressed values and actions must also be acknowledged: Chance, 'Anthropology of Honor and Shame', pp. 145-46.

61. Josephus, *War* 2.8.1 §118; cf. 2.16.4 §349, again; 2.16.4 §356-57, 361; 7. 8.7 §386; Mt. 17.25-26.

62. Cf. S.S. Bartchy, ΜΑΛΛΟΝ ΧΡΗΣΑΙ: *First-Century Slavery and the Interpretation of First Corinthians 7:1* (SBLDS, 11; Missoula, MT: Scholars Press, 1971), pp. 45-49. That selling oneself was practised as a career move is doubted by J.A. Harrill, *The Manumission of Slaves in Early Christianity* (HUT, 32; Tübingen: Mohr Siebeck, 1995), p. 31.

63. G.E.M de Ste Croix, *The Class Struggle in the Ancient Greek World from the Archaic Age to the Arab Conquests* (London: Gerald Duckworth; Ithaca, NY: Cornell University Press, 1981); S. Freyne, *Galilee from Alexander the Great to Hadrian 323 B.C.E.-135 C.E.: A Study of Second Temple Judaism* (Studies in Judaism and Christianity in Antiquity, 5; Wilmington, DE: Michael Glazier, 1980); J.H. Kautsky, *The Politics of Aristocratic Empires* (Chapel Hill: University of North Carolina Press, 1982); R.A. Horsley and J.S. Hanson, *Bandits, Prophets and Messiahs: Popular Movements in the Time of Jesus* (New Voices in Biblical Studies; Minneapolis: Winston, 1985).

apparently simple term conceals an incoherence. The honour they want (we have been told), and want more than anything, is the respect of their peers, honour in the community around them. Neyrey's Luke's Jesus offers them something other. We can give it the same name. But it still is not what we are told they would want more than anything. To parody Luke elsewhere, if your follower asks for respect in the community will you offer him nothing but your own? Rather is Luke's Jesus offering *alternative* goals, a redefinition of what makes life worth living, μακάριος. He is not offering an alternative fulfilment for prior expectations, coinage forged by himself to mimic a publicly recognised currency.

b. *Wealth before Honour*

At the outset Neyrey makes a distinction between 'sufficiency' (albeit meagre) and 'poverty', and then links this with a distinction between πένης and πτωχός, the hard-working poor over against the beggar. 'Peasants or artisans with little of this world's goods...are not called poor (they have enough to have honour).'[64] This distinction between πένης and πτωχός is also made by others, but still does not hold; the two terms can be used interchangeably, and their sense must be discerned from the context (as in discussions of Cynics).[65] Neyrey can only support the distinction itself (between a meagre but respectable sufficiency and 'real' but disgraceful poverty) by drawing two *obiter dicta* from a couple of wealthy essayists, Plutarch and Seneca, turning a Cynic conviction into a moral platitude: sufficiency should not be counted poverty. Neither writer intended to act on the axiom, neither indicates that others believed it. Mere sufficiency would for them have amounted to shameful indigence. The saying tells us nothing about peasant evaluations of wealth and respect.

The point is incidentally well illustrated by Dale Martin's remarks on wealth, slavery and status: wealth emerges as a more important indicator of well-being than (dishonoured) slavery or (honoured) freedom.[66] Much more realistic than Neyrey's wealthy idealists is Lucian's summary of the lot of even the most admired sculptor: 'you will be nothing but a labourer, toiling with your body and putting in it your entire hope

64. Neyrey, 'Loss of Wealth', pp. 139, 142.
65. Downing, *Cynics, Paul and the Pauline Churches*, p. 154 and n. 90.
66. D.B. Martin, *Slavery as Salvation: The Metaphor of Slavery in Pauline Christianity* (New Haven: Yale University Press, 1990), pp. 20-22.

of a livelihood, personally inconspicuous...one of the swarming rab-
ble.'[67] And it is noteworthy that livelihood comes before reputation,
whether the choice is for or against the sculptor's craft; and that is fully
allowing for the likelihood that skilled workers would have status
among their peers, and that this would be important to them.

c. *Poverty before Honour*
When Luke's Jesus makes poverty (not disrespect) his first concern, it
is because poverty is what counts, poverty is the real challenge, because
you go hungry and without shelter, and it hurts, and it threatens your
very life. And this Jesus is saying what the Cynics said (he may do so
independently or because Cynic tradition influenced our sources in some
way). It is this that constitutes 'the good life' (εὐδαιμονία), the life that
is happy (μακάριος). 'Come to what is really fine (τὰ καλὰ)...through
poverty (πενία) and ill-repute, with your parentage despised and yourself in exile...and you'll live happily (μακαρίως).'[68] Disrepute certainly
comes into the calculation (here and elsewhere in Cynic sources) but it
is not the entirety, and it is not the main point. Poverty, with hunger and
thirst and physical hurt inflicted on you can often be offered as the
happy life, without particular reference to the incidence of others'
disrespect.[69]

Neyrey takes the fourth Lucan beatitude first, arguing that as the climax it is the most significant, and imagines it, as we have seen, to refer
to followers of Jesus thrown out for that reason by their families, and so

---

67. Lucian, *The Dream or, the Life of Lucian* 9, in A.M. Harmon (trans.), *Lucian*,
III (LCL; 8 vols.; London: Heinemann; Cambridge, MA: Harvard University Press,
1921), pp. 213-33 (227).

68. Pseudo-Diogenes 31.4, trans. Fiore, in Malherbe (ed.), *Cynic Epistles*, p. 137;
and see also other passages collected in F.G. Downing, *Christ and the Cynics* (JSOT
Manuals, 4; Sheffield: JSOT Press, 1988), pp. 19-21. K.C. Harrison ('How Honorable! How Shameful! A Cultural Analysis of Matthew's Makarisms and Reproaches', in V.H. Matthews and D.C. Benjamin (eds.), *Honor and Shame in the
World of the Bible* [Semeia, 68; Atlanta: Scholars Press, 1966], pp. 81-111), argues
that μακαρίος *means* 'honoured', 'honorable'. If that were so the state of being
μακαρίος would have to count for Stoics as an 'external' (Epictetus, *Dissertations*
1.4.1-9; 3.20.12-15; 3.22.26-30), which it does not. Acknowledging someone's well-
being may honour them; but the word is not rhetorically interchangeable with conventional terms of respect; cf. also *Socratic Letter* 4.1; 6.4-5; Pseudo-Diogenes 32.2.

69. Pseudo-Diogenes 26, 32, 33. In 36.4 an ordinary man objects that poverty
causes 'hunger, cold, contempt' (in that order).

have been plunged into 'a total loss of honour', and only as a consequence of that, a loss of livelihood.[70] His suggestion is obviously not
impossible *a priori*, and Luke certainly does refer to trouble in families:
members set against one another (Lk. 12.51-53; 14.26-27) and the threat
of betrayal to death (Lk. 2.14-17). But there is nothing in Luke to suggest followers of Jesus in his lifetime were being thrown out by their
families for their 'loyalty' to Jesus (practical outcome unspecified).
Jesus is not thrown out by his family, nor are any of his followers. Jesus
and his followers *leave* house and family and so find poverty (Lk.
18.28). The younger son leaves home, then finds poverty, and then disgrace (Lk. 15.11-19).

The closest analogy from around New Testament times suggests just
the same sequence. According to Cynic sources, adopting the Cynic
impoverished lifestyle can *lead to* hatred, ostracism, reviling, a refusal
of respect from some (but, so what!). When 'Diogenes' has adopted
poverty and got his father upset, he is imagined reassuring him with
'You should rather be glad that your son is satisfied with little, and is
free from subservience to public opinion.'[71] In the same vein, we are
told of Crates leaving his family and adopting poverty, and only so
incurring disgrace; so, too, Hipparchia.[72] Parents do not initiate a sham-
ing break in response to their offspring's friendship with a radical
teacher, it is the disciple's acceptance of poverty that may create a
break, and will probably count as disgrace. This is the pattern we find
people around the time imagining, and the only pattern Luke suggests
when he presents any detail; and the other evangelists indicate the same
sequence.

In Luke, as in Matthew, and in Mark and in Q, Jesus issues an invitation to poverty. In the Lukan beatitudes we are told that poverty is an
important aspect of the happy life, of having a part in God's kingdom.
The invitation is very like that of some of our Cynic sources.[73] And as
in our Cynic sources, hostility, ill-treatment and disgrace may incidentally result. But disgrace is not the normal first step to poverty for disciples of a radical philosopher, nor is it the pivotal issue.

---

70. Neyrey, 'Loss of Wealth', pp. 145-47.
71. Pseudo-Diogenes 7.1, trans. Fiore, in Malherbe (ed.), *Cynic Epistles*, p. 99;
cf. Pseudo-Diogenes 30.
72. Diogenes Laertius, *Lives* 6.85-93, 96-98; on Crates, cf. Pseudo-Diogenes 38.
73. Downing, *Christ and the Cynics*; and *idem, Cynics and Christian Origins*.

4. *Conclusion*

Neyrey offers his interpretation as an hypothesis. Fresh hypotheses are always worth exploring, but there seems to be no good reason for adopting this one as our paramount clue (and still less as our exclusive key), no good reason to take a model based somewhat roughly and arbitrarily on the diverse findings from researches into some twentieth century people, and then to impose the simplified model universally onto first-century data. The issue of honour, of respect in community, is important, and may even *on occasion* be of prime importance. It does not help to assume—irrespective of the evidence—that it always must be dominant.

Even in the ancient world people do not fit neatly into the convenient moulds we may forge for them. We consider a further example in the next chapter.

Chapter 2

PERSONS IN RELATION

1. *Different Kinds of Persons?*

If 'honour' had turned out to have been as 'pivotal' as had been asserted, then further universal features of persons in relation to the ancient
east Mediterranean world might have seemed to be entailed.[1] Bruce
Malina and others invite us to envisage 'the self-image', 'the mind-set'
of the person who 'sees life nearly exclusively in terms of honor', and
assures us 'For starters, such a person would almost always see himself
or herself through the eyes of others.' And again, as with issues of 'honour', we are advised that we are being asked to envisage people quite
different from ourselves, people who 'did not share or comprehend our
idea of an "individual" at all'.[2] Further, this is not simply a matter of
intellectual abstractions, these are quite distinct lived definitions, which
we late twentieth-century individualists can only hope to grasp with the
help of percipient social anthropologists. We are 'monadic', seeing ourselves and others in terms of 'psychology, ...inner motivations that are
quite personal, reasons based on personality, childhood experiences,
personality development, interpersonal ability in terms of poise, IQ,
emotional control, personal story, highly personal reasons, and the
like', which is quite other than what we find in 'Plutarch, Josephus, Philo

1. 'Persons in Relation' is the title of the second volume of John MacMurray's
The Form of the Personal (Gifford Lectures for 1953–54; London: Faber, 1957).
2. Malina, *New Testament World*, pp. 63-64; see also B.J. Malina and J.H.
Neyrey, 'First Century Personality: Dyadic, Not Individualistic', in J.H. Neyrey
(ed.), *Social World of Luke–Acts: Models for Interpretation* (Peabody, MA: Hendrickson, 1991), pp. 67-96; J.H. Neyrey, 'Dyadism' in J.J. Pilch and B.J. Malina,
Biblical Social Values and their Meaning (Peabody, MA: Hendrickson, 1993), pp.
49-52; Esler, *First Christians*, pp. 29-30.

of Alexandria, Epictetus, Musonius Rufus and other writers of that period' (including those who produced the New Testament).[3]

2. *What Kinds of Persons in Relations are We, the Readers?*

One test (if only one) of any theory is whether it makes predictions that can be falsifed. We shall in the main in this chapter be concerned with ancient evidence that may seem to run counter to Malina's and other similar suggestions. But we need also to consider briefly the warrants for the conclusion that 'we' are to be defined by the quite distinctive individualism outlined above.

There are some items in Malina's list which may seem well warranted. It is often noted, for instance, that ancient 'Lives' do not portray the development of character, and, in particular, do not seem to see childhood as formative. Anecdotes and events are chosen to display 'character' (including complexities, strengths and weaknesses), not its development, and childhood episodes are only included to reveal what is to emerge more fully (as, for example, the boy Jesus with the experts in the Temple, the boy Josephus impressing community leaders in Jerusalem, the boy Moses outstripping his teachers...).[4]

Yet is it actually the case that 'we' are concerned solely with guilt feelings, with a privatized sense of shame, quite other than 'they' in their sole concern with 'actions they thought other people might say would be dishonoring', such as are no moment for us?[5] and that we are in no way like

> [t]he 'dyadic' person [who] is essentially a group-embedded and group-oriented person (some call such a person 'collectivity-oriented'). Such a group-embedded, dyadic personality is one who simply needs another continually in order to know who he or she really is...such persons internalize and make their own what others say, do, and think about them because they believe it is necessary, for being human, to live out the expectations of others.[6]

---

3.   Malina, *New Testament World*, p. 66.
4.   Lk. 2.46-47; Josephus, *Life* 9; Philo, *Vit. Mos.* 1.21. But I note a review by Andrew Marr (of Anita Desai's *Fasting, Feasting*) which takes this view of given 'character' to be 'the great tradition' among western novelists, taken up successfully by Indian writers: *Guardian Weekly* 1–7 July 1999, p. 23.
5.   Malina, *New Testament World*, p. 64.
6.   Malina, *New Testament World*, p. 67.

Malina then quotes Clifford Geertz in support of his account of our supposed clearly contrasting individualism. Philip Esler (who follows Malina at times) prefers an account of 'social identity theory' based on the work of Henri Tajfel, as being preserved from the excessive individualism of North American approaches. In particular Tajfel and associates point us to the ways in which groups anywhere may maintain their identity over against other groups, and where individuals find their 'socially derived selves', and 'little attention is paid to aspects such as individual moral dispositions, emotional make-up, abilities and interests which may characterize a particular person'. Since this theory is concerned primarily with the modern world, 'we' may seem already (according to Tajfel and associates) rather less distanced from the ancient eastern Mediterranean than we were with Malina. However, Esler soon brings us back again to Malina's generalized Mediterranean collectivism over against 'our' North Atlantic individualism.[7]

In response I would suggest it is worth according, at least initially, some counterweight to such conclusions about 'us' from, among others, Rom Harré, as a contemporary philosopher of social psychology (who, as it happens, also includes Tajfel among his sources). Harré offers:

> One final word of warning. The fact that much social psychological research has been conducted by and among North Americans has had an influence on how it has been assumed a knowledge base is located. The American moral universe is built on the idea of atomic individuals... Observational and participant studies of the ways knowledge bases are located in real life disclose a very different pattern of social distribution.[8]

Both 'practical' and 'expressive' knowledge of how to behave are socially given for us in modern western societies—and the expressive is (so Harré insists), paramount. 'It is the argument of this work that for most people, in most historical conditions, expressive motivations dominate practical aims in the energy and even in the time expended on co-ordinated social activities'; and 'expressive aspects of social activity' are where 'we make a public showing of skills, attitudes, emotions, feelings and so on, providing, sometimes consciously, the evidence upon which our friends, colleagues, neighbours, rivals and enemies draw conclusions as to the kind of person we are', the respect we hope for or the

7. P.F. Esler, *Galatians* (London: Routledge, 1998), pp. 40-47.
8. R. Harré, *Social Being* (Oxford: Basil Blackwell, 2nd edn, 1993), p. 21. For Tajfel I have so far only been able to consult H. Tajfel (ed.), *Social Identity and Intergroup Relations* (Cambridge: Cambridge Univeristy Press, 1982).

contempt we dread.[9] Harré, then, finds us, too, deeply concerned with others' opinions of us, whether or not as strong in practice as those posited for the ancient eastern Mediterranean. Our society, too, is 'ago-nistic', more weighted to drama than to work.[10] (In fact Harré also allows for differing intensities of collectivism, placing 'our Western self-theory' 'somewhere towards a mid-point'.)[11]

It may then also be worth citing Charles Taylor's *The Sources of the Self*, which Esler, for instance, supposes marks the shift to modern indi-vidualism. Taylor actually writes, with emphasis,

> A self exists only within what I call 'webs of interlocution'…it is impor-tant to see how this stance [the ideal of detachment], which has become a powerful ideal for us, *however little we may live up to it*, transforms our position within, but by no means takes us out of, what I have called the original situation of identity formation. It goes on being true of such [de-tached] heroes that they define themselves not just genetically but as they are today, in conversation with others.

Some of us may espouse individualist ideals, but that is an 'as if': 'as if the dimension of interlocution were of significance only for the gen-esis of individuality…to be left behind and play no part in the finished person'.[12]

In this connection is worth noting further that Harré can also readily use the jargon of 'dyads' for people at large today, for the sources of our selves are relational in origin and in sustaining performance. It is not a matter, either, of having a conscious 'concept of self'; rather, 'I claim that "the self" is acquired as a generalization and abstraction from the public person-concept, that is, in use in the public-collective dis-course of a community by a slide from one grammatical model to an-other, initiated by certain social-linguistic practices.'[13] If people in the ancient Mediterranean world were constructed out of others' past re-sponses and future expectations, then, it seems, no less are we.

9.   Harré, *Social Being*, pp. 162 and 26, and then pp. 27-29.

10.   Harré, *Social Being*, pp. 131-43, and ch. 6.

11.   Harré, *Personal Being* (Cambridge: Cambridge University Press, 1984), p. 86.

12.   Charles Taylor, *Sources of the Self: The Making of Modern Identity* (Cam-bridge: Cambridge University Press, 1989), pp. 36-37, emphasis added; the com-ment by Esler, *Galatians*, p. 12.

13.   Harré, *Personal Being*, chs. 4 and 5, and here citing p. 167.

3. *What Kinds of Persons in Relation Were they in the Past?*

I seem to have missed any detailed discussion of infancy among studies of 'the New Testament world' in the light of theoretical social anthropology. However, for today's world Harré argues persuasively for a universal 'dyadic' form to the construction of selfhood in babies, and our social anthropologists could hardly object to the discovery of an essential dyad at the very commencement of life also in the ancient eastern Mediterranean world defined by them in such terms (even if Harré himself is instancing North Atlantic children today). This is a summary account from Harré of the 'symbiotic dyad':

> Psychological symbiosis is a permanent interactive relation between two persons, in the course of which one supplements the psychological attributes of the other as they are displayed in social performances, so that the other appears as a complete and competent social and psychological being.[14]

Since people in our ancient world did grow up to interact socially, with complex linguistic and related skills, aware of others' expectations, our lack of much detailed information on the care of babies then is perhaps not so important for the case in hand. Then just as now (to quote Harré again) 'Mothers who continuously complement the psychological and social deficits of infants by talking to and of the child as if it had the full complement of of psychological capacities, in particular as if it were a fully competent self, seeing and acting upon the world from its own standpoint, eventually create adult human beings.'[15]

However, it is perhaps also worth including some illustrations, albeit very carefully composed, from the Graeco-Roman world. I have argued in elsewhere for the wider relevance of 'highbrow' writing;[16] and it will be noted that mother and wet-nurse are both included in what follows. Plutarch wrote a 'consolation' to his wife on the death of their baby daughter, and the conventionality of the form allows us to generalize with some confidence. This is how a man of sensitivity should appreciate what his contemporaries would recognize:

14. Harré, *Personal Being*, p. 105.
15. Harré, *Personal Being*, p. 41.
16. Downing, 'A bas les aristos', pp. 212-30; reprinted as Ch. 1 of Downing, *Doing Things with Words*.

> I know what great satisfaction lay in this, that after four sons the longed-
> for daughter was born and I was able to give her your name. Our affec-
> tion for children so young has, furthermore, a poignancy all of its own: it
> gives a delight quite pure and free from all anger or reproach. She had
> herself moreover a wonderful natural gift of mildness and good temper,
> and her way of responding to friendship and of bestowing favours gave
> us pleasure as well as affording an insight into her kindness. For she
> would invite her nurse to offer the breast and feed with it not only other
> infants, but even the inanimate objects and playthings she took pleasure
> in, as though serving them at her own table, dispensing in her kindness
> such bounty as she had and sharing her greatest pleasures with whatever
> gave her delight.[17]

Of course this delight in an infant daughter and sorrow at her loss
must be balanced against the practice among some of exposing girl
babies in particular. The fact remains that a positive dyadic relationship
seems to be the only basis then as now for growth into a person capable
of effective social interaction; and there are further illustrations available for this positive delight in the dyadic relationship, from such as
Musonius on the pleasure of seeing parents and children together cele-
brating some festival, or Epictctus on the impulse to get down on the
floor with babies, or images from Jewish sources of God's care for his
people in terms of parents with a nursling, to Jesus' simile of a mother
hen with chicks, or urging his followers to 'become as little children'.[18]

It was admitted above that ancient *Lives* display scant interest in the
childhood development of their subjects. But it would be wrong, then,
to deduce from this that no one at the time noticed, cared about or
thought to foster such growth. Cicero (in the voice of Piso) concedes,

---

17. Plutarch, *Consolatio ad uxorem* 2.608CD, in P.H. de Lacy and B. Einarson
(trans.), *Plutarch's Moralia*, VII (LCL; 16 vols.; London: Heinemann; Cambridge,
MA: Harvard University Press, 1959), pp. 573-605 (580-83). His wife had herself
breastfed at least one of their older children (5.609D). It is still difficult to find credible and detailed discussions of childhood in the Mediterranean world of the first
century. H.-R. Weber, *The Child and the Church* (Geneva: WCC, 1978) idealizes
the early Christian over against others. Perhaps especially significant is Dionysius
of Halicarnassus's sketch of a widowed single mother as 'not only a mother, but a
father, a nurse, a sister, and everything that is dearest'; *Roman Antiquities* 8.51.3
(trans. E. Cary; LCL; London: Heinemann; Cambridge, MA: Harvard University
Press, 1937).

18. Passages collected in Downing, *Strangely Familiar*.

I may risk being thought to lay undue stress on a field of observation sanctioned by the older thinkers, all of whom, and my own school (Academic) more than others, go to the nursery, because they believe that Nature reveals her plan to them most clearly in childhood...

Earlier he has noted,

Infants just born lie helpless, as if absolutely inanimate; when they have acquired a little more strength they exercise their minds and their senses; they strive to stand erect, they use their hands, they recognise their nurses; then they take pleasure in the society of other children, and enjoy meeting them, they take part in games and love to hear stories; they desire to bestow of their abundance in bounty to others; they take an inquisitive interest in what goes on in their homes; they begin to reflect and to learn...For every stage of this development there must be supposed to be a reason.[19]

That the Academic school supposed all this an innate programme does not detract from the observation, nor from the reinforcement that such expectations and pleased responses would afford. I would add only part of a consolatory note from the younger Pliny on the recent death of a teenage girl:

I never saw a girl so bright and lovable, so deserving of a longer life or even one to last for ever. She had not yet reached fourteen, and yet she combined the wisdom of age and dignity of womanhood with the sweetness and modesty of youth and innocence. She would cling to her father's neck, and embrace us, his friends, with modest affection; she loved her nurses, her attendants and her teachers, each one for the services given her; she applied herself intelligently to her books and was moderate and restrained in her play. She bore her last illness with patient resignation and real courage.[20]

Once more we are restricted, of course, to notes of children in aristocratic households (though slave-born children are there to be observed

19. Cicero, *De finibus* 5.20.55 and 5.15.42, in H. Rackham (trans.), *Cicero*. XVII. *De finibus* (LCL; London: Heinemann; Cambridge, MA: Harvard University Press, 1914), pp. 441-43, 457. Rackham supplies 'development' for 'quorum', but it seems the obvious word in context.

20. Pliny the Younger, *Letters* 5.16, in B. Radice (trans.), *Letters and Panegyricus*, I (LCL; 2 vols.; London: Heinemann; Cambridge, MA: Harvard University Press, 1969), pp. 349-81. On daughters' education see also Quintilian, *Institutio oratoria* 1.5.6-7, but also H. Marrou, *A History of Education* (ET; London: Sheed & Ward, 1956).

as well as the free). However, again the conclusions of our first chapter can be reinforced by further evidence and argument. The fact is that the educational 'system' was designed to produce as its most prized end-product an ability to interact with others in speech and body language and hearing in ways that met exacting expectations both for conformity and for novelty.[21] The importance of continuity and coherence from dyadic infancy to adolescent individuality is made explicitly in an essay on children's education mis-ascribed to Plutarch:

> Mothers ought, I should say, themselves to feed their infants and nurse them themselves, for they will feed them with livelier affection and greater care...just as it is necessary, immediately after birth, to begin to mould the limbs of the children's bodies in order that these may grow straight and without deformity, so, in the same fashion, it is befitting from the beginning to train the characters of children. For youth is impressionable and plastic, and while such minds are still tender lessons are infused deeply into them...servants and companions...should be sound in character and be Greek, and distinct in their speech, and not barbarians...[22]

Only through such early interaction would the final aims be likely to be achieved. (The extent of entry to 'primary' education is unsure; pseudo-Plutarch urged that even the most impoverished parents should do the best within their means.)[23]

Admittedly, a great deal of early learning was by rote, often with the 'help' of harsh physical punishment.[24] But the standard *progymnasmata* show that even at the grammar stage pupils were being taught to make their own choices of words and arrangements of words and gestures within the explicit but more importantly the tacit codes of what counted as good Greek or Latin and acceptable self-presentation.[25] Quintilian is aware that not all agree, but this is the ethos and practice that he has adopted and commends:

21. As further illustrated in Downing, 'A bas les aristos'.

22. Pseudo-Plutarch, *De liberis educandis* 5-6 (3C-4A), in F.C. Babbit (trans.) *Plutarch's Moralia*, I (LCL; 16 vols.; London: Heinemann; Cambridge, MA: Harvard University Press, 1927), pp. 1-69 (13-17), slightly amended, with 'train' instead of 'regulate' for ῥυθμίζειν); cf. Quintilian, *Institutio oratoria* 1.1.21, and 1.2.6-8.

23. Pseudo-Plutarch, *De liberis educandis* 11 (8E).

24. Quintilian, *Institutio oratoria* 1.1.25 is aware that others besides himself recognize the weaknesses of rote learning.

25. See again Marrou, *A History of Education*; and S.F. Bonner, *Education in Ancient Rome* (London: Methuen, 1977).

> I am not so blind to differences of age as to think the very young should
> be forced on prematurely or given real work to do. Above all we must
> take care that the child, not yet old enough to love his studies, does not
> come to hate them and dread the bitterness which he has now tasted,
> even later, when infancy is past. His studies must be made an amuse-
> ment: he must be questioned and praised and taught to rejoice when he
> has done well. Sometimes, too, when he refuses instruction, it should be
> given to some other to arouse his envy. At times he must also be engaged
> in competition and should be allowed to think himself successful more
> often than not; he should be encouraged to do his best by such rewards
> as may appeal to his tender years.[26]

The author of *De liberis educandis* makes similar points (9, 6EF and
12-13, 8F-9A). So, too, does a recent correspondent to a British news-
paper, advising 'that we go back to the method of Quintilian and follow
the learner, not the dogmas'.[27] So, too, does Philo:

> He (Moses) wished to show the independence of the learner. His purpose
> is that when the superintendence of the master is withdrawn, and no com-
> pulsion is applied, the pupil may make an exhibition of his own powers,
> and showing a diligence which is voluntary and self-imposed may work
> out by his own efforts what he has learned.[28]

A later aside from Quintilian is also worth noting: 'It is further of the
first importance that he [our teacher] should be on friendly and intimate
terms with us and make his teaching not a duty but a labour of love.'[29]
And a school is better than solitary home tuition, the learning in view is
essentially social and imitative and interactive, responsive to new challenges:[30]

> Pupils should learn to paraphrase Aesop's fables, the natural successors
> of the fairy stories of the nursery, in simple and restrained language and
> subsequently to set down this paraphrase in writing with the same sim-
> plicity of style: they should begin by analysing each verse, then give its
> meaning in different language, and finally proceed to freer paraphrase in

26. Quintilian, *Institutio oratoria* 1.1.20, in H.E. Butler (trans.), *Quintillian*, I
(LCL; 4 vols.; London: Heineman; Cambridge, MA: Harvard University Press,
1920–), pp. 29-31.
27. Dr Roland Meigham, Letter, *The Guardian*, 19 December 1998, p. 24
28. Philo, *De mutatione nominum* 270, in F.H. Colson and G.H. Whitaker (trans.),
Philo, V (LCL; London: Heinemann; Cambridge, MA: Harvard University Press,
1930).
29. Quintilian, *Institutio oratoria* 1.2.15.
30. Quintilian, *Institutio oratoria* 1.2.17-31.

which they will be permitted now to abridge, now to embellish the original, so far as this may be done without losing the poet's meaning.[31]

And this would seem to have been the method even of 'less enlightened' teachers, sharing the same aim: the pressure of the system was towards enabling and enhancing the individuality of the pupil in relation to peers and the wider public.

With all the real differences, both aims and methods seem analogous to those current in 'North Atlantic' countries and in other parts of our world today. The enabling—not restricting—of individuality-in-relationships for the adolescent cannot be reasonably supposed to be so very different, either. As we might put it,

> The basic premise of personal psychology is that cognitive activities are primarily public and collective, located in talk…personal appropriations occur…only in the course of the redistribution of demands upon individuals to make contributions to the public performances of thoughts and feelings put on them by psychologically symbiotic arrays, that is, socially structured groups of people.[32]

Such social production of adults as we have evidenced from the east Mediterranean of late antiquity is as interested in producing socially performed and socially reinforced individuality as is (for good or ill) the social production of adults in North Atlantic countries today.

With adolescence comes sexual awakening, as Quintilian, Pseudo-Plutarch and Plutarch himself, for instances, are well aware.[33] The general run of 'background' surveys, and the recently proliferating sociological studies, if they note sexual matters at all, tend to confine attention to formal marriage focused on property and legitimate (male) heirs, and possibly prostitution (male as well as female); all very impersonal role-playing, it would seem. It is ironic that North Atlantic society is coming round to seeing the value of written contracts between sexual partners, covering property and financial responsibility for children, such as were standard at quite lowly levels in society in Egypt at least. Portrayals of patterns of sexual congress in our own world as presented in novels and films and plays will often in fact allow little time for any

31. Quintilian, *Institutio oratoria* 1.9.2.
32. Harré, *Personal Being*, p. 21.
33. Quintilian, *Institutio oratoria* 1.2.1-5; 1.8.6, 2.2.14-15; Pseudo-Plutarch, *De liberis educandis* 7 (4B-5C); 15 (12BC); Plutarch, *Quomodo adolescencs poetas audire debeat* 3 (18AF).

complex interplay of the individuality of the partners, and the reluctant heroine may still be the one who 'succumbs' to the aggressive male. So even at this level it may be worth noting that women as portrayed in our ancient sources could be expected to take the initiative in erotic encounter, and aim for their own satisfaction, not simply be there as the passive objects of male desire, playing an imposed role (as opposed to a personally chosen or affirmed albeit, of course, socially acquired one). In concluding a very thorough survey, David Konstans notes: 'the sentimental conception of marriage offers an image of personal relations independent of patriarchal and civic interests [which are still powerfully obtained]. It expresses in a formulaic and condensed way the possibilities of individual and communal self-definition available...'[34]

Not everyone always sought a simple (as opposed to a complex and relational) sexual satisfaction. Although Pseudo-Lucian's Charicles, arguing in favour of heterosexual enjoyment, does have the woman passive, yet his crowning argument is that humans are sociable beings for whom a shared pleasure is an enhanced pleasure. (Some of Charicles's arguments against homoeroticism echo significantly Paul's in Romans 1.24-27.) Callicratidas, countering in favour of homosexual relationships, insists that they are based in high culture (not quick and easy pleasure) and blossom into long-lasting mutuality.[35] The arguments on both sides illuminate ancient ways of understanding personal being, and we are far more likely to find ourselves at home in such discussions than the abstract speculations of cultural anthoprologists would lead us to expect. We are as much the product of social expectations and reactions as people were then, and we as much as they come to such individuality as we attain and sustain as sexual persons in and through the same or very similar ranges of social interaction.

---

34. D. Konstans, *Sexual Symmetry: Love in the Ancient Novel* (Princeton, NJ: Princeton University Press, 1994), p. 231; cf. various contributions in R.F. Hock, J.B. Chance and J. Perkins (eds.), *Ancient Fiction and Early Christian Narrative* (Atlanta: Scholars Press, 1998); and see, for example, Lucian (?), *Lucius or the Ass* 5-11 (repeated in Apuleius' *The Golden Ass*); Longus, *Daphnis and Chloe*, 15-19; Petronius, *Satyricon* 16-26; and the erotica at Pompeii. Also relevant, of course, are the Pseudo-Clementine *Romances*.

35. Pseudo-Lucian, *Erōrtes*; *Affairs of the Heart*; *Amores* 27 and 48-49; cf. Achilles Tatius, *Leucippe and Clitophon* 1.8 and 2.35-38. For expectations of male friendship (and their relevance for the Fourth Gospel), see S. van Tilborg, *Imaginative Love in John* (BIS, 2; Leiden: E.J. Brill, 1993).

The possibility of a 'romantic' attachment (rather than one solely or primarily based in property and inheritance—or lust) burgeoning into a lifelong two-way relationship (albeit with initially reluctant parental permission) is presented as a cultural ideal in the ancient *popular* romances. Chariton's Chaereas and Callirhoe (in the eponymous work) are equally smitten on first meeting, survive arguments and suspicions and a host of perils through which they keep faith with each other, to be finally united to live their lives out together. Xenophon of Ephesus's *Ephesian Tale* has Anthia and Habrocomes also fall for each other on first sight, both maintain their commitment to each other through various trials, and live happily ever after (as, it seems, do Anthia's slave couple). Achilles Tatius allows Clitophon to attempt (unsuccessfully) to seduce Leucippe (who has, of course, fallen for him, anyway); they, too, are united finally after surviving dangers to life and to mutual commitment (as is Clitophon's sister and a noble captor). Though Daphnis is initiated into erotic play by an older woman (as we noted above), he and Chloe have grown chastely together for some time before perilous separation and final lifelong union when Daphnis can share with Chloe the skills to which the older women had introduced him. Theagenes and Charicleia survive even more troubles in Heliodorus's *An Ethiopian Story* before their final union.[36] These tales all seem to date from the first century CE or later; but similar motifs appear in the Hellenistic Jewish religious romance, *Joseph and Asenath*, possibly from the first century BCE. Both partners are 'helpless' at times in face of their passion for each other, which eventually includes but does not simply comprise coitus. In all these stories the woman is physically weaker, more likely to faint (but the man may also pass out);[37] but she is expected to have a mind of her own, courage, resolution, initiative. Both male and female characters risk being treated as 'sex-objects'.[38] But the important thing is that both are 'persons' in their relationship, persons with

36. See the translated collection edited by B.P. Reardon, *Collected Ancient Greek Novels* (Berkeley: University of California Press, 1989).

37. See K. Cooper, *The Virgin and the Bride: Ideological Womanhood in Late Antiquity* (Cambridge, MA: Harvard University Press, 1996), arguing more strongly than Konstans for an underlying 'conservative' ideology, which would, if anything, support my case.

38. Per contra, M. Aubin, 'Reversing Romance? The *Acts of Thecla* and the Ancient Novel', in R.F. Hock *et al.* (eds.), *Ancient Fiction and Early Christian Narrative* (Atlanta: Scholars Press, 1998), pp. 257-72 (258).

'their own stories', their own interests and concerns and interior dia-
logues. These have, of course, socially constituted roles: but the roles
expected in the narratives specifically involve individuality, similar
enough to the socially constituted individualities of today to be recognizable. For the relevance of all this among early Christians, particularly important is Loveday Alexander's essay, ' "Better to Marry than
to Burn": St Paul and the Greek Novel'.[39]

Such ideals (or idealizations) are not confined to the novelists. Dio
offers a sketch of two related peasant families whose son and daughter
respectively have fallen for each other, and whose union a visitor
prompts. ' "Don't let us permit the boy to be tormented any longer",
said his mother, and throwing her arms round the girl's mother, she
kissed her. "Let us do as they wish".' Dio then reflects critically 'on the
character of weddings and other things among the rich, on the match-
makers, the scrutinies of property and birth, the dowries, the gifts from
the bridegroom, the promises, the deceptions, the contracts and agree-
ments, and finally, the wranglings and enmities that often occur at the
wedding itself'.[40]

Without specifying whose consent might be involved, Musonius, too,
was sure a marriage should not be based on issues of family or wealth
or appearance. Children and the physical ability to engender them was
necessary, but 'in marriage there must above all be complete companionship and affection (συμβίωσίν...καὶ κηδεμονίαν) between husband
and wife, in health and sickness and all conditions'. This affection
should be 'perfect, where both share it completely, each striving to
outdo the other in devotion'. Failure, on the other hand, risks remaining together 'in worse than loneliness'.[41] (Their proper mutual sharing
—bodies specifically included—resonates with Paul in 1 Cor. 7.3-4.)

39. L. Alexander, ' "Better to Marry than to Burn": St Paul and the Greek
Novel', in R.F. Hock *et al.* (eds.), *Ancient Fiction and Early Christian Narrative*
(Atlanta: Scholars Press, 1998), pp. 235-56.

40. Dio Chrysostom , *Discourse* 7.65-80 (79-80).

41. *Musonius Rufus* (ed. and trans. C. Lutz; New Haven: Yale University Press,
1947), XIIIA. P. Veyne, 'The Roman Empire', in *idem* (ed.), *A History of Private
Life*. I. *From Pagan Rome to Byzantium* (Cambridge, MA: Belknapp/Harvard,
University Press 1987), pp. 37-45, focuses on roles and fails to note the relational
evidence. It is worth noting some recent writers' rediscovery of an appreciation of
personal relationships ('friendship') in marriage, in Augustine, especially in 'On the
Good of Marriage'; cf. P. Brown, *The Body and Society: Men, Women and Sexual
Renunciation in Early Christianity* (New York: Columbia University Press, 1988),

Pliny's Calpurnia might have to listen to his readings for friends herself from behind a screen, but he valued her opinion (and corresponded on equal intellectual terms with other women).[42] Seneca valued himself much more when he realized how much his wife valued him.[43] The young bride advised by Plutarch is certainly to be subordinate (as are the Christian wives in Ephesians, Colossians and the Pastoral Epistles), but her husband's responsibility is to 'delight and gratify her' and she will hold him 'by conversation, character and comradeship'.[44] And (whatever the reality, and however unequal in practice), epitaphs show how widespread was the social ideal of companionship between wives and husbands.[45] There is no need to exaggerate any part of this evidence to make the point here being urged. In a pastoral ministry of nearly forty years I have met many relationships (stable ones included) sustained by no richer hopes. Typical of socially given British expectations (in this case surpassed) was a young widow's lament, 'He wasn't just a husband. He was a friend.'

We noted at the outset a rather vague list of psychological factors Malina suggested would be included in any discussions among us of our contemporaries, factors he insisted would distinguish us from those of old time. I have allowed 'psychological development' as a theme that does not emerge noticeably in older thought (while registering Plutarch on the formation of character). For the rest, however, we may recall Quintilian on the importance of 'childhood experience'; and then the 'interpersonal relationship and poise', intelligence, 'emotional control, and personal story' in the popular romances. Of course the paucity and restrictions of our data leave us free to speculate about other strata of ancient society and so again create on the basis of theory persons much more foreign to ourselves than those we have been noting. But the evidence here adduced is drawn from a widespread urban culture shared by those early Christians whose writings have reached us. And it falsifies the general claims to a radical distinction between 'them and 'us', that we have cited, the claims made in some recent New Testament studies on the basis of social anthropology.

pp. 401-403, with further references.
    42. Pliny the Younger, *Letter* 4.
    43. Seneca, *Epistulae morales* 104.
    44. Plutarch, *Advice to Bride and Groom* 33, 22 (*Moralia* 142E, 141AB).
    45. S. Dill, *Roman Society from Nero to Marcus Aurelius* (London: Macmillan, 1905; repr. New York: Meridian, 1956), p. 257.

4. *Selves—Ancient and Modern*

With the help of Rom Harré I have been arguing that the dependency of our 'individuality' on our awareness of how others may or do react to us is as great as any dependency on others' opinions as Malina and associates find in the ancient Mediterranean world; but also that society then for which we have evidence was also geared to engender and sustain recognizable individuality. There still remains the question as to whether these ancients were self-aware selves, with a self-awareness at all closely cognate with what we suppose ourselves to possess. Harré himself, for example, allows for stronger and weaker 'self-theories', but also for the theoretical possibility of a sense of self in eastern cultures quite distinctive from our own.[46] Charles Taylor, allowing for various forms of self-reference, insists,

> But this is not at all the same as making 'self' into a noun, preceded by a definite or indefinite article, speaking of 'the' self, or 'a' self. This reflects something important which is peculiar to our modern sense of agency. The Greek were notoriously capable of formulating the injunction 'gnôthi seauton'—'know thyself'—but they didn't normally speak of the human agent as 'ho autos', or use the term in a context which we would translate with the indefinite article.[47]

And Clifford Geertz, cited by Bruce Malina (as noted above), distinguishes 'our conception of the individual' as '...a bounded, unique, more or less integrated motivational and cognitive universe, a dynamic centre of awareness, emotion, judgment and action organized into a distinctive whole and set contrastively both against other such wholes and against its social and natural background...' itself as 'a rather peculiar idea within the context of the world's cultures'.[48]

Taylor does not rest with his somewhat surprising Whorfian point from the incidentals of Greek vocabulary,[49] making a rather more substantial case to which we now turn. On the one hand stand Plato and

---

46. Harré, *Personal Being*, pp. 86-93.

47. Taylor, *Sources of the Self*, p. 113.

48. C. Geertz, ' "From the Native's Point of View": On the Nature of Anthropological Understanding', in K.H Basso and H.A. Selby (eds.), *Meaning and Anthropology* (Albuquerque: University of New Mexico Press, 1976), pp. 221-37, cited by Malina, *New Testament World*, pp. 66-67.

49. Compare the discussion in J. Barr, *The Semantics of Biblical Language* (London: Oxford University Press, 1961), pp. 37-38, *et passim*; and S.E. Porter, 'Two

successors, with a controlling vision of how things at large really are;
on the other, Descartes and ourselves, for whom 'the paramountcy of
reason is *made*, not found'.[50] However, Descartes has a predecessor in
Augustine. Taylor now makes a fresh distinction. Platonist though
Augustine is, he tell us to turn 'inwards' to divine reality, not 'outward'
to contemplation of the Good. And it seems not a little odd to suggest a
novelty or even an adumbration of novelty in Augustine at this point,
for it is hard to discern other than a concern for inwardness in many of
Augustine's philosophical predecessors, Roman Stoics in particular. We
may readily agree with Taylor that they, too, worked with 'a vision of
cosmic order'; aiming 'to be in accord with nature', but as clearly they
sought it by looking inwards. Taylor, however, dismisses them collec-
tively, without any detailed discussion, judging their inner concern for
'the soul' as no more than an interest in healthy functioning, akin to
telling a modern executive to look after his blood pressure.[51]

First-century examples of a concern for interiority are richly provided
by Epictetus, discussing 'the governing principle', τὸ ἡγεμονικόν, or
'the moral purpose', ἡ προαίρεσις, which is his true business, where
'neither shall a tyrant hinder me against my will, nor the multitude the
single individual, nor the stronger man the weaker; for this has been
given by God to each person as something that cannot be hindered'
(*Dissertation* 4.5.34).[52] (We may compare the very similar contrasts
with other individuals and with society which Geertz thought distinctively modern, just above.) It is this 'moral purpose' that constitutes
'you': 'because you are not flesh, nor hair, but moral purpose' (3.1.40).
'No one is dearer to me than myself', Epictetus insists unhesitatingly,
ἐμοὶ παρ' ἐμὲ φίλτερος οὐδείς, so I must maintain my moral purpose
(3.4.10), 'within me, in what is my own', (2.5.5); it is matter of every
thought that he thinks (3.22.95). So he can imagine reflecting on a day's

Myths: Corporate Personality and Language/Mentality Determinism', *SJT* 43 (1990),
pp. 289-307.
    50. Taylor, *Sources of the Self*, pp. 124-26, original emphasis.
    51. Taylor, *Sources of the Self*, p. 130; but compare pp. 152-53, where Epictetus
and Seneca are allowed to afford some precedents for Descartes' interiority; and
what Taylor then goes on to allow for in Descartes has still further parallels in the
passages above and other similar ones.
    52. In *Epictetus* (trans. W.A. Oldfather; LCL; 2 vols.; London: Heinemann;
Cambridge, MA: Harvard University Press, 1925), I, pp. 239, 353; II, pp. 19, 39,
165, 345.

'inner' experience: 'Today when I saw a handsome lad or a handsome woman I did not say to myself, "Would that a man might bed with her", and, "Happy the husband", for the one who says "happy" of the husband says it of the adulterer, too. I do not even picture to myself the next scene, the woman undressing with me there, and lying down beside me...' (2.18.15-16, LCL adapted).

This Stoic distinction, with the emphasis on the 'inner', on interiority, which Epictetus learned from Musonius Rufus, is widely available and deployed.[53] 'No one can fail to be supremely happy who relies solely on himself and who places all his possessions within himself alone', writes Cicero.[54] 'The supreme good', Seneca advises, 'is a clear and flawless mind which rivals that of God, raised far above mortal concerns, and counting nothing of itself to be outside itself.'[55] But followers of other schools shared similar concerns for 'inner' self-engagement, as for instance Plutarch arguing against the Stoics in *Progress in Virtue*, or Epicureans relying on the frank counsel of friends.[56] (Yet again we note that the *Lives* do not tell us everything about contemporary concerns: 'moral progress' is a proper topic for discussion in other contexts.)

Philo of Alexandria has his own reflections: 'The purpose is as important as the completed act. For as long as we only conceive of disgraceful actions with the bare imagination of the mind, so long are we not guilty of the intent, for the soul may, even against our will, move amiss...'[57] It may well be the case that 'the introspective conscience of the west' has been too easily read back into the New Testament writ-

53. Diogenes Laertius, *Lives of Eminent Philosophers* 7.96.

54. Cicero, *De paradoxa stoicorum* 17 in H. Rackham (trans.), *Cicero. IV. De Oratore III. De Fato. Paraodoxa Stoicorum. De Partitione Oratoria* (LCL; London: Heinemann; Cambridge, MA: Harvard University Press, 1942), p. 267; cf. all of *Paradox* 2, 16-19; and 5, 33-41; *Tusculan Disputations* 4.8-48.

55. Seneca, *Epistulae morales* 124.23 (trans. R.M Gummere; LCL; 3 vols.; London: Heinemann; Cambridge, MA: Harvard University Press, 1917–), p. 449 and the whole letter; cf. e.g., 9 and 108.

56. Cf. C.E. Glad, *Paul and Philodemus: Adaptability in Epicurean and Early Christian Psychology* (NovTSup; Leiden: E.J. Brill, 1996); and *idem*, 'Frank Speech, Flattery and Friendship in Philodemus', in J.T. Fitzgerald (ed.), *Friendship, Flattery and Frankness of Speech: Studies on Friendship in the New Testament Period* (NovTSup, 82; Leiden: E.J. Brill, 1995), pp. 21-60.

57. Philo, *Det. Pot. Ins.* 97, in F.H. Colson (trans.), *Philo*, II (LCL; London: Heinemann; Cambridge, MA: Harvard University Press, 1929–), p. 207; cf. *Jos.* 47.

ings, Paul's in particular.[58] But the metaphorical 'inside' remains an important issue in its own right, not simply as the source for overt activity (as in Mk 7.20-23 and other passages). Closer to Epictetus than to Philo is the condemnation of 'adultery in the heart' (Mt. 5.28, cf. 5.8), and we may compare Rom. 2.16, 7.7-25. Where your 'heart' is, or what is 'in' it, itself matters (Lk. 12.34; cf. 16.15; 1 Cor. 4.5, 14.25).

Quite how all—or any—of this is 'radically' different from Augustine's 'noli foras ire, in teipsum redi; in interiore homine habitat veritas' (Do not go outward; return within yourself. In the inward man dwells truth), cited by Taylor (p. 129), is quite unclear. It is difficult to read the above passages other than as of people reflecting on their own moral experience, 'present to themselves', something very like the 'radical reflexivity' Taylor proposes, 'experiencing our experiencing', using first person language reflectively and not just automatically. It may well be that it is through Augustine that an increased concentration inward reaches western European Christendom, and that such concerns intensified with Descartes, as Taylor proposes, and then become separated from their ground in a shared faith, to become largely subjective in an individualist and egotistic sense. None of that is at issue here. What I have hoped to show is that a willingness to engage in 'introspection' and to form our attitudes by reflecting on our own experience does not make us and our sense of being selves different in kind from some at least of our first century forebears.

In fact, what Taylor laments Harré would seem to reassure him is not so pervasively the case. Today as in times gone by (and for good or ill) most of us structure our attitudes and behaviour on the basis of the views, actions, expectations and reactions of those around us; we are not, by and large and in practice inventors of our own ethos and morality. It is not a distinctive and undue reliance on inwardness as such that would seem to have separated us (accepting that such seems to be the situation) from the roots of our understanding of the good.[59]

58. K. Stendahl, *Paul among Jews and Gentiles and other Essays* (Philadelphia: Fortress Press, 1976), pp. 78-96.

59. Taylor, *Sources of the Self*, e.g., p. 513, 'the basic moral standards of modernity...depend rather on goods to which we do not have access through personal sensibility'. For a critique of Cartesian dualism and an inner-outer dichotomy, from the point of view of a social psychology, Harré, *Personal Being*, pp. 38-41; and on our 'expressive' interdependence, *idem*, *Social Being*, *passim*.

On my reading Taylor does not engage with Gilbert Ryle's trenchant criticisms of any over-literal use of the metaphor of 'introspection', as if it were participant observation of one's own experience while experiencing it, entailing an implicit trust that there is no limit to the objects of one's synchronous attention to one's activities, intentions, reactions and concommitant observation of all these. Ryle argues that what we actually do is 'retrospect', as our common 'introspective' narratives show.[60] It may be that the use of the metaphor and others akin may affect the way we see things; but if what we are actually doing is looking back over past episodes, then, of course, still more people in the ancient world did that, and we have still more in common with still more of them.

People nowadays differ from one another, as people did in the first-century east Mediterranean; and we today are likely to find varying similarities and varying differences with people back then as conveyed to us by the available evidence. And we shall find both probable differences and plausible similarities only by painstaking comparisons, not by sweeping generalizations based in sociological or other theories, heuristically helpful though some of the latter quite certainly are. The ability of people back then and over there to deploy complex first, second and third person language, singular and plural, indicates that their social formation and sustenance as individual persons in relation had much in common with our own.

That does not mean that we necessarily use the words with which we translate theirs in the way they used the ones we translate. We need always to investigate carefully. But having found that we do have major aspects of life in common perhaps means that we can learn from them back there when they seem to see some things differently. To this possibility we now turn, for a consideration of an aspect of the relationships of persons: forgiveness.

60. G. Ryle, *The Concept of Mind* (London: Hutchinson, 1949; repr., Harmondsworth: Penguin Books, 1963), pp. 15-17 and pp. 156-60.

Chapter 3

FORGIVINGNESS?—OF FORGIVENESS?—
OR THE REMISSION OF OFFENCES?

1. *Remission*

'Forgive me!' 'Of course.' 'Forgive that bastard? I wouldn't, not ever.'
So we speak, and so victims of crime, or terrorist violence or family
breakdown express themselves when interviewed.

Commentators on the New Testament writings are fully aware that
the common idiom (following Septuagintal usage, itself echoing that
of the Hebrew Scriptures)[1] might more justly be rendered, 'someone's
faults, failings, offences, are dispatched, remitted, removed, sent away
for them', (ἀφέωνταί σοι αἱ ἁμαρτίαι σου, Lk. 5.20).[2] 'Vergebung
bedeutet den freiwilligen Verzicht, eine Shuldforderung einzutreiben.'[3]
(In other contexts, unconcerned with ἁμαρτίαι it is quite clear that
ἀφίημι demands 'dismiss', 'release', 'leave', or 'relinquish', Mk 1.20;
7.8, 10.28, etc.) The focus is on the 'removal', and then on what is removed; the beneficiary may be left implicit (especially when a general
offer is made: e.g. Mk 1.4). Only with the much rarer χαρίζομαι is the
offence more likely to be left implicit, and even then it is clearly entailed by the dative of the person (2 Cor. 2.10; Eph. 4.32 taken with
Col. 3.13). The direct object is the offence(s), την ἁμαρτίαν, τας ἁμαρτίας. *Persons* are not 'forgiven', persons are offered or given the re-

1. Ps. 103.12; Isa. 38.17; Mic. 7.19, etc.
2. 'ἁμαρτάνω, κτλ' (*TDNT*, I, Rengstorf), pp. 296-335; 'ἀφίημι, κτλ' (*TDNT*,
I, Bultmann); 'Debts' (*ABD*, II, Chilton), pp. 114-16; 'Forgiveness' (*ABD*, II,
Chilton), pp. 831-38; 'Sin, Sinners' (*ABD*, VI, Kselman, Charlesworth and
Shogren), pp. 40-47.
3. 'Vergebung' (*EKL*, B.4, S-Z, Gestrich and Zehner), cols. 1137-43; ' "Vergebung" (conventionally, "forgiveness") is the free remission or renunciation of the
exaction of a debt' (citing col. 1137). How that relates to everyday current German
usage I am not able to tell.

moval of their offence(s). Yet despite the widespread awareness of all this, the contraction to 'forgiveness', absolute, is taken, even in scholarly exegsis, as an unquestionably adequate term in English for what is being explained.[4] The implicit (ethic) dative of the personal pronouns in 'forgive me my sins', 'your sins are forgiven you', is tacitly ignored. I shall argue that the use of this apparently innocuous shorthand is likely to impose onto our reading of the New Testament texts a reading that fails to do them justice. (I shall not attempt to extrapolate from English to other current languages.)

I take as significant for this discussion an article entitled 'Forgiveness and Loyalty', by Piers Benn, published in the journal *Philosophy*. For Benn (writing as a 'secular' philosopher, while in fact paying some attention to aspects of classical Christian thought), forgiveness is 'forgiving an offender', and 'is quite distinct from forgetting the offence, or condoning it'.[5] Forgiveness, as Benn uses the term, is primarily a matter of dealing with the resentment which I legitimately feel (and even ought to feel) against someone responsible for some offence. Benn cites other contemporary philosophers' discussions, and himself instances people's publicly expressed attitudes to child killers, where, again, 'forgiveness' is commonly about one's attitude, and very much one's emotions, one's felt attitude to another person responsible (or held responsible) for some wrong (in this instance, a most heinous wrong). That in some (maybe most) modern English 'forgiveness' is about dealing with one's own resentment against another tallies with my own sense for common usage, even though I am in no position to offer a conclusive demonstration of its currency. I do note, however, that much the same was said some sixty or seventy years ago by H.R. MacIntosh in his now classic *The Christian Experience of Forgiveness*. Having made a clear distinction between remitting a penalty on the one hand and 'forgiveness' on the other, he is quite sure that 'forgiveness is an active process in the mind and temper of a wronged person, by means of which he abolishes a moral hindrance to fellowship with the wrong-doer;' and equally sure that it is this usage that reflects New Testament concerns.[6]

---

4. E.g. E.P. Sanders, *Jesus and Judaism* (London: SCM Press, 1985), pp. 200-204.

5. P. Benn, 'Forgiveness and Loyalty', *Philosophy* 71.277 (1996), pp. 369-83 (370).

6. H.R. MacIntosh, *The Christian Experience of Forgiveness* (London: Nisbet, 1927), pp. 24-29 (28).

I have also chanced on an example in William Thackeray's 1859 *The Virginians*, where the 'forgiveness' of which 'one or two sweet souls' are capable is explicitly distinguished from 'remitting a debt': 'I know how to remit, I say, not forgive.'[7] Since first drafting this piece I have also found L.G. Jones, *Embodying Forgiveness: A Theological Analysis*, who makes a similar point to mine in discussing current American usage, as exemplified in a popular work by an evangelical theologian, L.B. Smedes, *Forgive and Forget: Healing the Hurts we Don't Deserve*. 'It replicates some of the worst features of a therapeutic mind-set... He describes forgiveness as necessary for "coming to terms with a world in which, despite their best intentions, people are unfair to each other and hurt each other deeply".' Forgiveness has become a matter of salving my own inner hurt.[8]

The issues to which Benn so attends are certainly important, and in fact (if in other terms), not foreign to the concerns of some of our New Testament writers. Dealing with our own passions, feelings such as anger and hostility (Mk 7.20-23; Acts 24.25; Gal. 5.19-21; Eph. 4.30-31) is part of discipleship. We are encouraged to be loving and compassionate to one another, including our enemies; and that might well also, might well necessarily lead us to dispatch their offences for them. But nowhere is it suggested that dealing with our own feelings *constitutes* remitting others their wrongdoing, or even constitutes a major element in such remission of their offences and/or the 'debt' or penalty incurred. Even if it might reasonably be argued that resentment on my part could form a part or an aspect of the penalty from which release might be sought, that is nowhere stated. It may be relevant to note the way in which Paul talks about 'our hostility to God', as offenders—not any hostility on God's part towards us (Rom. 5.8-10). Contrary to the general contemporary usage which Benn presupposes and explores and which Jones finds so widespread, the emphasis in the New Testament writings is on removing the effects of the offence(s) on the offender, not on removing their offensiveness to the one affronted, to those offended. Yet Jones himself pays scant attention to the usage I am attempting to

---

7. W.M. Thackeray, *The Virginians* (Collins Library of Classics, London: Collins, n.d. [1859]); ch. 85, p. 794.

8. L.G. Jones, *Embodying Forgiveness: A Theological Analysis* (Grand Rapids: Eerdmans, 1998), p. 49, citing L.B. Smedes, *Forgive and Forget: Healing the Hurts We Don't Deserve* (New York: Harper & Row, 1984), pp. xi-xii. Jones also responds to some of the 'secular' studies noticed by Benn.

display and analyse, and continues to talk of 'forgiveness' (absolute) or 'forgiving people' (and that despite his complaint against another writer on the theme who 'devotes very little space to a discussion of Jesus' sayings and practices concerning forgiveness'). Jones himself does little more than glance at Luke, whose approach is anyway quite distinctive.[9]

A sole possible exception to my own generalization might seem to be Mt. 18.35, ἐὰν μὴ ἀφῆτε ἕκαστος τῷ ἀδελφῷ αὐτοῦ ἀπὸ τῶν καρδιῶν ὑμῶν, 'unless you each extend remission to his brother from your hearts'. Elsewhere in Matthew, however, καρδία seems to denote thought, reflection, will, intention, not emotional feelings.[10] In context here the sense seems to demand, 'unless you extend remission unreservedly, with total commitment, leaving no room for going back on it...' Of course, in all this the ending of resentment, as already said, would seem in all likelihood to be implicitly included; but there is still no suggestion that the removal of resentment constitutes or even predominates in what is urged.

For New Testament writers 'Forgiveness is the wiping out of offense from the memory of the one affronted, along with the restoration of harmony', we are told by G.S. Shogren.[11] It ought, rather, to be seen as significant that the hope that God may 'refrain from remembering offences', deployed from time to time in the Hebrew Scriptures (Ps. 25.7; 79.8; Isa. 64.9; Jer. 14.10; 31.34) recurs only in Hebrews among the New Testament writings, and there is rephrased as ἄφεσις (Heb. 10.17-18; cf. 8.12 with 9.22); while it is almost certainly the objective activating of the record that is deprecated in the older scriptural passages just cited, not the divine subjective awareness. Shogren offers no instances to support either part of his exposition. In the New Testament documents, the 'reification', the objectifying of the offence as some 'thing' both separable from and to be separated from both perpetrator and victim, seems to be consistently maintained.

It may be clear already, and is still more likely to be clear as the discussion proceeds, that I prefer what I take to be the usage I find in the

9. Jones, *Embodying Forgiveness*, p. 215, referring to C.R. Brakenhielm, *Forgiveness* (Philadelphia: Fortress Press, 1993); Jones on the New Testament, pp. 102-103, 110-11.
10. This seems to be the usage of καρδία for most New Testament writers. Even Rom. 9.2 is probably best rendered, 'it hurts me to think of' the situation of my fellow Jews.
11. G.S. Shogren, 'Forgiveness', *ABD*, II, p. 835.

New Testament and other near contemporary writings; but the modern illustrations offered are intended to clarify the distinctions I try to draw, not to persuade readers themselves to adopt one rather than another way of talking. Even if I am correct in my assessment of the ancient material, the reader remains free to prefer the more recent usage.

2. Debts

It is, of course, unsafe to build interpretation simply on grammatical structures or possibly 'dead' metaphor.[12] One needs to pay close attention to what seems to be being said with these patterns of words, in context. The most common fuller exposition in Matthew and Luke, by parable or metaphoric paraphrase, is in terms of debt, something owed, something quite objective which can be got rid of—maybe instantly dismissed—with no remainder. We are further reminded that the metaphor of 'debt' and its remission may well have stemmed from Aramaic usage.[13] Some further beholdedness may thereby be incurred by the person so favoured, gratitude perhaps, respect shown by emulating the behaviour of the benefactor. But the debt as such can be wiped out, nothing remains to be paid: ἄφεσις σοί τῶν ἁμαρτιῶν σοῦ, 'the remission of your offences', is like that.

So we find the following sequence in Matthew: Peter asks, 'How often is my brother going to offend against me, and I'm to extend forgiveness to him?' and Jesus responds with a tale of a king's slave deeply in debt to him, but whose debt the king cancelled, τὸ δάνειον ἀφῆκεν αὐτῷ (Mt. 18.21, 24, 27). Whether or not we suppose Matthew to have read the parable appropriately (perhaps its heavy punitive ending raises more questions than Matthew notices),[14] it is clear that for him 'cancelling debt' is a ready metaphor for remission of their offences extended to offenders. Where Luke's version of the Lord's Prayer has

12. Barr, *Semantics of Biblical Language*; more recently, S.E. Porter, 'Two Myths: Corporate Personality and Language/Mentality Determinism', *SJT* 43 (1990), pp. 289-307.

13. Chilton, *ABD*, II, 'Debts', pp. 114-16 (115) citing *idem, A Galiaean Rabbi and his Bible* (London: SPCK, 1984).

14. Downing, *Jesus and the Threat of Freedom*, p. 80; B.B. Scott, *Hear Then the Parable* (Minneapolis: Fortress Press, 1989), pp. 267-80; W.R. Herzog, *Parables as Subversive Speech: Jesus as Pedagogue of the Oppressed* (Louisville, KY: Westminster/John Knox Press, 1994), pp. 131-49.

ἄφες ἡμῖν τὰς ἁμαρτίας ἡμῶν και γὰρ αὐτοὶ ἀφίομεν παντὶ ὀφείλοντι ἡμῖν, with 'offences' and 'debts' in parallel (Lk. 11.3), Matthew has 'debts' in both clauses, followed by the further explanatory paraphrase, παραπτώματα, transgressions (Mt. 6.12-15).[15]

In similar objectifying fashion (though without the benefit of the 'debt' metaphor) Dionysius of Halicarnassus in his *Roman Antiquities* could commend relieving a repentant offender of a complaint (ἀφεὶς αὐτῇ τὰ ἐγκλήματα μετανοούσῃ), just as the Gods forgive human offences, and are readily reconciled (συγγνώμονεω τοῖς ἀνθρωπίνοις εἰσὶν ἁμαρτήμασι καὶ εὐδιάλλακτοι, *Roman Antiquities* 8.50.4). Josephus uses very similar language in his *Jewish War* (5.416); compare, too, the long section in *Ant.* 2.140-46, also assimilating divine and human remission of penalties. Then in his version of Ezra 9.6-15 and 1 Esdras 8.74-90 (where Ezra simply confesses his people's failings) Josephus specifically asks God to be disposed to be forgiving towards their offences (συγγνωμονῆσαι...τοῖς ἡμαρτημένοις), which means to remit the due punishment (ἀφεῖναι τῆς κολάσεως) (*Ant.* 11.144). In context it is clear that τὸ συγγνώμων in these passages quoted denotes an active disposition to remit. Nonetheless our New Testament writers bypass even dispositional terms such as this, to concentrate on the remission as such.

A further, and attractive illustration is afforded by Lucian of Samosata's account of his hero, Demonax:

> He was never known to make an uproar or excite himself or get angry, even if he had to rebuke someone; though he assailed sins, he forgave sinners (ἀλλὰ τῶν μὲν ἁμαρτημάτων καθήπτετο, τοῖς δὲ ἁμαρτάνουσι συνεγίνωσκεν), thinking one should pattern oneself on physicians, who heal sicknesses but feel no anger at the sick. He considered that it is human to err (ἁμαρτάνειν), the act of a God or a godlike human to set right what has gone wrong (Θεοῦ δὲ ἡ ἀνδρὸς ἰσοθέου τὰ πταισθέντα ἐπανορθοῦν; Lucian, *Demonax* 7).

The issue of one's emotional response is noted, but a clear distinction is drawn between that and dealing with offenders' offences. A distinction similar to the initial one above is also expressed in passing by Plutarch: one needs to have confidence that a complainant disapproves of some action, and is not simply expressing hatred for the agent (*De capienda ex inimicis utilitate* 9; *Moralia* 91A). The physician-and-sickness metaphor is deployed by Seneca, too, who insists that we have to reprove

15. Cf. also Lk. 7.41; 13.4.

failing fellow humans, but not angrily: 'Who gets angry with a patient he's trying to cure?' (*De ira* 15.1). I do not know when 'loving the sinner but hating the sin' first appears among Christians; Augustine is the first to be quoted, so far as I can find. In *Letter* 3.211.11, he counsels a nun to act in her community 'cum dilectione hominum et odio vitiorum', 'kind to the person(s) while hating the fault'.[16] Augustine himself had deployed variants of the commonplace healing metaphor (surgeon and infection), just a few lines earlier.

The physician image for dealing with people at fault is in fact widespread[17], implying this clear division of offence from offender, objectifying the former. One of Lucian's imaginary Cynic figures, the Cyniscus of *The Downward Journey* 7, is also a 'physician for human failings' (ἰατρὸν τῶν ἀνθρωπίνων ἁμαρτημάτων). The resonance with Mk 2.16-17 (and parallels) is clear, 'It is not the healthy who have need of a physician (ἰατροῦ), but those who are unwell. I have not come to call those who are all right, but failures, offenders (ἁμαρτωλούς).' Offences, failings are like sicknesses the offender is to be freed from, like debts to be cancelled. They are not part of the person (unless, one might guess, he or she clings on to them; but even this possible qualification is not articulated). Perhaps it is worth emphasizing that the point of this 'objective' model of healing is precisely to distinguish the disease from the patient; it is thus explicitly other than the 'psychotherapy' for the one offended which Benn espoused and against which I noted Jones arguing.

3. *Offenders*

As well as largely eschewing in the foregoing (other than in quotation) the words 'forgive' and 'forgiveness', the words 'sin' and 'sinner' have also been mostly avoided. In popular usage (if deployed at all) the terms relate primarily if not exclusively to sexual misdemeanours in such now rather dated phrases as 'living in sin', which also suggests a state of being. If any usage from the New Testament canon is recalled, it is likely to be the pseudo-Johanninne 'let him who is without sin...'

16. *PL* 33, 962 (I am told of a tradition that the wife of Rabbi Meir [late second-century CE?] suggested that Ps. 104 (105).34 be read as a prayer that 'sin' rather than sinners be banished from the earth.)

17. Diogenes Laertius 6.6; Diogenes 40.1; Pseudo-Anacharsis 9; Epictetus 3.22.72; 4.8.28-29; Dio Chrysostom 8.7-8; cf. Downing, *Christ and the Cynics*, pp. 122-23, 159.

('cast the first stone...' is often left unsaid; Jn 8.7). Echoing the kind of exegesis which I am here opposing, this, too, suggests 'sin' as an ontological ingredient. Any sin in your past characterizes you as 'sinner' and it is this (rather than particular unremitted offences—among which, perhaps, may have been involvement as accessory in the incident in question) which disqualifies you from condemning others to punishment. 'Sin' and 'sinner' carry too much of this sub-Augustinian luggage to be helpful.

In the usage which Piers Benn's article exemplifies we talk of someone as 'offender' (in the article, not even an 'ex-offender', where, however, the 'ex-' tends to be purely nominal).[18] Wickedness is part of that person's 'charcter' (371). 'Forgiveness' has no effect on this negative status of the one said to be forgiven; it is simply a matter of my changing my attitude to the offender. All legal penalties could be paid—or remitted—but if my attitude to the offender remained hostile, there would have been no forgiveness. Alternatively, an offender's society could change its attitude to him or her, could 'feel forgiving', and in this sense 'forgive', without remitting any penalties and while still categorizing her or him as an (ex-)offender. Western Christians, at least, have encouraged this way of seeing things in developments of the penitential system and in the Reformation reactions. They (we) encourage one another to categorize ourselves and others as 'sinners', as having that character, saddled with an undischarged debit balance for which we can at best ask God's continuing indulgence, but of which we are never rid. (We are still overdrawn, but God is now a friendly bank-manager; we are still offenders, but God is now a genial probation officer.)

The subjective individualism of 'forgiveness' in this sense is further emphasized in Benn's discussion of ways of inducing this changed attitude in myself. I might see the sinner as (nonetheless) having intrinsic worth, as loved by God, perhaps (this is how Benn interprets Augustine). Or, as proposed by another philosopher Benn cites, 'I try to make myself see that he is not wholly rotten; there is a core of decency in him that I should take account of.' Again, I might instead or as well recall the person he or she once was. Or I might try to change that person's character, so that there will be nothing there any longer to offend me.[19]

18. In general accord, Jones, *Embodying Forgiveness*, p. 275.
19. Benn, 'Forgiveness', pp. 370-72, citing Jean Hampton, 'The Retributive Idea', in J.G. Murphy and J. Hampton (eds.), *Forgiveness and Mercy* (Cambridge: Cambridge University Press, 1987), p. 155.

I am not for the moment concerned with assessing the rival merits of these different ways of using the vocabulary, nor of the sorts of behaviour articulated, though they are to be touched on as part of this argument. For the moment I mean only to point out that there is a difference, a marked difference; and to urge that any attempt to take the text seriously in English must involve a careful choice of English words.' Ἀφίημι just does not *mean* 'forgive' in the common usage of 'forgive' to which Benn's discussion bears witness.

The commentators are aware that ἀφίημι and ἄφεσις do not occur in the letters least disputedly ascribed to Paul, and other terms so translated are infrequent in these writings (e.g. Rom. 4.7-8, citing ps. 32.1-2). It remains clearly important nonetheless to represent Paul as concerned with this theme (as interpreted).[20] This is to miss what Paul seems to be saying.

It is in fact widely acknowledged that ἁμαρτία (sing.) most often in Paul seems to denote a sort of 'power' or field of force, one which is still very much around, and it is also widely but not universally accepted that this force is still able to affect those who have been hallowed, 'the saints', including Paul himself (Rom. 6.1; 7.22-25; 1 Cor. 15.56).[21] Whatever one makes of this, so far as ἁμαρτίαι (pl.) are concerned, Paul's 'saints' are no longer 'in their sins', 'sins' are in the past (Gal. 2.15; 1 Cor. 15.17).[22] That is 'dead and gone', we are free from all that (1 Cor. 6.11; 9.24-27; Rom. 6)—or should be. This is not to pretend that Paul and his saints are perfect, in no sense is that so (1 Cor. 4.8; 5-6; Phil. 3.13-16; Rom. 14; etc.). But whatever might be termed 'sins' have been got rid of, they have been dealt with. That is—or seems most probably—the reason why there is in Paul no place for talk of remission of offences for those who have 'come in'.[23] Whether or not Paul ever offered to anyone 'outside' ἄφεσις σοί τῶν ἁμαρτιῶν σοῦ, it

20. The same theme as is expressed overtly in Luke–Acts 'obviously underlies Paul', (Bultmann, ἀφίημι, *TDNT*, I, p. 512; Gestrich and Zehner, *EKL*, IV, 2.2, p. 1138; Shogren, *ADB*, II, pp. 835-36.

21. R. Bultmann, ἀφίημι, *TDNT*, I, p. 513, who unfortunately extends this Pauline usage to the New Testament documents as a whole. Cf. E.P. Sanders, *Paul, the Law and the Jewish People* (London: SCM Press, 1983), pp. 71-73.

22. Sanders, *Paul*, pp. 7-10.

23. Cf. J.D.G. Dunn, *The Theology of Paul the Apostle* (Grand Rapids: Eerdmans, 1998), pp. 326-33.

would certainly seem likely that he would not have seen it as appropriate to extend it to those whose offences had been expunged.

The approach in the synoptic tradition and in Acts is, then, somewhat different. There, ἄφεσις τῶν ἁμαρτιῶν clearly is offered to outsiders; but disciples, followers, are also expected to ask for it, and reluctance to extend it on their own part may well preclude them from receiving it from God, need it though they will (Mk 11.25; and Lk. 11.2-4 with Mt. 6.12-15 and 18.21-35, again; and compare 1 Jn 1.9-10; Jas 5.15-16). Deploying the metaphor of 'debt', we might allow that even those whose debts are cancelled may incur fresh ones, at least in this tradition. And we ourselves might well find such usage more acceptable than Paul's—more familar, at least.

But perhaps we may extend the metaphor. If your debts are cancelled you are no longer a debtor. In the modern western world a discharged bankrupt may well have a very low credit rating; but for both the synoptic tradition and for Paul, when offences have been expunged, got rid of, that is an end of it. You are an offender no longer, nor are 'ex-offender', 'forgiven offender' really appropriate designations: ἁμαρτωλός is no longer in any way an appropriate characterization of you or your status. 'While we *were* still sinners, Christ died for us' (Rom. 5.8) seems the appropriate translation.

4. *Forgivingness*

In attempting to clarify the distinction and its potential significance, it is worth imagining what difference it might make in practice. In the light of teaching in the New Testament as a whole we allowed we might well agree with Benn that if part or all of the penalty my debt had incurred were your resentment, and this in fact remained—you had not dealt with it or allowed it to be dissolved away—then your words of forgiveness would be hollow, void. You would not be in a state to make them a valid performative. But suppose you had achieved considerable self-mastery, and felt no resentment, yet nonetheless acted it out to express your disapproval of my offence, or to deter me from repeating it. In Benn's contemporary usage, because you now harbour no hostility, I am forgiven, while still suffering the penalties you—forgivingly—see fit to impose. If forgiveness is not to be the remission of penalties, the theoretical difference in accompanying practice is considerable. If society at large has no offended feelings towards me (having maybe no feelings towards me at all) I would seem in this sense to have to suppose I am forgiven—even if all the legal penalties remained to be inflicted. Compared with ancient usage, including that of the Jewish and Christian scriptures, modern usage, reducing forgiveness to (or, better, 'using the word forgiveness for') a matter of attitude, and (perhaps deliberately) failing to separate offender from offence, misses most of what the ancient terms so translated conveyed.

This is not to deny that what my attitudes to offenders do to me may be very important. Refusing to forgive in any sense, harbouring resentment and vindictiveness may destroy me.[24] And for sure, this may well be a proper concern, whatever its background. In terms of the ancient roots of western culture, an insistence on the value to oneself of 'forgivingness' seems in fact most akin to Stoic introspective concern to avoid inner turmoil. 'Otherwise you have destroyed within you the son, the respectful man, the man of honour.'[25] The Stoic tone does not have to disqualify it from our attention; but it does not help us much in our attempts to capture the early Christian talk we are here considering; though, again, if my resentment is part of the penalty imposed on you, then any full forgiveness in this sense must necessarily include removing my hostility.

5. *Offensiveness*

One further complication that modern usage involves emerges in Benn's discussion, and is further treated by Jones. It may well be the case that one continues to hate the offence, even that one accepts a strong obligation to hate the offence. It will then be difficult to offer any kind of forgiveness to the offender without seeming to condone his or her actions. So far from forgiveness being approved, it may readily seem morally reprehensible.[26]

However, guided, it would seem, by our modern usage which talks of 'forgiving the offender', rather than of forgiving the offender the offence

24. See, e.g., M.A. Coate, *Sin, Guilt and Forgiveness* (London: SPCK, 1994), pp. 82-89.

25. Epictetus, *Dissertation* 3.18.6; cf. *Encheiridion* 4-5; Seneca, *Epistulae morales* 81.25; *De constantia* 14.3; *De ira* 3.25.3; etc.

26. Benn, 'Forgiveness', p. 374; Jones, *Embodying Forgiveness*, pp. 225, 246-52, both citing Bishop Butler, *Sermons*; and also J. Hampton, 'Forgiveness, Resentment, and Hatred', in J.G. Murphy and J. Hampton (eds.), *Forgiveness and Mercy* (Cambridge: Cambridge University Press, 1987), pp. 35-85; also cited by Benn.

or penalty (or both), Benn quite explicitly does not wish to break the connection between them, insisting, rather, that 'we trace the immoral nature of the act back to the immorality of the agent.' The ancient world, with its alternative model, was, of course, fully sensitive to issues of responsibility and guilt. Clearly, if the sinner clings onto his or her sin, if the debtor refuses either to pay up or be released, if there is in fact no repentance in the full sense of no change, it may be very difficult if not impossible to make the separation, and the upshot may be a very similar situation of continuing retribution, including estrangement.

It is not appropriate to discuss in any detail here the conditions or lack of them for remission of sins. Stances on this issue seem to differ, but without apparently affecting the usage we are here considering. In Mark and in Luke John the Baptist preaches 'repentance', μετάνοια, 'for the remission of sins' (εἰς ἄφεσιν ἁμαρτιῶν), either as change of life and intentions or at least as commitment to such change. Matthew and Mark have people confess their sins at John's baptism, though Matthew does not allow John to offer them forgiveness of their sins. Mark has Jesus quote Isaiah to explain his use of puzzling parables, 'lest they repent and it be forgiven them' (Mk 4.12). Luke continues to emphasize repentance in the teaching of Jesus and of his first followers, and that would seem to include 'confession of sins' (Lk. 15.18, 21; 18.13-14). Elsewhere in the Markan tradition forgiveness is not linked to repentance (though repentance is still demanded), rather is Jesus portrayed offering forgiveness unconditionally (Mk 2.5-10). Though Luke insists (ch. 15) that the parables of the found sheep, found coin, and found son are about repentance, as noted, yet the first two (sheep and coin) can hardly be read that way, and for many commentators εἰς ἑαυτὸν δὲ ἐλθὼν, 'coming to his senses', in Luke 15.17 is at least ambiguous.[27] The woman in Lk. 7.36-50 has loved and has wept and her sins are forgiven her. The petition for forgiveness of sins in the Lord's prayer has the remission to others of their debts as its condition (Mt. 6.9-14; Lk. 11.4; cf. Mt. 18.21-35 and Mk 11.25). Paul, as we noted earlier, does not use the language of repentance or forgiveness much, and not at all at initiation; the only condition he seems to presuppose for 'justification' ('acceptance', 'setting right' etc.) is faith. In these

---

27. I have argued that Lk. 18.13-14 would also have seemed at least ambiguous if not caricature: F.G. Downing, 'The Ambiguity of the "The Pharisee and the Toll-Collector" (Luke 18.9-14) in the Greco-Roman World of Late Antiquity', *CBQ* 54.1 (1992), pp. 80-99: ch. 4, following.

passages where 'remission of sins' is spoken of it can be seen that the actual usage seems unaffected by differing thoughts about (pre-) conditions.

It might seem to us that the dispatching of offences then implies that no change in the actions and attitudes of the beneficiary are required (Bonhoeffer's 'cheap grace'). This seems nowhere to be the implication in practice. People have their sins forgiven them, or that is offered; and in response to the offer or the gift or both, considerable changes are expected. Mostly, in practice, it seems to be that people who still have a lot of desired changes ahead of them are accepted in advance of that (or much of that) already as friends, table-companions, followers, disciples, subjects of God's rule (in Paul, also as saints, limbs of the body). (Further) change is then expected to occur.[28] The offensiveness of past behaviour is by no means diminished (e.g., Rom. 1.28-32).

6. Changing the Penalty or Changing the Offender or Changing the One Offended

However, in connection with the theme of 'repentance', of questions of change, it is worth noting the insights assembled by Michel Foucault, focusing on the recent history and implications of the concentration of attention on the person rather than the offence, and the 'inner', rather than the bodily offender. 'Que le châtiment, si je puis ainsi parler, frappe l'âme plutôt que le corps.' 'Les juges, peu à peu...se sont donc mis à juger autres choses que les crimes: l' "âme" des criminels.'[29] The upshot is an attempt to recondition the offending human machine by more and more effective manipulation, by (supposedly) more and more 'humane' methods—including a forced awareness of total observation (Jeremy Bentham's 'Panopticon'—still the model for contemporary prisons). However we react to ever enhanced opportunities for surveil-

28. See, e.g., B. Chilton and J.I.H. McDonald, *Jesus and the Ethics of the Kingdom* (London: SPCK, 1987); Dunn, *Theology of Paul the Apostle*, pp. 326-33, again. On the context of reconciling practice, and on 'cheap grace' and Bonhoeffer, see Jones, *Embodying Forgiveness*, pp. 120-33 and more briefly, p. 31.

29. 'May the punishment strike the soul rather than the body, if I may put it so.' 'Judges, then, little by little, set themselves to judge something other than offences: the "souls" of offenders.' M. Foucault, *Surveiller et punir: La naissance de la prison* (Paris: Gallimard, 1975), p. 22, quoting G. de Mably, *De la législation* (*Œuvres complètes*, 1789), IX, p. 326; and then p. 24. I would call attention in particular to summaries on pp. 76, 128-29 and 240-42.

lance (for the public good, of course), it is clear that the choice of model for offence and offender can be very significant.[30] We cannot assume that an easy reduction of 'remission of offences' to 'forgivingness' leaves things as they were.

Were we consistently to objectify offences, conceptualize them as distinct from rather than necessarily integral to, even identified with the offender, then we might more readily think in terms of separating them in practice, enabling the offender to repudiate the offending course of action. But as things are, we make it clear that we see her misdeed(s) as essential to her character, she 'is' a thief, however much her 'debt to society' may have been 'paid'. We still cannot forgive *her*, because it now sounds as though we are condoning the offensiveness with which we have identified her. Perhaps it really could make a positive difference if we spoke of the offence as heinous, impermissible, but the offender's debt as wiped out, the record deleted?

This is clearly different from, and possibly better than, trying to find something 'lovable' in the offender, some strand(s) in his character to balance against the evil we see as also inherent, some present or past good as our required warrant for trying to persuade our offender to discard the offending aspect(s) of his character and 'earn forgiveness' (so, Benn, following Jean Hampton).[31] This is not to deny that there may be much that is likable and even admirable in many or most of all offenders, nor that discovering such goodness may help those offended. It is only to emphasize that early Christian talk of remission of sins involves no such search or preconditions, it constitutes a quite different practice from that articulated in the modern usage of 'forgiveness'.

Yet further distinct corollaries follow from a consideration of 'the right' to forgive, in the complex situation where I am only a minor victim, and someone else has suffered much more—perhaps a member of my family, perhaps simply a fellow human being, or a great many fellow human beings. Benn includes quite a helpful discussion, albeit in his questionable terms, and suggests what he terms 'quasi-forgiveness'. His reasoning is again significant for the discussion here. Benn notes that I can pay someone else's debt, if the creditor is willing; but I cannot *cancel* a debt owed to someone else, and concludes, 'the dis-

---

30. Foucault notes the contrast between the approach he is analysing and the traditional commonplace *payer sa dette*: *Surveiller et punir*, p. 235.

31. Benn, 'Forgiveness', pp. 370-72, citing Hampton, 'The Retributive Idea', p. 155.

analogy with forgiveness is clear enough, for an analogy would require
[me] to have the right to annual—i.e. literally 'forgive'—the debt'.[32] In
the Gospels, on the other hand, we are clearly told that Jesus has the
right to forgive people their sins against parties unspecified, and can
confer that right on others.

A little further on Benn concludes, 'If forgiveness is the overcoming
of resentment, it is plainly impossible that one person should literally
overcome another's resentment', and then argues the illegitimacy of
diminishing indignation against some wickedness, for that would under-
value the victim, treat him or her of no account.[33] In the New Testament
writings, an unrelenting opposition to 'sin' accompanies without strain
the ready remission of sins.

The ancient paradigm also discourages self-righteous censoriousness.
If we think of offensiveness as the inherent characteristic of deliberate
murderers, torturers, child abusers, thieves, all of whom fully deserve
our highly moral indignation, then they are the wicked to be buried
away, alive or dead, we are quite other. The ancient paradigm, by contrast, invites us to consider the debts we have all incurred and continue
to amass, as the beam in my own eye over against the mote in another's.[34] If just the motorists among us were to count up the debts to
society we incur in our lawless and antisocial and very destructive (but
respectable and admired) behaviour on the roads, we might be less ready
to condemn, more ready for others' debts to society to be written off.

It is on this basis that some in the ancient world argued that as people
with debts needing paying or cancelling, we had a duty to write off
debts of all kinds owing to us. This was not a duty to find offenses inof-
fensive, or to find offenders likable, but just to treat them as we expect
to be treated—or hope to be treated—ourselves. However often God
and others have remitted our offences, we are again and again in the
same state: not us guiltless and others criminals, but all discharged
debtors, as prone as others to fall back into our own favourite debts.[35]

32. Benn, 'Forgiveness', p. 375; cf. Jones, *Embodying Forgiveness*, pp. 101-105,
with reference to E. Levinas, *Difficult Freedom: Essays on Judaism* (Baltimore:
The Johns Hopkins University Press, 1990).

33. Benn, 'Forgiveness', pp. 378-81.

34. Musonius, frg. 22; Epictetus, *Dissertation* 3.22.98; Seneca, *De vita beata*
27.4; and, of course, Lk. 6.41-42; Mt. 7.3-5.

35. In addition to the above, Lk. 11.4 with Mt. 6.12 and Mk 11.25; and Lk.
11.13 with Mt. 7.11; Jn 8.7; Rom. 3.23.

7. Conclusion

It seems to me that the ancient paradigm of forgiving offenders their offences is clearly different from the modern one of achieving in one-self some sort of warranted 'forgivingness'. Whether the older is preferable—even workable—is another question.[36]

It is also worth recalling that 'remission of offences' itself is anyway not quantitatively a dominant theme in the New Testament canon, not even in the synoptic gospels. It is perhaps of positive significance that Bruce Chilton and Jim McDonald could write their account of Jesus' 'enactment of the Kingdom' without enough reference to 'forgiveness' for it to warrant a mention in the index. It is also worth noting Peter Och's brief appreciation of Gregory Jones as 'redescribing forgiveness as reconciliation'.[37] In Jones as in other writers the word 'forgiveness' becomes a token that must be deployed, irrespective of what it may be asked to denote: 'forgivingness', 'forgiven-ness', 'reconciliation'—or (least likely of all, it seems) 'the remission of offences'. Only this latter seems faithfully to represent the usage found among some of our New Testament writers.

Already we have noted instances of variety among people in the ancient east Mediterranean, and divergencies among early Christians, too (especially in our first two chapters). We now consider a wide range of people's differing attitudes to their own supposed balance of credit or debt in the eyes of their God or Gods.

36. Jones, *Embodying Forgiveness*, p. 151, reminds us of R. Swinburne's *Responsibility and Atonement* (Oxford: Clarendon Press, 1989), an elegant argument for Kant and against the New Testament.

37. Chilton and McDonald, *Jesus and the Ethics of the Kingdom*; P. Ochs, quoted on the back cover of Jones, *Embodying Forgiveness*.

Chapter 4

THE AMBIGUITY OF 'THE PHARISEE AND THE TOLL COLLECTOR'
(LUKE 18.9-14) IN THE GRAECO-ROMAN WORLD
OF LATE ANTIQUITY*

For most commentators Luke 18.9-14 is quite unproblematic. It is an authentic part of the Jesus tradition, though v. 9 ('He also told this parable to some who trusted in themselves that they were righteous, and despised others') and v. 14b ('for everyone who exalts himself will be humbled, but he who humbles himself will be exalted') may well have been added by Luke; and it expresses the heart of Jesus' teaching of the grace of God, anticipating the insights of Paul. There are a small number of varying exceptions to this widespread agreement, and their suggestions will be discussed in what follows. But even among these there is a widespread consensus that the toll collector is meant to engage our approval, and that this has been so from the very first telling of the story.[1] Whether the story comes from Jesus, as the majority avers, or

* Reprinted from *CBQ* 54.1 (1992), pp. 80-99, with kind permission. Among older commentators, J.M. Creed, *The Gospel According to St. Luke* (London: Macmillan, 1930); R. Bultmann, *Jesus and the Word* (ET; London: Collins, 1958), p. 142; T.W. Manson, *The Sayings of Jesus* (London: SCM Press, 1949), pp. 308-12; and, more recently, K. Rengstorf, *Das Evangelium nach Lukas* (NTD, 3; Göttingen: Vandenhoeck & Ruprecht, 1962), pp. 207-208; and I note the comments of H. Hendrickx, *The Parables of Jesus* (London: Geoffrey Chapman, 1986), p. 243. For this chapter I also consulted studies by F.R. Borsch, F. Bovon, E.E. Ellis, A. Feuillet, A.R.C. Leaney, A. Loisy, E. Linnemann, T.W. Manson, W. Manson, H. Merklein, A. Schlatter, R.S. Stein, D.L. Tiede, and D.O. Via, in addition to those referred to below. At the time of writing the only two dissertations I could find in the English, German or French lists were from the USA, by K. Drake and R.N. Wilken respectively, 1985; neither seemed to have said anything to pre-empt or disturb the argument that follows.
    1.   One recent exception near the time of writing was B.B. Scott, *Hear Then the*

from Luke himself, as some of late have argued, the toll collector and his reliance on and openness to the gracious forgiveness of God provide an example obviously meant for us to identify with and adopt. Certainly Luke makes it abundantly clear that this is how he means the narrative to be read. He has prepared us already in chs. 5–7 and at other points subsequently (e.g. 15.1) to expect to react negatively to Pharisees, but, by contrast, positively to 'toll collectors and sinners'. 18.14b on self-abasement has been anticipated at 14.11, and now 18.9 states unambiguously the judgment for which the following serves as illustration.

The questions that are raised about the toll collector mainly concern the authorship of the narrative. The genre of the 'example story' seems to be peculiar to Luke among the Gospels, and the theology (as just noted) is specifically Lukan: so perhaps the whole pericope is his?[2] However, if with the majority we take the story to be pre-Lukan and so to have circulated on its own without Luke's preparation for it, and at least shorn of vv. 9 and 14b, how then may we imagine it to have been read, standing on its own? If Luke felt it needed such introduction and conclusion, then it may be that even he did not find it as unambiguous as his early and modern commentators have done.

It is in fact quite rare to meet doubts about the details of the story itself. Luise Schottroff raised a number of queries about the figure of the Pharisee a few years ago now, suggesting that we meet here with a deliberate caricature, not a 'real' Pharisee, as most suppose.[3] Not many seem to have been persuaded by her arguments.[4] I shall be bringing forward some more in support of her contention.

Parable (Minneapolis: Fortress Press, 1989), pp. 92-98, to be discussed below. W.R. Herzog, *Parables as Subversive Speech*, takes a different line again, imposing (as I see it) an impressive materialist interpretation that pays insufficient attention to the cultural data available and here displayed; Herzog notes this present piece, pp. 175, 177.

2. So, for instance, M.D. Goulder, *Luke: A New Paradigm*, II (JSNTSup, 20; Sheffield: JSOT Press, 1989), pp. 667-70; see further below, but also F.G. Downing, 'A Paradigm Perplex: Luke, Matthew and Mark', *NTS* 38 (1992), pp. 15-36, repr. in Downing, *Doing Things with Words*.

3. L. Schottroff, 'Die Erzählung vom Pharisäer und Zöllner als Beispiel für die theologische Kunst des Überredens', in H. Betz and L. Schottroff (eds.), *Neues Testament und christliche Existenz* (Festschrift H. Braun; Tübingen: Mohr-Siebeck, 1973), pp. 439-61.

4. E.g. I.H. Marshall, *The Gospel of Luke* (NIGTC, 3; Exeter: Paternoster Press,

But what I mainly intend is to explore the very equivocal response from many quarters that the prayer of the toll collector would most likely have encountered in the first-century east Mediterranean world. Is he (by contrast with the Pharisee) quite so obviously 'ein Identifikationsonfigur' (Schottroff)? My conclusion will be that his prayer is at the very least ambiguous, and very likely as much a caricature of self-absorption as is that of the Pharisee, and both are warnings for us, quite plausibly from Jesus himself.

I intend to explore likely reactions to both prayers in the wider ('non-Jewish') Graeco-Roman world; in diaspora Hellenistic Judaism, among Luke's Christian contemporaries, and in the context of Luke–Acts; in Palestinian (but, of course, still Hellenistic) Judaism, including earlier Christians (supposing the story antedates Luke); and in the context of the traditions of the teaching of Jesus. I do not present these in any way as self-contained cultural spheres, but they do address distinctions used or assumed by other commentators, and they have a certain organizational utility.

1. *The Wider Graeco-Roman World*

The 'ideal audience' for Luke–Acts may well be taken to be Gentile.[5] How would the narrative of the two men at prayer have been heard if prior to its inclusion in Luke it had been told on its own, and in particular, without either v. 9 or v. 14b, in that pagan world? In fact the relevance of the material that follows remains even if the actual audience was always made up of people already Christian who had grown up in pagan and diaspora Jewish contexts. Such people also belonged within the wider Gentile culture.

1978), p. 678; Hendrickx, *Parables*, p. 237; F. Schnider, 'Ausschliessen und ausgeschlossen werden: Beobachtungen zur Struktur des Gleichnisse vom Pharisäer und Zöllner Lk 18, 10-14a', *BZ* 24 (1980), pp. 42-56.

5.   See, e.g., F.G. Downing, 'Ethical Pagan Theism and the Speeches in Acts', *NTS* 27 (1981), pp. 544-63; and 'Common Ground with Paganism in Luke and in Josephus', *NTS* 28 (1982), pp. 546-59; and 'Theophilus' First Reading of Luke–Acts', in C.M. Tuckett (eds.), *Luke's Literary Achievement* (JSNTSup, 116; Sheffield: Sheffield Academic Press, 1995), pp. 91-109, repr. in the companion volume to this, Downing, *Doing Things with Words*.

That people should go to a temple to pray is widely approved.[6] Though the toll collector would be a very unpopular figure,[7] it is easy to select data that would suggest likely approval for his prayer ('God, be merciful to me, a sinner!'). These are some examples from Dionysius of Halicarnassus' popular *Roman Antiquities*: 'Tullius told them…since they acknowledged their fault and had donned the traditional marks of suppliants and were humbly begging to be spared the resentment they deserved, they should receive clemency…' Decius counsels, 'Adopt the humble and piteous demeanour of one who has erred and is asking pardon, such a demeanour as your plight requires.' Veturia urges her son, Coriolanus, 'The Gods…are disposed to forgive the offences of men and are easily reconciled (εὐδιάλλακτοι). Many have there been before now who, though greatly sinning against them, have appeased their anger by prayers and sacrifices.'[8] Much the same emerges from Josephus's retelling of Scripture, where both ideal and intended audience are Gentile. To Ezra 10.1 Josephus adds, 'ashamed to look up'; Moses talks of 'despairing of other hope or resource'; Joshua eschews all self-confidence; and elsewhere Josephus echoes the conviction of Dionysius, when, in his imagined speech before the walls of Jerusalem under siege, he, too, insists, 'the deity is easily reconciled (εὐδιάλλακτον, again) to those who confess and repent'.[9]

For those who accept this standpoint, the story-teller who ended with 14a would be urging nothing new; he would simply be aligning himself with a contemporary commonplace, discerned in much the same way by Luke's contemporary, Josephus. Vv. 9 and 14b would hardly be necessary. Why should Luke bother to add them when he (supposedly) took the narrative over for his Gospel?

---

6. E.g. Arrian, *Dissertations of Epictetus* 3.21.14; and implicit in Plutarch, *De superstitione* 9, *Moralia* 169E (see p. 80 n. 11). Lucian, *Demonax* 27, suggests it is hardly necessary, but the story presupposes common use of temples for individuals' prayers.

7. Cicero, *De officiis* 1.150; Dio Chrysostom, *Discourses* 14.14; *m. Ned.* 3.4.

8. Dionysius of Halicarnassus, *Roman Antiquities* 4.27.5; 7.45.4; 8.50.4; cf. also 2.35.3; 11.12.3.

9. Josephus, *Ant.* 1, Proem 5, §2; 11.5.3 §142; 2.16.1.§336 (cf. Exod. 14); 5.1.13.§38 (cf. Josh. 7.6-9); and *War* 5.9.4.§415; in H. St.J. Thackeray, R. Marcus, A. Wikgren and L.H. Feldman (trans.), *Josephus* (LCL; 9 vols.; London: Heinemann; Cambridge, MA: Harvard University Press, 1926), IV, p. 5; VI, p. 381; IV, p. 313; V, p. 19; III, p. 331, respectively.

As it happens, there were others in Luke's world who would have indignantly rejected the toll collector's implicit understanding of God. What kind of deity would insist on being placated thus? So nervous a response, so lacking in trust that the speaker dared not even look up, would be nothing short of an insult. 'What can one say to the superstitious, how can you help such a person? He sits outside his house in sackcloth and filthy rags, often rolls naked in the mud, confessing various sins and errors...' 'The superstitious see the kindliness of the gods as cause for fear, their parental concern as despotism, their care as threatening injury...' 'How foolish are the words of Pythagoras, who said we reach our best when we draw near to the gods. For that is the time when the superstitious fare most miserably and wretchedly. They approach the halls and temples of the gods as they would bears' dens or snakes' holes...'[10] A similar refusal of any view of deity as demanding to be placated can be found earlier in Cicero and is echoed in Seneca, Epictetus and Dio.[11] Basic to this view is the conviction that the deity must be unchangeably good, unalterably benevolent, where both the goodness and the unchangeableness are essential to the understanding. To approach God or Gods in any way that suggests otherwise is grossly discourteous. Atheism may well be preferable. It would take far more than v. 14b to change the mind of someone who shared these convictions.

Luke may well suppose that this toll collector (like Zacchaeus, Lk. 19.8) will make restitution and mend his ways. Nothing in the story tells us that he will. The Gentile world was fully aware of the difference between 'mere' contrition on the one hand and repentance as undertaking amendment: 'the soldiers turned their eyes to the ground, but were sorrowful, rather than repentant'.[12]

The likely Gentile reaction to the toll collector's prayer is thus far from certain. Schottroff argues that the Pharisee is displayed as a caricature. We shall shortly consider this possibility in a little more detail. But perhaps the toll collector would also seem so to some, no less than

---

10. Plutarch, *De superstitione*, 7, 5 and 9; *Moralia* 168D, 167D, 169E.

11. Cicero, *De natura deorum, passim*; *De divinatione* 2.148-50; Seneca, *Epistulae morales* 73.16; 95.47-49; Epictetus, *Dissertations* 2.8.1-12; 3.16.6-7; 3.24.16; Dio Chrysostom, *Discourses* 12.61; 32.50.

12. Tacitus, *Histories* 1.82; from Tacitus, *Histories and Annals* (trans. C.H. Moore and J. Jackson; LCL; 3 vols.; London: Heinemann; Cambridge, MA: Harvard University Press, 1909), I, p. 139.

the craven suppliant in Plutarch. Luke's introduction and conclusion seem to show that he was aware of the likely ambivalence. Even given the careful Lukan preparation, some hearers might have found it hard to reconcile this prayer with the picture of deity implicit in Lk. 6; while for others it might have seemed so obviously right as to need no under-lining.

Among later and clearly Gentile Christians, Clement of Rome urges the recalcitrant Christians of Corinth to 'fall down before the Master and entreat him with tears' (1 Clem. 48.1); but no one seems to cite our example from Lk. 18 before Tertullian (*De Oratione* 17).[13] Luke 18.14b (par. 14.11) is frequently cited on its own (three times by Clement of Alexandria), but with no reference to the preceding narrative.[14] Perhaps it was not all that obviously or widely welcome. Origen has to defend it against Celsus who found it blasphemous (*Contra Celsum* 3.64).

At the opening of our narrative the Pharisee is introduced first, then the toll collector. We would probably expect a comparison.[15] Our cus-tomary dislike for toll collectors might lead us to expect to find our-selves in sympathy with the Pharisee, whether or not we knew what a 'Pharisee' was. He gives thanks, he keeps to his code, he is not parsi-monious.[16]

Nevertheless, Schottroff, as already indicated, argues that the Phar-isee of Lk. 18.9-14 would have appeared to at least some Gentile hear-ers not just as a negative figure in the story, but as a caricature from the start; and in opposition to the widespread consensus among Gentile scholars she insists that the figure in no way represents a serious sketch of the Pharisaic ethos within Judaism.

Schottroff quotes in illustration a story from the *Aesopica*: 'A certain man used to go late to the religious assembly and kneel down and say the following prayer, Lord God, be propitious to me and my wife and my two sons—and to no one else…' The introduction ('solitus erat tarde venire') shows 'Gleich kommt das falsche Gebet!' In the same way, the

---

13. Tertullian, *De oratione* 17; *Contra Marcionem* 4.36; cf. Cyprian, *De ora-tione* 6; Ireneus, *Adv. haer.* 3.14.

14. Lk. 18.14b or 14.11, quoted three times by Clement, and also in *Acts of Paul*, and *Prot. Ev. Jas.* (Biblia Patristica, 4 vols.; Paris: Centre de la Recherche Sci-entifique, 1975-87).

15. So Schnider, 'Ausschliessen', but see further, below.

16. On expressing thanks, keeping one's code, and generosity, see the many in-stances collected in Downing, *Strangely Familiar*, Chs. 8, 10 and 5, respectively.

words σταθείς and πρὸς ἑαυτὸν 'nur erwähnt, um den Hörer schon im voraus klarzumachen, dass mit diesem Beter nicht alles stimmt—sonst wären diese Worte in einer solche Erzählung überflüssig'.[17] But the response also makes clear what we shall note again, that a prayer so self-absorbed is also unacceptable, for a bystander then prays, 'Lord, Lord, God almighty, disrupt things for him and his wife and his sons—and no one else.' Persius reinforces the impression that private prayers intended to be overheard are likely to be hypocritical: '"A sound mind", "A fair name", "Good credit"—such prayers a man utters aloud so by-standers will hear. The rest he mutters to himself under his breath, "if only uncle would pop off..."'[18] It is probably apposite to include here as well as below Josephus's apologetic insistence, 'prayers for the welfare of the community must take precedence over those for ourselves. We are born for fellowship, and whoever sets its claims above his private interests is especially acceptable to God' (*Apion* 2.23 §196). Schottroff cites another example that both reinforces this point and makes another. In the pseudo-Platonic *Alkibiades 2*, an Athenian asks why the Gods pay so little attention to the Athenians' virtues and merits, which he details at length. The oracle replies that the Gods prefer the pious taciturnity of the Spartans.[19]

It is perhaps apposite to add that though a prayer of thanksgiving would itself be almost universally approved,[20] yet to thank God or Gods for one's own good deeds and virtues would not be thought appropriate. One's own deliberate actions are a matter of one's own responsibility, according to popular Stoicism (and even more in popular Cynicism). We may compare Cicero, 'Did anyone ever thank the gods because he

---

17. '"Now for a false prayer!" Then, the words "stood" and "to himself" are simply there so the hearer is clear in advance that all's not well with this prayer. Otherwise these words would be superfluous in a parable such as this one.' Schottroff, 'Erzählung', p. 448; citing *Aesopica* (ed. B. Parry; Urbana: University of Illinois, 1952), I, no. 666, p. 674; and other references given there.

18. Persius, Satire 2.8-10, in G.G. Ramsay (trans.), *Juvenal and Persius* (LCL; London: Heinemann; Cambridge, MA: Harvard University Press, 1913), pp. 334-35.

19. Schottroff, 'Erzählung', pp. 449-50, citing J. Burnett (ed.), *Alkibiades*, II, 148C-149C, from *Platonis opera*. II. *Parmenides*, etc (Oxford: Clarendon Press, 1901), pp. 138-51.

20. Dionysius of Halicarnassus, *Roman Antiquities* 6.71.3; Epictetus, *Dissertations* 1.16.15-16; Philo, *Plant.* 130-31 §31; Josephus, *Ant.* 4.13 §212; *m. Ber.*; and n. 17, above.

was good?' but also Epictetus, 'As a good king and in very truth a father...God has put the whole matter under our control without reserving for himself even the power to forestall or hinder.'[21] The Pharisee's prayer could only seem like a piece of baseless flattery addressed to God. If someone deems it appropriate to list their achievements, they should be open about them and accept responsibility. So Epictetus asks, 'Have I ever transgressed your commands, misused the resources you gave me...?' (*Dissertations* 3.5.8). On the other hand, it is not appropriate to compare your achievements with those of others; that is a 'vain and vulgar thing to do' (*Dissertations* 4.8.28-30).

In the Gentile world at least, the portrayal of the Pharisee would readily have been seen as a caricature. Schottroff has argued a strong case; I would hope that the additional evidence I have just adduced has made that case firmer still. But those who would most readily have agreed that the Pharisee's approach was obviously at fault would have been least ready to accept that the toll collector's was the only or a proper alternative. The more readily the Pharisee's approach was seen at fault, and a valid caricature, the more the likelihood that the toll collector would seem in the wrong, and also caricatured. The very questionable attitude of the toll collector would not be 'justified' simply by juxtaposing it with another that was even more clearly presented as mistaken. The narrative would do nothing for those debating the issue along conventional lines. The sheer assertion of v. 14a would have little or no persuasive force. It simply fails to address the common alternative piety. 'Why?' the hearers would still ask.[22] Not does the narrative really do much to reinforce the stance of those who, as we have seen, might be predisposed to self-abasement in prayer. To be assured that

---

21. Cicero, *De natura deorum* 3.36 §87, in H. Rackham (trans.), *Cicero. XIX. De natura deorum; Academica* (LCL; London: Heinemann; Cambridge, MA: Harvard University Press, 1933), p. 373; Epictetus, *Dissertations* 1.6.40, in W.A. Oldfather (trans.), *Epictetus*, (LCL; London: Heinemann; Cambridge, MA: Harvard University Press, 1925), p. 49. Compare Seneca, *Epistulae morales* 74.20. The Cynic recourse to *askēsis* was itself a refusal to submit to providence, fortune, fate; see M.-O. Goulet-Cazé, *L'ascèse cynique* (Paris: Vrin, 1986), pp. 49-50. On self-humiliation as a way of offering flattery, see Origen, *Contra Celsum* 3.63.

22. Scott, *Hear Then the Parable*, p. 97, has v. 14a as sheer assertion, but to make a different point from that which others have discerned: the criteria for being in with God or out, symbolized by the temple, are simply rejected. His view is briefly rebutted towards the end of this essay.

your preferred approach is better than one no one would defend is little gain.

In the Gospel itself, in context, Luke clearly intends the Pharisee's prayer to be taken seriously. It is an instance of an attitude which some people really do display. But he seems to feel the need to tell us so, in v. 9, as though without this we might indeed be tempted not to take it seriously (and that despite having prepared us so carefully to react negatively to Pharisees).[23] Luke also and as clearly approves of the second prayer. Yet even the firm insistence of v. 14a needs the further explanatory comment of v. 14b.[24] The narrative as such does not seem to have appeared even to Luke to have expressed his firmly held conviction sufficiently persuasively on its own without introductory and concluding support and interpretation.

We must, however, now consider whether anything of Luke's evaluation of the toll collector's and the Pharisee's prayers is at all more at home in the setting of the Hellenistic Jewish diaspora than in the wider Gentile world we have been considering.

2. Diaspora Hellenistic Judaism

There is plenty of evidence, again, that many would have approved in general the expressed attitude of the toll collector, certainly the prayer (see the commentaries). And we may legitimately note here as well as above the passages from Josephus earlier cited.

There are, however, no precise parallels to the full set of words and actions described. That the temple is a proper place for prayer goes without saying; that one may use it as a focus for prayer even from a great distance is stated in 1 Kings 8. What the toll collector is 'at a distance' *from* is not stated, but it often thought to be the sanctuary. Like the Pharisee, the toll collector stands, as does Solomon when praying for future divine forgiveness (LXX 1 Kgs 8.22, etc.).[25]

---

23. See J.T. Carroll, 'Luke's Portayal of the Pharisees', *CBQ* 50 (1988), pp. 604-21 (614-15): the Pharisees represent a false view of God's rule and are models of self-elevating behaviour.

24. That v. 14a itself is also Lukan will be argued below, with the help of Goulder, *Luke*, II, pp. 667-70. For the moment the decision does not much affect the argument.

25. I have found nothing to add to the usual illustration offered in the commentaries.

Josephus has Ezra 'ashamed to look up' (*Ant.* 11.5.3 §142f). There is a further instance, in the Prayer of Manasseh,[26] of a penitent unwilling even to look up to heaven; and we may note that Ezekias (Hezekiah) turns his face to the wall to pray in anguish (LXX 2 Kgs 20.2; Isa. 38.2). Closer still, Asenath 'was afraid to open her mouth and to name the name of God. And she turned away to the wall and sat and struck her head and her breast with her hand repeatedly...'[27] (As an expression of despair her breast-beating is paralleled in Josephus [*Ant.* 8.13.2 §325], as well as at Luke 18.3 and 23.38.) Jeremias claims that these gestures of despair are no usual part of prayer;[28] but, of course, praying (in any explicit sense) is what Asenath has for the moment desisted from. When she finally finds the courage to address God again, she adopts a quite different pose (11.19).

The words of the toll collector's prayer are quite like lines from a number of psalms (LXX 24.11; 77.38; 78.9, using ἰλάσκομαι and ἁμαρτία, though not ἁμαρτωλός),[29] as well as some lines in the Prayer of Manasseh (9, 10, 12, 14).

In (real or imagined) conversation with Trypho, next century, Justin Martyr says to this Hellenistic Jewish acquaintance, 'Who among you does not know that prayers accompanied by lamentations and tears, prostrate or kneeling, best propitiate God?' (*Trypho* 90). Clement of Rome suggests falling down with tears to induce God to become propitious (ἵλεως) and be reconciled (1 Clem. 48.1). Another early Hellenistic Jewish Christian, the author of James, would presumably have agreed (Jas 4.8-10). None of these Christians, though, at all clearly refers back to our passage from Luke (despite the similarity between Jas 4.10 and Lk. 18.14b and 14.11 parallel; see further below).

Luke himself, as a Christian with a considerable inheritance from Diaspora Hellenistic Judaism, is, as already fully allowed for, obviously able to use our story to express important convictions he holds about

---

26. On taking this as Greek, from the diaspora, see the list in J.H. Charlesworth, 'The Prayer of Manasseh', *OPT*, II, pp. 625-37, himself disagreeing. One may also compare Pseudo-Philo, *Antiquities* 50.5: 'perhaps I am not worthy to be heard'.

27. *Joseph and Asenath* 11.15; C. Burchard in *OTP*, II, p. 219.

28. J. Jeremias, *The Parables of Jesus* (ET; London: SCM Press, 1972), p. 143 and n. 59. Jeremias's elaborated reasons for the despair (the toll collector and family will starve if he truly repents and restores) have no basis in the text.

29. Closer than Ps. 50 [51], often cited, which uses other words.

sin, confession, and forgiveness, convictions he displays frequently else-where. A sense of people's sinfulness and their confession/repentance is expressed, for instance, at Lk. 5.8; 7.5, 37, 47; 15.7, 10 (cf. 15. 17, 20, as Luke understands that story). For Luke, the Markan phrase 're-pentance for the remission of sins' epitomizes the reality of salvation: Lk. 1.77; 24.47; Acts 13.38; 26.18; etc. (It is worth noting, however, that there is no expectation in Luke that the toll collector would go on repeating the prayer.)

Luke, we have suggested, must have assumed that the toll collector's penitence expressed a genuine repentance. It seems clear that could have been Diaspora Jews who would have read the second episode this way, and found nothing novel, nothing surprising or exceptionable about it.

It may be doubted, however, whether Philo would have agreed at every point. 'Humble entreaty to propitiate God and ask for remission of sins voluntary and involuntary' is entirely appropriate, as is discount-ing any merits of one's own; but so far from demanding any accom-panying expressions of despair, it is done 'with bright hopes' (χρηστὰ ἐλπίζοντες) confident in 'the gracious nature of him who sets pardon before punishment' (*Spec. Leg.* 2.196 §32, of the Day of Atonement); compare 'he who is resolved not only to commit no further sin, but also to wash away the past, may approach with gladness (γεγηθὼς)'; only 'let him who lacks this resolve keep far away' (*Deus Imm.* 9 §2).[30]

But it is not only Philo who might have been at least a little uneasy. Josephus, as we have seen, is convinced that 'the deity is easily recon-ciled to those who confess and repent' (*War* 5.9.4 §415, quoted above). 'To refrain from wrath in the case of offences that expose the culprit's life to his victim's vengeance is an attribute of God' (*Ant.* 2.6.8 §146). God accepts Joazos' repentance with prayer and supplication 'as a virtue' (*Ant.* 9.8.6 §175). Although, as we noted, Ezra was ashamed to look up, yet he did stretch his hands to heaven (and perhaps did look up, although ashamed?), insisting 'it was in keeping with the goodness of God to exempt even such sinners from punishment' (*Ant.* 11.5.3 §142).

To be ashamed to look up would be understandable; but then to refrain from drawing near (here contrast Jas 4.8) and also to beat your breast would strongly suggest a despairing lack of confidence in God's

30. Cf. *Spec. Leg.* 1.265 §49: 'he will abase his pride and become well-pleasing to God and claim the aid of his gracious power'.

preparedness and desire to forgive you your offences. Although many Jews might have seen this prayer as understandable, even initially appropriate for someone returning to God after a serious lapse, or for an outsider such as Asenath, others might well have found the approval in v. 14a of this untrusting attitude difficult to comprehend. As a Jew within God's covenanted mercy, even a toll collector should have known better.

In fact, the passages quoted above (and noted in many of the commentaries) to illustrate the standard interpretations of the toll collector's prayer are all short excerpts taken out of context. The penitential phrases in the Psalter (Pss. 24, 50, 77, 78) and in the Prayer of Manasseh, for instance, are all followed immediately by expressions of hope and confidence, as also is Asenath's initial expression of despair, with 'he himself will again heal me'; she then, as noted, adopts a fresh pose: kneeling up and looking up she prays, still contrite but with confidence (11.19-12.15).

The toll collector's prayer as interpreted by Luke certainly seems to contrast with the expressed attitudes of other early Christians likely to have had some roots at least in contemporary Hellenistic Judaism in the diaspora. Hebrews, Ephesians and 1 John all seem to share with Paul the trust that we are invited to 'approach with boldness (μετὰ παρρησίας) to the throne of grace' (Heb. 4.16; compare 3.6; 10.19, 35; Eph. 3.12; 1 Jn 3.21; 4.17; but also 1 Tim. 3.13).[31] Despite the quotations from *Trypho* included above, Justin by contrast stresses that the Christian communities he knows thank God in their liturgy for 'having been counted worthy' (*Apology* 1.65), a motif repeated in Hippolytus's *Apostolic Tradition* and in other later liturgies.

One might press the suggestion made above, and argue that the boldness of the ongoing Christian tradition need not preclude the extreme contrition of the outsider become aware of his or her situation as still not included within the sphere of God's grace. Luke, as we have noted, does not say that the toll collector needs to repeat this prayer. But following 18.1-8 on the ceaseless prayer of the elect, our vv. 9-14 would seem to be addressed to all disciples. And as an isolated pericope the narrative presents both characters as Jews, praying in the same part of the temple precincts, neither is an outsider as such. The two approaches,

---

31. Compare also S.B. Marrow, '*Parrhêsia* and the New Testament', *CBQ* 44 (1982), pp. 431-46.

boldness or self-humiliation, do seem to indicate different theologies, different understandings of God.

However, the Pharisee's prayer might on a superficial reading have seemed unexceptionable to Josephus, as also to Paul the Pharisee (Phil. 3.6). Josephus's Moses says, 'For my part, if the weighing of the matter had been left to me, I would have judged myself worthy of the honour [the high-priesthood], both from the self-love that is innate in all, and because I am conscious of having laboured abundantly for your safety' (*Ant.* 3.81 §190). If in his thanksgiving the Pharisee was genuinely ascribing his achievements to God, his prayer would probably have seemed quite correct to Philo, over against the Stoic and Cynic insistence on humans' sole responsibility for their own virtue. Philo writes, 'The righteous man exploring the nature of existence makes a surprising find…that all things are a grace of God' (*Leg. All.* 3.78 §24). All three, Philo, Paul and Josephus, would approve of prayers of thanksgiving.[32] However, if the Pharisee's thanks were shown to be insincere, and really an ill-concealed boast, then Philo and Josephus (and, most likely, Paul the Pharisee, too [Rom. 4.4]) would have joined in condemning him.[33] Philo might, however, have been rather surprised if Luke's Pharisee had found nothing to confess, for 'even the perfect man, in so far as he is a created being, never escapes from sinning' (*Spec. Leg.* 1.252 §46).[34]

But both Philo and Josephus would very likely have picked up the clues to which Schottroff points and the further ones I have indicated. As we have already noted, Josephus insists that prayer must be primarily for the community (*Apion* 2.23 §196), as the temple is and God is; in contrast with the Pharisee's concern with himself while explicitly excluding the toll collector. Josephus obviously approves strongly of the prayer he ascribes to Honi, 'O God, king of the universe, since these people standing beside me are your people, and those besieged are your priests, I beg you not to listen to them against these men, nor bring to pass what these men ask you to do to those others' (*Ant.* 14.2.1 §24). It is a prayer of that character that a true Jew would have prayed. Philo would have concurred. 'The prayer of good men is that if possible they may work a reformation in the lives of others, for virtue serves the

32. E.g., Philo, *Plant.* 130-31 §31; 2. Cor. 4.15; Josephus, *Ant.* 4.7.14 §212.
33. E.g., Philo, *Virt.* 178 §31; Josephus, *Ant.* 5.8.9 §301.
34. Cf. *Conf. Ling.* 178 §35; *Abr.* 6 §1.

common good' (*Omn. Prob. lib.* 63 §10).[35] Perhaps we may also note Rom. 9.1-5 (and the whole of Rom. 9-11), where Paul's Pharisaic Jewish heritage resurfaces so strongly in his passionate concern for his own people.

In the Hellenistic Judaism of the diaspora the narrative would most likely have been read much as in the wider Gentile world. The Pharisee's prayer is a caricature of what prayer should be, and the toll collector's is at least ambiguous, if not reprehensibly untrusting.

3. *Palestinian (still Hellenistic) Judaism (Including Early Christianity)*

Most commentators, as we have acknowledged, accept Lk. 18.10-14a as an authentic part of the Jesus tradition, obviously fitting well in the context of first-century Palestinian Judaism.[36] Schottroff raises questions but offers no verdict. Peter Fielder argues against authenticity, largely because, in his view, deploying so cruel a caricature of the Pharisees would not be consistent in a Jesus who preached the love of enemies. E.P. Sanders dismisses it with no further arguments; and J. Drury simply tells us that Luke composed it.[37]

In much more detail, Michael Goulder has more recently urged the same conclusion on the basis of the many 'Lukanisms' in the pericope, beside the very Lukan motif of contrite confession noted above.[38] His seems to me a strong argument, but not conclusive, and I shall attempt to counter it later. With his contentions still in mind, however, I now consider how the two characters and their respective prayers and actions might have appeared in a Palestinian setting, within the larger context of Hellenistic Judaism (however distinct or indistinct we may believe Palestinian and Diaspora Judaism to have been). I include here what we

35. For the righteous man as intercessor, concerned for others, e.g. *Migr. Abr.* 121 §21.

36. So, for instance, Marshall, *Luke*, p. 678; Hendrickx, *Parables*, p. 243; Schnider, 'Ausschliessen', p. 55; Scott, *Hear Then the Parable*, pp. 92-95.

37. P. Fiedler, *Jesus und die Sünder* (BBET, 3; Frankfurt: Peter Lang; Bern: H. Lang, 1985), p. 130; Sanders, *Jesus and Judaism*, pp. 175, and 285 with n. 6 (and cf. J.T. Sanders, *The Jews in Luke–Acts* [London: SCM Press, 1987], p. 206); J. Drury, *The Parables in the Gospels: History and Allegory* (London: SPCK, 1985), p. 130.

38. Goulder, *Luke*, pp. 667-70.

may discern of the earliest Christian communities, and the earliest Jesus traditions, insofar as we may seem to have relevant evidence. (We are now firmly treating the narrative as a free-standing pericope, with no Lukan context as yet to suggest a particular interpretation.)

Toll collectors would be no less unpopular in Galilee than elsewhere, even if (as S. Freyne argues)[39] the populace had grown used to the system.In Judaea the tolls would go to the Roman administration, and both toll and collector would be hotly resented. As Freyne also argues, in Galilee Pharisees would be known. And, as much as in Judaea, the Temple would be valued.[40]

On the other hand, the toll collector's prayer (if it signalled a genuine repentance, change of direction) might, again, have been seen as obviously correct and acceptable to God. In addition to the verses from the canonical Psalms and from elsewhere in the canon cited in the previous section, we may note such passages as 'Your servant has no righteous deeds to deliver him from the pit of no forgiveness. But I lean on the abundance of your mercies and hope for the greatness of your grace' (1QH 8).[41] And if (as J.H. Charlesworth argues) the Prayer of Manasseh can be used in evidence here, we may note the following: 'Because my sins multiplied in number more than the sand of the sea, and on account of the multitude of my iniquities, I have no strength so that I can lift up my eyes'.[42] If we may use evidence from the *m. Yom.* 8, then just as clearly sincere repentance would have been approved and assured of divine forgiveness—if accompanied by restitution. (When Luke incorporates this narrative he will follow it a little later with another toll collector's assurance of restitution, Lk. 19.8, and the narrative could presume as much here, though there is, of course, no mention of it.) If sincere contrition is intended and effective restitution is implied, then Jesus in this narrative would be saying nothing new, simply affirming the Pharisaic and wider piety he is so often thought here to be

39. Freyne, *Galilee from Alexander*, pp. 191-94; compare his *Galilee, Jesus and the Gospels* (Dublin: Veritas, 1988), e.g. p. 147.
40. Freyne, *Galilee from Alexander*, pp. 259-93 and 319-23. See Mt. 18.17; 23; 5.23-25; but contrast Mt. 6.1-6. This is a somewhat different picture from the more conventional one in Scott, *Hear Then the Parable*, p. 92.
41. From the translation by G. Vermes, *The Dead Sea Scrolls in English* (London: Penguin Books, 1987) p. 185; and there is much else in this vein.
42. Charlesworth, 'Prayer of Manasseh', 9a (*OTP*, II, pp. 636-37).

attacking. And so Abrahams argued a century ago, as Fiedler points out.[43]

In the narrative as it stands in vv. 9-14, approval of the toll collector and contrasting disapproval of the Pharisee are very clearly signalled, as we have had occasion to note more than once. We then tend to fill in any gaps we discern. The toll collector is truly penitent, he displays a proper contempt for himself, he will make restitution, he trusts God's forgiveness: he does what is necessary, and it suffices, as v. 14a indicates.[44]

But it is important to recall how lonely stands this narrative in the entire Jesus tradition in the synoptics (and the Fourth Gospel). People confess their sins in John's baptism (we are not told in what form). Apart from Luke's Peter (Lk. 5.8), no one ever actual confesses their sin or sinfulness before being assured of forgiveness by Jesus. In fact, where forgiveness is explicitly offered it seems as explicitly to preclude confession (Mk 2.5). No one is shown, let alone approved of, for keeping their distance, literally or metaphorically from God (or from Jesus as God's plenipotentiary—apart, that is, from Luke's Centurion [Lk. 7.3, contrast Mt. 8.5]). Without other exception, elsewhere we find a trusting approach that is met with acceptance. No one else, in non-Lukan tradition, is encouraged to express despair or contempt for themselves.

And there is very little sign of other strands of the early Christian tradition having picked up or even independently developed the kind of spirituality displayed by Luke's toll collector. If James is seen as Palestinian and early, then Jas 4.8-11 and 5.16 are the closest available to us; yet, as we have already noted, James encourages drawing near, confident of forgiveness, not a despairing standing away. For the rest the confidence encouraged in the deutero-Pauline literature, to which attention has already been drawn, is well prepared for in Paul himself.[45] We may take as instances 2 Cor. 3, quite explicitly asserting that Christians approach God boldly; and, as significantly, Rom. 14.1-4 and 15.7, where we are made welcome and 'stand' accepted. Nowhere in Paul's allu-

---

43. Fiedler, *Jesus*, p. 231; I. Abrahams, *Studies in Pharisaism and the Gospels* (2 vols.; Cambridge: Cambridge University Press, 1917; repr., New York: Ktav, 1967), II, pp. 57-58.

44. So, e.g., Jeremias, *Parables*, p. 143.

45. Abrahams, *Pharisaism*, pp. 58-59.

sions to peoples' acceptance into the Christian community (Rom. 6.1-11; 10.9-10; 1 Cor. 6.11; Gal. 3.1-4; 1 Thess. 1.9-10) is there any hint that a despairing contempt for oneself has been accepted or offered. And then one may recall again the deutero-Pauline passages noted above (Col. 2.10-13; I Pet. 1-2; Tit. 3.5-7; Heb. 10.22-23). Though release or cleansing from sin and its defilement are believed to be part of Christian initiation, the ethos that appears is quite other than than of Luke 18.13.

And while it has clearly been easy to quote penitential phrases from non-Christian Jewish Palestinian sources, it must again be realized that these again have been taken out of their fuller context. The confession of sin in the Qumran *Hôdâyôt* is always set within expressions of hope and trust, as is the psalm attributed to Hezekiah (5ApocSyrPs. 3) and as is also the Prayer of Manasseh: 'You are the God of those who repent... You will save me... I shall praise you' (13-15—accepting again, and with Charlesworth, that it may be allowed into this Palestinian section of our discussion). *M. Yom.* 8.9 insists, 'For graver transgressions repentance suspends punishment, until the Day of Atonement comes and effects atonement.'

If reflective Jewish contemporaries of Jesus or members of the early Jewish-Christian communities in Galilee and Jerusalem and Judaea had listened sympathetically to this story, filling in its many gaps, then, as has been suggested, they could possibly have found it quite acceptable, for Jesus would be saying nothing new or different. But if they took it as it stood, they would have found it very odd in itself, and very much at odds with other stories of Jesus' approach to 'sinners'.

The Pharisee, in turn, would have been as likely to have appeared a caricature in this setting as in the others we have considered. It is clear, of course, that many have not been persuaded of this by Schottroff, any more than by Montefiore before her.[46] We are still asked to take the first prayer as a serious example, intended to be and in fact an accurate representation of contemporary Pharisaic and perhaps wider Jewish spirituality.[47] In support is often adduced the Talmudic prayer given at *b. Ber.* 28b:

---

46. Schottroff quotes C.G. Montefiore, *The Synoptic Gospels*, II (2 vols.; London: Macmillan, 1927), p. 556.

47. See again n. 36, above.

> I thank you, O Lord my God, that you have given me my lot with those who sit in the seat of learning, and not with those who sit at the street corners; for I am early to work, and they are early to work; I am early to work on the words of the Torah, and they are early to work on things of no moment. I weary myself, and they weary themselves; I weary myself and profit by it, while they weary themselves to no profit. I run, and they run; I run towards the life of the Age to Come, and they run towards the pit of destruction.[48]

Quite apart from doubtful questions of the relevance for the first century of matter from Mishnah and Talmud, I think we need to accept here that the distinction to be drawn is a fine one, perhaps less obvious than Schottroff argues. Both praying persons give thanks (universally approved of), both are concerned with Torah, and both compare themselves with others. But the ethos is nonetheless different. Here in the Talmud the thanks are for divine predestination, for where the praying person is set;[49] in Luke's narrative the thanks are for the Pharisee's own achievement; the comparison in the former is with what we might term 'the educationally disadvantaged', in the latter with people condemned as 'greedy, dishonest, adulterous', and a specific individual is singled out for condemnation. In further contrast we may cite Hillel in *m. 'Abot* 2.5: 'Keep not aloof from the congregation and trust not in thyself until the day of thy death and judge not thy fellow until thou art come to his place.'[50]

But we ought also to note a variant of the above much quoted prayer:

> I (who study the law) am a creature (of God), and my fellow man is a creature (of God). My work is in the city, his in the field; I rise early to my work, he rises early to his. Just as he cannot excel in my work, so I cannot excel in his. Perhaps thou wilt say, I do much and he does little (for the Torah). But we have learned...he who offers much and he who offers little are equal, provided each directs his heart to heaven (*b. Ber.* 17a).[51]

48. Jeremias, *Parables*, p. 142; others (Linnemann, Marshall) simply quote Jeremias.

49. I note a paper by E.P. Sanders, British New Testament Conference, Bristol, 1989, on 'Predestination in Josephus and in Paul'; for Josephus, of course, see the well-known accounts of Pharisaic belief (e.g. *War* 2.8.14 §§162-63; but also such passages as *Ant.* 4.3.2 §47; *Apion* 2.16 §166); cf. e.g. *Gen. R.* 10.7 with 76.4.

50. As noted by Manson, *Sayings*, p. 309.

51. Abrahams, *Pharisaism*, II, p. 57; Scott, *Hear Then the Parable*, p. 95, also adduces *Ber.* 7.18 (acknowledging E. Linnemann as source) where a male praises

Here the contrast with Luke's Pharisee is much clearer. But even the more often quoted prayer from *b. Ber.* 28b may well seem to indicate a genuine compassion: others, too, are early to work, hard at it, weary, yet to no valid end. The Pharisee in Luke refuses any fellow-feeling at all. The prayer from *b. Ber.* 28b is akin to what we find in Paul (self-proclaimed Pharisee, if not Palestinian), lamenting the ignorant falling-away of his fellow Israelites under God's providence (Rom. 9–11). By contrast, Luke's Pharisee is entirely self-concerned. We saw earlier from Josephus (with his Palestinian roots, even if his writing is influenced by Diaspora tradition) that prayer should be concerned with all one's fellows; and that point, too, can be supported from the Mishnah, in a lament that 'there is none that seeks compassion for Israel, none that enquires for his fellow's welfare' (*Soṭ.* 9.15).

The Pharisee's prayer, then, does not represent a genuine Jewish piety that is being rebuked in the story. It is, as Schottroff argues, a caricature, and it is so in every plausible setting we have considered. A first century Pharisee would join with others in saying, 'So betet kein frommer Mann!' ('No one of true piety prays like that!')

The toll collector's prayer is at best ambiguous. It, too, could well also be a caricature, mocking what is in effect just another kind of unacceptable self-absorption. That possibility we must now consider in a little more detail.

4. *Luke 18. 10-13 in the Tradition of the Teaching of Jesus*

Two men went up into the Temple to pray, one a Pharisee and the other a toll collector. The Pharisee stood and prayed thus with himself: 'God, I thank you that I am not like other people, extortioners, unjust, adulterers, or even like this toll collector. I fast twice a week, I give tithes of all I get.' And the toll collector, standing afar off, would not even lift up his eyes to heaven, but beat his breast, saying, 'God, be merciful to me, a sinner.' [I tell you...]

As we noted at the outset, most commentators see the intention of this narrative as exemplary. Even those who agree that vv. 9 and 14 are Lukan editorial additions to a prior tradition almost all suppose that he was right to interpret it so. One significant exception is Bernard Brandon Scott. 'We cannot find in the tax collector merit or fix blame on the

God for not being made a woman, a heathen, or unlearned: but the same distinctions hold.

Pharisee... Despite Luke's use of the parable as an exemplary story, it is not. There is no lesson to learn...' The parable he supposes Luke to have received points us to what Scott calls the 'map', the set of values symbolized by the Temple, and simply proclaims, 'the map has been abandoned, it can no longer predict who can be an insider or outsider. The parable subverts the metaphorical structure that sees the kingdom of God as temple.'[52] In all probability the parable is to be read as subversive, but its challenge, it is here being argued, would in Jesus' day most likely have been heard rather differently.

On the basis of a small selection of the 'parallels' normally adduced, Scott insists that up to the end of v. 13, 'Nothing about this parable would have struck the original hearers as out of the ordinary.'[53] We have been noting, on the contrary, that there is much in both prayers that would have been likely to raise questions in contemporary hearers' minds. Neither sits comfortably among the examples of the approach to prayer each initially seems to resemble and is taken to exemplify. The more comparisons we make, and in detail, the more we realize that there is something ambiguous, something not quite right about each character's utterance; there is a strong element of caricature, albeit subtle enough perhaps to deceive at first glance and then effect all the more powerful an impact.

And there is a further difficulty in the way of accepting Scott's reading. The whole weight of his interpetation (along with those he rejects) rests on v. 14a. We have already recalled the common conclusion that v. 14b is a 'free-floating' addition (and have noted that it is treated so in the tradition elsewhere).[54] It is even clearer that v. 9 is no part of the original telling.[55] Luke elsewhere appears to add such introductions (Lk. 14.7; 15.2; 19.11). That leaves us with only v. 14a, the explanatory ending, to resolve the ambiguity of both prayers, and either to 'reverse the temple map'—or (more conventionally) affirm a grovelling though still self-absorbed approach to deity. But explanatory endings tend to arouse our suspicions (or should do).

---

52. Scott, *Hear Then the Parable*, p. 97. Scott overpresses 'distance' in favour of his 'inside–outside' dichotomy. In the parable both are in fact in the same part of the Temple precincts. 'Inside–outside' does not seem to be at issue.

53. Scott, *Hear Then the Parable*, p. 97, again.

54. P. 83 above, and nn. 13 and 14.

55. Marshall, *Luke*, p. 678.

If the narrator has control of his or her material, the narrative should make its point without more ado—as is the case with many of the Synoptic parables, anyway. V. 14a looks like an 'oracular response'[56] added by someone quite unconvinced that the story on its own is enough.

There is no other third-person narration with a change to an emphatic λέγω ὑμῖν, 'I tell you', concluding address, in shared Synoptic tradition. At Mt. 5.25-26 (Lk. 12.58-59 par.) there has been direct address from the start, as there has been in Mt. 18.12-13 (Lk. 15. 4-7 par.), though here the oracular response differs. On the other hand, Luke adapts his 15.8-10 (third-person from the start) to the same form as he has used in the preceding parable. He also includes 'I tell you' in the cluster of comments following 16.1-8a (and note vv. 19, 26). Then, after concluding the narrative of 18.1-6, he adds an extended address, ending with 'I tell you that he will vindicate...(v. 8)' The last word there comes from the same cluster as the 'justified' (δεδικαιωμένος) of v. 14, and δικαιοῦν in this kind of context does seem to be purely Lukan among the Synoptics (Lk. 10.29; 16.15; 18.14; Acts 13.39). It echoes, of course, the δίκαιοι of v. 9. Michael Goulder notes that παρά used for comparison is also Lukan. Whether or not the rest of the parable is a Lukan construction (so, Goulder), certainly v. 14a very much looks to have been his work. It is not the original teller's 'reversal of the temple map' but part of Luke's reinterpretation of the narrative he received. For if there is so much reinterpretation (v. 14a as well as vv. 9 and 14b) then surely the original itself cannot also have been Luke's construction.

In Lk. 18.9-14 as it stands we have 76 words of narrative and a further 41 of explanatory gloss. It must be allowed that it would be very strange indeed for an author to compose and deploy a parabolic narrative that he or she saw as so inadequate on its own for its intended purpose as to need more than half as many extra words as were used for the narrative itself then to resolve its ambiguity and make it say what the narrator meant. It does look very much more as if Luke received from the tradition a tale of two people praying, where (irrespective of original intention) the second example met with his own strong approval which we have argued is not at all impossible in the religious culture of his day. Yet he was also sufficiently aware of contemporary discussions of prayer to realize that as it stood many might on reflection find both men equally obtuse. The narrative could be rephrased a little (perhaps

---

56. Schottroff, 'Erzählung', pp. 455-56; Origen, *Contra Celsum* 3.64, sees this as an addition, albeit, of course, from Jesus himself.

adding some details of the Pharisee's self-appraisal, and the contrasting ὁ δὲ at the start of v. 13).[57] But, as with other parables in the tradition, the story had to remain recognizable. So it would demand a very clear and emphatic commentary to turn the still recognizable but deliberately ambiguous and mocking narrative into a comparison in which only the first prayer stood condemned, while the second would appear unqualifiedly commended. It took 41 words (or a few more) to impose the new meaning on the 76 (or less) of the original. At least from Tertullian onward the frame has dominated the picture with complete success.[58]

My suggestion, then, is that we agree to take the parable as presenting us with twin caricatures. Both have initial plausibility, sufficient for the allusions to register. But then the ambiguity of each dawns on us, for the prayer of the apparently pious and respectable Pharisee is as self-absorbed as is the prayer of the despised toll collector.[59] Hearers are then left puzzling, left to decide for themselves how to respond. Both characters are sure that God's welcome is restricted and conditional, and both are sure God holds public offenders at arm's length. So both are wrong? Thus the intention of the narrative, shorn of its frame, must be to suggest that the second prayer is as much a parody in its own way as is the first.[60] The ambiguity is deliberate. The hope is we may

57. See Goulder, *Luke*, II, pp. 688, 670.

58. See, again, n. 13, above.

59. That the toll collector's prayer is not beyond criticism is acknowledged by Henrickx, *Parables*, p. 240, quoting from J.S. Glen, *The Parables of Conflict in Luke* (Philadelphia: Westminster Press, 1962), pp. 57-61: 'It is important, however, not to misconstrue the nature of the tax-collector's confession as if it were a pre-occupation with sin comparable to that of the Pharisee with piety...the degree of egotism would be the same, but its direction would be opposite. Under these circumstances the spiritual significance of such self-depreciation—still an egotistical confession—would be remarkably similar to that of the Pharisee's self-exaltation.'

60. Schnider, 'Ausschliessen', has argued (against Schottroff) that the structure of the story clearly focuses our attention entirely on the improper comparison the Pharisee draws, arrogating to himself the right to limit God's grace: the rest of what he says is not criticized. Doubtless the narrative can be read that way, as Schnider shows; but it is so far from obvious that no one seems to have noticed it before he did in 1977. In fact the structure of the story as it stands in its Lukan context much more clearly encourages us to make precisely the kind of comparison the Pharisee himself makes, and we 'self-righteously' distance ourselves from 'that horrid Pharisee' or from those prigs who condemn the Pharisee, in an apparently infinite regress.

prefer Jesus' offer of God's quite unconditional welcome, and ourselves respond appropriately.

Yet we may be reluctant to allow a parable to end so abruptly, without even a question of the 'Which of them?' kind (Mt. 21.31; Lk. 7.42; 10.36) to conclude it (though even with such a question the ambiguity would remain). But we might then compare at least Lk. 7.32, the Children in the Market Place: as contextualized in the tradition, neither response is appropriate.

We may well be reluctant to admit a parable that makes no positive point, robs us of an appealing guilt-ridden figure to admire, identify with and emulate. We expect to be given exemplary heroes. We find one in the Good Samaritan, one or even two in the Prodigal, and so on. But, as we know from the Unjust Steward, we may be wrong always to expect such; and perhaps the usurious master and his favoured servants in the Pounds/Talents are as wrong as the disgraced one; perhaps even the king and his lackeys are as wrong as the Unforgiving Servant; and what are we to make of the disastrous behaviour of the man who let out his vineyard?[61] On the proposal advanced here we just gain one more disquieting parable that subverts our expectations. Not every parable, not even every Lukan parable, has to be an example story.

We may also not be happy to have a tradition of self-attentive prayer lose its dominical support; but we also need to recognize that it is not only here that Luke has ideas about prayer that are at odds with other strands of the tradition (compare his commendation of persistence in prayer, Lk. 11.5-13 and 18.1-6, with Mt. 6.7). In proposing his alternative to the much more common early Christian insistence on bold and confident access to God, Luke also stands on his own.[62]

Freed from apparently Lukan additions we find a narrative whose internal integrity Luke seems to respect. It presents us with two figures, both of whom are ambiguous, subtly effective parodies. If we chose to reject the words and actions of the second figure as well as those of the

---

61. Compare J.D. Crossan, *In Parables* (San Francisco: Harper & Row, 1973), though he offers a very conventional interpretation of Lk. 18.9-14; and Scott, *Hear Then the Parable*, on the parables cited; and perhaps my own *Jesus and the Threat of Freedom*, pp. 60-70.

62. Marrow, '*Parrhêsia*', pp. 440-46, again, on 'the Christian's ready access to God in prayer'.

first, we find ourselves affirming the kind of approach to God that Jesus in the tradition elsewhere teaches. By the criterion of coherence it seems to have as good a claim as any other to be Jesus' own.

For an example of the 'boldness' which the early Christian tradition often proposes, we next reflect on the woman from Syrophoenicia and her shameless behaviour.

Chapter 5

THE WOMAN FROM SYROPHOENICIA, AND HER DOGGEDNESS:
MARK 7.24-31 (MATTHEW 15.21-28)*

A woman in late antiquity approaches a strange male and speaks first,
without being invited to. Then, in the ensuing exchange, apparently she
comes out best. There are not many parallels in ancient texts to the bold
approach; very few instances indeed where a woman wins an argument
with a man (or, for that matter, where a teacher loses a debate to any
but a fellow teacher).

* Reprinted from G.J. Brooke (ed.), *Women in the Biblical Tradition* (Studies in
Women and Religion, 31; Lewiston: Edwin Mellen Press, 1992), pp. 129-49, by kind
permission. I do not claim an exhaustive search of the secondary literature. The
following are works actually used in what follows: H. Anderson, *Gospel of Mark*
(NCB; London: Oliphants, 1976), pp. 188-92; F.W. Beare, *The Earliest Records of
Jesus* (Oxford: Basil Blackwell, 1962), pp. 132-33; R. Bultmann, *The History of the
Synoptic Tradition* (ET; Oxford: Basil Blackwell, 1963), pp. 38-39; T.A. Burkhill,
'The Syrophoenician Woman: The Congruence of Mark 7 24-31', *ZNW* 57 (1966),
pp. 23-37; *idem*, 'The Historical Development of the Story of the Syrophoenician
Woman (Mark vii:24-31)', *NovT* 9 (1967), pp. 161-71; P. Carrington, *According to
Mark* (Cambridge: Cambridge University Press, 1960), pp. 156-58; C.E.B. Cranfield,
The Gospel According to Mark (Cambridge: Cambridge University Press, 1954),
pp. 245-49; A. Dermience, 'Tradition et rédaction dans la péricope de la Syro-
phénicienne: Marc 7, 24-30', *RTL* 7 (1977), pp. 15-29; J.D.M. Derrett, 'Law in the
New Testament: The Syrophoenician Woman and the Centurion of Capurnaum',
NovT 15 (1973), pp. 161-86; M. Fander, *Die Stellung der Frau im Markus-
evangelium* (Altenberge: Telos, 1989), pp. 63-84; R.A. Harrisville, 'The Woman of
Canaan: A Chapter in the History of Exegesis', *Int* 20 (1966), pp. 274-87; E. Lohmeyer, *Das Evangelium des Markus* (KEK, 1.2; Göttingen: Vandenhoeck & Rup-
recht, 10th edn, 1937), pp. 144-48; O. Michel, 'Kuwvn', *TWNT* 3 (1938), pp. 1100-
1104; D.E. Nineham, *Saint Mark* (London: Penguin Books, 1963), pp. 197-201;
R. Pesch, *Das Markusevangelium*, I (HTK, 2; Freiburg, 1976), pp. 129-31, 385-95;
J. Schmid, *The Gospel According to Mark* (RNT; Cork: Mercer, 1968), pp. 142-44;
E. Schüssler Fiorenza, *In Memory of Her* (London: SCM Press, 1983) pp. 137-38;

The story is discussed in commentaries and articles, but there do seem to be aspects of it, especially of its cultural context, that warrant further exploration. I shall touch on the issues most commonly discussed, but concentrate elsewhere. We shall be concerned mainly with Mark, only glancing at Matthew in passing.

1. *Textual Variants*

καὶ Σιδῶνος (Mk 7.24) is omitted by most; variants on συροφοινίκισσα (v. 26) are regularly dismissed; some alternative to ναὶ κύριε (v. 28) is occasionally adopted. As far as I can perceive, only the last has any bearing on my interpretation. Previous commentators do not seem much exercised over these textual variations.

2. *Matthew*

Matthew brings the disciples into the scene, and they back the woman's plea, perhaps to get rid of her harassment of the party. The woman cries out, from a distance it seems, rather than falling at Jesus' feet and asking him from close to. Jesus replies by repeating from 10.6 his conviction that he has been sent only to the lost sheep of the house of Israel. He lacks Mark's 'let the children be filled first' (Mk 7.27). The final exchange is similar, but Matthew has Jesus commend the woman's faith.

Some have argued that Matthew must have had an independent source;[1] C.E.B. Cranfield actually supposes Matthew's the more authentic account.[2] But T.A. Burkhill argues cogently that the amount of

E. Schweizer, *The Good News According to Mark* (London: SPCK, 1967), pp. 151-53; A. Stock, 'Jesus and the Lady from Tyre: Encounter in the Border District', *Emmanuel* 93 (1987), pp. 336-39; B.H. Streeter, *The Four Gospels: A Study in Origins* (London: Macmillan, 1924) p. 260; R.S. Sugirtharajah, 'The Syrophoenician Woman', *ExpTim* 98 (1986), pp. 13-15; H.B. Swete, *The Gospel According to St. Mark* (London: Macmillan, 3rd edn, 1953), pp. 155-59; V. Taylor, *The Gospel According to St. Mark* (London: Macmillan, 1953), pp. 347-51; G. Theissen, *Lokalkolorit und Zeitgeschichte in den Evangelien* (NTOA, 8; Göttingen: Vandenhoeck & Ruprecht, 1989), pp. 62-85; J. Wellhausen, *Das Evangelium Marci* (Berlin: Georg Reimer, 1903), pp. 56-57.

1. Beare; *Earliest Records*, p. 132; Streeter, *The Four Gospels*, p. 425; Swete, *The Gospel According to St. Mark*, p. 347; V. Taylor, *The Gospel According to St. Mark*, p. 347.
2. Cranfield, *Mark*, p. 245.

Matthew-pleasingness in his variants suggest they are all from his reflection.[3]

3. *Mark*

Mark's 'let the children be fed first (πρῶτον)' is often linked with Paul's 'to the Jew first but also to the Greek' (as in, e.g., Rom. 1.16; 2.10), and is seen as indicating the use or even origin of the story; or otherwise, as a Markan addition to make this Pauline point.[4] This rejoinder could also seem somewhat to soften Jesus' main saying, and in a way that the woman could be held to have discerned: at least the dogs will be fed, even if they have to wait. She is then insisting that they may expect to eat the fallen crumbs even before the meal is over. I don't see any way of deciding the question of the originality to the story of this sentence. The harsher tone of the story without it would suit my interpretation better, but its absence is not necessary to my reading.

Verses 24 and 31 are normally accepted as Markan editorial links. The story could easily have begun, 'a certain woman had a daughter… she heard…she came' (cf. Mk 5.25, 27; Jn 4.46; 12.20); and it would end with the δαιμόνιον gone, the woman's plea met in full.

4. *Genre*

a. *Form.*
Bultmann classified this as an apothegm, and most commentators agree that the whole stress is on the verbal exchange, as with the (Q) Centurion's Servant (which Bultmann actually suggests is a variant of the Woman from Syrophoenicia). We might again compare John 4.46-54, the Nobleman's Son. R. Pesch, however, suggests that dialogue is merely part of the distance-healing *Gattung* ('form', or 'genre').[5]

For my part, I would suggest that this should make us reflect critically on the standard disjunction between apothegm and miracle story (with inconvenient 'mixed examples'). Perhaps this division should now be replaced by 'verbal *chreia*' and 'tacit action *chreia*' on a spectrum with various 'mixed *chreiai*' in the middle.[6] Both in terms of the

3.   Burkhill, 'The Syrophoenician Woman', pp. 25-28.
4.   Pesch, *Markusevangelium*, p. 388; Schweizer, *Good News*, p. 152.
5.   Pesch, *Markusevangelium*, pp. 385-86.
6.   On the *chreia*, R.F. Hock and E.N. O'Neil, *The Chreia in Ancient Rhetoric*.

data and of more abstract considerations of speech-act theory, the 'saying-doing' dichotomy is probably untenable.[7] To utter a striking saying, clinch an argument, win a dispute, are all to *do* something, just as healing and even more exorcism can only be perceived, certainly can only be narrated in terms of socially constituted meaning. Even prior to narration, the action speaks, very likely 'louder than words'.

However, here the occasion for the verbal exchange is patently a plea for an exorcism. G. Theissen has suggested an analysis of the characters, motifs and themes (clusters of motifs), as well as of the 'functions' (socio-cultural and economic, religious and existential functions) of miracles of healing, whether exorcistic or not.[8]

b. *Structure*

For the 'character set' Theissen suggests:

		Companion	
[Demon]	[Sick]		[disciples] Main Character
		[crowd]	
		[opponent]	

But as it stands, even as a healing, this exorcism is so underplayed, with so few of the expected characters appearing, that the healer is almost a secondary character (a situation rectified by Matthew).

On an actantial analysis of this as a restoration of well-being, some of the peculiarities of the narrative emerge even more clearly:

I. *The Progymnasmata* (SBLTT, 27; Atlanta: Scholars Press, 1986); K. Berger, *Formgeschichte des Neuen Testaments* (Heidelberg: Quelle & Meyer, 1984), pp. 80-93; V.K. Robbins, 'The Chreia', in D.E. Aune (ed.), *Greco-Roman Literature and the New Testament* (SBLSBS, 21; Atlanta: Scholars Press, 1988), pp. 1-23; B.L. Mack and V.K. Robbins (eds.), *Patterns of Persuasion in the Gospels* (Sonoma, CA: Polebridge Press, 1989).

7. 'Speech-Act' theory, stemming from J.L. Austin, has of late been taken up widely by others; but see, e.g., J.R. Searle, *Speech Acts: An Essay in the Philosophy of Language* (Cambridge: Cambridge University Press, 1969); and also my companion volume, *Doing Things with Words*.

8. G. Theissen, *Miracle Stories of the Early Christian Tradition* (ET; Edinburgh: T. & T. Clark, 1983), chs. 2 and 3, pp. 47-121. In Appendix 1 to this chapter I suggest, on the basis of Theissen's inventory of motifs, that apothegms/pronouncement stories/*chreiai* are formally almost indistinguishable from exorcisms or other healing miracles. Cf. also the discussion in Fander, *Die Stellung*, pp. 67-72.

[Sender] Woman   ⟹   [object] exorcism   ⟹   [receiver]
                                                                    woman/daughter
                                    ⇑

[helper(s)]   ⟹   [subject] Jesus   ⟸   [opponent] Jesus
Woman   (cf. Jn 4.48) or the
                                                                     woman's non-
                                                                     Jewishness; or both

We might even have:

[helper] Jesus   ⟹   [subject] Woman ⟸   [opponent] Jesus
                                   who obtains her
                                   desire from ⟹

And the fact is that as a mixed *chreia* (or apothegm) it now has as its
main character the woman: she wins the verbal exchange (controversy
chreia):

[Sender] Woman   ⟹   [object] verbal   ⟹   [receiver] Woman
                                   victory
                                    ⇑

[helper(s)]   ⟹   [subject] Woman ⟸   [opponent] Jesus
Woman
wit/repartee

If one accepts that this is a mixed word-and-deed *chreia*, or if one still
prefers terms such as 'apothegm' or 'pronouncement story', an actantial
analysis displays the woman as the chief protagonist, and the victor.

5. *Details*

a. *A Woman*

The commentators do realize that it is a female person who approaches
Jesus, but most seem to find it quite unremarkable,[9] and prefer to stress
her foreignness. In the story it is her femaleness that is emphasized
(ἀκούσασα γυνὴ...ἧς εἶχεν τὸ θυγάτριον αὐτῆς...ἐλθοῦσα...ἡ δὲ
γυνὴ ἦν Ἑλληνίς, Συροφοινίκισσα). Her religio-cultural and ethnic
otherness are important additional facts. 'She heard of him, a woman
did, a woman with a daughter...and she came to him and furthermore
she was a Greek woman, a Syrophoenicianness...'

---

9.   Exceptions: Fander, *Die Stellung*; Schüssler Fiorenza, *In Memory*; and John
Chrysostom, to whom we return later.

As already noted, it is in fact difficult in antiquity (even in the Christian tradition it is difficult) to find other stories where a woman approaches a strange man and opens a conversation with him, rather than waiting to be spoken to. There is no other in Mark. At Mk 14.3-11 the woman says nothing (nor does the woman in Luke 7), nor does Mark's poor widow (Mk 12.42), nor do the women at the tomb question the young man (Mk 16.1-8). Matthew, as we have already noted, has the disciples approach Jesus on the woman's behalf, she only cries from a distance until Jesus responds to the disciples' initiative (Mt. 15.22-25); Zebedee's wife falls as Jesus' feet and waits to be asked what she wants (Mt. 20.20). The woman in John 4 only speaks when she is spoken to. Although L. Alexander has suggested an attractive re-reading of Martha and Mary (Lk. 10.38-42),[10] it still seems most likely that Luke saw Mary as the model woman, silently attentive: Martha who speaks out is reprimanded. In John 11 both Martha and Mary do address Jesus, but we have been told he is already known to them. Among strangers the conventional etiquette holds, as expressed in 1 Cor. 14.34-35, 1 Tim. 2.11-12, Plutarch, *Coniugalia praecepta* 31 (142D).

There are a number of Old Testament passages involving women who do not speak first, or at all. I recall that Josephus, retelling the story of Rachel at the well, allows her to open up the conversation, but excuses this as what you might expect from a child (*Ant.* 1.287). However, in extreme need a woman may speak first, if she has no male representative to speak for her (2 Sam. 14.4; 2 Kgs 4.2; 6.6), and perhaps one might assume a similar situation here, for the initial approach. But it remains uncommon, unexpected.

And then the woman answers back, and wins the argument. At least, so I shall argue, along with a number of commentators. And I can think of no analogies for that, save the Cynic Hipparchia (Diogenes Laertius, *Lives of Eminent Philosophers,* 6.97-98). And Cynics, and Cynic-tinged Stoics, of course, allow that excellence (ἀρετή) is the same for women as for men; they are just as capable of 'philosophizing', living and articulating life as it should be lived and understood.

b. *A Woman, of Greek Culture and Religion, Racially Syrophoenician*
The commentators, as remarked above, ignoring her femaleness, jump

10. L. Alexander, 'Sisters in Adversity: Retelling Martha's Story', in G.J. Brooke (ed.), *Women in the Biblical Tradition* (Studies in Women and Religion, 31; Lewiston: Edwin Mellon Press, 1992)), pp. 167-86.

to her ethnic and religio-cultural and possibly (free) civic status.[11] G. Theissen's quite lengthy study makes much of this as a 'boundary-crossing', *Grenzüberschreitung*.[12] R. Pesch notes that distance healings in the gospel tradition are (perhaps seem to be) all of Gentiles.[13] It is clearly the primary issue in Mark's use of the narrative, as we shall note again below. But I shall argue further that such analyses leave much more that is relevant to be said.

c. *Exorcism*
We obviously have here explicit reference to an exorcism, although we have also seen that this is not where the emphasis lies, either in Mark's use of the pericope, or in the pericope as a self-contained unit. Both the condition and the healing are off-stage, and played-down. A further suggestion is made that πνεῦμα ἀκάθαρτον is Palestinian, δαιμόνιον Hellenistic, but also that unclean spirits indicate foreignness from the story's standpoint.[14] Mark 5.1-20 may carry some such suggestion, but Mark himself does not make this generalization. I seem to recall meeting the suggestion that the idea of demon-possession as such is primarily Palestinian-Jewish. Philo in *De gigantibus* is dismissive of the idea. John, often thought to have strong Palestinian roots, only mentions the idea in passing invective. Dio of Prusa (c. 100 CE) can use the idea metaporically—but metaphor suggests a more literal sense is well-known. Plutarch (c. 100 CE) refers to such beliefs incidentally.[15] An exorcism at a distance related in Philostratus's *Life of Apollonius of Tyana* is adduced by some, but comes from rather too late in time to be illuminating here.

If only in our minds there may be some tension between a belief in demon-possession and what I shall suggest is the Cynic wit and vigour of the woman's reply, but the story betrays no sense of unease at this combination of themes. It seems entirely possible for ideas of demons and demon-possession to be mentioned in passing in texts whose main thrust lies elsewhere. (On collocations of what we might see as credulity and scepticism, see ch. 10, below.)

11. E.g., Nineham, *Mark*, pp. 198-99; Wellhausen, *Marci*, p. 56.
12. Theissen, *Lokalkolorit*, pp. 62-63.
13. Pesch, *Markusevangelium*, p. 386.
14. Pesch, *Markusevangelium*, p. 387.
15. Plutarch, *De defectu oraculorum* 417C; *De iside et osiride* 369EF.

d. *Faith?*

'The woman shows all the signs of faith and reverence we have met in similar cases before.'[16] Many commentators, though by no means all, do perceive faith here: 'Although the word 'faith' does not occur, that is what the story is about...no personal merit...'[17] Faith is not in fact so obvious that Matthew could let it pass without making it explicit. The woman would seem to trust Jesus just enough to bother to ask. How sure she is in the story of Jesus' power or willingness to exorcize the δαιμονιόνó from her daughter, or whether this is a desperate 'try anything' gamble are not discussed, and cannot be the point of the tale.[18]

e. *Respect*

The respect shown is fairly standard in an approach to a teacher with a reputation, as it is the normal way to ask for attention from an acknowledged superior, and we may compare Mk 10.17. It is not specifically honorific, it is not προσκύνησις. Even Crates the Cynic in one mixed *chreia* can make a request on his knees to a gymnasiarch (although he then mocks the convention).[19]

f. *The Harshness of the Response*

Most commentators are embarrassed by Jesus' response. Much of the discussion of other issues often seems at least in part aimed to reduce this harshness. Perhaps the harshness stems from the early church, from controversies then. Perhaps it is in thick quotation marks: 'You know what they say...' Perhaps Jesus is testing the woman's faith and/or demanding humility. Perhaps he is really just working things out in his own mind. Perhaps with his 'Let the children be fed first' and perhaps, too, with his 'puppies', 'housedogs', he is already softening the harshness of what is to follow and providing a clue for the woman to pick up.[20] There is no widespread agreement.

---

16. Nineham, *Mark*, p. 198; cf. Pesch, *Markusevangelium*, p. 386.

17. Schweizer, *Good News*, p. 153.

18. As already argued by means of the actantial analysis above; but see further below; and Carrington, *Mark*, p. 157.

19. Diogenes Laertius, *Lives of Eminent Philosophers* 6.89. In the context of Jesus' 'defeat' in argument, the κύριε of v. 28 is no title of glory, even if it is taken to be so in Mark's use of it (so, e.g., Fander, *Die Stellung*, pp. 78-81).

20. Wellhausen, *Marci*, p. 56; Swete, *Mark*, pp. 157-58; Taylor, *Mark*, p. 350.

g. *The Kind of Dog*
If we took v. 24 as part of the story, we could envisage Jesus in a Gentile house, careless of purity laws, surrounded by fawning puppies, playfully teasing the woman who comes in, and, as already suggested, feeding her a cue for her smart—or humble—rejoinder.[21] 'Thus the term, which on Jewish lips was usually a reproach, is used by the Lord to open a door of hope through which the suppliant is not slow to enter.'[22] The words are chosen 'not to extinguish the woman's faith, but rather to whet her zeal and inflame her ardour'.[23] Other commentators say that is a load of nonsense, and the diminutive κυνάριον is simply in line with the style of Greek Mark is used to—cf. δαιμόνιον, θυγάτριον, earlier.

The prevalence of domestic hounds among Jews is debated, as are both Jewish and general Greek ambivalence concerning dogs. While canine faithfulness may be admired, applying the term to a human is generally insulting, and 'puppy', most conclude, is no better. Among Jews there is some (late) evidence for 'dog' being an abusive term reserved for Gentiles. Wellhausen quotes Eliezer on dogs and idolaters.[24] S.T. Lachs quotes R. Joshua ben Levi comparing the righteous to the guests invited to the king's table, and the wicked heathen to the dogs who obtain the crumbs that fall from it.[25] Also noted is the enigmatic injunction against giving what is holy to dogs (Mt. 7.6), which can readily be interpreted along the same lines as Jesus' saying here.

h. *Food, Purity, Gentiles*
'Why does a request for exorcism elicit a response in terms of food?' some ask. It should in fact be obvious that a woman, foreign, idolatrous, from a household with an unclean spirit, raises most forcefully issues of purity and distinctiveness, for which food is the symbolic focus.[26]

21. Schmid, *Mark*, p. 143; Lohmeyer, *Markus*, pp. 146-47.
22. Swete, *Mark*, p. 157.
23. John Calvin, in Cranfield, *Mark*, p. 248; per contra, Nineham, *Mark*, p. 201; Pesch, *Markusevangelium*, p. 389.
24. Wellhausen, *Marci*, p. 56; Theissen, *Lokalkolorit*, p. 64, gives the reference as *Pirqe R. El.* 29.
25. S.T. Lachs, *A Rabbinic Commentary on the New Testament* (Hoboken, NJ: Ktav, 1987) p. 249.
26. Theissen, *Lokalkolorit*, pp. 71-73, with reference to the pseudo-Clementine *Homilies*, on which, see further below; and, e.g., M. Douglas, *Purity and Danger* (London: Routledge & Kegan Paul, 1966).

It is widely accepted that Jesus made no systematic attempt to take his message to Gentile communities (Rom. 15.8; Mt. 10.6; 15.24), and that the present tale provides no exception to this conclusion. But on most issues of detailed interpretation the discussion remains indecisive, lacking as it does sufficient contextual controls to enable an objective choice among the options canvassed.

i. *Socio-Cultural and Economic Context*

The most thorough discussion of the 'local colour', local in time and space, that seems available to date, is provided by Theissen.[27] He discusses the ethnic question: the area is mixed, not as clearly 'heathen' as Mark suggests. But there are tensions. This woman is quite clearly Greek in culture and religion as well as language (by birth she could well be native Phoenician, of course). Ἑλληνίς probably indicates social status, too: from a free citizen family. Tyre is the powerful urban centre carrying on the normal exploitation of its agricultural hinterland, of which northern Galilee formed a large part. There were long-standing and closely connected disputes over political control in the area. All in all, there was a considerable basis for hostility.

I shall argue that some decisively significant issues still remain unexplored.

j. *The Woman's Response*

So, is the woman's response trusting, or humble, or so desperate she will eat dust, or what is it? As already noted, some commentators are sure that she evinces faith, and that this faith is the point of the story. 'Die gläubige Demut der Frau...[die] von ihm alles glaubt und alles erhoft.'[28] 'Ihr Glaube ist "Grenzüberschreitung", der die Überschreitung der Heilsgrenzen rechtfertigt.'[29] 'She acknowledges Israel's privilege... and simply appeals to Jesus' kindness unconditionally.'[30] Her great humility overcomes Jesus' reluctance.[31]

---

27. Theissen, *Lokalkolorit*, pp. 62-85.
28. 'In humble faith the woman puts her complete trust and hope in him', Theissen, *Miracle*, pp. 137-38.
29. 'Her faith crosses boundaries, it justifies a breach in the limits of salvation', Pesch, *Markusevangelium*, pp. 389-90; cf. Schweizer, *Good News*, p. 151.
30. Cranfield, *Mark*, p. 249.
31. Schmid, *Mark*, p. 142; Taylor, *Mark*, p. 351.

But faith is not mentioned here any more than at the outset. As Carrington insists, there is no question of faith or of humility. The story makes it clear that 'The woman had actually got the better of him in the encounter.'[32] And on the latter point quite a number of commentators agree. It is a conflict story. 'But here, by an unusual turn of events, the one who is vanquished in the argument is Jesus himself.' Taylor acknowledges the woman's witty reply, and the pleasure it gives Jesus (though Taylor omits ναί).[33] Schüssler Fiorenza concludes, 'Jesus does not have the last word. Rather, the woman's argument prevails over that of Jesus.'[34]

k. *Dogs at Table?—Yes!*

There is a lot about dogs in the commentaries, very little about dogs at table: just two passages are cited: the late passage in Lachs, and another passage, also late, from Philostratus, who quotes a critic of his source, Damis, Apollonius of Tyana's original biographer. The critic allowed that Damis had recorded well enough his specimens of his master's sayings and opinions. But collecting such trifles 'reminded one of dogs who pick and eat fragments which fall from a feast'.[35]

I have found no one who asks whether there is any instance where anyone else agrees to be called 'dog'. Yet there are in fact many.

In the Greek-speaking world there is just one most likely reaction to this story. A woman boldly approaches a strange man to beg for help, is told it would be throwing children's food to dogs, accepts the metaphor, turns it to her own advantage, and wins the point. This is an encounter with a woman Cynic.

In the Appendix to this chapter, I display a number of instances of the acceptance of the term κύων, always by Cynics, and references to 'dogs of the table' in particular, also explicitly and apparently conventionally referring to Cynics. Admittedly, κυνάριον as such is not included: but a range of other variants is, and the absence of this one variant is prob-

---

32. Carrington, *Mark*, p. 157; cf. Taylor, *Mark*, p. 350.

33. Schmid, *Mark*, p. 142; Taylor, *Mark*, p. 351.

34. Schüssler Fiorenza, *In Memory*, p. 137. Literally, of course, Jesus does say the last words, but the woman says the conclusively winning words.

35. Philostratus, *Life of Apollonius* 1.19; quoted by, e.g., Theissen, *Lokalkolorit*, p. 84.

ably fortuitous.[36] I quote here a few examples, retaining the numbering from the Appendix:

(1)   When Plato styled Diogenes a dog, 'That's right (ναί)', he said, 'I keep coming back to the people who sold me.'[37]

(12) Do not turn back, even if they call you a dog.[38]

(9)   [Crates writes to his woman/wife Hipparchia] Stand fast, and live the Cynic life with us, for you are by nature no whit inferior to us [males]. Bitches are by nature in no way inferior to dogs.[39]

(16) Some admired Diogenes as the wisest man in the world. To others he seemed crazy. Many scorned him as a beggar and poor good-for-nothing, and some jeered at him, some tried to insult him grossly by throwing bones at his feet as they would to a dog...[while] he really resembled a royal lord who in the guise of a beggar moved among his slaves and menials.[40]

(20) Leucus, if you have any scraps of bread, give them to these Dogs [the Cynics who have come to the feast].[41]

(19) 'It is the custom to throw the remnants to the dogs', as Euripides said [again, the Cynics present are under discussion].[42]

It seems quite clear that in any urban Greek-speaking setting (Rome, or south Syria or wherever else Mark is placed) the story would most likely have been taken, initially at least, as deploying a Cynic *topos*.[43] Further warrants for this conclusion will be offered below.

36. κυνάριον as a word is used by Epictetus, among others. The other variants are κύων ('dog/Cynic'); κυνίκος (Lucian); κυνοῦλκος (Athenaeus); σκυλάκιον ('puppy', Pseudo-Crates); see Appendix.

37. Diogenes Laertius, *Lives of Eminent Philosophers* 6.40. (For full references, see Appendix 2).

38. Pseudo-Diogenes 44.

39. Pseudo-Crates 29.

40. Dio Chrysostom, *Discourses* 9.9.

41. Athenaeus, *Deipnosophists* 6.270CD in C.B. Gullick (trans.), *Athanaeus*, III (LCL; 7 vols.; London: Heinemann; Cambridge, MA: Harvard University Press, 1927), pp. 214-15.

42. Athenaeus, *Deipnosophists* 3.96F-97A, in C.B. Gullick (trans.), *Athenaeus*, I, pp. 416-17.

43. On the wide dispersion of popular Cynics, and not just the literary ones whose material has come down to us, see M.-O. Goulet-Cazé, 'Le cynisme à l'époque impériale', *ANRW*, II, 36.4 (1990), pp. 2722-24, 2731-34; and, further, Downing,

l. *Jesus' Final Response*

Matthew, as we have noted, has Jesus commend the woman's faith. Mark just has him respond to her utterance as such, διὰ τοῦτον τὸν λόγον. Many of the commentators, as noted, want to have Jesus 'just testing', quoting a known line, even sorting things out in his own mind. Just as they do not want him really wishing to put her off at the outset, so they also do not want him really defeated at the end. Yet, whatever tacit intention we may choose to imagine, that which in the story he clearly says would not be proper (οὐ γάρ ἐστιν καλὸν) is what he does.

Are we to take Jesus' words as effecting the healing? Vermes quotes Hanina ben Dosa when Gamaliel II's son is ill, 'Go home, the fever has departed from him.'[44] There is no agreement. With no word of healing, this can be taken simply as reassurance, or even as telepathy,[45] while Pesch, as we have noted, argues that the whole tale is still basically a distance healing in which conversation is a necessary but incidental motif. Yet there are conversations and significant sayings in other healings, too; and here it is the healing that is incidental.

Again, do themes of possession and exorcism run counter to a Cynic interpretation? I have indicated that such motifs are quite widespread, even appearing as metaphor in a Cynic-influenced writer such as Dio Chrysostom. I cannot pretend that these themes help a Cynic interpretation of the pericope, but as played down as most find them to be in the story, the dominant thrust is clearly the Cynic *topos*, 'dogs of the table'.

6. *Mark's Use of the Tale*

It is widely accepted that the story plays a significant part in the Markan sequence. Mark has just dealt with issues of food laws and so of table-fellowship, and so now can have Jesus proceed into Gentile territory, stay in a Gentile house, and be approached by a Gentile woman. Mark

---

Cynics and Christian Origins, pp. 57-76; and *Cynics, Paul and the Pauline Churches* (London: Routledge, 1998); and 'Deeper Reflections on the Jewish Cynic Jesus', ch. 7 of this collection; but also J.S. Kloppenborg Verbin, 'A Dog among the Pigeons: The "Cynic Hypothesis" as a Theological Problem', in J. Asgeirsson, K. de Troyer and M.W. Meyer (eds.), *From Quest to Quelle* (Festschrift James M. Robinson; BETL; Leuven: Peeters, 1999), forthcoming.

44. G. Vermes, *Jesus the Jew* (London: Collins, 1973), p. 75, citing *b. Ber.* 34b; *y. Ber* 9d; as do others.

45. Assurance: Schmid, *Mark*, p. 144; telepathy: Taylor, *Mark*, p. 348.

has already told us that there are ample crumbs for the picking (Mk 6.43), and soon re-emphasises this motif (Mk 8.8, 19-21); many can be be filled (χορτασθῆναι; Mk 6.42; 7.27; 8.4, 8). It seems clear to most that this is an anticipation of the mission to the nations.

I would accept this common analysis, but stress that in particular Mark must himself have recognised this as the approach of a woman, an Ἑλληνίς, who was Cynically bold and outspoken, and content to be styled as such. And this is not an isolated Cynic *topos* in Mark. I have pointed to them in a number of studies elsewhere,[46] and here would instance only Mark 10.17-31, which portrays an attitude to wealth that in the Graeco-Roman world was seen as distinctively Cynic. Mark is addressing those Greeks who have been 'prepared for the Gospel' by Cynic preaching: Jesus accepts you, and especially the women among you.

7. *The Story before Mark*

Was this tale created by the later church, in a dispute over the Gentile mission? Theissen follows Roloff in pointing out that nowhere else in the New Testament documents do we find traces of a post-resurrection rejection of the mission as such, however much the details were disputed; and if there had been, this brusque encounter and the woman's dogged rejoinder would have constituted a pretty ineffectual response.[47] An informal 'criterion of dissimilarity' persuades most that Mark or anyone else starting from scratch with any pro-Gentile purpose in mind that we are aware of or can readily imagine, would have produced something more serviceable than this.

So, the story goes back in something like its present form to Jesus himself. As I argue in much more detail elsewhere, we probably need now, among our various reconstructions of the Jesus of history, to allow for a Jesus who saw himself as healer and exorcist within a Jewish-and-Cynic understanding of human flourishing, as including mental and physical well-being, but also a distinctively Cynic conviction that such well-being could be enabled and enhanced by a simple and trusting social lifestyle under a parental God. Already aware of Cynic tradition,

46. See n. 44, above; but also Downing, *Christ and the Cynics*, pp. 117-49.
47. Theissen, *Lokalkolorit*, p. 66, citing J. Roloff, *Das Kerygma und der irdische Jesus* (Göttingen: Vandenhoeck & Ruprecht, 1974), pp. 159-61.

Jesus recognizes Cynic traits in the woman who approaches him, and is content when she responds in character.

8. *Ancient Interpreters*

a. *Luke and Matthew*
Luke does not include the tale, but, of course, neither does he include anything else from Mk. 6.45–9.50. We need not speculate here as to his likely response to this individual pericope in particular.

Matthew certainly seems to read the pericope as significant for the Gentile mission, as Mark had done, fully aware that Jesus himself undertook no such project. As we have seen, Matthew does not allow the woman to confront Jesus directly, and he responds only when her importunity arouses the men to back her request; even then, it is only they who are now addressed, the women being allowed merely to overhear. Indirectly acknowledged, she can now at last herself speak to Jesus; and her reply is one of faith, not a winning repartee. It makes it even more noteworthy that the Cynic flavour is still apparent to some among later readers, even though it is Matthew's version that they use. This we shall now see.

b. *Tertullian, the Pseudo-Clementine Romances, Origen, and Others*
Tertullian concentrates on Matthew's version and its relevance for the debate with Marcion. Jesus is sent to the lost sheep of the house of Israel, compared with whom the Gentiles are dogs: God is clearly the God of the Jews.[48] It is the woman's faith that is stressed by other early writers such as Theodore of Mopsuestia and Apollinaris of Laodicea.[49]

As just a few of the modern commentators note, the tale is taken up in the Pseudo-Clementine *Romances* (*Homilies and Recognitions*), stemming from a Christian group who maintained at least some Jewish purity rules. The link with food purity is made, and the bread signifies healing only available to pure sons of Israel, not to Gentile 'dogs' who do what they please in matters of eating and other activities (the basis for the term 'Cynic'). The woman, now given a name, Iusta, may, then, be thought to have abandoned some Cynic anarchy, but is still portrayed with a Cynic attachment to poverty, and in one of the two

---

48. Tertullian, *Adversus Marcionem* 4.7.5; *De fuga* 6.3; etc.
49. In J. Reuss, *Matthäus Kommentare aus der Griechen Kirche* (TU, 61.V.6; Berlin: Akademie Verlag, 1957), pp. 61, 126-27.

accounts, ensures for her foster sons a 'philosophical' education that is clearly ascetic.[50] A woman concerned with an ascetic philosophy that includes an insistence on poverty, she is still being interpreted as near-Cynic.

Origen picks out the Gentile mission, and the woman's faith, and discerns humility. The 'bread' is a Johannine intellectual awareness of God, for which Jesus has the power to transform even irrational κυνάρια/κυνίδια. But in a final comment on the passage, Origen explains that it is 'shamelessness' (ἀναίδεια) which warrants calling someone a κύων: and such 'shamelessness' is, of course, part of the distinctive reputation of the more radical Cynics. Origen's closing summary begins, 'One who is reproached as being a dog, and yet is not indigant...' with which we must compare, of course, the Cynic *chreia* quoted above and in the appended note. It is Cynics who so far from being indignant, relish the term.[51]

c. *Chrysostom*

The last patristic source I have traced for this discussion is John Chrysostom, at the end of the fourth century. He knew pagan Cynics in his own day, and had little good to say of them. He refers quite often in surviving writings to this passage, and holds the woman up as an example. The fullest treatment is in ch. 52 of his *Homilies on Matthew*. He makes many of the points repeated by modern expositors. But he also stresses that this is a woman (ἡ γυνὴ) time and again, and contrasts her both with the nobleman of John 4, and also with ἐκεῖνοι, the male disciples. He notes the 'shamelessness' of her approach to Jesus (while also allowing for the propriety of her earlier behaviour as given by Matthew). 'What's this, woman,' he asks, rhetorically, 'greater boldness (παρρησία, another catchword in descriptions of Cynics) than the male disciples?' The woman is then made to reply, 'Not boldness of my own strength, I am really full of modesty.' Clearly, boldness is the natural reading, and in fact Chysostom then has her say, 'Well, yes, I do offer my entreaty shamelessly. He will validate (αἰδεσθήσεται) my boldness.'

50. Pseudo-Clementine, *Homilies* 2.19-20 (*PG*, XI, 87-88); cf. *Recognitions* 7.32.

51. Origen, *Commentary on Matthew* 11.16-17 (*PG*, XIII, 959-66); cf. Athanasius, *Festal Letter* 7.7 (*PG*, XXVI, 1394).

In response to Jesus' 'It is not right to take the children's bread and give it to the dogs', the woman says, 'So, if I am a [house-]dog, I am part of the household.' Chrysostom then comments, 'She is not indignant at the insult. He says κυνάριον and she points to how things are for dogs. The woman responds as a philosopher (ἡ γυνὴ φιλόσοφει).' It was, of course, only the Cynics who had a tradition of women philosophizing in public (Epicureans included women, but kept themselves apart.) The woman shows her endurance (καρτερία, claimed by others, too, but especially by the Cynics) in the face of insult. Christ, explains Chrysostom, said all this to allow the woman to display her excellence (ἀρετή; where it was Cynics who claimed women could display the same ἀρετή as men), her understanding (σύνησις), her effective strength (εὐτονία; where to have τόνος is a Cynic claim, later shared with Stoics).[52] So she would win her crown: as Cynics claimed they did by their dogged perseverance and unconcern for convention. Chrysostom concludes, the male disciples made bold to approach Jesus, but ineffectively. The woman had the real endurance.

That the Cynic resonances have remained, despite being muffled by Matthew, must indicate just how strong they were in the earlier version, in Mark.

9. *Conclusion*

To allow oneself to be called κύων, 'dog', 'dog of the table', in the Graeco-Roman world of late antiquity is obviously to render oneself liable to be interpreted as κύων, Cynic. The non-Christian sources make it clear that this would be the most likely interpretation. The Christian sources, and especially John Chrysostom, show this potential actualized. We may well not take too seriously the ancient commentators' historical critical judgments. But they lived in a culture that continued to have a lot more in common with the world of the first century than ours has, they were much more naturally attuned to the nuances of culture and convention in the time of Jesus and of Mark than we are.

The Jesus of the story is aware of at least some aspects of Cynicism and of at least one Cynic *topos*. He challenges the woman in the light of

52. John Chrysostom, *Homilies on Matthew* 52 (*PG*, LVIII, cols. 521-22; and cf. 23 (*PG*, LVII, cols. 306-308). For these themes as characteristically and often distinctively Cynic, see Goulet-Cazé, *L'ascèse cynique*, pp. 17-76; and her 'Le cynisme', pp. 2721-2763; and see again, n. 43, above.

this awareness, she accepts his assessment, and wins the encounter—and her request. It may be difficult to fit such an interpretation into conventional reconstructions of the story of Jesus; but it is even harder, I have argued, to find a setting for its creation in this form by the early church. Perhaps we need to include among our serious reconstructions a Cynic interpretation of Jesus the Jew; and perhaps this tale of this woman, this Ἑλληνίς, this Syrophoenicianess with her dogged perseverance, will embolden us. 'Deeper Reflections on the Jewish Cynic Jesus' sketches and defends recent work of my own along these lines.

APPENDIX[53]

Dogs, crumbs and tables in some Graeco-Roman writings

(1)   When Plato styled him a dog, 'That's right (ναί)', he said, 'I keep coming back to the people who sold me' (Diogenes Laertius [D.L.], *Lives of Eminent Philosophers* 6.40).[54]

(2)   When some boys clustered round him and said, 'Watch out in case he bites us', he replied, 'Don't be scared, dog don't eat beet' (D.L. 6.45). This *chreia* is repeated at D.L. 6.61, and is expanded in Pseudo-Diogenes *Epistle* 2 (in *The Cynic Epistles*), where the reply initiates a positive relationship with the mockers.[55]

(3)   At a certain feast people kept throwing all the bones to him as they would have done to a dog. In response he wetted them as a dog would do (D.L. 6.46).

(4)   Asked what kind of dog he was, he replied, 'When hungry, a Maltese, when full, a Molossian' (D.L. 6.55).

(5)   Asked what he did to be called a dog, he said, 'It's by fawning on those who give, yapping at those who don't, and sinking my teeth into wrong'uns' (D.L. 6.60).

(6)   He was breakfasting in the market place [unseemly behaviour], and the bystanders gathered round him, shouting 'Dog!' 'It's you who are the dogs,' he replied, 'standing round watching me eat' (D.L. 6.61; the only instance in the tradition, I think, when the term is thrown back).

53. In the original version, in Brooke (ed.), *Women in the Biblical Tradition*, this appeared as Appendix 2. The contents of the first Appendix, 'Parallel Motifs in Apothegms and Healings', appeared more fully in F.G. Downing, 'Words as Deeds and Deeds as Words', *BibInt* 3.2 (1995), pp. 129-43, and this is reprinted in the companion volume to this one, Downing, *Doing Things with Words*, Ch. 2.

54. My own translation; but cf. Hicks (trans.), *Diogenes Laertius*, II (LCL).

55. As conveniently collected in A.J. Malherbe (ed.), *The Cynic Epistles* (SBLSBS, 12; Missoula, MT: Scholars Press, 1977); Pseudo-Diogenes 2, pp. 92-93.

(7) Do not be distressed when taking the short cut to philosophy is said to be 'living like a dog' (Pseudo-Crates 16; *Cynic Epistles*, pp. 66-67).

(8) So long as you fear the name 'Dog' I am going to call you by it; and you are plainly still afraid of it (Pseudo-Crates 21; *Cynic Epistles,* pp. 70-71).

(9) Stand fast then [Hipparchia], and live the Cynic life with us, for you are by nature no whit inferior to us [males]. Bitches are by nature in no way inferior to dogs (Pseudo-Crates 29; *Cynic Epistles*, pp. 78-79).

(10) Take care of our little puppy [σκυλάκιον] (Pseudo-Crates 33; *Cynic Epistles*, pp. 82-83).

(11) Don't be upset, father, at my being called a dog (but he is uneasy, the name and the actions may not match up; Pseudo-Diogenes 7.1; *Cynic Epistles*, pp. 98-99).

(12) Do not turn back, even if they call you Dog (Pseudo-Diogenes 44; *Cynic Epistles,* pp. 174-75).

(13) ...our contemporary Cynics, 'dogs round the table, round the gates' (Epictetus, *Dissertations* 3.22.80).

(14) Diogenes said he was like a Spartan dog. Plenty of people were ready to pat them when they were shown at popular gatherings, but no one was willing to buy one, they didn't know how to deal with them (Dio Chrysostom, *Discourses* 8.11).

(15) When taxed for behaving like a dog, he would jokingly reply, 'Well, dogs follow people along to festivals, without doing them any wrong. They bark and attack rogues and thieves, and when their masters are in a drunken stupor stay awake and guard them' (Dio Chrysostom, *Discourses* 9.3; cf. 9.7).

(16) Some admired Diogenes as the wisest man in the world. To others he seemed crazy. Many scorned him as a beggar and a poor good-for-nothing; some jeered at him, others tried to insult him grossly by throwing bones at his feet as they would to a dog...[while] he really resembled a royal lord who in the guise of a beggar [like Odysseus] moved among his slaves and menials (Dio Chrysostom, *Discourses* 9.9).[56]

(17) Let your language be barbarous, your voice discordant, just like the barking of a dog (Lucian, *Philosophies for Sale* 10; cf. 7).

(18) ...barking, gluttony, thievishness, excessive interest in females, truckling and fawning on those who give them things, hanging around tables (Lucian, *Runaways* 16).[57]

(19) 'It is the custom to throw the remants to the dogs', as Euripides said in *The Women of Crete* (νόμος δὲ λείψαν' ἐκβάλλειν κυσίν) (Athenaeus, *Deipnosophists* 3.96F-97A).[58]

---

56. Oldfather (trans.), *Epictetus*, II (LCL), pp. 158-59.
57. Cohoon (trans.), *Dio Chrysostom*, I (LCL), pp. 382-83; 402-403; 406-409.
58. Hartman (trans.), *Lucian*, II (LCL), pp. 468-69; V, pp. 72-73.

(20) …he turned to his slave and said, 'Leucus, if you have any scraps of bread, give them to these Dogs' (δὸς τοῖς κυσίν; Athenaeus, *Deipnosophists* 5.270CD).[59]

59. Gullick (trans.), *Athenaeus* (LCL).

Chapter 6

DEEPER REFLECTIONS ON THE JEWISH CYNIC JESUS[*]

In his 1998 'Reflections on the Cynic Jesus Thesis' Paul Rhodes Eddy reassembled a number of adverse criticisms of 'the thesis' in general that have been advanced by various authors, a sort of litany with set versicles and responses.[1] Burton Mack, John D. Crossan, Leif Vaage and others are able to respond for themselves. F. Gerald Downing is at times singled out by Eddy for particular mention, and so I was grateful for being allowed to rehearse and elaborate a little in the same *Journal of Biblical Literature* some of the arguments I had deployed to counter in advance many of the rebuttals Eddy parades, but which he appears to have missed in the books and essays of mine which he cites.

Cynicism, repeats Eddy, had at best 'a low profile' until the mid-first century, and only then a 'revival', 'after the death of Jesus'.[2] It is true, named, educated Cynic authors emerge only then in that century. It is, however, also true that many scholars have, for instance, been finding Paul confidently deploying Cynic *topoi* in a way that indicates a wide-spread popular currency already in his century, along with much more

*   Reprinted from *JBL* 17.1 (1998), pp. 97-104, with kind permission.

1.   Paul Rhodes Eddy, 'Jesus as Diogenes? Reflections on the Cynic Jesus Thesis', *JBL* 115.3 (1996), pp. 449-69. Other works critical of 'the Thesis' cited by Eddy and known to the present author include H.D. Betz, 'Jesus and the Cynics: Survey and Analysis of a Hypothesis', *JR* 74.4 (1994), pp. 453-75; B. Withering-ton, *Jesus the Sage: The Pilgrimage of Wisdom* (Minneapolis: Fortress Press, 1994); C.M. Tuckett, 'A Cynic Q?', *Bib* 70.2 (1989), pp. 349-76. There is an admirably measured rejoinder to Betz in particular by D. Seeley, 'Jesus and the Cynics: A Response to Hans Dieter Betz', *JHC* 3.2 (1996), pp. 284-90; and to Eddy, *idem*, 'Jesus and the Cynics Revisited', *JBL* 116.4 (1997), pp. 704-12. Not defending 'the Thesis' but querying the opposition, Kloppenborg Verbin, 'A Dog among the Pigeons'.

2.   Eddy, 'Reflections', pp. 451 and 467.

evidence for the prevelance of popular Cynicism in the first century.[3] Eddy makes no attempt to dispute or reinterpret this evidence, apparently preferring simply to repeat such received opinion as supports his case. Marie-Odile Goulet-Cazé, on whose authority Eddy elsewhere relies, herself concludes from given evidence that the continuity of Cynicism was in no way broken over the centuries.[4]

'It is generally recognised that great diversity existed among Imperial Cynics themselves', Eddy rightly assures us; but is also able to list for us their defining characteristics, which they supposedly shared so uniformly among themselves as to be readily distinguished from early followers of Jesus.[5] (Eddy is not alone it wanting to have it both ways: Cynics are so diverse that comparison is difficult, but also so uniform as to be easily contrasted with the first followers of Jesus.) The much repeated contrast centres on the lack of bag, staff and sandals in the mission charge in Q/Lk. 10.4. If one looks at the Cynic sources in detail (rather than at today's or yesterday's generalizations), there was even more variety in Cynic get-up than we find among the sets of instructions in the synoptic gospels; this, too, is explained in some little detail in my *Cynics and Christian Origins*. 'Mark allows...both sandals and staff, which many Cynics would carry; Matthew forbids the staff, as Luke does in one list, an Matthew forbids sandals, as Luke does in his other list.' 'Barefoot' is how Dio Chrysostom describes Diogenes; on this sculptors vary in their depictions of Cynics. (Particularly significant in fact are the photographs of [acknowledged] statues of Cynics

3.   Studies in Paul: e.g. A.J. Malherbe, *Paul and the Popular Philosophers* (Minneapolis: Fortress Press, 1989); S. Vollenweider, *Freiheit als neue Schöpfung* (Göttingen: Vandenhoeck & Ruprecht, 1989); M. Ebner, *Leidenlisten und Apostelbrief* (FzB, 66; Würzburg: Echter Verlag, 1991); as well as work by R.F. Hock and others, cited by Eddy himself; to all of which attention is already drawn in Downing, *Cynics and Christian Origins*, pp. 61-63 (a work Eddy implies he has read). The evidence is in fact much stronger than I then argued: see my 'A Cynic Preparation for Paul's Gospel', *NTS* 42.4 (1996), pp. 454-62; and my *Cynics, Paul and the Pauline Churches*.

4.   Goulet-Cazé, 'Le cynisme', p. 2724, 'la chaîne ne s'était point interrompue'; and now also R.B. Branham and M.-O. Goulet-Cazé (eds.), *The Cynics* (Berkeley: University of California Press, 1996), 'Introduction', pp. 13-14: any concentration on the emergence of eminent Roman Cynics in the first century is potentially misleading, for 'most Cynics lived...in the Greek cities of the east'.

5.   Eddy on variety, 'Reflections' p. 459; on common 'defining elements', pp. 461-62.

available in various published collections, but perhaps now especially those in Diskin Clay's recent essay.)[6] Some Cynics forgo a staff; for some the begging bag (or, for some, bowl) is a positive symbol, others would prefer to earn their keep. Though Jesus' followers do not beg (αἰτεῖν), they are expected to depend on others' hospitality, like some Cynics.[7] Eddy (along with other critics of 'The Cynic Jesus Thesis') makes no attempt to discuss such inconvenient data. To appear poorly dressed, to draw attention to yourself with a message encouraging poverty while relying on others' support, is, in the first-century east Mediterranean world, certainly quite enough to risk being seen as a Cynic.[8]

Eddy also reiterates the common conviction that Cynics deployed a common set of 'concepts' (and he quotes some of the 'slogans' often referred to in summaries) and 'a characteristic set of behaviors', which also, he avers, distinguish Cynics from early followers of Jesus.[9] In fact, as I was able to show in detail, the terms cited (whether as indicating 'concepts' or as 'catchphrases') are most often used by others discussing the Cynics, and often do not appear at all in Cynics' own works.[10] Eddy makes no reference to this evidence, let alone attempting to counter it. As he himself elsewhere allows, Cynics tended to individualism. They made their own selections from the traditions of doggish behaviour (including dress and language). Some items or motifs may be sufficient to attract the designation 'Cynic', no one (nor any one particular cluster) is necessary to warrant it.

6.   D. Clay, 'Picturing Diogenes', in R.B. Branham and M.-O. Goulet-Cazé, (eds.), *The Cynics* (Berkeley: University of California Press, 1996), pp. 366-87; especially fig. 9, p. 381, naked with bowl; and fig. 10, p. 384, with no cup, staff or satchel, but here with sandals and cloak draped around his midriff.

7.   Downing, *Cynics and Christian Origins*, pp. 10-11, 32-33, 133-34 for some long lists; but cf. Dio Chrysostom, *Discourses* 6.15 and 60; Musonius 19; Pseudo-Lucian, *The Cynic* 3; Teles, Stobaeus IVA, Hense 44; Philostratus, *Lives of the Sophists* 488; Pseudo-Crates 2, 19, 2; Pseudo-Diogenes 38.4; R.F. Hock, *The Social Context of Paul's Ministry* (Philadelphia: Fortress Press, 1980), pp. 37-42; but also Ebner, *Leidenlisten*, pp. 39-42, on the Cynic sound of Paul's account of his poor clothes.

8.   Jesus' followers do not beg ('ask'); but they expect support: Lk. 10.7, and cf. Pseudo-Crates 2.19, 22; Pseudo-Diogenes 38.4.

9.   Eddy, 'Reflections', pp. 451-52.

10.   Downing, *Cynics and Christian Origins*, pp. 45-50, with a table.

This factor—of diversity—is itself essential for any proper understanding of first century Cynicism, as 'received' by Roman or Greek aristocrats, or by plebeians. Cynics (self-styled and/or so styled by others) varied widely in their actual behaviour, and argued vigorously among themselves as to what was appropriate. As Branham and Goulet-Cazé have recently emphasized, the 'reception' of Cynicism in the first century (by those making a positive claim to appropriate the tradition) is very diverse.[11] If one takes 'shamelessness' as an expected (even if not 'necessary') feature of a Cynic's behavior, then shabby dress, eating in public, expecting support from others, disturbing the peace with caustic witticisms, are all instances. Outrageous sexual conduct was an option for some—but not noted, as it happens, for any named first century Cynic.[12] It is worth emphasizing this particular point.

There is no indication that Demetrius, Epictetus, Musonius, Dio Chrysostom, or Demonax in their (albeit often 'idealized') appropriation of Cynicism felt that a lacuna on this issue would invalidate the claim; nor does Dio in his criticism of plebeian Cynics in Alexandria (Dio Chrysostom, *Discourses* 32.8-9) include any such; nor in the next century does Pseudo-Lucian in *The Cynic*, nor Lucian in *The Fugitives*, nor in any of his Menippaean pieces (though he does, once, in his *Peregrinus* 17, and in his *Philosophies for Sale* 10). (It is intriguing to find how consistently modern western and apparently sophisticated commentators pick on excretory and even more on sexually shocking conduct as an 'essential' mark of Cynicism, as though only these counted —one can only guess it may be that only these might shock—or titillate—them or their circle.)[13] In the ancient world, however, to attack wealth, property, family, status and 'honour' would be quite enough to gain a reputation for Cynicism. Tales of such behavior would be quite enough to make the Jesus of the synoptic tradition appear Cynic, even if

11. Branham and Goulet-Cazé, *The Cynics,* 'Introduction', pp. 12-18; 'disparate', p. 16.

12. Eddy, 'Reflections', p. 463, refers confidently to 'the sort of "doggish" shamelessness that *characterised* the Cynics' public behavior', (my italics) without apparently checking the evidence. Again, a sweeping generalization ignoring the variety which Eddy elsewhere allows when it is convenient for his case.

13. For the fascinated concentration on excretion and coitus to the exclusion of wider ancient proprieties, see also D. Krueger, 'The Bawdy and Society: The Shamelessness of Diogenes in Roman Imperial Culture', in R.B. Branham and M.-O. Goulet-Cazé (eds.), *The Cynics* (Berkeley: University of California Press, 1996), pp. 222-39 (and in other writing).

(with Eddy) we minimize any critique of 'the Law' in the Jesus tradition.[14]

Eddy does once hazard an original guess: refusing to exchange greetings (Q/Lk. 10.4) would distinguish a follower of Jesus from any bold Cynic; yet 'exchanging greetings with no one' is precisely what Lucian expected of a Cynic.[15] Mostly Eddy continues to repeat received but unsupported generalities. So, Cynics were urban, we are told, while Jesus' followers kept to the countryside. There is actually much more evidence for Cynics out of town in the sources, even if not in the standard generalizations. And many moved around—that is, through the countryside, on foot, at walking pace; where else and how else?[16]

Eddy and I agree on rebutting any stratification of 'Q', or any sharp division between wisdom on the one hand and either prophecy or apocalyptic or both on the other. We would both in fact allow Jesus to have maintained a rich heritage from a diverse, argumentative, but not disjointed Judaism, long open to Hellenism. First-century Jews could make very different selections from their own varied national tradition and pervasive Hellenistic culture. For example, I think I have been able to show that such very nationalistic eschatological works as *4 Ezra* and *2 Baruch* deploy what is in origin an Epicurean motif, of the world as an ageing woman.[17] There are many other features in common among very diverse Greek, Roman and Jewish 'sages' who are authors of eschatologies, sharing each in his (or just possibly her) own way selections of motifs of whose origins they may or may not have been aware, using them maybe in very different ways in their respective contexts. Jesus' Jewish Cynicism as reconstructed by me is (on one level) just one other mix to put alongside the *Sibylline Oracles, 4 Ezra, 2 Baruch*, 4 Maccabees, Josephus, Philo—and later Rabbinic tradition. Jesus' Hellenistic and oral 'sources' are (on this thesis) mainly from popular Cynicism, despite (for instance) its present rather than future 'kingdom'. Jesus—I

---

14. Eddy, 'Reflections', p. 463.

15. Eddy, 'Reflections', p. 462; Lucian, *Philosophies for Sale* 10 (which could readily have been found to compare with Lk. 10.4 in my *Christ and the Cynics*, p. 48, had Eddy perused it more thoroughly).

16. Eddy, 'Reflections', pp. 451-52 and 463; for the counter, Downing, *Cynics and Christian Origins*, ch. 2, pp. 26-56, 'Definition: Who or What Counts as Cynic?' but especially pp. 26-30 and 45-52; on rural Cynics, pp. 82-84, 148-49; but note in particular, Lucian, *Demonax* 1; cf. also 9; and Dio 33.13.

17. Downing, 'Cosmic Eschatology', pp. 99-109. See also ch. 9, here.

take it—did not himself accept that particular restriction. However, it is worth noting on the other hand that the idea of a sage with authority as judge in a next life appears (*with whatever meaning*) in Cynic writings just as it does in the gospels (Q/Lk. 12.8-9; Mk 8.38).[18] Some strands of Cynic teaching are chosen, some are not. Analyse the elements in the Jesus tradition as a whole and some strands may seem very Jewish in origin, others very Cynic, while many motifs from each are certainly missing in Jesus' teaching as recorded. Mix them, as in the synoptic tradition, and in the fresh intertwined context the Cynic of course becomes Jewish, the Jewish gains a Cynic flavour. It is a very eclectic age.

We are assured, however, that 'one of the most characteristic forms of Jesus' teaching style—the parable—has no real Cynic parallels'.[19] In fact, most of the short metaphors and similes in the synoptic tradition do have close parallels in Cynic and related sources; and that is most of the material.[20] In the synoptic gospels we can also see longer and shorter versions (of, for instance, The Thief in the Night, The Sower, and The Mustard Seed; and different 'expansions' of The Pounds/Talents). Longer figurative constructions are admittedly not frequent in our Cynic materials (they are not frequent in the gospels); but when we do find such in Cynic sources, we realize how readily the short forms may have been condensed from the longer ones or shorter ones expanded. We may instance Antisthenes on 'strongholds' in Diogenes Laertius compared with the preserved fragment of his Odysseus; or the brief example of 'athletic prizes' in Paul compared with the treatment of the same model in Dio Chrysostom; and in Dio in particular do we find other 'expansions' of metaphors and similes found in brief elsewhere. The metaphor of 'fighting with wild beasts' used with reference to controlling the passions can be used in Cynic writing as briefly as by Paul (1 Cor. 15.32), or as expanded by Dio into his 'Libyan Myth'.[21] Dio's

---

18. Eddy, 'Reflections', pp. 454-57; against 'strata' in Q; F.G. Downing, 'Word-Processing in the Ancient World: The Social Production and Performance of Q', *JSNT* 64 (1996), pp. 29-48, ch. 4 in the companion volume to this, Downing, *Doing Things with Words*; and the Cynic sage as judge, Downing, *Cynics and Christian Origins*, p. 140 n. 122: Pseudo-Heraclitus 5.2 (cf. 9.3, 5); Pseudo-Diogenes 39; *Socratic Epistle* 25.1; Epictetus, *Encheiridion* 15 (of Heraclitus and Diogenes); cf. Lucian, *Downward Journey* 23.

19. Eddy, 'Reflections', p. 461.

20. See Downing, *Christ and the Cynics*.

21. Arguing that the metaphor is shared, A.J. Malherbe, 'The Beasts at Ephesus', *JBL* 87 (1968), pp. 71-80, repr. in *idem*, *Paul and the Popular Philosophers* (Min-

'Good Euboean' has formal as well as substantial similarities with Luke's 'Good Samaritan'. Dio Chrysostom here writes at very much greater length, but uses an everyday rural setting and an unexpected generous 'hero' to challenge narrow-minded expectations (besides portraying a rural Cynic 'natural' simplicity).[22] Dio says that people come to men dressed as he was (as a Cynic) expecting such stories. To quote an earlier conclusion of my own, 'the sheer quantity of parable, metaphor and simile [in the synoptic tradition] would strongly reinforce the impression that anyone repeating this material was some sort of Cynic'.[23]

We may wonder, then, where it is that we find much more closely similar but exclusively Jewish parables to provide a cultural context for the longer or shorter ones in the gospels. It is, of course, only in the much later rabbinic writings. We have no independent evidence that others in Galilee in Jesus' day were using this varied form. On the other hand, we might indeed feel it is unlikely that Jesus invented the genre, still less that the rabbis learned it from him. So the gospels themselves come to persuade some that the (rabbinic) parable mode, otherwise unevidenced in the first century, 'must have been' part of Jesus' cultural setting. (The same argument applies to precedents for healing and for exorcism by Jewish sages.) 'By extrapolating from such generalities… theorists have constructed…a milieu for Jesus and his followers' (to quote Eddy). It is a circular argument, though not lacking in cogency, whether applied to 'Jewish Sage Theorists' *or* to 'Jewish Cynic Theorists'. Just so would some of us conclude that strands of the Jesus tradition which to us look quite Cynic indicate that Cynicism 'must have been' a part of Jesus' cultural context, even though Cynicism, too, is not directly evidenced in the Galilee of the early first century. (*Of course* the literary Cynic tradition in Gadara—better evidenced though

neapolis: Fortress Press, 1989), pp. 79-89. Q/Lk. 11.24-26 (the returning unclean spirit) also affords an interesting comparison with Dio's Libyan Myth, *Discourses* 5.

22. A.J. Malherbe discusses the Antisthenes passages in 'Antisthenes and Odysseus and Paul at War', now in his *Paul and the Popular Philosophers* (Minneapolis: Fortress Press, 1989), pp. 91-119; H. Funke discusses the prizes, in 'Antisthenes bei Paulus', *Hermes* 98 (1970), pp. 459-71; the passages can be found in G. Giannantoni, *Socratis et Socraticorum Reliquiae*, II (Naples: Bibliopolis, 1990); the 'Good Euboean' is in Dio Chrysostom, *Discourses* 7.1-80.

23. Dio Chrysostom, *Discourses* 55.9, 11, 22; cf. 72.13; quoting Downing, *Cynics and Christian Origins*, p. 139.

it is there than anywhere other than in Athens—could never on its own show that there were Cynics passing through Galilee, let alone making their presence felt; only that there could have been, should the gospel evidence in any measure itself suggest their presence. The presence of the rabbis' pharisaic forebears in the gospels similarly suggests to Eddy and others what could have been, what is not inconceivable for the context of this aspect of Jesus' teaching.)[24]

It is then also worth noting how pervasive is the Diogenes tradition in particular in the *progymnasmata*, the manuals for elementary education. Anyone learning Greek in Palestine would be likely to be introduced to Cynicism, in this way if in no other, and provided with good stories and witty comments—and the radical ethos—to pass on, in the original or in translation.[25] If any Jews in Galilee learned to read and write Greek the way Greek was normally taught, Cynic tradition would be known in Jewish Galilee. On the other hand, although 'Jesus as Diogenes?' makes for a bright, eye-catching title, I am not aware that this phrase has been used by any of the scholars cited by Eddy (who certainly advances no such suggestion). More importantly, I do not think any of us has argued that Jesus had any direct awareness at all of the *literary* Cynic tradition with its focus on the figure of Diogenes himself (or even that a Cynic Jesus would have known the name). No one, so far as I know, supposes that Jesus had, for instance, read Menippus or Meleager, or Diocles, or any of Diogenes Laertius' sources for book six of his *Lives of Eminent*

24. Eddy, 'Reflections', pp. 460-67; Downing, *Cynics and Christian Origins*, pp. 143-49. There are no first-century Jewish sources preserved for us that include the quantity of figurative writing we find both in the synoptic tradition on the one hand, and the Cynic on the other. At best we find solitary parables or allegories, in the whole of the occasional longer work a meagre tally of one. Eddy cites B.B. Scott with approval on some issues. In his *Hear Then the Parable* (Minneapolis: Fortress Press, 1989) Scott notes the absence of any evidence for a widespread use of parables in first-century Judaism, pp. 63-65; while also denying that the 'form' is used in Hellenistic literature of the day.

25. I am grateful to a reader for *JBL* for suggesting this point be made; see Hock and O'Neil (eds.), *The Chreia in Ancient Rhetoric*, I; cf, Dio Chrysostom, *Discourses* 72.11; but on Cynic influence among later Rabbis, also H.A. Fischel, 'Studies in Cynicism', in J. Neusner (ed.), *Religion in Antiquity: Essays in Memory of Edwin Ramsdell Goodenough* (Leiden: E.J. Brill, 1968), pp. 372-411; and *idem*, *Essays in Greco-Roman and Related Talmudic Studies* (New York: Ktav, 1977); and C. Hezser, 'Die Verwendung der hellenistichen Gattung Chrie im frühen Christentum und Judentum', *JSJ* 27.4 (1996), pp. 371-439.

Philosophers; nor, for that matter, any of the *Cynic Letters*. A Jewish Cynic Jesus is not a literary figure at all, not in Greek, not in Aramaic, not in Hebrew.[26]

The alternative Eddy offers instead, is, as might be expected, that 'the model of Jewish sage offers the most apparent parallel.'[27] 'Apparent' in what sense and to whom? This Jewish sage is to be found in Jewish wisdom *literature* (*sic*), a composite figure drawn from (among other sources) the scepticism of Qoheleth, the prudential ethics of Proverbs, and the establishment ethos of ben Sirah. So now we have Jesus as a collator of literary wisdom sources, despite the absence of any significant quotations from (emergent) canonical wisdom texts in the synoptic tradition—even in passages where 'wisdom' is referred to.

That we have not a shred of evidence for a single instance of this composite (and very literary) figure in the time of Jesus seems to be of no moment. We may glean charismatic miracle workers, bandits, prophets and messiahs from Josephus, and he even on occasion tells us of 'sophists' (but these turn out to be interpreters of Torah), and of one ascetic (Bannus). Nowhere do we find a sage, neither commoner nor patrician, touring the countryside with followers, drawing on the extremely diverse resources of the Jewish wisdom literature. And if we were to, how close in *content* would the 'parallel' be? In Proverbs poverty may be better than strife, but poverty *per se* is never demanded, nor is homelessness admired. In his *Jesus the Sage*, Ben Witherington counters my emphasis on Q/Lk. 12.22-31 with Prov. 6.6, also a lesson from 'nature'.[28] Prov. 6.6 actually advises 'Go to the ant, you sluggard!'—precisely the opposite of the *insouciant* emulation of ravens and anenomes that Jesus demands. Nowhere from the Jewish Wisdom tradition (nowhere in any 'core' Jewish tradition culled in centuries of scholarship) has any such carefree injunction been adduced. But in Cynic and Cynic-influence sources there are numerous examples—some of which also, as it happens, link such carelessness with reliance on divine provision.[29] We do have two Jewish ascetics: Bannus, noted above, and the synoptic (not the Josephan) John; but they are not por-

26. Cynic motifs are found by A.J. Malherbe and others in Paul without any reference being made—or the absence noted—to any named Cynic.

27. Eddy, 'Reflections', p. 460.

28. Witherington, *Jesus the Sage*, pp. 133-34. Eddy relies on Witherington's authority.

29. Downing, *Christ and the Cynics*, pp. 68-71.

trayed as sages.[30] Essenes lived simply—but their community retained
the wealth members brought in, maintained buildings, it seems, and
traded; and they are not seen as concerned with the wisdom traditions;
nor do they travel the countryside relying on the hospitality of non-
members, displaying their poverty.

Of course it is possible to ransack prior and later Jewish wisdom
teaching for 'parallels' with which to construct an a posteriori 'model'
non-Cynic Jewish sage for Jesus to have emulated, and of course, some
of the selected parallels are apposite. Jesus clearly was a Jew and assimilated and deployed considerable elements of his core inheritance. But
of this purely Jewish sage assembled for Jesus to model himself on
there is no other instance recorded than Jesus himself, and many of
Jesus' recorded concerns still remain unrepresented in the constructed
model. Neither, of course, do we have any individual Cynic to provide
a precise model for Jesus—but that has never been suggested by the
various proponents of 'the Thesis'.[31] In my own, as in others' reconstructions, Jesus makes his own selection and offers his own innova-
tions within a culture that includes significant Cynic along with much
core Jewish tradition.

'Jewish Sage Theorists' just as much as 'Jewish Cynic Jesus Theorists' agree in a tacit or explicit assumption that for even the most inno-
vative public speaker (and performer) to be effective, he or she must
needs produce variations in a shared language of concepts in words and
significant actions. First-century Judaism as reconstructed solely from
core Jewish texts just does not seem to provide an adequate 'langue', an
adequate cultural context for the full range of the synoptic Jesus tradition, and especially for those parts where even opponents of the Cynic
thesis agree the Cynic 'parallels' are most striking.

Would these Cynic ascetic and disruptive strands in the gospel tradition really look Cynic to native Greek speakers of whose varied culture
'pagan' Cynicism was a part (and not just to snappers up of superficial
similarities, as I and others are made out to be)? Eddy cites approvingly
an essay by Gilles Dorival. Dorival has himself concluded that Cynicism was the most significant 'pagan' philosophical movement for
Christians in the early centuries, as the one closest to it in ethos, both as
support against common foes and as rival with similar aims. And I have

30. In older tradition, maybe the Rechabites, and Elijah, perhaps; Elisha main-
tains a home and a servant.
31. Seeley, 'Jesus and the Cynics'.

further warranted this conclusion. Those who knew Cynicism in all its varieties as a living contemporary family of ideas and practices knew that the ascetic strands in Jesus' teaching sounded very similar. It was not a matter of superficial coincidences.[32] (One part of this exploration of the 'reception' of early Christianity constitutes the next chapter of this volume.)

In many discussions of cultural context, 'my' parallels are apposite in form, content and ethos, 'yours' are superficial, and 'his' are parallelo-maniacal. Eddy and others prefer the 'parallels' afforded by the model of a Jewish sage that they have constructed. In my case, it is averred, 'the mass of surface parallels have proven to be mesmerizing'.[33] Eddy's argument would be a little more impressive if he could adduce even superficial parallels in the Jewish wisdom tradition to Jesus' asceticism (in which, in his own way, Paul seems to have followed him). It is the content (not the form, not the surface) of much of the Jesus tradition that demands an interpretative comparison with contemporary Cyni-cism. Of course, Witherington and Eddy and others could be right. Per-haps there were ascetic Jewish sages around the turn of the era pro-viding a world of enacted discourse within which Jesus could compose his own variations while still being understood by those around him; and these hypothetical Jewish sages quite independently within the Hel-lenistic world had reached many Cynic-like conclusions for Jesus perhaps to develop in his own way. Or, perchance, it was totally inde-pendently and innovatively that Jesus hit on ideas and practices that would then a little later look very Cynic to people in the Hellenistic cities, even happening to phrase them similarly. Perhaps similar socio-economic circumstances produce similar individual phenomena, even down to details of imagery. It could be, and it has been suggested.[34] These and other possible imaginative constructs some do find plausible.

Eddy has convinced himself that no version of a Cynic Jesus is viable. In fact the only certainty is that we are all dealing with constructs that

32. Eddy, 'Reflections', p. 452 n. 22; G. Dorival, 'L'image des Cyniques chez les pères grecs', in M.-O. Goulet-Cazé and R. Goulet (eds.), *Le cynisme ancien et ses prolongements* (Paris: Presses Universitaires de France, 1993), pp. 419-43; and *idem*, 'Cyniques et Chrétiens aux temps des pères grecs', in MS given to author; and Downing, *Cynics and Christian Origins*, pp. 169-301.

33. Eddy, 'Reflections', p. 467.

34. M. Goodman, review of Downing, *Jesus and the Threat of Freedom*, *JJS* 12.1 (1990), p. 127.

appear more or less plausible to their creators and to some others around, while no construct is certain, not even certainly wrong. Eddy's own (shared) construct is not certainly wrong, but his opposition to mine might be strengthened by a keener attention to evidence rather than to citations of uncritically received opinions.[35]

I have outlined a still fuller defence of the theoretical basis for an interpretation of Jesus as a 'Jewish Cynic Jesus' in another essay set to appear about the same time as this collection.[36] In the next chapter, as already promised, we consider one strand of the evidence of outsiders seeing Christianity as a form of Cynicism.

---

35. It is only fair to admit that some proponents of 'the Cynic Jesus Thesis' can be as cursory in their reading of the Cynic sources as Eddy seems on this showing to be, and that does afford him some excuse—but not justification. (My own early essays in Christian Cynicism are at times similarly flawed. I have tried to correct them in later essays. Most recently, as noted above, I would now allow for much more Cynicism in Paul than I did in my *Cynics and Christian Origins*—while finding in Paul often rather different Cynic strands from those in the Jesus tradition; see my *Cynics, Paul and the Pauline Churches*).

36. 'The Jewish Cynic Jesus', in M. Labahn and A. Schmidt (eds.), *Jesus, Mark and Q: The Teaching of Jesus and its Earliest Records* (JSNTSup; Sheffield: Sheffield Academic Press, forthcoming). But for a more general and less 'committed' discussion of the issues, see J.S. Kloppenborg Verbin, 'A Dog among the Pigeons' (n. 2, above).

Chapter 7

CYNICS AND CHRISTIANS, OEDIPUS AND THYESTES[*]

Justin and the other second-century Christian apologists endeavour to present their beliefs and lifestyle as a 'philosophy', and Christians as a philosophical sect. This was a 'quite implausible' suggestion according to R.L. Wilken, commenting on Justin.[1] Yet a number of outsiders in the second century do seem to have seen the Christians in such terms, although not as intellectually respectable as the apologists would have liked. 'What distinguished them from wandering Cynic philosophers?' asks Stephen Benko, and replies, 'Outwardly, probably nothing.'[2] The evidence for these preliminary assertions will be sketched at the end of this discussion. But if this is a plausible reading of the reaction to Christians of such outsiders as Aristides, Galen, Celsus and Crescens, and of Lucian's Peregrinus, it provides a context in which better sense may be made of the charges widely evidenced at least from Justin's time onwards and levelled against the Christians, of indulging in Oedipoean intercourse and Thyestean feasts.[3] Accused of incest and cannibalism,

*   Reprinted from *JEH* 44.1 (1993), pp. 1-10, with kind permission.
1.   R.L. Wilkin, 'Towards a Social Interpretation of Early Christian Apologetics', *CH* 39 (1970), pp. 437-58 (445); but see further below, on Galen; and L. Alexander, 'Paul and the Hellenistic Schools: the Evidence of Galen', in T. Engberg-Pedersen (ed.), *Paul in his Hellenistic Context* (Minneapolis: Fortress Press, 1995), pp. 60-83.

2.   S. Benko, *Pagan Rome and the Early Christians* (Bloomington: Indiana University Press, 1984), p. 45. Tertullian actually complains about contemporaries who would insist in seeing Christianity as no more than a set of philosophical opinions: *Apology* 46.2; cf. J. Whittaker, 'Christian Morality in the Roman Empire', *VC* 33 (1979), pp. 209-25 (213).

3.   Justin Martyr, *Apology* 1.26, 29; *Trypho* 10; Tatian, *Oratio* 23; Athenagoras, *Legatio* 3.32; Theophilus, *Autolycus* 3.3-6; Eusebius, *Historia ecclesiastica* 5.1.14-15, 26, 52; Origen, *Contra Celsum* 6.27; Tertullian, *Apology* 7-9; *Ad nationes* 1.7; Minucius Felix, *Octavius* 11; *Clementine Homilies* 4.15-23; 5.11-14; other references in Benko, *Pagan Rome*, ch. 3.

the Christians are thought to be practising a Cynic philosophical 'naturalism' that deliberately flouts mere social conventions. This affords a more plausible explanation of the indictment than that generally offered, namely the suspicions thought likely to have been aroused by any secretive religious group, a suggestion for which the evidence proffered is far from convincing.

The examples are too well known to need rehearsing exhaustively, but as a reminder I quote from the fullest account preserved for us, as found in the *Octavius* of Minucius Felix:

> they despise temples as dead-houses, they reject the gods...half-naked themselves, they despise honours and purple robes... They despise present torments, although they fear those that are uncertain and future... they love one another almost before they know one another. Everywhere also there is mingled among them a certain religion of lust, and they call one another promiscuously brothers and sisters...I hear that they adore the head of an ass...an infant covered over with meal, that it may deceive the unwary, is placed before him who is to be stained with their rites. This infant is slain by the young pupil...Thirstily—O horror! they lick up its blood, eagerly they divide its limbs...on a solemn day they assemble at the feast with all their children, sisters, mothers, people of every sex and every age. There, after much feasting, when the fellowship has grown warm and the fervour of incestuous lust has grown hot with drunkenness, a dog that has been tied to the chandelier is provoked by throwing a small piece of offal beyond the length of the line by which he is bound, to rush and spring. And thus, the conscious light being overturned and extinguished in the shameful darkness the connection of abominable lust involves them.[4]

Again it is well known that Tertullian was sufficiently confident to make a grim joke of the charges:

> While you recline at table, take notice of the places which your mother and sister occupy. Mark them well, so that when the dog-made darkness has fallen on you, you may make no mistake, for you will be guilty of a crime unless you perpetrate a deed of incest.[5]

But the martyrs of Lyons and Vienne paid for this reputation with their lives: 'Some of the heathen domestics...fearing the tortures inflicted on God's people, at the soldiers' instigation falsely accused us of

---

4.   Minucius Felix, *Octavius* 9 (*ANF*, IV, pp. 177-78); also quoted in Benko, *Pagan Rome*, pp. 55-56.
5.   Tertullian, *Apology* 8 (*ANF*, III, p. 24); cf. *Ad nationes* 1.7.

Thyestean banquests and Oedipean incest.'[6] (The speech by Fronto to which Minucius Felix's Caecilius refers focused on legends of the house of Pelops, including both Thyestes's 'banquet' and also tales of incest.)[7]

The usual explanation adduces 'standard accusations' levelled indiscriminately against minority religious groups, always suspected of the worst by prurient outsiders. W.H.C. Frend stresses the language in which the second-century BCE suppression of the Bacchanalia is recounted.[8] Benko suggests more recent analogies: Canidia in Horace's *Epode* 5, rumours involving Apollonius of Tyana, Commodus, Elagabalus, Valerian and Antinous, as well as episodes in popular fiction, in Achilles Tatius's Leucippe and Cleitophon, and in Lollianus's Phoinika.[9] R.M. Grant adds Dio Cassius on the rites of Bellona.[10]

Orthodox Christians were themselves willing to believe such things of the 'gnostic heretics'; Clement charges the Carpocratians with promiscuity, and Epiphanius the Phibionites with both promiscuity and cannibalism.[11]

So, 'incest and cannibalism' are to be seen as standard denunciations directed against esoteric religious groups. And yet not one of these

6. Eusebius, *Historia ecclesiastica* 5.1.14; trans. G.A. Williamson, as *Eusebius: The History of the Church* (Harmondsworth: Penguin Books, 1965), pp. 64-66.

7. E. Champlin, *Fronto and Antonine Rome* (Cambridge, MA: Harvard University Press, 1980), pp. 64-66.

8. W.H.C. Frend, 'The Persecutions: Some Links between Judaism and the Early Church', *JEH* 9 (1958), pp. 141-58 (153-54); cf. *idem, Martyrdom and Persecution in the Early Church* (Oxford: Basil Blackwell, 1965), pp. 162-64.

9. Benko, *Pagan Rome*, pp. 61-63.

10. R.M. Grant, 'Charges of "Immorality" Against Various Religious Groups in Antiquity', in R. van den Broek and M.J. Vermaseren (eds.), *Studies in Gnosticism and Hellenistic Religions presented to Gilles Quispel,* (Leiden: E.J. Brill, 1981), pp. 161-70; one may also note de Ste Croix, *The Crucible of Christianity*, pp. 345-51; A. Heinrichs, 'Pagan Ritual and the Alleged Crimes of Christians', in P. Granfield and J.A. Jungmann (eds.), *Kyriakon* (Festschrift Johannes Quasten; Munich: Kösel, 1970), pp. 18-35; P. Keresztes, 'The Emperor Antoninus Pius and the Christians', *JEH* 22 (1971), pp. 1-19; R.L. Wilken, *The Christians as the Romans Saw Them* (New Haven: Yale University Press, 1984), pp. 16-21.

11. Clement, discussing Carpocrates in *Stromateis* 3.2 suggests a thoroughgoing Cynic egalitarianism based in 'nature', in which incest is simply a part: *Stromateis* 3.2.5, 10; 3.4.27; 3.6.54; Epiphanius, *Panarion* 26.4-5; in Benko, *Pagan Rome*, pp. 64-65; cf. Grant, 'Charges', pp. 165-68; R.L. Wilken, *The Christians*, pp. 19-21; and similar charges by Christians against other 'heretics'. To his credit, Jerome would not believe charges of infanticide: *Letters* 41.

instances that have been collected over the years to support this thesis does in fact combine them. At most we find accusations either of cannibalism or of promiscuity; and the promiscuity is never, in the passages quoted, incestuous. Incest as such is not mentioned, and cannibalism and promiscuity do not appear to be linked in any of the examples cited.

The explanatory point that is often added must of course be well taken. Common Christian words and cultic practice could have been enough to give credence to such suggestions once made, or to arouse suspicions in the first place. The Christians called each other brother and sister (1 Cor. 7.15; Jas 2.15; Ignatius, *Polycarp* 5; etc.), they exchanged a kiss, made an offering of fine flour (Justin, *Trypho* 41) in their 'love feasts' with 'new-born' members (1 Pet. 2.2), sharing in the body and blood (flesh and blood, Jn 6) of their founder who had declared all foods clean (Mk 7.19). If Christian groups used or were thought to use these terms, people might well think the worst.[12] But the fact remains that no other religious sect or cult is to be found in our surviving literature accused of both incest and cannibalism together.

The one movement that did have a reputation for approving both and even practising both was that of the Cynics. In his doxography for Diogenes of Sinope, Diogenes Laertius tells us that the Cynic 'advocated community of women, recognising no other marriage than the union of the man inviting and the woman who consents'.[13] With no further restrictions specified, this could only look like an invitation to incest (as becomes clear later). Two sentences further on Laertius tells us that Diogenes saw no impropriety in eating the flesh of any living thing (ζῷον) whatsoever; and this explicitly includes the eating of human flesh, as Diogenes (or some other member of the school) made clear in his Thyestes. As well as a Thyestes Diogenes is also credited with a version of Oedipus, and Dio Chrysostom makes a point of having Diogenes discuss the acceptability of incest with reference to Oedipus in particular.[14] Cannibalism is defended as the custom of other nations in Laertius's doxography, as is incest in Dio. The unforced custom of foreign nations is taken by Cynics an an indication of accord with nature.

---

12. Benko, *Pagan Rome*, p. 60; Wilken, *The Christians*, pp. 16-17.

13. *Lives of Eminent Philosophers* in R.D. Hicks (trans.), *Diogenes Laertius*, II, 6.72, pp. 74-75.

14. Laertius 6.80; Dio Chrysostom, *Discourses* 10.30-33; cf. R.G. Andria, 'Diogene Cinico nei papiri ercolanesi', *Cronache ercolanesi* 10 (1980), pp. 129-51 (144 and n. 67).

Animal—especially canine—behaviour may well have been adduced to show the 'naturalness' of both, as against the artificiality of Greek *mores*.[15]

Laertius adds that community of women, and also cannibalism, were both considered acceptable, at least in theory, by the early more Cynic-minded Stoics. He does not suggest that either group put theory into practice.[16]

When Philodemus in the first century BCE wished to tar the reputation of contemporary Stoics, he did so by stressing Zeno's original close dependence on the *politeia* ascribed to Diogenes (though it seems widely accepted that Philodemus had no direct access to work itself). At paragraph 11.2 of the second manuscript, 'p', we meet a reference to (men) having children in common. This echoes the similar clause of Laertius's doxography for Diogenes which immediately follows his prior reference to having women in common. In Philodemus there is a lacuna; but the text of 'p' (soon joined by paragraphs 8 and 9 of 'P') goes on straightaway to interpret having women in common specifically in terms of incest; men are to have coitus with their sisters and mothers and (other) kin, and (they) with brothers and sons, eschewing no sexual intercourse whatsoever. There even seems to be a very similar rhetoric in the pairing here to that in the later charges brought against Christians: it is sisters and mothers (entailing, of course, brothers and sons) who are specified, while (for no obvious reason) fathers and daughters escape attention.[17]

Philodemus's Cynics are also accused of proposing unisex clothing and common naked exercise (after Plato). The 'p' papyrus next says that the Cynics kill and eat dying members of their own families, and 'P' says they are especially obliged to kill their fathers. Cannibalism as such has already been referred to in 'P' before this. Although it is not in fact babies that are said to be eaten (as in the accusations against Chris-

15. Laertius 6.72-73; cf. Goulet-Cazé, *L'ascèse cynique*, pp. 61-66.

16. Laertius 7.121, 131. Andria, 'Diogene', argues that the proposal would have been restricted to cases of dire necessity; compare Goulet-Cazé, *L'ascèse cynique*, p. 41; R. Hoïstad, *Cynic Hero and Cynic King* (Uppsala: Lundeqvist, 1948), p. 148. Augustine, *De civitate dei* 14.20 was of the same opinion.

17. W. Cronert, *Kolotes und Menedemus* (TU, 6; Leipzig: J.C. Heinrichs, 1906), pp. 53-65; cf. T. Dorandi, 'Filodemi. Gli Stoici', *Cronache ercolanesi* 12 (1982), pp. 91-133; and cf. Lucian, *Philosophies for Sale*, 10.

tians) we clearly have here Cynics taken both to advocate and to practise incest and cannibalism. Their common tradition is interpreted so, and these are the most serious charges to be levelled against them. Cynicism (and early Cynic-tainted Stoicism) is represented 'as a barbarism that would destroy every conceivable human society',[18] much as Christianity was later described by such as Tacitus or Celsus.

If Christians are accused of advocating and practising incest and cannibalism, it probably means that they are being seen as some kind of Cynic group. The dress and the poverty ordered by their founder, along with much of his recorded teaching, would anyway suggest this.[19] Once the connection was made they would automatically be thought likely to espouse a crude 'naturalism' of the kind under discussion. And then the language of their liturgy—'body and blood', 'new-born babes', 'brothers and sisters', 'kiss of peace', 'love-feast'—would simply confirm that they were putting philosophical theory into practice.[20]

When Theophilus of Antioch, two centuries after Philodemus, turns to responding to the charges levelled against Christians, it is in these terms: 'that the wives of us all are held in common and made promiscuous use of, and that we even commit incest with our own sisters; and, most impious and barbarous of all, that we eat human flesh'. He repudiates the latter as Stoic and Cynic, the former as taught rather by Plato, Epicurus and Stoics.[21] It would have been more convenient for the present thesis had he stuck to Cynicism. But he supports the general point being made here. No Christian we know of responds to these allegations by saying, 'No, that is what happens in your [*pagan*] mysteries.' Theophilus mentions traditional Homeric mythology, but as taken up by Plato, not as rubrics for some cult. Tatian rebuts the charge with reference to philosophers.[22] Athenagoras discerns and rejects the implicit philosophical appeal to 'nature' that might be thought to justify such customs.[23] The Clementine *Homilies* talk of 'grammarians and

18. Hoïstad, *Cynic Hero*, p. 149.
19. Benko, *Pagan Rome*, pp. 44-45; Downing, *Christ and the Cynics*, pp. 47-48 and *passim*; and *idem, Jesus and the Threat of Freedom*, pp. 51-57; and *idem, Cynics and Christian Origins*.
20. See above, and n. 12.
21. Theophilus, *Autolycus* 3.3-6.
22. Tatian, *Oration* 25.
23. Athenagoras, *Legatio* 3.32, again.

sophists' who might imitate the immorality of the gods, and it is among philosophers that such practices have been held to be 'indifferent'.[24]

Justin does refer to 'mysteries of Cronos' which Christians could have claimed to be enacting, if they had wanted to justify such a philosophy,[25] but with no suggestion that any such were currently celebrated. Minucius Felix mentions quite other unattractive pagan rites of human sacrifice, but does not suggest incest or cannibalism were being practised.[26] Tertullian can think of public cults which in earlier centuries offered children for sacrifice (but not for eating); he suggests none that was thought to require incest. He also mentions the likely rationalizing philosophical argument from foreign practice.[27] Ready as they are to bounce charges back, none suggests a pagan cult anywhere that enacts such rituals or is commonly charged with so doing. There is no sign at all among the Christians themselves that this is 'a standard accusation levelled against minority religious groups'. L.T. Johnson has reminded us that recriminations of disgraceful behaviour were common coinage precisely between competing philosophical groups, insisting that their theory was the only one that led to true virtue.[28] 'Incestuous cannibals' would be an appropriate slur against any group affecting what appeared to be a Cynic lifestyle.

We must conclude, then, that the espousal and practice of incest and cannibalism combined together were seen as philosophical aberrations, and the Christians as a perverse Cynic sect. And although Cynics are not alone in being (correctly) seen as having countenanced incest and cannibalism as 'natural', our evidence (Philodemus, Dio Chrysostom, Diogenes Laertius) suggests that it is they in late antiquity, rather than the Stoics after the time of Panaetius and Posidonius, who have this reputation.[29] Subjected to these allegations, Christians are being castigated as all too consistent Cynics.

24. *Clementine Homilies* 4.16-17, 20; 5.18-19.

25. Justin, *Apology* 2.2.

26. Minucius Felix, *Octavius* 24.

27. Tertullian, *Apology* 9, including reference to Oedipus; Oedipus and Thyestes figure at *Ad nationes* 1.7.

28. L.T. Johnson, 'The New Testament's Anti-Jewish Slander and the Conventions of Ancient Polemic', *JBL* 108 (1989), pp. 419-41.

29. Andria, 'Diogene', pp. 144-45; Goulet-Cazé, *L'ascèse cynique*, Ch. 3 §2, pp. 179-91; on Panaetius (and Cicero): 'il dénonçait le manque de pudeur et les outrances', p. 176.

It would be unwise to put too much weight on the 'dogs' that appear in many of the accusations. But κύων as well as κυνικός, 'dog' as well as 'doggish', continue to be used of Cynics throughout the period; and this certainly does not detract from the suggested identification. Even 'throwing morsels' to the dogs would match.[30] Other incidental items in Caecilius's descriptions of Christians would also fit: their plebeian character, the prominence of women, the disreputable dress (Cynics go '[half-]naked'), the despising of honours and purple robes, the disregard for present pain (and even the talk of after-life, a Cynic topos, although classically probably intended not literally but as 'myth').[31]

It is commonplace to conjecture that Pliny's enquiries into the Christians' behaviour, to find out whether or not they were commiting any of 'the crimes associated with the name', and his noting in particular his finding that they took 'ordinary, harmless food', and, among other things, swore to abstain from adultery[32] implies that the charges we have been considering were around earlier in the second century CE than Justin's time. 1 Pet. 2.11-17; 4.4, 15, can be taken in support. By then Christians would have already gained this reputation for Cynic immoralism among the public at large.[33]

It must, however, be admitted that the earliest references to Christians from outsiders available to us do not immediately support the position argued here. In fact, the 'wicked superstition' of Suetonius' note, with much the same in Tacitus, combined with 'abominations' and 'hatred of the human race', together with the sentence of death by fire under Nero[34] have usually been pressed into service to support the 'commonplace slandering of secretive cults' theory. 'Superstition' itself, of course, readily suggests to us a religious cult rather than a philos-

---

30. Cf. e.g., Dio Chrysostom, *Discourses* 9.9; Athenaeus, *Deipnosophists* 5.270CD; 3.96F-97A; and the Appendix to Chapter 6 above.

31. E.g., Menedemus, Laertius 6.102; but also Mennipus, whose *Satires* seem often to have taken this form, as witness both Varro and Lucian; cf. R.F. Hock, 'Lazarus and Micyllus: Greco-Roman backgrounds to Luke 16:19-31', *JBL* 106 (1987), pp. 447-63.

32. Pliny the Younger, *Letters* 10.96.3, 7.

33. Grant, 'Charges', pp. 161-63; Wilken, *The Christians*, pp. 15-23; Heinrichs, 'Pagan Ritual', pp. 19-24.

34. Suetonius, *Life of Nero* 16.2; cf. Pliny the Younger, *Letters* 10.96.8; and Tacitus, *Annals* 15.44.2-5. Christian 'atheism' is also best explained as Cynic, against J.W. Walsh, 'On Christian Atheism', *VC* 45 (1991), pp. 255-77.

ophy, especially in the light of the usual Greek word used, δεισιδαι-
vονία. L.F. Janssen has in fact argued cogently that the Latin *superstitio* indicates astrological and magical practices with political over-
tones, rather than a *religio* as such. 'Superstition' is more likely to have
been a reaction to some awareness of Christian eschatological expectations.[35] What has perhaps come to official notice is a different aspect,
and even a different strand of early Christianity, and neither 'cult asso-
ciation' nor 'philosophical sect' is at issue.[36] Then again, the Christians
encountered by Pliny recognized that their meetings came within the
scope of the edict against collegia, at least potentially a subversive political club, a view later espoused by Celsus.[37] Celsus also saw them as a
disloyal Jewish sect;[38] others may have seen them as a rather more
respectable burial society, and so forth.[39] Christianity was diverse; people are likely to have noticed diverse aspects of the strands they encountered, and interpreted them in terms of differing models from their
respective social contexts. But when outsiders levelled charges of incest
and cannibalism they were most probably identifying Christianity as a
kind of radical Cynicism.[40]

From outsiders themselves within the first century we have no evidence at all for any views they may have held of nascent Christianity.

35. L.F. Janssen, ' "Superstitio" and the Persecution of Christians', *VC* 33
(1979), pp. 131-59.
36. For indications of variety in the first-century church—or churches—see, eg.,
W. Bauer, *Orthodoxy and Heresy in Earliest Christianity* (ET; Philadelphia: Fortress Press, 1971); M. Werner, *The Formation of Christian Dogma* (ET; London:
A. & C. Black, 1957); J.D.G. Dunn, *Unity and Diversity in the New Testament*
(London: SCM Press, 1977).
37. Pliny the Younger, *Letters* 10.96.7, again; Celsus in Origen, e.g., *Contra
Celsum* 1.1.
38. R.L. Wilken, 'The Christians as the Romans and Greeks Saw Them', in E.P.
Sanders (ed.), *Jewish and Christian Self-definition*, (London: SCM Press, 1980), pp.
100-125 (119-23); commenting on Origen, *Contra Celsum* 2.4, etc.
39. Wilken, 'Social Interpretation', pp. 449-51; and *idem*, *The Christians*, pp.
31-47. On this issue see now, J.S. Kloppenborg and S.G. Wilson (eds.), *Voluntary
Associations in the Graeco-Roman World* (London: Routledge, 1996).
40. Cf. the judgment of Dorival, 'L'image des Cyniques chez les Pères grecs',
in M.-O. Goulet Cazé and R. Goulet (eds.), *Le cynisme ancien et ses prolongements*
(Paris: Presses Universitaires de France, 1993), pp. 419-44: Cynicism is for the
ancient Fathers the most important philosophical school.

For its first-century origins, obviously, we have to rely on the Christian writings that have come down to us. But here, too, Cynic-seeming motifs and possible influences are (again) being increasingly discerned.[41]

One sub-plot in this discussion that warrants more than a footnote is the suggestion that the charges originated among Jews who were both distancing themselves from Christians and also trying to transfer to them the malicious calumnies to which they had long been subjected.[42] 'Hatred of the human race' was one (rebutted by Josephus).[43] 'Worshipping an ass's head' is another (Josephus, again, and Minucius Felix as quoted above).[44] Heinrichs notes in particular the accusation that Jews shared in human sacrifice and cannibalism.[45] Origen suggests that the twin accusations against Christians of incest and cannibalism may first have been laid by Jews.[46] But there is still no evidence for Jews themselves having faced this combined slur. It is only to Christians, so far as our evidence shows, that such charges of 'immoral Cynic naturalism' are transferred.[47] And if we accept that this is what lies behind the widely evidenced popular opinion that Christians encountered in the second century CE, it then tallies rather than conflicts with a standard reading of other important indications available to us, as intimated at the beginning of this article.

Justin Martyr was harassed and later prosecuted by a Cynic philosopher, Crescens. Justin in fact suggests that Crescens may be attacking him for fear of himself being identified as a Christian.[48] The possibility seems quite obvious to Justin. A.J. Malherbe has suggested,

41. See the discussion and bibliographies in Downing, *Cynics and Christian Origins*, and *idem*, *Cynics, Paul and the Pauline Churches* (London: Routledge, 1998); and Ch. 6 in this volume.

42. Frend, 'The Persecutions'; Heinrichs, 'Pagan Ritual'.

43. Tacitus, *Histories* 5.5; Josephus, *Apion* 2. 121 §10.

44. Josephus, *Apion* 2. 80, 95 §§7-8; Minucius Felix, *Octavius* 11.

45. Heinrichs, 'Pagan Ritual', p. 23, citing Josephus, *Apion* 2. 89 §8.

46. Heinrichs, 'Pagan Ritual', pp. 18-24; Origen, *Contra Celsum* 6.27; cf. Justin, *Trypho* 10.

47. B.L. Visgotsky, 'Overturning the lamp', *JJS* 28 (1987), pp. 72-80, believes he can find (separate) 'charges of incest, magic, and wife-sharing levelled against heretics, probably Jewish Christians, by the Jews' in some widely dispersed sources. His case is intriguing, but the evidence very allusive, and he offers no text combining charges of cannibalism with incest.

48. Justin, *Apology* 2.3.

> Both Justin's reason [for wanting to put some distance between himself and the Cynics] and Crecens' for opposing the Christians may be due to the fact that Cynics and Christians were beginning to be lumped together by the opponents of both…[and] the disputatious Justin in his philosopher's cloak could easily have appeared to have Cynic characteristics.[49]

Certainly his pupil Tatian, for all his angry denunciation of the founders of the Cynic way, was for Hippolytus, a little later, himself a Cynic.[50]

Justin's contemporary, Peregrinus, had, according to Lucian, spent some time as an eminent member of a Christian group, and had had a spell in prison for it. His Christian associates saw him as 'the new Socrates', Lucian tells us. While still in good standing with the Christians Peregrinus returned to his home town, according to Lucian's narrative, and donated his patrimony to his fellow citizens, who saw him as a splendidly consistent Cynic. Only later did he carry his Cynic disregard for convention—Christian scruples over meat offered in temples?—too far, and was excommunicated.[51]

At around the same time, Aelius Aristides in a lengthy attack on the Cynics for their abusive begging, 'base and wilful, behaving like those impious men of Palestine', also appears to be making this connection. There seems to be no other group linked with Palestine apart from the Christians to which this can refer.[52] Galen is less dismissive. The Christians display an ascetic self-mastery as strong as any philosopher's, in their sexual self-restraint, their eating and drinking, and their contempt for death. The only other recognized group that 'philosophized' so, by the 'short-cut' of practice rather than by intellectual reflection, was that

---

49. A.J. Malherbe, 'Justin and Crescens', in E. Ferguson (ed.), *Christian Teaching: Studies in Honor of Lemoine G. Lewis*, (Abilene: Abilene Christian University Bookstore, 1981), pp. 312-27 (316); cf. also Frend, *Martyrdom*, p. 275, referring to Apollonius Saccas (?Cynic 'bagman'), in conflict with another Cynic.

50. Hippolytus, *Elenchos* 10.8, as discussed in Frend, *Martyrdom*, p. 275, again; F.G. Downing, *Cynics and Christian Origins*, pp. 182-89 (186).

51. Lucian, *Peregrinus* 11-16; see the discussion in Frend, *Martyrdom*, pp. 273-75. There are interesting similarities between Lucian's mocking account of Peregrinus' Hercules-style death, and the Smyrneans' admiring description of the death of his contemporary, Polycarp: *Peregrinus* 35-40; *Martyrdom of Polycarp* 12-19.

52. Aelius Aristides, *Oration* 3, 'To Plato, in Defence of the Four' 670-71, in C.A. Behr (ed. and trans.), *Aelius Aristides: The Complete Works*, I (2 vols.; Leiden: E.J. Brill, 1986), p. 275; discussed in Frend, *Martyrdom*, p. 275; and Benko, *Pagan Rome*, p. 46.

of the Cynics.[53] And it is clear to Origen that when Celsus around the same date mocked the Christians' plebeian teachers, women among them, 'those people who gather in market places and perform the most disgraceful tricks, gathering crowds round them', he is likening them to Cynics, (as classically described by Dio Chrysostom).[54]

As W.H.C. Frend concluded, 'The evidence for similarity between the two groups is drawn from too wide a range of sources to be brushed aside. Outwardly some Christian preachers, with their old philosopher's cloak and few worldly goods, must have resembled their [Cynic] rivals. So, too, did their disciples.'[55]

It seems that we have to accept that as soon as we find distinctive public reactions to Christians in the second century (and perhaps earlier) the less prurient see them as a kind of vulgar ascetic (or hypocritical) Cynic, and those with the nastiest minds see them as Cynics who were bound to be doing naturally what every decent person saw as unnatural but deeply fascinating vice. Either way it is as followers of a Cynic philosophical lifestyle that Christians first appear in the reactions of those outsiders whose opinions are preserved for us in any detail.

Whether this assessment of the early Christians from outside may have been justified internally at all, and, if so, to what extent, are questions too large to be argued here. If warranted at all, this identification may still have been more appropriate for some, less for others; least for

---

53. Galen can arguably be included in this survey if *De peccatorum dignotione* 3.12-13 on Cynic philosophy aiming for virtue and foregoing logical theory is put alongside the Arabic excerpt on Christians who also eschew demonstrative argument but still live 'philosophically': in R. Walzer, *Galen on Jews and Christians* (London: Oxford University Press, 1949), p. 15; Walzer's translation from the Syriac of Ḥunain ibn Isḥāq, of *Six Books on Hippocrates' Anatomy*, in G. Bergsträsser (ed.), *Abhandlungen für die Kirche des Morgenlandes*, XVII.21 (Leipzig 1925; repr. Nendeln, Liechtenstein: Kraus, 1966). The 'self-discipline and self-control' of that passage are also paralleled at *Peri ton peponthon topon* 7.519/3.515, in *Medicorum Graecorum opera quae extant*, ed. D.C.G. Kuhn (Leipzig: Cuoblochii, 1823), 6.419, on Cynics, again; Benko, *Pagan Rome*, p. 40; and for this interpretation of Galen's comments, see also Wilken, 'Social Interpretation', pp. 447-49; and *idem*, 'Christians as the Romans and Greeks Saw Them', p. 108; though Wilken fails to notice the Cynic parallel.

54. Celsus as understood by Origen, *Contra Celsum* 3.50, using the language of Dio Chrysostom, *Discourses* 32.9.

55. Frend, *Martyrdom*, p. 275; compare the similar judgment of Benko, *Pagan Rome*, p. 45, cited above; and A.J. Malherbe's comment, cited above.

Jewish or for gnostic Christians.[56] But there are other strands in addition to these in early Christianity such as those represented by the 'Q' tradition used by Matthew and by Luke, or as represented by James, or, in his own way, by the early Paul; there are many more besides. Others than I have argued that many of the earliest Jesus traditions are Cynic in character from the earliest discernible stages.[57] And later Christians, through to the fifth century at least, often seem able happily and naturally to interpret and elaborate the teaching ascribed to Jesus in Cynic terms, often tacitly adopted, sometimes quite explicitly. They would all (bar Clement's Carpocratians, perhaps) have repudiated the extreme Cynic naturalism of which they were accused, and though many had an un-Cynic attachment to speculative metaphysics, yet Jesus' ascetic ethics were to them obviously Cynic; clearly that was the language and practice to which they saw themselves committed in response to him.

I argue this at greater length elsewhere, as already indicated.[58] But some lines in the *Sentences of Sextus* may serve to make the point in brief: 'The tough training a virile Cynic does is fine, but his public lifestyle is best avoided; do not accept the outward show, but emulate the strength of character.' Sextus's eclectic composition was accepted as Christian by Origen and others.[59] If a great many of those early Christians whose writings we have preserved for us shared this outlook, then outsiders were entirely warranted in seeing the movement (or some strands of it) as a kind of Cynicism, albeit neither Oedipoean nor Thyestean in either theory or practice.

Cynic resonances make early Christianity appear part of the wider Graeco-Roman world. Early Christian eschatology can seem to set it apart, as distinctively Jewish (its eschatology can even be adduced to counter the Cynic material). In fact the diverse early Christians are of

56. In the earlier version of this article in *JEH* I included in this bracket, Pauline Christians; but have now revised this judgment: see my *Cynics, Paul and the Pauline Churches*, and for the retraction, p. 31. On variations among early Christians, see n. 37, above.

57. See, again, Downing, *Cynics and Christian Origins*, and the references there; and, again, Chapter 6 in this volume.

58. Downing, *Cynics and Christian Origins*, Chs. 6-10, pp. 169-301; and note the reference to G. Dorival, n. 41, above; also many of the essays in Branham and Goulet-Cazé, *The Cynics*.

59. *Sentences of Sextus* 461-62, ed. and trans. H. Chadwick, *The Sentences of Sextus* (Cambridge: Cambridge University Press, 1959), p. 64.

course both: distinctively Jewish in many aspects, clearly part of their wider east Mediterranean world in others. And so, too, are their eschatologies, to which we now turn in the next two chapters: first, the themes of exile and the final end of exile (Ch. 8), and then common strands in ancient Mediterranean eschatologies (Ch. 9).

Chapter 8

EXILE IN FORMATIVE JUDAISM

1. *Introduction*

Jews (some, most, all) in the first century, in *eretz Israel* as much as
elsewhere, believed (so it is averred) that they were living in an ongoing (punitive) exile. Their study of their ancient texts in the light one
shed on another, and in the light of contemporary circumstance, convinced them there had been no 'return' worth noting, no 'restoration'
worthy of the name. Or so we are assured by a number of scholars.
Some, Tom Wright in particular, would assure us that this conviction
(a) of a continuing exile (or 'exile') also entailed (b) living with a supposedly defective temple from which (c) their God was thought absent,
and (al)so (d) living with a sense of unavailable forgiveness (d is
perhaps restricted to Wright). (e) a 'real' return from this protracted
punitive exile lies in the future. And Jesus of Nazareth is to be interpreted within this context.[1]

By no means all agree. Maurice Casey, for instance, while welcom-
ing much of Wright's work, especially for its attention to Jewish
sources, finds the arguments for this particular motif 'quite spurious'.
Many Jews lived in Israel and in Jerusalem itself and attended the
major festivals in the Temple where 'the Tamid was sacrificed twice a
day, a special symbol of God's presence with Israel'.[2]

---

1. N.T. Wright, *The New Testament and the People of God* (London: SPCK,
1992), pp. 268-72 *et passim*; and *idem*, *Jesus and the Victory of God* (London:
SPCK, 1996), pp. xvii *et passim*. For an early statement of the theory, see M.A.
Knibb, 'The Exile in the Literature of the Intertestamental Period', *HeyJ* (1976), pp.
253-72.

2. M. Casey, 'Where Wright is Wrong', *JSNT* 69 (1998), pp. 95-103 (99); cf.
J.D.G. Dunn, review of Wright, *The New Testament*, *JTS* NS 46 (1995), pp. 242-45
(243), 'most dubious of all, however, is the argument…that most first century Jews
thought of themselves as still in exile'.

In fact not all those whom Wright claims in support agree even on the issues of 'exile', 'return' and 'restoration'—let alone on the supposed entailments. Anthony Harvey, for instance (whose *Jesus and the Constraints of History* Wright cites in his own favour in *The New Testament and the People of God*) himself expresses doubts on this score.[3] J.A. Goldstein, cited by Wright, has a much less sweeping picture of a continuing 'Age of Wrath' in response to further sin. On Goldstein's view it is in response to further sin that the glorious prophecies of restoration were not being fulfilled, despite the return of exiles and the rebuilding of the Temple.[4] S. Talmon, also cited by Wright, limits his ascription of an idea of a delayed return and 'restoration' (in some sense), to the Qumran community.[5] I shall argue that this latter more restricted conclusion, but only this, is sustainable.

Obviously we need to ask again what controls we have that may warrant or exclude the kinds of ancient 'scribal' inter-textual readings that are being proposed. Can we tell how much of the immediate or wider context of a line or sequence, quoted or apparently 'in mind', was also influential in the interpretation we are studying? And are we able to tell whether implications that seem to us to follow are actually accepted by an ancient author?

2. *Suggested Clarifications*

a. *Terminology*
First I shall present what I hope is a clearer terminology and at the same time a summary of what seem to me the most plausible conclusions to be drawn from the evidence currently adduced and the interpretations offered.

3.   Wright, *The New Testament* p. 114 n. 68 citing A.E. Harvey, *Jesus and the Constraints of History* (London: Gerald Duckworth, 1980) but with no page reference: perhaps p. 61, quoting Sirach 48.10, where Elijah is expected to 'restore the tribes of Jacob'. For Harvey's dissent, see his review of Wright, *Jesus and the Victory of God,* in *Theology* 100.796 (July/Aug. 1997), p. 296.

4.   J.A Goldstein, 'How the Authors of 1 and 2 Maccabees treated the "Messaianic" Prophecies', in J. Neusner *et al.* (eds.) *Judaisms and their Messiahs at the Turn of the Christian Era* (Cambridge: Cambridge University Press, 1987), pp. 69-96; cited by Wright, *The New Testament*, p. 270, n. 108.

5.   S. Talmon, 'Waiting for the Messiah: The Spiritual World of the Qumran Covenanters', in J. Neusner *et al.* (eds.), *Judaisms and their Messiahs at the Turn of the Christian Era* (Cambridge: Cambridge University Press, 1987), pp. 111-37.

(i) 'Exile' can refer to an initial movement or an ongoing state. Either or both may be voluntary, or forced (or involve some measure of both). It may sometimes help to use a word like 'deportation' for the inception of forced exile and retain 'exile' for the continuing state.

(ii) There may be or have been a return involving actual surviving deportees themselves; or a 'return' for some (or all or most or a few) of the deportees' near or distant descendents.

(iii) 'Restoration' may imply a very close reproduction of the situation obtaining prior to the deportation and its attendant circumstances (which had involved the destruction of buildings, etc.) or scholars today may use the word 'restoration' in an extended sense, for something similar but much better happening, or even for something quite different but very good. In the case of hopes or assurances held out to those deported from Jerusalem and to their descendents scholars use 'restoration' indifferently for some supposed later common amalgam of the diverse and in some instances mutually exclusive schemes of the books of Jeremiah, Isaiah, Ezekiel, Haggai–Zechariah, Chronicles–Ezra–Nehemiah. One needs to be much clearer as to precisely *which* expectations (prophecies) interpreted in which ways *may* have been held to have been fulfilled or to be awaiting fulfilment, and by which groups.

b. *Some Possibly Agreed Data*
(i) There was no independent Judaean state in the first century CE, nor had there been since the early sixth century, apart from the brief Maccabaean–Hasmonaean flowering.

(ii) There were a great many Jews ('Israelites' might be better, that including people with Judaean roots and others with northern roots) living beyond the borders of *eretz Israel* in the period of 'Second Temple' Judaism. This seems widely accepted, even if the estimated numbers are not agreed.

(iii) Some—even, a great many—of these were the descendants of people forcibly removed in the first place, in various deportations, of which the one most often referred to in subsequent Jewish writings available to us was that enforced by the Babylonians, and conventionally dated 587/6 BCE. It involved, we are told, the wealthiest and the most skilled of the population of the devastated city of Jerusalem, who were then made to settle in Babylonia. This is widely agreed, even among those most sceptical as to the historical value of the canonical documents purporting to relate to the events in question;[6] and I find no reason to doubt it.

(iv) Jerusalem seems to have remained very little populated for some time after 586 BCE, although other towns and villages in Judaea continued in effective occupation, albeit at a reduced level.[7] There is the important analogy of the conditions of the northerners (as pieced together from the Elephantine papyri, Josephus, the Samaritan Pentateuch, and archaeology): we should assume a continuing community in the south just as there was from earlier on in the north, with continuous traditions (despite the hostile propaganda of 2 Kgs 17).[8]

(v) Initially, at least, those involved in this deportation (to Babylonia), and their progeny and later descendents were prevented by the authorities (by order backed up by force or the threat of it; and perhaps by distance and uncertainty as to their likely reception) from returning 'home'. This, too, seems widely agreed. This is involuntary exile—and does not need inverted commas.

(vi) One explanation for this situation (devastation, and exile for some) was always possible, that their God had failed them, and they were not to blame. They had been faithful to the covenant, they had trusted God, and put no trust in themselves, let alone in any other deity; yet their God had scattered them among the nations (Ps. 44. 3, 17, 20, 11).

(vii) On the one hand, some of those who remained (Ezek. 11.15-16) took the view that the land was theirs, they had not been driven out. On the other hand some seem to have supposed that deportation was a sign of comparative approval from God: they were the 'good figs', the core of a renewed people (Jer. 24; Ezek. 11.17-20).

6.   G. Garbini, *History and Ideology in Ancient Israel* (ET; London: SCM Press, 1986); P.R. Davies, *In Search of Ancient Israel* (Sheffield: JSOT Press, 1992); E. Nodet, *A Search for the Origins of Judaism from Joshua to the Mishnah* (JSOTSup, 248, Sheffield: Sheffield Academic Press, 1997); L.L. Grabbe (ed.), *Can a 'History of Israel' be Written?* (JSOTSup, 245, ESHM, 1; Sheffield: Sheffield Academic Press, 1997).

7.   D.L. Smith-Christopher, 'Reassessing the Historical and Sociological Impact of the Babylonian Exile (597/587–539 BCE)', in J.M. Scott (ed.), *Exile: Old Testament, Jewish and Christian Conceptions* (Leiden: E.J. Brill, 1997), pp. 17-36 (17-21).

8.   Cf. H.M. Barstad, *The Myth of the Empty Land: A Study in the History and Archaeology of Judah during the 'Exilic' Period* (Symbolae osloenses, 28; Oslo: Scandinavian University Press, 1996).

(viii) However, this enforced absence, this involuntary exile, in the case of the 586 BCE deportees and their descendents (in common with at least some other deportations) certainly was interpreted at the time and subsequently by some as a punishment inflicted by their God (2 Kings; Jeremiah; Ezekiel; 2 Chronicles; Ezra–Nehemiah). Conditions are unclear, and may have varied at different times. There may have been forced labour; on the other hand, some may have settled happily (Jer. 29); some may have prospered (the Murasu Archive).

(ix) The conviction was expressed to some of the exiles (probably early on) that their God had abandoned his Temple, allowing it to be destroyed (Ezek. 11; Isa. 49.14[?]).

(x) The Deuteronomic historians, on the other hand, were sure that exiles could pray towards the temple (and not just the site) and be heard (1 Kgs 8.46-53; cf. Dan. 6.10). Cultic activity was continued by some (Jer. 41.4-6; Zech. 7.1-7; 1 Kgs 8.46-53 [?]).

(xi) Hope of a glorious return for the deportees and/or their descendents led by their God to a renewed homeland were expressed by at least one prophet during this exile, who probably persuaded some to share these hopes: the city (and Temple?) would be rebuilt (Isa. 49.17; 54.11-12). The penalty had been paid, the punishment, these insisted, was over (Isa. 40.2). Similar hopes were expressed by Ezekiel. At some point some shared the conviction that this would be seventy years after the first fall of Jerusalem, 597 BCE (Jer. 25.12; 29.10).

(xii) Permission for any who wanted to, to leave Babylonia and take up residence in the ancestral homeland, and renew its cultus, was apparently granted by the Persian authorities sometime after their defeat of the Babylonians (538 BCE). This was the end of any externally enforced stay. (If this is rejected in favour of some alternative in which a 'return' of those who claimed ownership of the land is a pure invention in their interest, it makes little difference to the use of these writings in the period where this present essay focuses.)[9]

(xiii) A number of descendants of the Judaean deportees (or soi-disants deportees) presumably travelled (or claimed to have) to the ancestral homeland, around 520 BCE (?Ezra 1.1-6), and the dominant tradition

9.   See the discussion in L.L. Grabbe (ed.), *Leading Captivity Captive* (JSOTSup, 278; ESHM, 2; Sheffield: Sheffield Academic Press, 1999), between T.L. Thompson, 'The Exile in History and Myth: A Response to Hans Barstad', pp. 101-18; and Barstad's rejoinder, 'The Strange Fear of the Bible: Some Reflections on the "Bibliophobia" in some Recent Ancient Israelite Historiography', pp. 120-27.

is theirs; but others remained in Babylonia. There was no glorious 'translation' of people from Babylonia to Judaea (but we do not know how literally Isaiah's words were intended or were taken). We have no indication that those remaining were waiting for a miracle to assure them that their God really wanted them in Judaea, no indication that they thought they must continue in Babylonia to serve out a punitive sentence, to purge ancestral guilt, await a miracle as a sign that all was forgiven, no indication that at that time or later those remaining thought those who removed to Judaea guilty of hubris. They just stayed where they were settled, as did many others elsewhere, who nonetheless maintained a version or, more likely, versions of their ancestral traditions.

(xiv) One strand of explanation among the reverse settlers (Chronicles–Ezra–Nehemiah) maintained that Judaea had had to remain fallow for the 70 years of the enforced exile, catching up on its Jubilee years (2 Chron. 36.21). Those who meanwhile (and perhaps all along) had been living and farming in Judaea (including the ancestral land of those moving back and reclaiming it?) are not likely to have seen it this way. There are many signs of tension among people with different interests and traditions (3 Isaiah; Haggai–Zechariah; Nehemiah; the Elephantine papyri).[10]

(xv) Those who were comfortably (re)settled in *eretz Israel* may well have felt no unease in the face of the extravagant hopes of 2 Isaiah; those less blessed—even, dispossessed by the incomers?—may have adopted or retained hopes of some richer fulfilment of those assurances (elements in 3 Isaiah). There is no clear sign of a uniform ideology of any sort emerging, no uniform reinterpretation of inherited discussions of the deportation, or of the past forced exile; nor of the ongoing voluntary absence from the promised land of many, nor of the presence in the promised land of others, whether descendants of deportees or not. We have no evidence for any sub-group insisting *all along* (and against the evidence) that a punitive enforced exile—enforced absence from *eretz Israel*—was still in progress. Robert Carroll allows that an idea of dispersion with no return may lie hidden in some of the prophets (Amos, Micah), but concludes 'What is significantly missing in the prophetic literature [Isaiah, Jeremiah, Ezekiel, and the 'minor prophets' as they

10. P.R. Ackroyd, *Exile and Restoration* (London: SCM Press, 1968), pp. 20-31 and 144-45 with n. 29; P.D. Hanson, *The Dawn of Apocalyptic* (Philadelphia: Fortress Press, 1979).

stand] is any sense of the permanence of the diaspora experience…My sense of its absence is that what we have is the point of view of the Jerusalem community.' B. Halpern concludes, 'The elite community regarded Jeremiah's prophecy as so entirely fulfilled, so thoroughly vindicated as to be no longer relevant…'[11]

(xvi) Cultic activity may have been continuous on the sacred site in Jerusalem (as also on Mount Gerizim) and was certainly operative in Jerusalem by the end of the century, with some attempt under way to build a stone sanctuary on the original site to replace the one that had been destroyed (Haggai–Zechariah).

(xvii) Even though there seem to have been other sanctuaries (contrary to Deuteronomy), such scant evidence as we have indicates that the Jerusalem site and temple were highly valued (Haggai–Zecchariah–Nehemiah; ben Sirach; the Maccabee rebellion) as important for their God and for his devotees.

(xviii) Some Jews (Israelites? Judaeans?) during this period may well have hoped for a final ingathering of all 'their people' to *eretz Israel*. We do no know how many did; but see what follows.[12]

3. *The Second Century* BCE

(i) Ben Sira, early in the second century BCE, is fully aware that 'the prophecies spoken in [God's] name' still await fulfilment (36.1-17) but at no point suggests the failure of fulfilment to date constitutes the continuation of a past punitive sentence. He is sure that some of the hopes inspired by 'the twelve prophets' 'delivered the people' and that a valid Temple 'holy to the Lord' was erected in the time of Zerubbabel and Joshua (49.10-12). As obviously, sin is forgivable, and blessing is readily available (2.9-11; 3.15, etc.)

(ii) The composition of Tobit is usually dated around the same period, while the story itself is set in the time of the northern tribes' forced exile under the Assyrian Shalmanesar. Tobit's prayer for mercy on the

---

11. R. Carroll, 'Deportation and Diasporic Discourses in the Prophetic Literature', in J.M. Scott (ed.) *Exile: Old Testament, Jewish and Christian Conceptions* (Leiden: E.J. Brill, 1997), pp. 63-85 (83, 85); B. Halpern, 'The New Names of Isaiah 62:4: Jeremiah's Reception in the Restoration and the Politics of "Third Isaiah"', *JBL* 117.4 (1998), pp. 623-43 (630).

12. Cf. I.M. Gafni, *Land, Centre and Diaspora: Jewish Constructs in Late Antiquity* (JSPSup, 21; Sheffield: Sheffield Academic Press, 1997).

dispersed (ch. 13; see v. 5) is often quoted in support of the 'prolonged punitive exile' theory. In fact the writer knows that the Temple will have had a first rebuilding by the hands of those whom God has brought back, though an incomparably more splendid sanctuary lies ahead, along with a total 'return' (14.5-7 and 13.15-18). But God has already shown his greatness where the Israelites are scattered, mercy and forgiveness have already been granted, and Tobit already has cause for thanks (13.4, 6) as have the inhabitants of Jerusalem (13.8). There is no indication at all that the delay of completion of restoration is seen as a continuing punishment by enforced exile.[13]

(iii) Clearly the events under Antiochus IV—the assault on then established traditions, and the desecration of the current Temple in particular—stimulated a great deal of anguished reflection. Perhaps Isaiah's and Ezekiel's assurances of an invulnerable divine sanctuary were recalled. Be that as it may, the self-blame device was redeployed; clearly his people had gone back to, or gone on with displeasing their God. One prophecy to be reinterpreted was that of Jer. 29.10. The 70 years there mentioned was now reinterpreted as 490 years (of which some 434 had already passed); and the 'return to this place' at the end of that period was also reinterpreted as the end of all rebellion and sin, when all iniquity would have been expiated and everlasting right ushered in (Dan. 9.3, 24). It is important to recognize the extent of the reinterpretation. Neither the term 'exile' nor any idea of exile recurs at all, not even as metaphor. In fact the author of Daniel 9 of course knows that Jerusalem was restored centuries before, and remained so, as promised; and is sure it had a fully valid sanctuary which was then again desecrated. It is *other* aspects or implications of the prophecy in Jeremiah that remain to be fulfilled (9.24, again).[14]

13. Ben Sira and Tobit are both claimed for the continuing exile thesis by, among others, C.A. Evans in 'Exile and Restoration in the Proclamation of Jesus', in J.M. Scott (ed.) *Exile: Old Testament, Jewish and Christian Conceptions* (Leiden: E.J. Brill, 1997), pp. 299-328 (305-306). Evans also claims 1 Baruch. As it stands it is complex, likely composite, and of a date hard to determine. But, as it stands, the author or editor knows that the Temple is restored and operational (1.6-10), even though he imagines the scribe recalling its dereliction (2.26). The exiles have admitted their forefathers' wickedness, and have themselves repented (ch. 2), the condition for the return (3.7, past; even if 2.33, future), the outcome for which 'Baruch' prayed. It still remains appropriate, however, to recall the past misdeeds that were the occasion for the punitive destruction and deportation.

14. D.J. Bryan, in correspondence (26 October 1998), very likely speaking for

(iv) *The Apocalypse of Weeks* (*1 Enoch* 93.1-10; 91-11-17) dated by James VanderKam to just prior to the Maccabee times,[15] divides Israelite history into periods, with Solomon's Temple built in the fifth week, and then, at the end of 'a time of blindness' (the sixth period), the Temple is burnt and the whole race of the chosen is scattered. It is true, there is no reference to any reversal of the scattering under Ezra or any-one else, nor to the rebuilt Temple, by the time of writing. Clearly, this author saw nothing good in the intervening period. But when the 'times of righteousness' do come (including an everlasting house for the King of Glory) we are *not* also told that the chosen race once scattered is 'only now' to be reassembled. Any theme (or metaphor) of an end to as yet unended forced exile has to be argued from silence. The writer in fact seems only concerned with his own very recent past, with 'the apos-tate [fallen away] generation' which 'arose' and which (on this dating) can only be the hellenizing collaborators in Judaea. No earlier period or wider geographical horizon is indicated, and by implication the pre-decessor generations of the recently arisen 'apostates' had been in good standing.

(v) VanderKam dates *The Animal Apocalpyse* (*1 Enoch* 85–90) to 164 BCE. This also summarizes Israelite history. 'The Lord of the Sheep' abandons 'the house and the tower', giving the flock over to the (Baby-lonian) lions and other ravenous creatures (89.56). Although E. Isaac's translation inserts a sub-heading, 'From the destruction of Jerusalem to the return from exile', the writer's concern is with the sheep who 'aban-don' their Lord's house, and with the beasts into whose death-dealing power the sheep are given, but not with where the sheep are. He does

others, similarly points out that texts such as this (and others to be noted below) 'are evidence that in situations of reversal Jewish groups in the Second Temple period drew upon the traditions associated with exile and were prepared to say that their current experience made sense against the background of the changes intro-duced in the exile'. I am not disputing this; what I am asking is that we should note which elements and associations are used, which are not, and not assume without good evidence from somewhere that what is *not* said is nonetheless intended. And one thing that is not said in any overt way (save in the Qumran exceptions to be discussed)—is that exile continues. (Bryan argues his case in more detail in his *Cos-mos, Chaos and the Kosher Mentality* (JSPSup, 12; Sheffield: Sheffield Academic Press, 1995), which I have not been able to study.)

15. J. VanderKam, 'Exile in Jewish Apocalyptic Literature', in J.M. Scott (ed.), *Exile: Old Testament, Jewish and Christian Conceptions* (Leiden: E.J. Brill, 1997), pp. 89-109 (94-96).

have three sheep 'return' and rebuild 'the tower' despite opposition (89.72-73; and the reference might seem to be to something like the sequence in Haggai–Zechariah–Ezra); he also tells us that 'the table before the tower' had polluted food on it (89.74), which some take to be a dismissal of the rebuilt Temple as worthless; but which need not be anything more than a reflection of Mal. 1.6-10, or some such liturgical shortcoming. Or is not the reference more precisely to pagan sacrifice under Antiochus IV? for at 89.75 the sheep are dispersed *afresh* into the forests, and then sacred items from this rebuilt Temple are taken away and carefully stored (90.28) before a fresh and more glorious edifice is erected (cf. 1 Macc. 4.41-58?). Prior to that the oppressors have been brought (resurrected?) to be condemned (cf. Dan. 12.2). Those who had been 'destroyed and dispersed' are able to 'return' to the house, but the reference seems only to those recently scattered into the forests. Attention is still directed to freedom from oppressive rulers for true worshippers. Deportation, forced exile, continued dispersion to and return from further abroad, are details insufficiently important or even apposite for explicit mention.

(vi) Most of the *Testaments of the Twelve Patriarchs* 'forecast' sin–exile–return. There is a lot of heavy Christian editing, inserting references to the events of 30 and of 70 CE. So when a few passages as they now stand omit reference to any past 'return' (but without adding any note of a future 'return', either) it is again unsafe to argue from such silence to an implicit but significant 'continuing exile' motif in the pre-Christian strata. VanderKam supposes he has found such an allusion beneath the Christian editing in the sequence 'for seventy weeks...you will wander astray and profane the priesthood...[and] you will be a curse and a dispersion among the nations until he will again have regard for you and will take you back in compassion' (*T. Levi* 16.1, 5); but as the passage stands there is no antecedent for the 'he' other than the Christ, and the entire passage could just as well or more likely be the Christian editor's response to 70 CE and/or 134 CE, akin to what we find in Origen: it is recent exile in Christian times that is at issue in the text.[16] VanderKam's excisions are too conjectural to be safe in the absence of further supporting clues in context. He himself notes (against M. Knibb) that the next chapter, *T. Levi* 17, refers clearly to the sixth–fifth-century return and the renewed Temple; and while the priesthood

16. Origen, *Contra Celsum* 2.8; see further, below.

is again criticized for its subsequent conduct, there is no suggestion here
of a prolonged exile.

(vii) *Jubilees* 1.15-18, though very 'delphic' is perhaps more promising. After the punitive scattering of his people among nations, so God
tells Moses,

> they will turn to me from among the nations with all their heart and with
> all their soul and with all their might. And I shall gather them from the
> midst of all the nations. And they will seek me with all their heart and
> with all their soul... And they will be head and not tail and I shall build
> my sanctuary in their midst, and I shall dwell with them.

As VanderKam argues, this does not tally very obviously with other
accounts of the original return, and so could refer to some future reversal of an ongoing exile. If that is correct the motif remains nonetheless
a very minor one, nowhere picked up again in the lengthy remainder of
the work, even though exile and return as such seems to be a recurrent
motif, as Betsy Halpern-Amaru points out.[17] And on the other hand the
interpretation offered is itself not so clear as to be inevitable.[18] The
book seems to take a very positive view of the early successes of the
Maccabees (chs. 34, 38), as (among others) VanderKam himself has
previously concluded. By the time of writing the nation is receiving
signs of divine favour. If that is so, then perhaps we should read 'will
turn to me...And I shall gather them' as referring to the Haggai–
Zechariah–Ezra events (and the end of punitive exile as such), with
'And they will seek me' then referring to the recent resistance and renewal of which the book approves. This is how Betsy Halpern-Amaru
also seems to interprets this passage: 'Repentance ends the exile. But
repossession of the Land is no longer the culminating point. It is followed by a more thorough-going repentance, by a spiritual regeneration.' Exile is not the focus. 'The crucial issues of the author's day—
spiritual return and regeneration—stand in its place.' 'Restoration of a
lost purity, not exile and return to the Land, is the signature of the

17. Betsy Halpern-Amaru, 'Exile and Return in *Jubilees*', in J.M. Scott (ed.),
Exile: Old Testament, Jewish and Christian Conceptions (Leiden: E.J. Brill, 1997),
pp. 127-44.

18. J.C. VanderKam, 'Exile', p. 104; cf. O.S. Wintermute, 'Jubilees', in J.H.
Charlesworth (ed.), *The Old Testament Pseudepigrapha*, II (London: Darton, Long-
man & Todd, 1985), p. 44; referring to J.C. VanderKam, *Textual and Historical
Studies in the Book of Jubilees* (Harvard Semitic Monograph, 14; Missoula, MT:
Scholars Press, 1977), p. 283.

imminent eschaton' in Jubilees;[19] for which exile and return are not even a metaphor.

(viii) However, for the Qumran community Martin J. Abegg, following many others, has argued, I think convincingly, that an idea of prolonged exile (punitive, purgative, educative), a full 390-year-long 'era of wrath' plus twenty of 'groping', is clearly expressed in CD 1.4b-11 (taking the latter as originating in the Qumran community at some stage of its development):

> [God] left a remnant of Israel and did not allow them to be exterminated. In the era of wrath—three hundred and ninety years from the time he handed them over to the power of Nebuchadnezzar king of Babylon—he took care of them and caused to grow from Israel and from Aaron a root of planting to inherit his land... They considered their iniquity and they knew they were guilty men, and had been like the blind and like those groping for the way twenty years...

That brings us to 176 BCE or thereabouts. Similarly (if using a different set of symbolic figures) 4Q390 1.7b-10 talks of a remnant escaping in the seventh jubilee.[20]

It seems quite consistent to allow that the idea may herefore also be there in other Qumran writings in references to those who composed the community as 'the captives of Israel'. Once that is agreed, then it would at least be consistent to suppose that 'Damascus' may in fact refer to Babylonia, from which this group had made its way to Judaea early in the second century BCE, 390 years after the fall of Jerusalem. *For this group* there had been no valid 'return' before theirs with their lived convictions, and no valid 'return' apart from theirs, or their group's together with any who shared its ideas and practices.[21] For this group at some period at least, the implication (albeit unstated) would be

---

19. Halpern-Amaru, 'Exile', pp. 140, 141, 144.

20. M.G. Abegg Jr, 'Exile and the Dead Sea Scrolls', in J.M. Scott, *Exile: Old Testament, Jewish and Christian Conceptions* (Leiden: E.J. Brill, 1997), pp. 111-25, here quoting from and referring to 119-20. For other studies, P. Garnet, 'Some Qumran Exegetical Cruces in the Light of Exilic Soteriology', in E.A. Livingstone (ed.), *Studia Evangelica*, VII (Berlin: Akademie Verlag, 1982), pp. 201-204; M.A. Knibb, 'Exile in the Damascus Document', *JSOT* 25 (1983), pp. 99-117; P.R. Davies, 'Eschatology at Qumran', *JBL* 104.1 (1985), pp. 39-55.

21. Cf. also, J.M. Scott, 'Exile and the Self-understanding of Diaspora Jews in the Greco-Roman Period', in *idem* (ed.), *Exile: Old Testament, Jewish and Christian Conceptions* (Leiden: E.J. Brill, 1997), pp. 173-208 (188).

that others of Israelite/Judaean stock resident in *eretz Israel* were none-theless in continuing (metaphorical) 'exile'. Even so, that this state was also and currently punitive is not stated.

If this much is allowed, ought we not now agree that the hints of such a 'prolonged punitive exile' discerned by VanderKam and others in Tobit, in *The Apocalypse of Weeks*, the *Animal Apocalypse*, and the *Testament of Levi*, *Jubilees* (and elsewhere) should then also be al-lowed? It does not seem to me to follow at all. In these Qumran writ-ings it is *clearly* stated and then resumed elsewhere in frequent hints. That is in no way true of the other documents adduced, not even of *Jubilees*. It is specifically a minority, sectarian position clearly taken and stated only by the Qumran community, precisely *un*representative of the majority view.

4. *The First Centuries* BCE *and* CE

(i) James VanderKam himself very properly allows that *Sibylline Ora-cles 3* and *Assumption of Moses* both accept clearly that a punitive Babylonian exile lasted seventy years and ended. Earlier writings taken to emanate from the Jewish Diaspora (Tobit and ben Sira) have been discussed above. Wisdom of Solomon, Esther, Susanna, *Aristeas*, and *Joseph and Asenath* contain no hint of a notion of a prolonged punitive exile .

(ii) How the Jewish Diaspora was understood by others involved is debated. Louis Feldman argues that Philo, for instance, is aware that being sent into exile (φυγή) was a heavy punishment, but avoids that penal terminology in discussions of Jews living in 'colonies' ('abroad'); and Josephus, too. James Scott notes, however, that the wider usage is more ambivalent, and *can* cover what we might indeed term 'penal' colonies.[22] Clearly Josephus has an apologetic interest, and would not be likely to welcome any suggestion of indefinite punishment. How-ever, detractors of the Jews might be expected to have picked hold of such a notion, had it been current: a Jewish admission of unassuaged guilt—yet Josephus does not have to defend himself against any such claim relating to the Babylonian deportation (whereas in relation to the departure from Egypt Josephus has to respond to various scurrilous

22. J.M. Scott, 'Exile', pp. 178-218; augmenting the study of W.C. van Unnik, *Das Selbstverständnis der jüdischen Diaspora in der hellenistidch-römischen Zeit* (AGJU; Leiden: E.J. Brill, 1993); and cf. I.M. Gafni, *Land, Centre and Diaspora*.

accounts from Manetho and others).[23] Rather, according to Josephus, is the diaspora a positive divine success, ensuring a wide dissemination of the divine Law,[24] and the whole known world is promised to the Jewish people as homeland.[25]

That Josephus and Philo were both sure that God's presence was effectively focused in the contemporary Temple, and that forgiveness and other blessings were currently obtainable there is quite clear. Philo notes how Jews come on pilgrimage to every feast to the Temple 'to give thanks for blessings received or to ask pardon and forgiveness for their sins'.[26] Josephus himself is as certain that forgiveness is readily available, and of the Temple's validity; the divine presence was focused there until the desecration in 70 CE.[27]

In the first century CE, Judaeans are willing to die to preserve the sanctity of the Temple, determined enough to persuade the Roman governor Petronius to disobey Gaius (Caligula)'s orders.[28] Josephus notes that many thought the destruction of the Temple in 70 CE had been preceded by an explicit divine departure, implying a prior settled presence. Josephus as well as Philo is writing with fellow Jews in mind,[29] and both can take these convictions as needing no argument. It is incredible that *2 Baruch* and *4 Ezra* (both often cited for the 'ongoing exile' thesis) should see the events of 67–70 CE as a catastrophic repetition of 586 BCE, if Herod's rebuilt Temple had no positive divine significance,

23. Josephus, *Apion* 1.227-320 cf. 1.128-60, on the Babylonian exile and return.

24. Josephus, *War* 6.442, 7.43; *Ant.* 14.114; *Apion* 2.284; L.H. Feldman, 'The Concept of Exile', in J.M. Scott (ed.), *Exile: Old Testament, Jewish and Christian Conceptions* (Leiden: E.J. Brill, 1997), pp. 143-72 (149).

25. Josephus, *Ant.* 1.280-83; 4.115-16; Feldman, 'The Concept', pp. 152-53.

26. Philo, *Spec. Leg.* 1.67-70; cf. 168. P. Borgen, in his 'Two Philonic Prayers in their Context: An Analysis of *Who is the Heir of Divine Things (Her.)* 24-29, and *Against Flaccus (Flac.)* 170-75', *NTS* NS 45.3 (1999), pp. 291-309, argues that Abraham is made to represent himself as driven away, expelled, renounced; and that this 'reflects the precarious situation of the Jewish people in Diaspora situations' (p. 298). Even if that were correct, they are not being punished by God who remains Abraham's 'country...his kinsfolk...etc'. However, it is more likely that Abraham is here primarily the model proselyte punished for 'converting' (cf. *Migr. Abr.* 1, on Gen. 12.1-3; and *Abr.* 62-67; and *Praem. Poen.* 152).

27. Josephus, *Apion* 2. 193-98; *Ant.* 8.166; *War* 4.323; 5.19; 20.166.

28. Philo, *De legatione* 207-60; Josephus, *Ant.* 18.261-308.

29. Feldman, 'The Concept', pp. 164-72; T. Rajak, *Josephus: The Historian and his Sources* (London: Gerald Duckworth, 1983), p. 178.

comparable to that of Solomon's. (It is worth noting that diaspora synagogue buildings are all aligned with Jerusalem and its Temple, as still
the most effective focus for devotion and prayer.)[30]

(iii) It is also worth noting that there is no sign of any motif of prolonged punitive exile and its entailments in the criticisms of the Jewish
people discussed by Justin Martyr with Trypho and by Origen responding to Celsus; indeed Origen says of the state of affairs in his own day,
that no such prolonged expulsion of the Jews from their homeland had
ever been previously recorded.[31] It is only the 70–134 CE banishments
that are picked out as punitive.[32]

(iv) J.M. Scott enters into a three-way discussion with A.T. Kraabel,
who proposed a very positive view of their situation among diaspora
Jews, and W.C. van Unnik, who had argued that 'dispersion' was normally a negative idea, 'decomposition'; while in neither account does
'exile' as such figure. Scott wants to combine both negatives, while
admitting, 'Some Diaspora Jews may well have viewed their situation
in a far more positive light.'[33] However, all his data come from later
than 70 CE, and in the light of the evidence from Justin and especially
from Origen just quoted, cannot usefully be read back to any part of the
earlier period.

(v) Many passages in Jewish writings, not least in the emergent
'canon' promised a glorious future for the Jewish people in or ingath-
ered to the land of Israel. Beyond dispute many Jews (Israelites, Judaeans; probably a great majority) were not there in the first century CE,
nor was Judaea free nor dominant.[34] One could always argue that the
withholding of a promised good is itself punitive. But for the most part
people seem to distinguish quite clearly between rewards and punishments. One significant instance is Philo. The final rewards promised in

---

30. Scott, 'Exile', p. 177; citing A.T. Kraabel, 'Unity and Diversity among Diaspora Synagogues', in L.L. Levine (ed.), *The Synagogue in Late Antiquity* (Philadelphia: American Schools of Oriental Research, 1987), pp. 49-60.

31. Justin Martyr: cf. *Dialogue with Trypho* 133; and especially Origen, *Contra
Celsum* 3.3 and 4.22. In early days the Jews maintained their law *despite* deportations.

32. Origen, *Contra Celsum* 2.8

33. Scott, 'Exile', p. 181.

34. Cf. the recognition of this in the LXX translations cited by Scott, 'Exile', pp.
186-88, referring to Deut. 29.27, 2 Kgs 17.23, 1 Chron. 5.26, 2 Chron. 29.9. These
passages do *not* say that prolonged absence is itself punitive, nor a continuing
penalty for ancestral guilt.

Deuteronomy in particular await 'the reformation working in those who are being brought to make a covenant of peace'. Then,

> even though they dwell in the uttermost parts of the earth, in slavery to those who led them away captive, one signal, as it were, one day will bring liberty to all. This conversion in a body to virtue will strike awe into their masters, who will set them free, ashamed to rule over men better than themselves...they who but now were scattered...will arise and post from every side, guided in their journey by a superhuman divine vision...'[35]

But there is on the other hand no indication that Philo supposed he and his contemporaries were suffering the punishments threatened in Deuteronomy, 'poverty, dearth and lack of necessities, conditions of absolute destitution...', together with cannibalism, barren fields and cattle, chronic disease;[36] especially so when he instantly contrasts these threats to Israelites by birth with the happy lot of the contemporary proselyte.[37] Philo does not consider conversion to Judaism as joining a penal colony, nor that staying put in the Diaspora was an expected penitential self-discipline.

(vi) Scott allows that at times Jews living outside *eretz Israel* were free to come and settle there, and that the fact that so many did not might suggest they were content with their lot, counter to his overall argument. He suggests 'it is doubtful whether the Romans would have allowed whole Diaspora communities unilaterally to initiate unscheduled returns to the land, even if such moves were economically feasible.' The only evidence he cites in support is action against mass movements within Judaea, as reported by Josephus (see further, below).[38] Philo's account of pilgrims from abroad attending festivals in large numbers, referred to above, suggests no such worry among the authorities. Other things being equal, pilgrims could readily have stayed. The economic reason is much more likely. Short of the divine 'eschatological' miracle, there was small chance for large numbers of Jewish immigrants to find land or make a living any other way in Palestine.

35. Philo, *Praem. Poen.* 163-67; cf. 117.
36. Philo, *Praem. Poen.* 127, 134, 141, 143.
37. Philo, *Praem. Poen.* 152.
38. Scott, 'Exile', p. 211 and n. 119. C.A. Evans argues a similar point at greater length, 'Exile and Restoration in the Proclamation of Jesus', in J.M. Scott (ed.), *Exile: Old Testament, Jewish and Christian Conceptions* (Leiden: E.J. Brill, 1997), pp. 300-305.

But there is no sign at all that such as did return were criticized for evading an unremitted penalty, or were expected to be struck down for their hubris—nor that they were admired for being counted worthy to 'return' scot-free.

(vii) Craig Evans interprets the programmes of Theudas and the Egyptian, and others unnamed, narrated by Josephus, as enactments of a return from exile represented by Transjordan or 'the desert'.[39] It is often supposed that they hoped to repeat Joshua's conquest of the land.[40] The accounts are so sparse that almost any interpretation could be imposed; but it was local Jews who formed the following in each case, not Diaspora Jews. Had they believed themselves already in exile they would hardly have needed this charade—or, alternatively, they might have been expected to go to Babylon and Egypt at least, to collect a representative following. Evans assures we are given 'glimpses of their true purpose'. For this supposedly dominant motif it seems strange that it is only ever 'glimpses' that we get—apart from the two assured passages from Qumran.

(viii) Scott wonders whether the Diaspora rebellion of 115–17 CE may not have constituted an attempt to realize the promise of the longed-for 'return'. He admits there is no clear evidence to support this conclusion;[41] and it has to be said that no such venture got underway even at the most promising stages of the 67–70 CE revolt, in the records we depend on from Josephus.

(ix) *The Jesus Tradition.* Craig Evans picks out six items from the Gospels to show that Jesus presupposed just such an extended punitive (geographical and metaphorical) exile thesis.[42] If the thesis were otherwise established—if most Jewish sources from the period and the preceding centuries had clearly stated the conviction claimed—then these passages from the Gospels might validly be taken to allude to it. None of the Gospel passages themselves can be said to *state* it; and I think I have shown it does not constitute a commonplace ready to support supposed tacit allusions.

(ix.a) The tradition tells us of 'the twelve' appointed by Jesus, and this is often taken to symbolize in some sense or other a new Israel,

39. Evans, 'Exile and Restoration', pp. 300-305; Josephus, *Ant.* 20.97-98, 167-72.

40. E.g., Horsley and Hanson, *Bandits, Prophets and Messiahs*, p. 166.

41. Scott, 'Exile', pp. 214-18.

42. Evans, 'Exile and Restoration', pp. 316-28.

with the twelve as 'judges' (Mt. 19.28//Lk. 22.30). None of the twelve are said to have come from abroad, nor (for instance) to have been given names symbolizing the northern tribes; there is nothing in the appointment to suggest a reversal of exile, rather (if anything) the opposite. A new Israel could be inaugurated (if that was the intention) from Jews already in the land.

(ix.b) Jesus is faced with a demand to produce a 'sign' (or signs), perhaps of an expected kind (Mk 8.11-13; Mt. 12.38-39//Lk. 11.29-32). Josephus tells us of such (very varied) expectations, and of the assurance of Theudas and of 'the Egyptian' that some such 'signs' would be forthcoming. We have found nothing in Josephus's accounts to indicate that the miraculous end to a prolonged punitive exile would be in the mind of either set of followers or their leader.

Philo awaits a divine vision to prompt and guide the final ingathering (a passage Evans ignores).[43] Philo expected an internalised vision, unseen by outsiders; we might conjecture that other contemporaries may have expected something more public. There is still nothing in the tradition to suggest that asking for '*a* sign' was shorthand for asking for *the* ingathering. And none of this, anyway, supports a notion of a prolonged punitive exile.

(ix.c) Mark's version of the Temple 'incident' has Jesus allude, it seems, to Isa. 56.7 and Jer. 7.11, 'Is it not written, "My house shall be called a house of prayer for all the nations"? But you have made it a den of robbers' (Mk 11.17). Evans shows that the wider context of the passage in Isaiah, in the LXX and in the later Isaiah Targum versions, includes reference to the final ingathering. Jesus may well have shared the hope which Philo expresses, of such an outcome of a moral and spiritual renewal of his people (see the next paragraph), but the accounts as we have them afford no warrant for interpreting Jesus' symbolic renewal of the Temple (if such it was) as also the reversal of a prolonged punitive (literal and/or metaphorical) exile. And, whatever may have been amiss with the Temple and its ways in Jesus' eyes, the Matthaean and Lukan traditions still find it a valid focus of the presence of God.[44]

(ix.d) Mk 13.27 promises the ingathering of the elect. In the light of Mt. 10.6 and Rom. 15.8, on Jesus' lips this former assurance would have at least to involve if not simply comprise Israel as a whole. It still

43. Philo, *Praem. Poen.*162, again.
44. Mt. 5.23-24; 23.16-22; and Lk. 1–2; Acts 1–3.

does not say that residents of *eretz Israel* are in (metaphorical) exile; nor that they or dispersed Israel are currently subject to unremitting punishment.

Evans also follows Wright in the latter's interpretation of the story of the spendthrift and his homecoming (Lk. 15.11-32) as a 'reading' of (if not allegory on) exile and return.[45] Yet even allowing the initial sugges-tion, the 'reading' that Jesus then proposes does not seem to support the thesis. The authority figure, the father, is never punitive; the journey away from home is voluntary (and any criticism of it has to be read in); the only behaviour conventionally disapproved of ('riotous living', herd-ing swine) follows rather than prompts the departure, the elder brother is always at home and even if shown as 'alienated' himself makes no 'return'...

(ix.e) Jesus threatens various towns, including Jerusalem, and such threats in scripture often involve exile. Evans tacitly admits the argu-ment is not very promising. Jesus' desire to gather Jerusalem's children as a mother hen her chicks 'could imply hopes of gathering the exiles of Israel'.[46] Again, even if that is allowed it has as little relevance for the issues here in contention as the other data adduced.

(ix.f) The exile (but not any return) is referred to in Matthew's genealogy (Mt. 1.11-12, 17), and the reference *might* betoken a convic-tion that such an exile remains in force until the time of Jesus the Messiah, and that *might* be a pre-Easter conviction.

(ix.g) Of clear evidence that Jesus held the beliefs attributed to him by Evans there is none.

(x) *Paul.* (x.a) Paul hopes that 'all Israel' will be saved (Rom. 11.26); but nowhere does he indicate any expectation of an ingathering of his people to *eretz Israel.*

(x.b) Does the 'slavery' of Gal. 4.1-7 refer to an ongoing exile seen as extended childhood, under the Law and under cosmic powers, as proposed by Scott Hafemann?[47] Paul does not say so. He speaks of Jeru-salem being in bondage (Gal. 4.24)—but *not* 'in exile'; of his fellow Jews as veiled, blinded—but *not* 'in exile'; (2 Cor. 3.14; 4.4); ignorant,

---

45. Wright, *Jesus and the Victory of God,* pp. 125-31.

46. Evans, 'Exile and Restoration', pp. 325-26.

47. S.J. Hafemann, 'Paul and the Exile of Israel in Galatians 3-4', in J.M. Scott (ed.), *Exile: Old Testament, Jewish and Christian Conceptions* (Leiden: E.J. Brill, 1997), pp. 329-71.

stumbling, hardened, enemies, even—but *not* 'in exile'; (Rom. 10.3; 11.11, 25, 28). Perhaps it is significant that Paul so often fails to say what Hafemann says he means.

(x.c) For Paul the present is a time when God's wrath is revealed (Rom. 1.18). In the past God's wrath was thought to have been displayed in the forced exile of his people, as James Scott reminds us.[48] But Paul does not say exile is the only demonstration of divine wrath; in fact it is perverse sexual over-indulgence that currently shows God's severe displeasure, and there is no hint that this is an implicit by-product of exile (Rom. 1.24-27).[49] Whether or not 1 Thess. 2.15-16 is by Paul, the non-specific wrath of God that has come upon the Jews in Judaea (εἰς τέλος) is not renewed exile from the land. In Rom. 9–11 Paul explicitly deploys Deuteronomy with its accusations of continuous disobedience and punishment (Rom. 11.7-8). He does not say that the punishment of enforced exile is what is meant; nor does he hint that he as a Diaspora Jew is paying the penalty or was trying to escape it (cf. Phil. 3.5-6); nor that as servant of Jesus Christ has he been returned from it.

5. *Conclusions*

In the Preface to his *Jesus and the Victory of God*, Tom Wright asks rhetorically,

> would any serious-thinking first-century Jew claim the promises of Isaiah 40–66, or of Jeremiah, Ezekiel, or Zechariah, had been fulfilled? That the power and domination of paganism had been broken? That YHWH had already returned to Zion? That the covenant had been renewed, and

---

48. J.M. Scott, 'Paul's Use of Deuteronomic Tradition', *JBL* 112.4 (1993), pp. 645-65.

49. Akio Ito, 'Romans 2: A Deuteronomic Reading', *JSNT* 59 (1995), pp. 21-37, apropos of Rom. 2, ventures, '[Paul] is almost saying that Israel is now in a state of "exile"', p. 31. The fact is that Paul never does quite gets round to saying what Ito and others think he must nonetheless have meant. On this 'Deuteronomic' schema see especially O.H. Steck, *Israel und das gewaltsame Geschick der Propheten: Untersuchungen zur Überlieferung des deuteronomistischen Geschichtsbildes im Alten Testament, Spätjudentum und Urchristentum* (WMANT, 23; Neukirchen-Vluyn: Neukirchener Verlag, 1967); and 'Das Problem theologischer Strömungen in nachexilischer Zeit', *EvT* 28 (1968), pp. 445-58.

Israel's sins forgiven? That the long-awaited 'new exodus' had happened? That the second Temple was the true final and perfect one? Or—in other words, that the exile was really over?[50]

It is risky to accept the terms of a rhetorical challenge. Perhaps only an imaginary Jew who agrees with Wright qualifies as serious, etc. But one would have to answer, prophecy fulfilled to the letter? Of course not completely fulfilled. Pagan power broken? Undermined but of course, not abolished. YHWH had returned? Not everyone thought he'd left, and of course it's in the Temple that we've gone on praying to him, maintaining the cult. Covenant renewed? He never reneged on his covenant (Rom. 9.4), and many of us think we've been keeping to its terms pretty well, certainly we've meant to. Our sins awaiting forgiveness? Of course he forgives; why else do you think we all share in *yom kippur* (even if it's the only day in the year some observe)?[51] The final ingathering (your 'new exodus'!), of course not. The final Temple? (before 70 CE) We can always hope it will never be desecrated again (after 70 CE). Clearly it wasn't final, but it was fully valid till we lost it. And, the exile's not really over? Oh, you're one of those Qumran fanatics, think your lot are the only true Israelites, your founders made the only valid return from exile? No one else agrees with you…

The interpretative device of 'protracted punitive exile' has no place in our interpretation of formative Israel, so neither has it any place in our understanding of Jesus and his first followers.

However, for other eschatological themes in the ascribed and recorded thought of Jesus and his first followers there is a weight of evidence. And here we find ideas and expressions widely shared among Jews, Christians and many others in the Graeco-Roman world of late antiquity.

50. Wright, *Jesus and the Victory of God*, pp. xvii-xviii (Preface).
51. Cf. Philo, *Spec. Leg*. 1.186.

Chapter 9

COMMON STRANDS IN PAGAN, JEWISH AND CHRISTIAN
ESCHATOLOGIES IN THE FIRST CHRISTIAN CENTURY*

> You can almost see that the stature of the whole human race is decreas-
> ing daily, with few men taller than their fathers, as the crucial conflagra-
> tion which our age is approaching exhausts the fertility of human semen.[1]

Pliny the Elder makes this reference to the approaching conflagration,
exustio, simply in passing in a discussion of babies and their growth. It
seems to express a commonly accepted view that needs no further
argument or explanation at the date (around 70 CE) when he is writing.
And it would seem to have much in common with the conviction an-
nounced perhaps twenty years later in *4 Ezra*:

> You and your contemporaries are smaller in stature than those who were
> born before you, and those who come after you will be smaller than you,
> as if born in a creation which is also aging and passing the strength of
> [its] youth.[2]

With this second passage one may also take 'the world is hastening
swiftly to its end' (*4 Ezra* 4.26), and 'For the age has lost its youth and
the times begin to grow old' (*4 Ezra* 4.26). Not much later, we may
suppose, we find something very similar in *2 Baruch*:

* Reprinted from *TZ* 51.3 (1995), pp. 196-211, with kind permission.

1. *In plenum autem cuncto mortalium generi minorem in dies fieri prope-*
modum observatur, rarosque patribus proceriores, consumente seminum exustione
in cuius vices nunc vergat aeves (Pliny the Elder, *Hist. nat.* 7.16.73) from W.H.S.
Jones (trans.), *Pliny: Natural History* (trans. R. Rackham, W.H.S. Jones *et al.*;
LCL; 10 vols.; London: Heinemann; Cambridge, MA: Harvard University Press,
1927), VII, pp. 552-53; cf. E. Schilling, *Pline l'ancien: Histoire naturelle* (Paris:
Belles Lettres, 1977).

2. *4 Ezra* 5.51; from M. Stone, *Fourth Ezra* (Hermeneia; Philadelphia: Fortress
Press, 1990), p. 142.

> The youth of this world has passed away, and the power of creation is
> already exhausted, and the coming of the times is very near, [indeed] has
> passed by. And the pitcher is near to the well and ship to the harbour and
> the journey to the city and life to its end.[3]

Discussions of Jewish and then Christian cosmic, universal eschatology have mostly ignored contemporary 'pagan' ideas, or mentioned
them only in contrast.[4] In other areas of apocalyptic parallels have for
sure occasionally been noted with pagan views, for instance in discussions of individual eschatology, of the topographies of Heaven and
Hades, and tales of journeys to or visions of 'the beyond'.[5] But by and
large, expectations of imminent end-time catastrophe have been depict-
ed as important distinguishing features of homeland Jewish and early
Jewish-Christian beliefs and attitudes; and then the apparent abandon-
ment of a belief in an end at hand marks the disappearance of original
Christianity into 'Early Catholicism', often seen also as its assimilation
to its Hellenistic environment.[6]

---

3.   *2 Baruch* 85.10; in A.F.J. Klijn, '2 (Syriac Apocalypse of) Baruch', *OTP*, I,
p. 651.
4.   Just such a failure seriously diminishes the value of U.H.J. Körtner's otherwise interesting 'Weltzeit, Weltangst und Weltende. Zum Daseins- und Zeitverständnis der Apokalyptik', *TZ* 45 (1989), pp. 32-42. I note only two recent exceptions: D. Georgi, 'Who is the True Prophet?' in G. Macrae (ed.), *Christians among
Jews and Gentiles*, (Philadelphia: Fortress Press, 1986), pp. 100-26; and H. Koester,
'Jesus the Victim', *JBL* 111 (1992), pp. 3-15; though both are concerned with
'realized' eschatology, not 'cosmic catastrophe', the main theme of this chapter.
But see also J.H. Neyrey, n. 29, below. Most recently, D.C. Allison, *Jesus of Nazareth, Millenarian Prophet* (Minneapolis: Fortress Press, 1998), pays scant attention
to contemporary eschatology, preferring to press the Jesus material into a chosen
'universal' millenarian mould, and that, despite a reference to this present discussion, p. 154.
5.   Especially T.F. Glasson, *Greek Influence in Jewish Eschatology* (London:
SPCK, 1961), but he, too, is concerned to stress parallels with 'realized' eschatology. D. Hellholm (ed.), *Apocalypticism in the Mediterranean World and the
Near East* (Tübingen: Mohr-Siebeck, 1983), deals interestingly with accounts of
revelations of the beyond, but barely touches revelations of an imminent end.
6.   On 'Early Catholicism' see for instance Dunn, *Unity and Diversity*, Ch. 14,
pp. 341-66; and see p. 171, below. Disappointingly, Allison, *Jesus of Nazareth*,
continues this unsubstantiated theme: in the Gentile world Christians lost this eschatological enthusiasm, p. 169—still despite his previous reference to this present
discussion, p. 154.

This chapter is primarily concerned with forecasts of cosmic catastrophe in various Jewish, Christian and 'pagan' sources. It asks how distinctive in fact, if at all, were Jewish and Christian cosmic and imminent eschatologies. Perhaps some motifs were shared, and others, maybe, were restricted to one or another group. Then, if some motifs at least were shared, how far might such eschatologies, 'imminent' and 'consistent', or 'inaugurated' or 'realized' have seemed to constitute an alien field of discourse in the wider Graeco-Roman world, and how far common, even commonplace? If they were commonplace, then a shift in emphasis or even a more radical change can hardly betoken a surrender to a Hellenism which itself entertained a similar range of ideas. And if these common motifs were used in various contexts by such diverse groups, can one single 'interpretation' serve them all (as strongly argued, for instance, by U.H.J. Körtner)?[7]

A very sharp distinction was asserted between the 'the eschatological premiss of the primitive Christian sense of imminence', and subsequent 'Hellenization' by M. Werner, in his *Die Entstehung des christlichen Dogmas* (1941),[8] where this undifferentiated 'Hellenism' is belatedly re-titled 'neo-Platonism', still without further warrant or explanation. There is no attempt to survey the varieties of Graeco-Roman eschatology, nor to relate them in detail to 'late Jewish apocalyptic'. There is brief reference in passing to varieties of views among Christians in the following centuries (especially Cyprian, to whom we return later)[9] but this has no impact on the main argument. We find much the same in O. Cullmann, *Christus und die Zeit*: 'Wohl aber lässt sich die im Neuen Testament vorausgesetzte *Vorstellung* vom Verlauf der Zeit gegenüber der typisch griechischen eindeutig bestimmen, und wir müssen von dieser Grunderkenntnis ausgehen, dass das Symbol der Zeit für das Urchristentum wie für das biblische Judentum und die iranische Religion die *aufsteigende Linie* ist, während es im Hellenismus der *Kreis* ist'.[10]

7. Körtner, 'Weltzeit', n. 4, above.

8. M. Werner, *Die Entstehung des christlichen Dogmas* (Bern: Georg Lang, 1941); ET, *The Formation of Christian Dogma* (London: A. & C. Black, 1957), pp. vii; 52-53; 292-94.

9. Cyprian, *Ad Demetrianum* 35, noted by Werner, *Entstehung*, p. 109, *Formation*, p. 42; and there is also a reference to *4 Ezra* 2.13, but with no further comment. On Cyprian, cf. C.J.M. Bartelink, 'Le thème du monde vieilli', *Orpheus* 4 (1983), pp. 342-54.

10. O. Cullmann, *Christus und die Zeit* (Zollikon-Zürich: Evangelischer Verlag,

More recent writers seem to pass over the issue in silence, simply concentrating on Jewish and Christian material to the all but total exclusion of any other contemporary literature when eschatology as such is under discussion.[11] Thus, to take a particularly relevant example, in his commentary on *4 Ezra*, Michael Stone cites in a note a passage from Lucretius (98–55 BCE), *De rerum natura*, 'Even now the power of life is broken, and earth exhausted scarce produces tiny creatures, she who once produced all kinds and gave birth to the huge bodies of wild beasts',[12] without further comment; while it is important for him to conclude that the metaphor of ' "world history in the terms of the aging of an individual"…seems to have originated in Jewish (perhaps Jewish apocalyptic) thinking'. On this point he cites A. Momigliano: but the latter only noted that he had not found the idea in pagan Greek historians, not that it was absent from Graeco-Roman writers as a whole.[13] That a near contemporary, Pliny the Elder, seems to have shared with the authors of *4 Ezra* and *2 Baruch* a very similar conviction, that a final end for a perceptibly senescent cosmos was imminent, is ignored.[14]

1946), p. 44; 'Indeed, we can clearly define the conception of the course of time which the New Testament proposes by stating it in opposition to the typical Greek idea, and we must start from this fundamental perception, that the symbol of time for Primitive Christianity as well as for Biblical Judaism and the Iranian religion is the *upward sloping line*, while in Hellenism it is the *circle*', ET, *Christ and Time* (London: SCM Press, 1951).

11. C. Rowland, *The Open Heaven* (London: SPCK, 1982), mentions the *Sibylline Oracles* in passing, p. 20, with no further discussion of any of the links with the wider cultural context; and mentions *2 Baruch* 85.10 and *4 Ezra* 4.50, p. 27, just once each in a preliminary survey of the field. There is a similar neglect in G.W.E. Nicklesburg, *Jewish Literature between the Bible and the Mishnah* (London: SCM Press, 1981). On the other hand, by identifying 'Apocalyptic' so closely with its eschatological strand, Körtner misses a large proportion of the matter of Apocalyptic, with its dominant fascination with 'heaven open now' (Rowland), only according a line in passing: 'Man denkt nur an die Himmelreisen und Thronsaalvisionem' ('One thinks simply of heavenly journeys and throne-visions') ('Weltzeit', p. 38 n. 4). But see, now, E. Adam, 'Historical Crisis and Cosmic Crisis in Mark 13 and in Lucan's *Civil War*', *TynBul* 48 (1997), pp. 329-44; with, hopefully, more to come.

12. Lucretius, *De rerum naturae* (trans. W.H.D Rouse and M.F. Smith; LCL; London: Heinemann; Cambridge, MA: Harvard University Press, 1924), p. 185.

13. Stone, *Fourth Ezra*, pp. 152-53, on *4 Ezra* 6.50; referring to A. Momigliano, 'The Origins of Universal History', *ASNS* 3.12.2 (1982), pp. 533-60.

14. It is particularly disappointing to find R.L. Fox, *Pagans and Christians in*

How, in a little more detail, then, are we to understand the passing comment from Pliny the Elder with which we began? In his critical edition of book 7 of the *Historia naturalis*, R. Schilling concludes, without supporting argument, 'cette allusion conforme à la doctrine stoïcienne de l'alternance de cataclysmes', adding a reference to a previous passage where Pliny inferred from the fires of Etna that 'nature threatens the world with conflagration'.[15] And when Graeco-Roman eschatologies are discussed this is the usual interpretation. The Stoics accepted the idea of recurrent conflagration (ἐκπύρωσις) or of conflagration and flood, taking place when the planets returned to their supposed original alignment. In one often repeated version, the universe would be absorbed into fire, then melt into liquid, out of which there would be a rebirth of the world and a repetition of at least the main strands of its previous history: very much, it would seem, a 'cyclical' view, with which to contrast the contemporary Judaeao-Christian schemes.[16]

None of the Stoic accounts that have come down to us give a date for the next cataclysm. The expected intervals of 'The Great Year' are vast, around 10,000 years or more. There is no suggestion in the scholarly discussions that ancient Stoic writers saw themselves as nearing the end of such a period. This might afford yet another contrast with first century Jewish and Christian expectations: but it also affords a contrast with Pliny.

the Mediterranean World from the Second Century AD to the Conversion of Constantine (London: Viking, 1986; Harmondsworth: Penguin Books, 1988), writing as though only Jews and Christians had traditions of eschatological myths (e.g., pp. 266-67).

15. 'This allusion is in keeping with Stoic teaching on alternating cataclysms', R. Schilling, *Pline l'ancien*, p. 159, referring also to *Hist. nat.* 2.236.

16. As noted by, for instance, M. Lapidge, 'Stoic Cosmology', in J.M. Rist (ed.), *The Stoics*, (Berkeley: University of California Press, 1978), pp. 180-85; E. Zeller, *Die Philosophie der Griechen* 3.1 (Leipzig: Reisland, 1923), pp. 152-63; R. Hoven, *Stoïcisme et stoïciens face au problème de l'au-delà* (Paris: Les Belles Lettres, 1971), pp. 31-37; J. Mansfeld, 'Providence and the Destruction of the Universe in early Stoic Thought', in H.J. Vermasseren (ed.), *Studies in Hellenistic Religion*, (Leiden: E.J. Brill, 1979), pp. 129-88; and A.A. Long, 'The Stoics on World-Conflagration and the Everlasting Recurrence', *SJP* Supp. 23 (1985), pp. 13-37. None of these suggests that a possible imminence of the end of the present period is at issue in any of our sources.

'*Exustio*' in Pliny *prima facie* might well suggest the Stoic ἐκπύρ-ωσις. However, Pliny the Elder emerges as a fairly critical eclectic, with little patience for Stoic dogmatic theory (e.g., on astrology, *Hist. nat.* 2.54; and on prophecy, *Hist. nat.* 7.178).[17] He is unlikely to have accepted the notion of a cosmic conflagration, *exustio*, simply on the basis of Stoic teaching; and the rest of the passage shows no clear signs of Stoicism. Epicureans as well as Stoics believed this world would come to an end, over against Platonists and Aristotelians, who dis-agreed.[18] I would argue that Pliny here echoes at least in part an Epicurean commonplace, as found repeatedly in Lucretius; for instance, the passage already quoted: 'Even now, indeed, the power of life is broken, and earth, exhausted, scarce produces tiny creatures, she who once produced all kinds, and gave birth to the huge bodies of wild beasts.'[19] It would mostly likely be prompted by Epicureanism, directly or indirectly, that Pliny had learned to interpret apparent diminutions in natural forces, and especially the diminishing size of those being born, as a sign that the world as such was coming to its end. The spontaneous stoking-up of elemental fires was absorbing the thermal energy needed in procreation.

Another sign of the coming end which again anyone might recognize, was volcanic eruption. In Etna and other volcanoes 'nature threatens the world with conflagration' (*exustio*, *Hist. nat.* 2.236), as we have already noted. There is always fire under the earth, ready to break out, affirms Lucretius (*De rerum natura* 6.654-720). (Epicureans and Stoics could anyway adopt and adapt one another's ideas: Lucretius himself seems

17.   On Pliny the Elder as far from credulous, see M. Beacon, *Roman Nature: The Thoughts of Pliny the Elder* (Oxford: Clarendon Press, 1992). On his eclecti-cism, W. Kroll, 'Plinius der Älter', *PRE* 21.1, cols. 271-439.

18.   F. Solmsen, *Aristotle's System of the Physical World* (Cornell Studies in Classical Philology; Cornell: Cornell University Press, 1960), pp. 434-39; A.-H. Chroust, 'The "Great Deluge" in Aristotle's On Philosophy', *AC* 43 (1973), pp. 113-22; Mansfeld, 'Providence and Destruction', pp. 138-42.

19.   *De rerum natura* 2.1150-52. This link is argued more fully in Downing, 'Cosmic Eschatology', pp. 99-109. For Lucretius, see W.M. Green, 'The Dying World of Lucretius', *AJP* 63 (1942), pp. 51-60; F. Solmsen, 'Epicurus on the Growth and Decline of the Cosmos', *AJP* 74 (1953), pp. 34-51; J.M. Rist, *Epicurus: An Introduction* (Cambridge: Cambridge University Press, 1972), pp. 64-73 and Appendix C, pp. 169-70; Bartelink, 'Le thème'; H. Jones, *The Epicurean Tradition* (London: Routledge, 1989); C. Segal, *Lucretius on Death and Anxiety* (Princeton, NJ: Princeton University Press, 1990).

to have 'borrowed' the idea of a final fire or flood, *De rerum natura* 5.380-415.)

But there is further confirmation for this 'popular Epicurean' reading of Pliny the Elder's *Hist. nat.* 7.73, in the account that his nephew, Pliny the Younger, has left us of the eruption of Vesuvius in 79 CE. The hot dust and fumes that overwhelmed Pompeii and Herculaneum reached the younger man and his uncle's household in Misenum, and earthquake shocks were continuous. They joined the crowd of terrified refugees. Many sought the the aid of the Gods, 'but still more imagined there were no Gods left and that the universe was plunged into eternal darkness for evermore.' That sounds like a popular version of Stoic belief, in which all the divine powers, the Gods, are to be absorbed into the one divine fire, prior to rebirth. So, given a big enough catastrophe, the end of the current cycle could be thought to be happening now (wherever the planets stood!). Pliny the Younger did not believe the myth, he tells us, but did believe the end was upon him, seen, again, in the Epicurean terms of a 'dying world': 'I derived some poor consolation in my deadly peril from the belief that the whole world was dying with me and I with it' (*omnia mecum perire... mortalitatis solacio*).[20]

This way of interpreting appearances of change and decay may, then, have come directly or indirectly from Epicurean tradition. Yet Pliny the Elder in particular is far from being a consistent Epicurean, as witness his attitude to deity (*Historia naturalis* 2.14), and the way he eschews Epicurean empiricist positivism. But neither does he align himself consistently with the scepticism of the New Academy affected by Cicero. I think we have to take seriously the implication that the senescence of the age was in fact a commonplace idea, one that could indeed readily be referred to in passing, on the assumption that it was part of many people's vocabulary of ideas, whether or not they took it 'scientifically' as Pliny seems to have done, or as 'religiously' and 'mythically' as his

20. Pliny the Younger, *Letters* 6.20.17, in B. Radice (trans.), *Pliny: Letters and Panegyricus*, I (LCL; 2 vols.; London: Heinemann; Cambridge, MA: Harvard University Press, 1969), p. 447; the earlier passage in full runs: *plures nusquam iam deos ullos aeternamque illam et novissimum noctem mundo interpretabantur*. A.N. Sherwin-White, *The Letters of Pliny* (Oxford: Clarendon Press, 1966), p. 360, comments only on (Stoic) ideas of conflagration, and not on the world's 'dying'. It is worth noting that a Jewish writer, the author of *Sibylline Oracles* 4.130-35 also saw this eruption as a sign that the final conflagration was at hand; cf. M. Simon, 'Sur quelques aspects des Oracles Sibyllins', in Hellholm, *Apocalypticism*, pp. 218-33.

nephew's fellow refugees seem to have done. It was not only some Jews and many Christians who were used to reading the signs of the times in expectation of the end of the world as they knew it. And obviously the 'existential' meaning would differ among such varied people as these.

Although, as we have said, the Stoic discussions of the end of the age never seem concerned or willing to suggest a date, let alone an imminent one, still the imagined details are worth considering further, especially in the light of the lines from Pliny the Younger. The ἐκπύρωσις is alluded to a few times in passing and in brief by Epictetus. A fuller account from our period is to be found in Dio Chrysostom's *Discourses*[21] and in Seneca's *Naturales questiones*.[22] But there is no attempt to describe the death-throes of the previous form of the universe, no indication of how the end might be imagined.

However, in tragedy Seneca allows himself to be more graphic. The dreadful death of Hercules must involve the death of all else:

> Now, now, to the universe there comes the day when [natural] laws are overwhelmed, the southern skies fall on the Libyan plain and all the lands of the scattered Garamantians. The northern heavens overwhelm all that lies beneath that sky, subject to Boreas' withering blasts. [Fallen] from the stricken sky the fearful Titan [sun] banishes day. The palace of heaven collapses, dragging down east and west, as death of sorts overwhelms all the Gods/divine powers in a shared destruction, and death executes a final sentence on itself (*et mors fata novissima se constituit sibi*).[23]

In a similar passage of Seneca's *Thyestes*, the Chorus imagines the response of the universe to the enormity of Thyestes's unwitting crime, when the sun will cease to shine, and the moon, too, will fall, and asks,

> Have we of all humankind been deemed deserving to have heaven's pillars shattered and ourselves crushed in its fall? has the last age come upon us? (*in nos aetas ultima venit?*)... Greedy indeed for life is one who would not rather die when the world is perishing around him.[24]

21. See Dio Chrysostom, *Discourses* 36.42-62.

22. Seneca, *Naturales questiones* 13.1.

23. Seneca, *Hercules Oetaeus* 1102-1117, in F.J. Miller (trans.), *Seneca's Tragedies*, II (LCL; 2 vols.; London: Heinemann; Cambridge, MA: Harvard University Press, 1917), pp. 183-341 (275).

24. Seneca, *Thyestes* 835-84, quoting only 875-84, in F.J. Miller (trans.), *Seneca's Tragedies*, II (LCL; 2 vols.; London: Heinemann; Cambridge, MA: Harvard University Press, 1917), pp. 89-181 (163).

We may remark the resonance with Pliny the Younger's 'the whole world was dying with me and I with it', quoted above.

It is probably worth noting, however, that Seneca is not bound by a single imaginative picture of the future catastrophe. A little later in *Naturales questiones* 27 he foresees an initial destruction of the world by flood, rather than the collapse of the heavenly firmament; but compare *Ad Marciam, de consolatione* 26.6, where the flood is accompanied by 'clash of star with star'.[25] And then again there is a picture more like that from Seneca's *Thyestes* in Pseudo-Seneca, *Octavia*. Human wickedness must be resulting in a catastrophe, if, as it seems, 'this sky is growing old, doomed wholly once more to fall into blind nothingness. Then for the universe is that last day at hand which shall crush sinful humankind beneath heaven's ruin…' (*aetheris magnis… qui si senescit…*).[26]

People who were aware of this imagery would, I suggest, recognize it if they heard Mark's fellow Christians repeat,

> In those days, after that tribulation, the sun will be darkened, and the moon will not give its light, and the stars will be falling from heaven, and the powers in the heavens will be shaken…heaven and earth will pass away…(Mk 13.24; cf. Mt. 24.29; Lk. 21.23-26).[27]

Even though the Markan passage most likely depends at least in part on Isaiah 13.10; 34.2-4; 51.6; and Ezekiel 32.7, there is nothing here that would appear unusual to those used to popular Stoic teaching, or even aware of Epicurean science. We may conclude much the same for Revelation 6.12-14.

But more striking still is 2 Peter 3.5-7, 10-13:

> By the word of God the heaven existed long ago, and an earth formed out of water and by means of water…but by that same word the heavens and earth that now exist have been stored up for fire, and the earth and the works that are upon it will be burned up. Since all these things are to be dissolved…the heavens kindled and dissolved, and the elements melt with fire…a new heaven and a new earth…

25. Seneca, *Ad Marciam, de consolatione,* in J.W. Basore (ed.), *Seneca: Moral Essays*, II (LCL; 3 vols.; London: Heinemann; Cambridge, MA: Harvard University Press, 1932), pp. 2-97 (95).

26. Pseudo-Seneca, *Octavia* 391-94, in F.J. Miller (trans.), *Seneca's Tragedies*, II (LCL; 2 vols.; London: Heinemann; Cambridge, MA: Harvard University Press, 1917), pp. 399-489 (439).

27. There is, of course an anticipatory disappearance of sunlight in Mark's account of Jesus' death (Mk 15.33) as for the death of Hercules in Seneca.

Christians who said and wrote such things could but be aware that this was common parlance.

The assembly of ideas in 2 Pet. 3.3-13 in particular has too much in common with the ideas I have been drawing attention to, for them to be understood simply in terms of Jewish and ancient Mesopotamian tradition, with the Graeco-Roman material set aside. That the Stoic 'end' was only the end of a to-be-repeated cycle, while 1 Peter seems concerned with a once-for-all 'linear'[28] end is not all that important: other, Epicurean-influenced eschatologies, were, as just explained, also *not* cyclical. And for individuals, divine ones included, the end envisaged by Stoics was final so far as any self-awareness was concerned.

That some contemporaries of the author of 2 Peter say 'All things have continued as they were from the beginning of creation' seems to indicate a further awareness of Graeco-Roman controversies over cosmogony and eschatology: it is, as we noted, a characteristic position of Aristotelians and Platonists which both Epicureans and Stoics felt they had to counter. Taking into account creation ἐξ ὕδατος καὶ δι᾿ ὕδατος, ('out of water and by means of water') the burning up to come both of the earth and all the elements, and the counter to the suggestion that we are in a totally stable universe (πάντα), we have too many elements additional to known independent Jewish traditions for them to be either coincidental or incidental (even though other strands again do seem specifically Jewish: creation by word, the fire as judgment, and so forth; but see further, below). In the *Sibylline Oracles* 2 we read:

> And then a great river of blazing fire
> will flow from heaven, and will consume every place,
> land and great ocean and gleaming sea,
> lakes and rivers, springs and implacable Hades
> and the heavenly vault. But the heavenly luminaries
> will crash together, also into an utterly desolate form...
> and then all the elements of the world will be bereft
> ...at once all
> will melt into one and separate into clear air.[29]

So it seems that we must accept that by the first century CE these close

28. J.H. Neyrey, 'The Form and Background of the Polemic in 2 Peter', *JBL* 99 (1980), pp. 407-31, argues for an Epicurean provenance for some of the ideas being discussed—and mostly combatted—in 2 Pet. R.J. Bauckham, *Jude, 2 Peter* (Word; Waco: Word Books, 1983), p. 314, disagrees, but without much argument.

29. *Sib. Or.* 2.196-213, trans. J.J. Collins, *OTP*, I, pp. 345-61 (350).

assimilations of the various traditions (whether or not sharing ancient Mesopotamian roots) are widely known and accepted as part of many people's common conceptual stock—however varied their use of it may turn out on close inspection to be.[30]

It is also worth recalling that we have found at various points in these accounts of a physical decline a sense, justified or not, of moral decline. It is in fact already there in Lucretius: although agonizing death for early humans is presupposed, yet in those first days 'never were many thousands of men led beneath the standards and done to death on a single day' (*De rerum natura* 5.999-1000)...'thereafter property was invented and gold found, which easily robs the strong and beautiful of honour' (*De rerum natura* 5.1113-1115)...'so did gloomy discord beget one thing after another...and day by day increase the terrors of war' (*De rerum natura* 5.1300), so 'The greater fault lies with us' (*De rerum natura* 5.1425). And this deterioration of human society (despite or because of its technological advances) is just one aspect of the inevitable senile decay of our world as a whole.[31]

In Seneca, as we saw, cosmic catastrophe is expected as a result of, not simply a concomitant with the wickedness that has been experienced. Pliny the Elder is similarly convinced of the corruption of his age (e.g. *Hist. nat.* 2.158-59).[32] Much the same was said in Pseudo-Seneca, *Octavia*—the senescence of the heavens is expected to 'crush sinful man beneath heaven's ruin' (393-94). The theme is taken up particularly vigorously in the late pagan Asclepius apocalypse (from Egypt, probably early third-century CE), where it is again explicitly combined with the idea of the world's senescence:

> Egypt will allow herself to be brought into a still worse condition—much worse. She will be defiled by still more heinous crime...she will be a model for atrocious cruelty...the earth will no longer be firm, the sea no longer navigable, the sky no longer decked with stars...this will be the world's senescence: irreligion, disorder, confusion...[33]

---

30. A number of writers are willing to allow that the earlier Jewish Sibyllines may in fact have influenced later Roman authors: Georgi, 'The True Prophet', pp. 110-11; Koester, 'Jesus the Victim', p. 11, citing E. Norden; J. Carcopino, *Virgile et le mystère de la IVe eclogue* (Paris: Artisan du Livre, 1930), pp. 38-40.

31. Cf. Jones, *Epicurean Tradition*, pp. 40-48.

32. Cf. W. Kroll, art. 'Plinius der Älter', *PRE*.

33. *Asclepius Apocalypse* 25, in A.D. Nock and A.-J. Festugière, *Corpus Hermeticum*, I-XII (Paris: Belles Lettres, 1945), pp. 326-31 (326-27).

And moral decline is, of course, also a sign of the imminence of the end in our world as we know it, in Jewish eschatological apocalyptic: 'friends will make war on friends like enemies' (*4 Ezra* 6.24); 'honour will change itself into shame...jealousy will arise, passion will take hold of those who were peaceful, and many will be agitated by wrath to injure many' (*2 Bar.* 48.35-37); 'the land will be corrupted on account of their deeds' (*Jub.* 23.18). So, too, among Christians we are told, 'In the last days there will come times of stress, for people will be lovers of self, lovers of money, proud, arrogant, abusive, disobedient to their parents, ungrateful, unholy, inhuman, implacable' (2 Tim. 3.1-5); 'many will fall and betray one another, and hate one another...and because wickedness is multiplied, people's love will grow cold' (Mt. 24.10-12; cf. Mk 13.12-13); 'in the last days false prophets and corrupters shall be multiplied, and the sheep shall be turned into wolves, and love shall be turned into hate' (*Did.* 16.3-4).

The theme of the world's senile decay to a now imminent end, the strand with which we began, appears as a commonplace, an assertion made without argument and with the apparent expectation that it will be accepted without demur, in two of our contemporary Jewish sources, and in pagan ones. The way the end, the final destruction, is pictured, seems very similar in various pagan, Jewish and Christian writings. The world's senescence as such is also taken up in similar terms by later Christian writers, Cyprian, Lactantius, Augustine and others. Lactantius almost certainly quotes Asclepius, while most likely also being aware of the similar Epicurean motif in Lucretius.[34]

In the light of this widespread common acceptance of the idea of the world's senescence, it is this motif that ought most plausibly to guide our reading of Romans 8.21-22, where Paul writes of creation, ἡ κτίσις, about to be 'freed from bondage to decay' (ἐλευθερωθήσεται ἀπὸ τῆς δουλείας τῆς φθορᾶς).

The interpretation of the passage has, of course, been much argued over. Recent commentators, however, report a widespread agreement that ἡ κτίσις refers to the non-human creation, the entire cosmos (per-

---

34. Bartelink, 'Le thème', p. 346. Some of the passages noted by Bartelink appear also in B.E. Daley, *The Hope of the Early Church* (Cambridge: Cambridge University Press, 1991), but here categorized as 'traditional Roman sentiment' (pp. 99, 133) with no note of the parallel Jewish antecedents.

haps including non-Christian humanity) as contrasted with Paul's fellow Christians (v. 23).[35]

There is also widespread but in this instance quite unargued and unsubstantiated agreement that the 'subjection' of creation to 'futility' (v. 20) and to 'decay' (v. 21) alludes to Gen. 3.17, to God's curse on the ground. Yet there is in fact no verbal link whatsover with the LXX 'cursed is the ground for your work, in sorrow you shall eat of it', and no obvious common imagery; and no evidence is offered for the Genesis passage being so reinterpreted by Paul's contemporaries.[36] The only explanatory context available for Paul's assumption that his hearers will 'know' that all creation is in decay is the popular Epicurean-based observation to which attention has here been drawn.

The 'groaning in travail' is readily taken as a metaphor for birth, and we are referred to passages in both Testaments and in the Dead Sea Scrolls. But all of these apply the metaphor or simile either to various (male) humans who are in trouble, or to the Israelite community; never to creation. Nor can 'the whole creation groaning in travail until now' (ἄχρι τοῦ νῦν) allude to 'pangs of the Messiah', which would (*ex hypothesi*) only recently have begun.[37]

(If this be accepted, then 1 Cor. 7.31, 'the form of this world (τὸ σχῆμα τοῦ κόσμου τούτου) is passing away', should probably be read along similar lines.)

Really there is no call to scratch around for hints of similar ideas in our canonical texts, when Paul himself displays no sense of need for

35. Commentators include M.J. Lagrange, *St. Paul: L'épître aux romains* (Paris: J. Gabalda, 1950); E. Käsemann, *Commentary on Romans* (ET; London: SCM Press, 1980); C.E.B. Cranfield, *A Critical and Exegetical Commentary on the Epistle to the Romans* (ICC; Edinburgh: T. & T. Clark, 1975); U. Wilckens, *Der brief an die Römer* (EKKNT, 6.2; Zürich: Benziger Verlag, 1980); together with J. Lambrecht, 'The Groaning of Creation: A Study of Rom. 8.18-30', *Louvain Studies* 15 (1990), pp. 3-18.

36. Käsemann, *Romans*, p. 233, cites *Gen. Rab.* 12.6, a saying ascribed to R. Shemuel, whom he dates to 260 CE: 'Although things were created in their fullness, when the first man sinned they were corrupted and they will not come back to their order before ben Perez (the Messiah) comes.' But, quite apart from the time-gap (if the given date is allowed) the saying seems to be concerned with a lack of order, not with decay.

37. Passages often cited are Isa. 26.17; 66.8; Jer. 4.31; Hos. 13.13; Mic. 4.9-10; together with Mk 13.8; Jn 16.21; 1 Thess. 5.3; and 1QH 3.7-10, 'I am in distress like a woman in travail...'

any such. We have here a commonplace, Epicurean in origin, but in Paul's day widespread, one which he could obviously incorporate into his scheme of things without needing any inter-textual allusions or further elaboration. Its nearest parallels are in *4 Ezra* and in *2 Baruch*: we are born of a creation ageing and long past her youth; this physical creation is an exhausted mother in apparently terminal decay, but (Paul is sure) in fact waiting to see the glorious outcome of her prolonged labour, the revelation of the children of God in whose liberation she will share.

Paul is sure, quite explicitly, that creation can validly be seen as expectant, hopeful: that is the Christian conviction countering the common pessimistic awareness of decay. The notion of total decay and/or disastrous decline is often accompanied by the idea of a period when things were very much better, as well as (in some instances) the hope that the good times may be ahead, may return: stories of a good past and hopes for a good future, one or both. The myth of the past Golden Age was widely shared. Hesiod had spoken of one, and Plato, too.[38] But how that better state was to be described differed considerably. In some accounts it is thought of as a time of great simplicity and peace, before life has been corrupted by property, technology, luxury, power. For others, the discovery of the arts of civilized living constitute an initial advance, rather than the first downward step. There is some ambivalence found in this respect in Lucretius.[39]

We meet a lively debate between these two attitudes in Seneca, *Epistulae morales* 90, where he argues a Cynic case against the Stoic Podeidonius. We cannot choose both Diogenes with his cupped hands and Daedalus with his advanced technology (90.14). The account in *1 Enoch* 7–8 of humans seduced by Azazel and others instructing them in the crafts (cf. also 52.7-8) echoes one side of this sort of debate, while *Jubilees* is closer to Poseidonius's Stoic line: angelic technological ex-

38. A.O. Lovejoy and G. Boas, *Primitivism and Related Ideas in Antiquity* (Baltimore: The Johns Hopkins University Press, 1935; New York: Octagon, 1965); H. Schwabl, art. 'Weltalter', PRE Supp. 15, cols. 784-850; P. Vidal-Naquet, 'Plato's Myth of the Statesman, the Ambiguities of the Golden Age and of History', *JHS* 98 (1978), pp. 132-41.

39. Lovejoy and Boas, *Primitivism*, pp. 222-42; H. Jones, *Epicurean Tradition*, pp. 40-48; for a critique of seeing any simple utopian primitivism in Lucretius, Rist, *Epicurus*, ch. 4, 'Man and the Cosmos', pp. 67-73.

pertise is imparted before the corrupting union of angels and human females (4.15).[40]

But even without or before complications of crafts and property, there are differing accounts. Hesiod pictures a time of natural luxury, when the fish fried themselves and the fruit jumped into humans' mouths.[41] Cynics, on the other hand, pictured a time of radical and strenuous simplicity, a hard life but a good one, humans at peace with one another, and with the animals and with the environment.[42]

For Stoics there was, of course, a succession of Golden Ages ahead, though none but the divine pervasive rational power would recall the experience of it.[43] For Epicureans it was a matter of chance whether another fortuitous agglomeration of atoms would produce a replica of a Golden Age that once obtained on earth. The precise conditions could not, of course, be expected to return for this world.

Cynics and others could, however, conceive of a fresh Golden Age, the Age of Cronos or Saturn, within present history. Cynics claimed that it could be anticipated, by living again life according to nature: a radically 'realized' eschatology.[44] I have argued at some length elsewhere that the teachings of Jesus on simplicity, poverty, dependence may have been shaped in part by Cynic teaching in the tradition of Gadara, a few miles south of the Sea of Galilee. Certainly many later Christians explicitly acknowledge the analogies.[45] (And here again, a later Epicurean, Diogenes of Oenoanda, adopts a similar hope: something of life as once it was may be lived now if people allow themselves to be saved by the teaching and example of Epicurus.)[46] In contrast to

---

40. T.F. Glasson, *Greek Influence*, pp. 67-73.

41. See the collection of references in J.J. de Jonge, 'ΒΟΥΤΡΟΣ ΒΟΗΣΕΙ: The Age of Cronos and the Millennium in Papias of Hierapolis', in M.J. Vermasseren (ed.), *Studies in Hellenistic Religion* (Leiden: E.J. Brill, 1979), pp. 37-49.

42. Cf., again, Lovejoy and Boas, *Primitivism*, pp. 117-54.

43. See the discussion in Long, 'Stoics on World-Conflagration'.

44. Lucian, *The Runaways* 17; Epictetus, *Dissertations* 3.22.79, and 4.8.34; L. Vaage, 'The Ethos and Ethics of an Itinerant Intelligence' (PhD thesis, Claremont Graduate School, California, 1987), argues that *Runaways* 12 is also relevant to a Cynic 'realized eschatology'; cf. also B. Mack, *A Myth of Innocence: Mark and Christian Origins* (Philadelphia: Fortress Press, 1988), pp. 69-74; and next note.

45. Cf. Downing, *Cynics and Christian Origins* and Dorival, 'L'image des Cyniques', pp. 419-44.

46. Cf. M.F. Smith, 'Thirteen New Fragments of Diogenes of Oenoanda', *Ergänzungbände zu den Tituli Asiae Minoris* 6 (1974), frg. 21, pp. 21-27.

Jesus' invitation to simplicity, however, other Christians soon adopted for preference something closer to Hesiod's hedonist ideal, when 'every vine will bear ten thousand branches, every branch ten thousand shoots, every shoot ten thousand clusters...and when one of God's holy ones takes hold of a cluster, another will call out, I am better, take me...' But something of this strand had already been taken up into Jewish apocalyptic eschatology (eg., *2 Bar.* 29.5).[47]

Others again saw a renewed Golden Age as part of a cycle within human 'political' history, as the 'Great Year' came round. How far the hope was seen as a realizable possibility, how much as a dream only to be approximated to, how much merely exploited as political rhetoric, it is hard to tell. It certainly seems to many commentators that it must have appeared ideologically powerful, witness its use by Virgil and by Horace.[48] When Jewish and Christian writers deployed similar motifs these are likely to have been in conscious response to and competition with Roman imperial propagandists.[49]

Golden Age themes are used, without apparent sarcasm, by Philo, looking back to the early days of Gaius's reign. 'It was not a matter of people hoping that they would have possession and use of good things public and private, they considered that they had already the plenitude of good fortune... In those days the rich had not precedence over the poor, nor the distinguished over the obscure, creditors were not above debtors, nor masters above slaves... Indeed, the life under Cronos, pictured by the poets, no longer appeared to be a fabled story, so great was the prosperity and wellbeing, freedom from grief and fear, the joy which

47. Papias, in Ireneus, *Adv. haer.* 5.33.3-4; as discussed in de Jonge, 'ΒΟΥΤΡΟC ΒΟΗCΕΙ', along with similar references in early Christian texts. De Jonge argues that Papias's expectation must stem from a prior Hebrew source, already influenced by the Greek myth.

48. On the latter see Georgi, 'The True Prophet' and Koester, 'Jesus the Victim'. On 'The Great Year' see, for instance, H. Schwabl, 'Weltalter'; A.-H. Chroust, 'The "Great Deluge"', pp. 113-22; B.L. van der Waerden, 'The Great Year in Greek, Persian and Hindu Astronomy', *AHES* 18 (1977/78), pp. 359-83; G. Roca Sera, *Censorinus: Le jour natal* (Paris: Vrin, 1980); J. Bels, 'Le thème de la grande année d'Héraclite aux Stoïciens', *RPA* 7.2 (1980), pp. 169-83; and the discussion of Stoicism listed at n. 16.

49. See, again, Georgi, 'The True Prophet', and Koester, 'Jesus the Victim'.

pervaded households and people.'[50] But Philo can also use this imagery
to expound an immanent Jewish hope for the future: there will be peace
among all animals 'when the Uncreated judges that there are some
people worthy of salvation…because their will is to bring their private
blessings into the common stock to be shared and enjoyed alike'.[51] The
peace among animals finds precedent in Isa. 11.6-9; Lev. 26.6; Job
5.23; Hos. 2.18. But linking that hope with a willingness to share possessions clearly echoes Golden Age traditions.

It is quite obvious, then, that the same or very similar motifs appear
in futurist or inaugurated or realized eschatologies, the context in each
affecting the use of shared motifs in another. And so the early Christians had a large and varied popular, widely shared vocabulary of proto-
logical as well as of eschatological ideas on which to draw, to explore
and express their emerging and diverse convictions.[52] In a situation
where all sorts of protologies and eschatologies were current cultural
coinage there is no justification for producing interpretative schemes in
which one posited original Christian view (imminent, inaugurated or
realized or whatever) is then supposed to have been changed under
pressure from gnosticism, Hellenism, evangelistic failure, or some other
source.[53] Much the same range of views as were available to Jews in
Palestine were readily available and current and certainly comprehensible in the Graeco-Roman world cultural context—where a fair number of them probably originated, anyway.

Most attention has been paid here to ideas of imminent cosmic catastrophe, in Jewish, Christian and other Greco-Roman sources. But there

50. Philo, *De legatione* 11-13 in F.H. Colson and J.W. Earp (trans.), *Philo*, X
(LCL; 10 vols., 2 supplements; London: Heinemann; Cambridge, MA: Harvard University Press, 1962), pp. 1-187 (9).

51. Philo, *Praem. Poen.* 87, in F.H. Colson (trans.), *Philo*, VIII (LCL; 10 vols.,
2 supplements; London: Heinemann; Cambridge MA: Harvard University Press,
1939), pp. 309-423 (365).

52. Cf. C.F.D. Moule, 'The Influence of Circumstances on the Use of Eschatological Terms', *JTS* NS 16 (1964), pp. 1-15; and L.W. Barnard, 'Justin Martyr's
Eschatology', *VC* 19 (1965), pp. 86-98; also D.E. Aune, *The Cultic Setting of Realised Eschatology* (Leiden: E.J. Brill, 1972).

53. See the references above to M. Werner, O. Cullmann, etc. It is perhaps also
worth commenting that expectations of cosmic disaster do not necessarily die young
(against P. Fredriksen, 'Judaism, the Circumcision of the Gentiles and Apocalyptic
Hope', *JTS* NS 42 (1991), p. 559, 'Millenarian movements tend, of necessity, to
have a short half-life.'

are many more common features besides, which can now be no more than noted in passing. There are similar combinations in each of the strands that may be labelled 'sapiential' or 'prophetic': both so regularly occur together that it is almost certainly unhelpful to distinguish them, let alone oppose them to one another.[54] There are competing 'focal' figures in at least some 'pagan' writers to match the 'messiah' of some sort in some Jewish and most Christian writing.[55] There is talk of life to come, of souls discarding bodies and of tombs being emptied and their occupants assumed to heaven; there are prospects of punishment and reward.[56] Even Cynics can imagine eminent philosophers as judges or prosecution witnesses in some life to come (like the Son of Man in the Gospels).[57] Particular variant combinations of motifs may appear (so far) in only one strand of tradition: for instance, the emptying of tombs for most or all of humankind as a prelude to judgment, bliss, punishment or annihilation appear only in some Jewish and many Christian schemes, and not in the rest. But each selection from the common stock is likely to display some unique features, a distinctive *parole*. The *langue*, the vocabulary of motifs is still largely common and commonplace. This is how communication can happen. Early Christians would certainly not have been under any pressure from outsiders' incomprehension to change their eschatological speculations or convictions.

But the fact that this *langue* could be shared by such different people from such different social contexts and with such varied concomitant beliefs means that it is very unlikely that just one interpretative scheme for understanding each and every instance will suffice. Some of those that U.H.J. Körtner canvasses but then discards may be apposite, and his preferred one may indeed fit some examples well. For some it could well be the case that 'Noch einmal zeigt sich an dieser Stelle, dass Apocalyptik auf einer präsentischen Erfahrung von Welt und Zeitlich-

54. Noting the over-hard disjunctions between wisdom and apocalyptic eschatology in Mack, *A Myth of Innocence*, pp. 58-59 and 70-72; and in J.D. Crossan, *The Historical Jesus* (San Francisco: HarperSanFrancisco; Edinburgh: T. & T. Clark, 1991), pp. 227-28.

55. Koester, 'Jesus the Victim'; Georgi, 'The True Prophet', again.

56. F. Cumont, *Afterlife in Roman Paganism* (New Haven: Yale University Press, 1992); Glasson, *Greek Influence*.

57. In the *Cynic Epistles*, Pseudo-Heraclitus, 5; 9; Pseudo-Diogenes 39; Socratic Epistle 25.1; and in Epictetus, *Encheiridion* 15; Lucian, *Downward Journey* 23; see Downing, *Cynics and Christian Origins*, p. 140, to which the last two references are an addition.

keit beruht.'[58] But it is hardly so for all. A proper estimate of the existential import of various eschatologies must wait upon a much greater awareness of their similarities and differences (and this already lengthy article is no place for such an attempt).

In any more detailed investigation of eschatologies (including then also the gnostic ones to which Körtner refers), the contrast between Jewish and early Christian linear eschatologies on the one hand, and necessarily cyclical Graeco-Roman views on the other is one that should be deliberately dispensed with, along with the outworn notion of a movement (often 'decline') from an original eschatological purity into 'Early Catholicism'. And we should certainly no longer even subconsciously censor our choice of illustrative comparison in studies of Christian or Jewish eschatologies from around the beginning of our era so as to exclude what was in all probability a common currency.

In the foregoing we touched only in passing on the Platonic tradition which was to become so important in later Christian metaphysical reflection, especially through the work of Philo of Alexandria. The latter in particular is regularly used as foil against which to set the earliest Christological speculations of Paul and his followers, the author to Hebrews, and John. Philo's neo-Platonic speculation turns out to be rather more subtle than the desire for a quick and easy comparison has often allowed.

58. 'Once again it is clear here that Apocalyptic is set in a present experience of reality and temporality', Körtner, 'Weltzeit', p. 52: a matter of the quality of current experience, the pressures of experienced reality. Also too simplistic is the generalizing interpretation of Jewish and Christian eschatology in Wright, *The New Testament* , ch. 10, pp. 280-338; and *Jesus and the Victory of God*, e.g, pp. 467-72: it always refers to a dramatic change expected in the world as it is.

Chapter 10

ONTOLOGICAL ASYMMETRY IN PHILO, AND CHRISTOLOGICAL REALISM IN PAUL, HEBREWS AND JOHN*

> It was no small matter, it was the greatest possible disturbance of things
> as they are when created and corruptible human nature was made [sc., by
> Gaius] to appear to have become deified, uncreated and incorruptible...
> for it would be easier for God to become human, even, than for a human
> to become God.[1]

So wrote Philo in his *De legatione ad Gaium*. Philo is interesting enough
in his own right to warrant close attention. But he is also widely used to
illustrate early developments in Christian theology, or at least to suggest the likely parameters of those developments; and especially is that
so in Christology.

In what follows I shall first display some examples of the use recently
made of Philo by J.D.G. Dunn in his rightly influential *Christology in
the Making*.[2] Dunn (and many others) argue that the 'metaphor' of the
'Logos' allows Philo to bridge the 'gulf' he is taken to believe subsists
between God and all creation. I shall argue, rather, that between God
and us there is for Philo neither gulf nor barrier; yet we, for our part,
cannot reach God: there is an 'asymmetry of knowing'. I shall then
argue further that there is for Philo an 'asymmetry of truth': though
what we say cannot be true of God, yet are able to speak truly of that

* Reprinted from *JTS* NS 41.1 (1990), pp. 243-440, with kind permission. This
paper was originally presented to the SNTS Philo Seminar, Dublin, 1989. I am
grateful to its members for their generous and helpful discussion.
   1. Philo, *Leg. Gai.* 118, in Colson and Earp (trans.), *Philo*, X, p. 59. The translations in what follows are my own revisions of LCL.
   2. J.D.G. Dunn, *Christology in the Making* (London: SCM Press, 1980), to
which the following refers. The second edition (London: SCM Press, 1989) does
not seem to add anything substantial to the discussion of Philo with which I am here
concerned.

reality as we perceive it. In the next stage of my discussion I hope to show that for Philo this reality that we perceive (especially the Logos) really 'is'; it is not a matter of 'mere metaphor'. Yet this perceived reality does not exist as God exists: there is an 'ontological asymmetry'.[3] Fifthly and finally, I shall relate the conclusions I have urged to more of what Dunn says on Philo and the Logos, briefly noting possible implications for our understanding of some of the earliest developments of Christology.

1. *Philo and Christology in J.D.G. Dunn*

Dunn refers to Philo frequently in his *Christology in the Making*, but especially in ch. 7, 'The Word of God'.

> Philo has no thought of the Logos as a real being with particular functions distinct from God... Philo was using the Platonic conception of a world of ideas to bridge the gulf between God and creation, between God and man...in the end of the day, *the Logos seems to be nothing more for Philo than God himself in his approach to man, God himself insofar as he may be known by man* (pp. 227-28, original italics).

And Dunn concludes: 'Our task in this section has been to fill out the context of meaning within which many at least of the Fourth Gospel's readers would interpret the prologue to that Gospel' (pp. 228-29). Dunn has already used Philo in a similar way in discussion of 'Son', 'Man', and 'Wisdom' in particular. Philo is taken as showing that it is very unlikely that early Christians would have come at all quickly to identify the risen Christ with any 'pre-existent' divine figure, for 'even Philo (as one might say) did not *really* believe in any such figures'.[4]

---

3. Many writers on Philo find ambiguity or paradox. I would accept David Runia's warning against 'imposing any measure of systematization on the diffuseness of Philo's thought', in D. Runia, *Philo of Alexandria and the TIMAEUS of Plato* (Leiden: E.J. Brill, 1986), p. 450, n. 247. I hope that my chosen term 'asymmetry' will be seen to allow something of the complexity of Philo's thought to emerge, without forcing on it an extraneous clarity.

4. Cf. J. Drummond, *Philo Judaeus*, II (2 vols; London: Williams & Norgate, 1886), pp. 102-104; E.R. Goodenough, *By Light, Light* (New Haven: Yale University Press, 1935), p. 64; L.W. Hurtado, *One God, One Lord* (Philadelphia: Fortress Press, 1988), pp. 37, 45-48; unchanged, I think, in the second edition (Edinburgh: T. & T. Clark, 1998, at the same pp.); S. Sandmel, *Philo of Alexandria* (New York: Oxford University Press, 1979), p. 98, argues that there is 'no decisive clarity in Philo's presentation'; cf. *idem*, 'Philo Judaeus: An Introduction to the

In the passages quoted just above, then, Dunn claims to find in Philo ideas of 'the gulf between God and creation, between God and man', 'nothing more than God himself in his approach to man, God himself insofar as he may be known to man', and 'no thought of a real being with particular functions distinct from God'. It is to what Philo himself has to say on these three issues of access, knowledge and being, that we now turn, to see whether 'asymmetry' better interprets what Philo actually writes. In this discussion I shall try to follow the important advice that David Runia has urged, and indicate how the main passages of Philo to which I refer operate in their own immediate contexts (especially where the exegesis of Scripture is at issue), and only then introduce passages from elsewhere in Philo.[5]

2. A Gulf between God and Creation— or Simply an 'Asymmetry of Access?'

There sems to be nothing in Philo to correspond either word-for-word or conceptually with the 'gulf' that Dunn (and others) suggest.[6] In fact in a whole variety of contexts Philo seems to insist on denying any such possibility.

Man, his Writings and his Significance', *ANRW* 2.22.1 (1977), pp. 3-46 (24), 'the Logos is not a real reality [sic] but is only a manner of speaking.'

5.   D. Runia, 'How to Read Philo', *NTT* 40 (1986), pp. 185-98; and, for an example of his approach, *idem*, 'God and Man in Philo of Alexandria', *JTS* NS 39 (1988), pp. 48-75. Runia also sets Philo in a wide Neoplatonic context in his *Philo*. I am not equipped to set what follows in as wide a range of Neoplatonists, but shall refer occasionally to Plutarch and a few others for illustration.

6.   Drummond, *Philo* 1.312; L.K.K. Dey, *The Intermediary World and Patterns of Perfection in Philo and Hebrews* (Missoula, MT: Scholars Press, 1975), p. 96; G.D. Farandos, *Kosmos und Logos nach Philon von Alexandria* (Elementa, 4; Amsterdam: Rodopi, 1976), p. 175, 'die Kluft zwischen Gott und sinnlicher Welt'; R. Mortley, *From Word to Silence. I. The Rise and Fall of the Logos* (Bonn: Peter Hanstein, 1986), p. 44; even Runia, 'God and Man', p. 61; and R. Williamson, *Jews in the Hellenistic World: Philo* (Cambridge, Cambridge University Press, 1989), p. 42, citing *Sacr.* 92, discussed below. In disagreement, H.A. Wolfson, *Philo: Foundations of Religious Thought in Judaism, Christianity and Islam*, I (2 vols.; Cambridge, MA: Harvard University Press, 1947), pp. 284, 289; E. Osborn, 'Negative Theology and Apologetic', in R. Mortley and D. Dockrill (eds.), *The Via Negativa*, *Prudentia* Supp. (Auckland, NZ, 1981), pp. 49-63 (55); L. Hurtado, *One God*, p. 23; and D. Winston, *Logos and Mystical Theology in Philo of Alexandria* (Cincinnati: Hebrew Union College Press, 1985), p. 49.

At one (and I think, only one) point in his LCL translation, F.H. Colson offers in the text the following translation: 'The gulf that separates God from what comes next to him is one of kind and nature' (*Sacr.* 92). However, in a footnote he writes, 'Literally "everything that comes after God is found to have descended by a whole genus"'. The text he prints runs, ἀλλ᾽ ὅλῳ γένει καταβεβηκὸς ἅπαν τὸ μετὰ θεὸν εὑρίσκεται. There is no warrant in Philo's Greek here for importing the word 'gulf'. The context in Philo is a discussion of the embarrassment caused by God's swearing an oath in the passage of Exodus (13.11-13) that Philo has adduced to help him comment on Gen. 4.4 (Abel's sacrifice). Talk of God's oath, says Philo (as he often does with similar embarrassments in the text) is simply a concession to our human weakness. 'We cannot always be recalling to mind the text so appropriate to the Cause, "God is not as human is" (Num. 23.19), transcending all human conceptuality' (οὐ γὰρ δυνάμεθα διηνεκῶς τὸ ἄξιον τοῦ αἰτίου κεφάλιον ἐν ψυχῇ ταμιεύεσθαι τῇ ἑαυτῶν, τὸ ᾽οὐχ ὡς ἄνθρωτιος ὁ θεός᾽ ἵνα πάντα τὰ ἀνθρωπολογούμενα ὑπερκύψωμεν, *Sacr.* 94). Yet this discussion of the oath ascribed to God, and then of God's transcendence, in fact itself forms a parenthesis in a lengthy disquisition on God's effective providential guidance as the owner and giver of every gift we have (*Sacr.* 76-97).

As we shall see in further passages, God's transcendence certainly entails great—insuperable—difficulties in the way of any attempt on our part to reach him. But it is precisely because he is transcendent that God himself can and does reach everywhere, without anything—let alone any gulf—being able to hinder him. The transcendence that precludes our reaching him is the transcendence that ensures that he reaches us. It is an anthropomorphism that suggests the deity could be limited or hindered. However we try to express Philo's thoughts about the disparities in kind of God and creation, the tempting word 'gulf' is entirely inappropriate. Philo does use various Greek words that may be so translated (βαθύς, ὄρυγμα, χάσμα),[7] but he does so only in ordinary literal contexts. These words never appear as metaphors for any division between God and creation, God and humanity. In fact, as already indicated, there are many settings where Philo makes a point of insisting on just the opposite. Where there seems to be a suggestion of anything that might separate God from any human (e.g. Gen. 3.8; Num. 11.23, etc.)

7. See G. Mayer, *Index Philoneus* (Berlin: de Gruyter, 1974).

Philo cites Exod. 17.6, 'Here I am stood, before ever you had being', and tells us that it means, 'He who is here is also there and everywhere, filling everything entirely and completely, leaving nothing bereft of himself' (*Sacr*.67-68; *Leg. All.* 3.4; *Conf. Ling,* 6-8, 138; *Migr. Abr.*183; *Somn.* 1.241, 2.221). The same point is insisted on even more emphatically in a similar setting at *Det. Pot. Ins.* 150-58, on Gen. 4.14, where Cain is suggesting that he may be hidden from God's presence (though here Philo does not quote Exod. 17.6).

So far from Philo seeking some device to bridge any 'gulf' between God and creation, what we find is that whenever any kind of divide might seem suggested in scripture Philo immediately repudiates it, and does so in the interests of insisting on the very transcendence that talk of a 'gulf' is meant by modern commentators such as Dunn to affirm. As we shall illustrate in more detail later, it is true that for Philo God is in a very strong sense inaccessible to humans (even though Philo does not talk of a 'gulf' in this connection, either). But humans are obviously not inaccessible to God, and there is certainly no place for Dunn's talk of 'the gulf between God and creation, between God and man'. What there is is an asymmetry of access. An aspect of this asymmetry of access is an asymmetry in knowing, and underlying that there may well be an asymmetry in being. But there is no gulf. Clearly this does leave Philo with problems for safeguarding his conviction of God's transcendence when he is talking of God's involvement in creation. But Philo has other devices than any kind of 'gulf' talk with which to deal with this issue, as we shall note a little later.

3. *An Asymmetry in Knowing*

For Philo God exists in a way we humans cannot apprehend, but can only acknowledge) e.g. *Det. Pot. Ins.* 160; *Poster. C.* 13-14; *Quod Deus Imm.* 55). Even Moses could reach no further, despite his proper reliance on God alone in his search (*Fug.* 164-65; *Mut. Nom.* 7-10). 'From his quest comes the one great benefit of comprehending that God in his being is incomprehensible to all' (*Poster. C.* 15). Thus no human conceptuality, and certainly no human language, not even scriptural language is adequate. The best we can achieve is a negative theology, 'God is not as human is' (Num. 23.19); he is without quality (ποιότης), that is, without any defining characteristics (*Deus Imm.* 53-54; cf. *Leg. All.* 1.91; 2.1-2; 3.206; *Leg. Gai.* 6, etc.) There thus seems no warrant for Dunn's emphatic assertion that '*the Logos is what is knowable of*

God...God himself insofar as he may be known by man.[8] God himself is not known. Besides our acknowledgment that 'he is', all we can know are his effects, and how most appropriately to respond to him (*Poster. C.* 166-69). That is all that even Scripture enables (*Fug.* 165, again; cf. *Sacr.* 60). And in this sense at least we already note Philo accepting something like 'asymmetry of being': God's existence is quite other than ours, so alien that we cannot hope to comprehend it.

Philo is also sure that, without betraying or diminishing or in any way sullying his essential otherness, 'the truly existent' (τὸ ὄντως ὄν) achieves his purposes in the world (e.g. *Gig.* 45). To do this the unknowable God does not need any vice-regent, anyone to deputize for him. Citing perhaps Isaiah 40.13 Philo insists it was 'with no counsellor (for who else was there?)' that God created (*Op. Mund.* 23). He needs no one else, for he can do everything himself (*Op. Mund.* 46; cf. *Cher.* 77; *Plant.* 50-51; *Conf. Ling.* 175; *Somn.* 1.158).[9] He is entirely self-sufficient (*Leg. All.* 3.205). As we have seen, God has no need of any gap between himself and his cosmos so as to preserve his own integrity, and thus has no need of any plenipotentiary representative to make connections for him (cf. *Somn.* 1.142). Moreover, since God (and God alone) understands God, he obviously needs no human metaphors to make himself intelligible to himself (*Leg. All.* 3.206-207; *Praem. Poen.* 39-40). It is not only 'realist' language about divine intermediaries that would seem ruled out by such assertions; there would seem to be no warrant for using the terms even metaphorically to talk of God (or of 'what is knowable of God') either, for about God (as opposed to his 'effects') there would really seem nothing knowable but that he is. There would seem nothing else to say, even in metaphor.[10]

Yet Scripture does try to allow us at least to articulate an appropriate response to the God we cannot hope to comprehend. It does itself use human language of God; it does (paradoxically) at times talk as though 'God is as human is', in such passages as Deut. 8.5, 'as a father...so God'. Philo insists, 'It is for education and instruction that such words are used, not because they are appropriate to the nature of God's being' (*Deus Imm.* 54; *Quaest. in Gen.* 4.4-8). There is no other language available, and God mercifully condescends to our human feeble-mind-

8. Dunn, *Christology*, pp. 226, 228. Dunn's italics.
9. Wolfson, *Philo*, I, pp. 281-82; cf. Josephus, *Apion* 2.192.
10. Goodenough, *By Light*, p. 64, on Philo's obvious dissatisfaction with his conceptuality.

edness, for 'we cannot always be calling to mind the text so appropriate to the Cause, "God is not as human is" [Num. 23.19, again], transcending all human conceptuality...[but such talk of God is there] to help us in our weakness' (*Sacr.* 94-96, again; cf. 101; and *Quaest. in Gen.* 2.54).

In the passage just quoted (and as we noted earlier) Philo is dealing with the embarassment of finding God said to have sworn an oath. Later, in a text of Genesis in the Septuagint (Gen. 31.13) Philo reads 'I am the God who appeared to you in the place of God' (where 'Bethel' is translated, not transliterated). The 'God' appearing 'in the place of God' is his Word. And in much the same way, Philo goes on to say, God takes on the appearance of angels so we may be aware of his presence, in such a way that we take what represents his presence not as an image of it but as the original reality (*Somn.* 132). He then ventures this bold explanation:

> The old story is still current that the deity goes the rounds of our cities resembling now one person, now another, making a tally of wickedness and law-breaking. Though the story may well not be true (καὶ τάχα μὲν οὐκ ἀληθῶς), it is certainly to everyone's clear advantage that it goes on being told. And although [our scriptural] narrative prefers more reverent and hallowed concepts for the one who is, still it tries very hard to provide education for life for ignorant humans, and so likens the one who is to human kind (though not to any one person in particular)...By and large we can say that [these] two strands run through the Law code, one concerned with the truth (τὸ ἀληθὲς), stressing 'God is not as human is', the other concerned with the attitudes of the less intelligent, for whom there are sentiments like, 'the Lord God will discipline you as if a human were disciplining his son' (*Somn.* 1.233-34, 237).[11]

Can we discern any more clearly, positively and consistently the status of talk about God, his Word and his powers that Philo accepts from Scripture and tradition? He has insisted that there is no affirmative

---

11. On this see Runia, *Philo*, p. 438, on κατάχρησις, the (necessary) misuse of language, with references given (*Cher.* 121, etc.); and *idem*, 'Naming and Knowing', in R. van den Broek, T. Baada and J. Mansfeld (eds.), *Knowledge of God in the Greco-Roman World* (Leiden: E.J. Brill, 1988), pp. 82-98. On the place of such use in our spiritual progress, see *Det. Pot. Ins.* 56; *Deus Imm.* 116; *Migr. Abr.* 174-75; and also Dey, *Intermediary World*, esp. p. 12. 'Unmediated Access' (Dey, *Intermediary World*, pp. 42-46) is, however, not for physical beings (see below). Note also E. Bréhier, *Les idées philosophiques et religieuses de Philon d'Alexandrie* (Paris: Vrin, 1950), pp. 76-78.

human way truly to 'characterize' the one who is; there are even places where he says explicitly of Scripture what he allows in *Somn.* may be the case with Homer, that the narrative is 'mythic' and literally untrue (e.g. *Op. Mund.* 154 [but cf. 156]; *Leg. All.* 2.19). Yet for the most part he talks of 'the Word' and 'the powers' without further excuse. As we have noted, he is happy to take such language as directed to shaping our attitudes and conduct. Yet, although it is not descriptive of the one who is, it does not seem for the most part elsewhere to be labelled 'convenient ethical fiction', either. It seems to be taken as genuinely *appropriate*, corresponding in some way to reality as we perceive it. It would not be enough to say that it is authoritative (though that is relevant), for Philo in effect refuses to take as appropriate anything that might seem to attempt to describe God, however firmly entrenched in authoritative scripture. We might have to conclude that Philo is simply arbitrary and inconsistent. Yet we ourselves ought not simply to opt for that conclusion before we have explored all the avenues Philo opens for us.

The one solution that seems to remain to the puzzle with which Philo faces us here is as follows. When (especially with the help of Scripture) we try to think about God, and/or try to respond to him, we are not left in a trackless morass of indifferently inappropriate ideas. Some are better than others, Jewish and Platonic ones in particular. They are not 'the truth'; they are not at all adequate to the truth. But they are still not as inappropriate as much current mythology or indifference (e.g. *Spec. Leg.* 2.165-66). As we have already noted, they do genuinely articulate our response to God and our apprehension of the activity of God in the world, the effects God has on his world. But they are also true of our guided and inspired apprehension of reality as our minds move Godwards—even though our apprehension is still not the truth of the one who is. We can talk truly of our perceptions of divine reality, even though our perceptions are not themselves true of the one who is.

We must consider further evidence in support of this conclusion, from Philo's exegesis read in context. Philo wonders why Scripture represents the Father of the universe as saying, 'Let us make humankind in our own image and in our own likeness' (Gen. 1.26), when in fact he has no need of anyone to help him. God alone *knows* why it is said, and so Philo can only offer 'by probable conjecture what seems plausible and reasonable'. He notes that the plural is only used of the creation of humans, the creation of beings capable of choosing and doing evil, when that must be hateful to God (*Op. Mund.* 72-75; cf. *Spec. Leg.*

1.329). A platonist such as Philo can only plausibly conceive of such creation at one remove.[12] Scripture allows him to conceptualize things this way, and the conjecture may even represent the truth of how the creation of humans took place. It still does not represent the truth of the one who is, who needs no intermediaries.

At *Leg. All.* 3.96 Philo includes in a list of recipients of God's prevenient grace, Bezeleel. Allowing his standard etymology of the name to suggest the word 'shadow', and without anything in the text at all obviously demanding further explanation, he then (it seems, gratuitously) introduces a reference to God's Word as God's 'shadow'. In other contexts 'shadow' is clearly a derogatory term, designating a very poor second to the reality that 'casts' it (*Migr. Abr.* 12; *Somn.* 1.206) if not, indeed, positively misleading (*Poster. C.* 112; *Deus Imm.* 177; *Agr.* 42). And, compared with God, 'the Word' is a 'mere' shadow. Philo uses the term again in his explanation of the three divine figures in Genesis 18: two are ('merely') shadows cast, and Philo insists, 'no one should think the shadows can properly be spoken of as God' (*Abr.* 119-20). Yet it is by this shadowy Word that, as by an instrument, God made the world (*Leg. All.* 3.96, again). This seems to mean that our conception of God's creative activity is at best a shadow of the reality of God's creativity. But it is still more true than not. It is better to conceive things so than in some other way or not at all. It is true to our best (and guided) theologizing. Perhaps we should discern that the Word, although 'only' a shadow is nonetheless a 'real' shadow, provided by God for us, not a figment of our imagination, or a mere rhetorical play of our own.

This certainly seems to be the import of the impressive sequence *Poster. C.* 13-21. Philo is discussing Gen. 4.16, with its implausible suggestion (as we have seen) that one can put any sort of distance between oneself and the God who has 'filled the universe with himself'. Philo considers kinds of moral and perceptual distance and closeness. Closest, of course, has been Moses. Yet Moses' request to God (Exod. 33.13) to reveal to him his nature is noble but doomed (*Poster. C.* 13, 18, 21).

---

12. On the Platonic background, see F.H. Colson's note to *Op. Mund.* 72-74, *Philo*, I, p. 475; Wolfson, *Philo*, I, pp. 200-274; Goodenough, *By Light*, pp. 60-63; Runia, *Philo*, pp. 242-49; and cf. Plutarch, *De iside et osiride* 369AB.

[Moses] entered into the darkness where God was (Exod. 20.21), that is, into the sacred realm of formless apperception of the one who is (εἰς τὰς ἀδύτους καὶ ἀειδεῖς περὶ τοῦ ὄντος ἐννοίας, 14)[13] When this lover of God seeks to understand the being of the one who is...he gains the one great benefit of comprehending that God in his being is incomprehensible to all... (15). Our mind which can move faster than anything else we know would be bound to fall incalculably short of comprehending the Cause (16).

And yet it is precisely in this context of emphatic agnosticism, where we are intellectually far from God that Philo then reaffirms that God is 'intensely close' (ἐγγύτατα) to each one of us (20). We are far from him, not he from us, for he has 'filled the universe with himself through his powers...' 'he takes hold of us through his creative and punitive powers which exist as close neighbours to each of us...' (16). God is close and active, we can and do envisage this close activity; it is as close to the truth as we can get to talk of things in this way—and this is so, even though God himself still escapes us.

Philo returns to the theme of our possible awareness of God towards the end of the treatise, and re-emphasizes the same point. When Scripture talks of 'seeing' God it means being aware of the divine activity, the powers—and at the same time being aware that God in himself is not being apprehended. 'When we say that the one who is is seen, we are not using language accurately, but are in a figure of speech transferring the reference to each of the powers respectively' (*Poster. C.*166-68). We may compare 'The soul who honours the one who is with him, the one who is, ought to honour him alone in view, not irrationally or ignorantly, but with knowledge and reason. And our reasoning about him recognises (ἐπιδέχεται) partition and division into each of the divine powers and excellencies' (*Spec. Leg.* 1.209).

It would then not be appropriate to attempt to survey all the many (and varied) accounts in Philo's extant writings of Word, Powers, Wisdom, and so forth. Perhaps one more passage may suffice for the present purpose. At *Somn.* 1.228, where he begins to deal with Gen. 31.13, 'I am the God who appeared to you in the place of God' (see above),

---

13. In the SNTS Philo Seminar, Dublin, 1989, *Poster. C.* 14 and *Vit. Mos.* 1.158 were considered at length. Is Philo hinting at an identification of Moses with the Logos as the world of undifferentiated ideas, Moses as the 'incarnation' so to speak of the Philonic Logos? Perhaps 'assimilated into' would be more apt. It is an intriguing line of thought, but it cannot be further pursued here.

Philo says that Scripture 'gives the title "God" to God's primal Word, not offering a grand title out of any superstitious flattery, but with the clear aim of speaking of things as they are' (ἕν τέλος προτιθειμένος, πραγματαλογῆσαι (230)). No name, not even the name 'God' is appropriate for the one who is and belongs to no genus; but it is fully appropriate to apply it to God's Word.

It is here that Philo goes on to talk of God making himself like angels (ἐν σώματι ἀγγέλοις εἰκαζόμενον), so that we may have a way of envisaging his presence (232). Angels are ideas (*Somn.* 142, 147) and ideas really exist, for Philo (*Spec. Leg.* 1.327-28). The language he uses he takes to be true to the realities we do perceive, true to beings which truly 'are'. We can know these realities, from Scripture interpreted and from experience and from Platonic and other reflection. Yet this knowledge of divine realities affords us no knowledge of the one who really is (τὸ ὄντως ὄν). Time and again Philo insists no one, not even Moses, has such knowledge. And that means that the knowledge we have is not in fact knowledge of what is really real. It is only true to our perceptions of reality, but not true to reality as such.

We may well assume that for Philo there is a coherent and rational relationship known to God between God as Cause and all that we perceive. God is cause of all and knows and understands all (*Deus Imm.* 28-32). But there is no way in which we can trace that relationship back towards God, from effects to rationally entailed Cause, not even from our valid perceptions of his Word or his (other) powers. There is no possible effective analogical move from the entirely genuine knowledge we may have of our perceptions of other existent realities to the unknown ultimate reality of the one who is. 'To God alone is it permitted to know God' (*Praem. Poen.* 40). There is an asymmetry between God's total knowledge and our partial knowledge, even though ours genuinely is knowledge of what we perceive.

The conclusion is the exact opposite of that urged by Dunn. Rather than what is said of the Word being true of what we know of God while untrue of the Word (where 'Word' is only metaphor), Philo would seem to be insisting that what we say of the Word is true of the Word—but untrue of God, of whom we know nothing save that he 'is'. There is an asymmetry between our knowledge of reality and God's knowledge of reality. It points to an asymmetry in 'being', in 'existence'. It is to Philo's understanding of 'existence', and to possible asymmetries in existence as he understands it that we must now turn.

4. *An Asymmetry in Being?*

The quotation from *De legatione* 118 with which this paper begins does certainly, in its own immediate context, suggest something which might usefully be termed 'an asymmetry of being'; 'it would be easier for God to become human, even, than for a human to become God'.[14] This could be an off-the-cuff rhetorical aside. But it turns out to have been carefully prepared for (114) by a discussion using technical terms important to Philo elsewhere: φύσις, προαίρησις, οὐσία. And the assertion does not stand alone; much the same is said briefly at *Somn.* 2.130, and at a little greater length at *Mut. Nom.* 181. So *De legatione* 118 is probably best taken as in fact expressing an illuminating entailment of a consistent strand in Philo's thought. We may well be justified in taking it that there is an asymmetry in his understanding of how things are. I shall now try to provide further support for this provisional conclusion.

Only God truly exists. It is to make this point that Moses is ordered, 'First tell the people that I am the one who is, so they may learn the difference between what is and what is not, and the further corollary that [therefore] no name may properly be applied to me to whom alone existence belongs' (*Vit. Mos.* 1.75; cf. *Det. Pot. Ins.* 160). This sole true existence is simple, undifferentiated, in contrast with all that is multiple, constituted by its relatedness (*Cher.* 114); and is in total opposition to the imprecision of disorder (*Poster. C.* 26-31; *Gig.* 48).[15]

Bringing non-being into being is a matter of bringing order out of chaos: the more orderly and unified, the nearer the result is to God's true existence. 'As the one who alone truly is he is undoubtedly the maker, bringing into being what was not' (τὰ μὴ ὄντα ἤγαγεν εἰς τὸ εἶναι, *Vit. Mos.* 2.100; cf. 2.267). 'He called the non-existent into being: order out of disorder, distinctiveness out of indifference, similarity out of confusion, identity out of heterogeneity, shared harmony out of disjunction and discord, equality from inequality, light from darkness' (*Spec. Leg.* 4.187; *Somn.* 2.45). Philo retains the Platonic concept of the

---

14. That some ancient Greek thought could work with the notion of 'degrees of being' is obvious enough; cf. D. Morrison, adding Aristotelian instances to the common Platonic ones, in his 'Evidence for Degrees of Being in Aristotle', *CQ* 37 (1987), pp. 382-401.

15. Cf. Plutarch, *De animae procreatione* 1024A-C. On the undifferentiated true being of deity, *De communibus notitiis* 1085B-C; and cf. Winston, *Logos*, p. 15.

'non-existent' ὕλη as 'formless raw material' for creation as organization (*Spec. Leg*. 1.329), accepting the conventional axiom that nothing
could come from 'pure' unbeing, 'ex nihilo nihil' (cf. *Spec. Leg* 1.266;
Aet. Mund. 5).[16] God's primacy in all this is safeguarded by taking him
to be the originator of the ideas (*Op. Mund*. 10; *Leg. All*. 1.22, even
more emphatically). God is not simply an artificer (δημιουργός) putting
independent ideas into practice, as it were, but their creator (κτίστης,
Somn. 1.76).[17] But this is also in some measure to give this formless
matter a share in 'his own excellent nature' (*Op. Mund*. 21-22; *Cher*.
86; cf. *Fug*. 112, of the Word). The 'non-existent' seems then to be
totally undifferentiated (ἄποιος, *Leg. All*. 1.36; *Spec. Leg*. 1.48, etc.) In
between come various kinds of order, and so of existence, 'real' compared with total chaos, 'unreal' compared with the inexpressible unity
of God.[18] Closest to the reality of God are the ideas which he formed.
Ideas subsist in God's mind, and so are 'real' (*Leg. All*. 1.22; *Spec. Leg*.
1.327). They are created first, as incorporeal. Then follow the sense-
perceptible objects for which they are the models (*Op. Mund*. 16, 130;
Quaest. in Gen. 1.19; *Leg. All*. 1.22-23; *Somn*. 1.186-88). Through these
alone can the ideas be approached (*Poster. C*. 18-20).

The real existence of the ideas themselves Philo asserts most emphatically:

> Some maintain that the 'incorporeal ideas' exist in name [only], in a name
> with no basis in fact, so doing away with the most necessary and basic
> reality of everything there is, the archetypal patterns...the holy tables of
> the law refer to such persons as 'crushed'. Anything crushed has lost its
> qualities and its form, and can quite accurately be said to be nothing but
> formless matter; and in the same way, the argument that does away with
> the ideas confuses everything and reduces it to the undifferentiated and
> formless state it was in before any order was imposed (*Spec. Leg*. 1.327-
> 28).[19]

---

16. Cf. Plutarch, *De animae procreatione* 1014C; and Runia, *Philo*, pp. 105-
106; 140-48, with reference to Plato, and further, Plutarch again, 550D, 1016C-D;
Winston, *Logos*, p. 48.

17. Plutarch, *De animae procreatione* 1014B; *De communibus* 1073DE.

18. Cf. Plutarch, *De communibus* 1085BC, again; and Morrison, 'Evidence'.

19. Cf. Plutarch, *De communibus* 1073D-1074D: 'To hold that what is true is
not existent and does not subsist but that what is apprehended and apprehensible
and credible has no part in the reality of what exists (τῆω οὐσίας τοῦ ὄντος)—how
can there be any absurdity unsurpassed by this?' (1074D).

Human minds are 'breathed into' by God, 'stamped' with an impress of God himself, 'inseparable portions of the divine and blessed soul' [sc., of God] (*Det. Pot. Ins.* 86-90; cf. *Op. Mund.* 77, 135; *Leg. All.* 1.36; 3.161). Only so can it be that they are able to escape for a while from their bodies and contemplate the underlying realities represented in the sense-perceptible universe. And because they are thus 'stamped' or 'inbreathed' they may indeed come to an awareness of the fact (though not the manner) of divine reality (e.g. *Op. Mund.* 143-44; *Plant.* 18-22; *Fug.*91-92; *Ebr.* 99). After death they may even gain unmediated awareness of that reality (*Cher.* 115; *Migr. Abr.* 174-75, as above; *Fug.* 100-104).[20] The way we are thus constituted means that our best ideas of divine organization are God-given and orderly, and correspond to the divine impress or image, to the reality created and guaranteed by God. Yet even the best of these distinct ideas are 'less real' than God, for they are themselves differentiated, and make merely relative order out of physical pluriformity. As such they are complex, 'mixed' (*Deus Imm.* 77), in contrast with the undifferentiated simple being of God. Compared with physical pluriformity itself they are nonetheless highly organized and rational, and as such 'exist' more objectively than we do. Closer to the divine originating reality than we are ourselves, sharing more fully in that reality, they are 'more real' than we are (*Cher.* 51; *Gig.* 61; *Migr. Abr.* 193).

If 'the one who is' is of his sheer goodness to share existence, to create other beings by shaping formless matter, he can only do so by first forming effective, powerful, creative ideas (powerful and creative in their own subordinate right) which are other than himself and necessarily less than himself in his undifferentiated unity, though still in some sense contained within himself (e.g., *Op. Mund.* 15-25; *Spec. Leg.* 1.329; *Deus Imm.* 77-80; *Mut. Nom.* 27-28). As distinct ideas they are 'less real' than God, who, as we have emphasized, alone truly 'is'; but as his creative and effective ideas, his powers, they are, of course 'more real' than what they form.[21] So Philo can write of God as the 'most

20. Dey, *Intermediary World*, pp. 44-46, writes as though for Philo the progress to perfect awareness was possible in this physical existence, whereas it seems that the requisite shedding of the physical before death was achieved only by Moses (see above, n. 14, on *Poster. C.* 14, etc., and Runia, 'God and Man', pp. 69-71.

21. As a possible illustration from a later Platonist, Origen's *De principiis* 1.2.6 appears in Jerome's *Letter* 124.2 as: *filium, qui sit imago invisibilis patris, conparatum patri non esse veritatem; apud nos, autem, qui dei omnipotentis non possumus*

generic' (himself of no genus, but the supreme source of all generic orderly differentiation 'into existence') 'and next to him, God's Word, with everything else existing in word only, and some things so ineffectual as barely to exist at all' (or, 'in effect, barely existing at all', τὰ δ'ἄλλα λόγῳ μόνον ὑπάρχει, ἔργοις δὲ ἐστιν οὗ ἴσα τῳ οὐχ ὑπάρχοντι, *Leg. All* 2.86; cf. *Deus Imm.*77; *Abr.* 119-23).

If this is an appropriate characterization of Philo's thought, we would expect him at times to stress the 'objective reality' of the divine forms, agencies and powers suggested to him by Scripture and other Jewish tradition (with some prompting from Plato and from the Stoics); and at times to stress their comparative 'unreality': their reality in our appraisal of their effects in their impact on our minds, their unreality compared with an abstract definition of unitary divine being. And we might also expect the scriptural context of a meditation to have some part in determining which line Philo takes. Dunn looks for 'vigorous metaphorical style' (p. 220), personifications that are to be taken as our own creative figures of speech. Philo's ontology leads him to expect divinely created and effective ideas 'more real' than we are who receive them and are informed by them. We have certainly found some of them on occasion in Philo characterized as 'unreal'; but that is only in comparison with God, not because they are 'only ideas'. As God's ideas they enjoy a very high level of existence indeed, for Philo.[22]

---

recipere veritatem, imaginariam veritatem videri ('The Son, who is the image of the invisible Father, compared with the Father is not the truth; but for us, who cannot receive the truth of God the all powerful, he is to be seen as imaginary truth.'). Rufinus' text offers a less striking contrast: *quantum ad ipsum quidem patrem veritas, quantum autem ad nos...imago est* ('In relation to the Father himself [our Saviour] is the truth; in so far as he relates to us, he is the image.'); cf. H. Görgemanns and H. Karpp (eds.), *Origines: von den Prinzipen* (Darmstadt: Wissenschaftliche Buchgesellschaft, 1976), p. 136; and compare, further, R. Mortley, *From Word to Silence*, II, pp. 100-104, on Proclus.

22. Runia, *Philo*, p. 450: 'When the Logos is regarded as "the embodiment" of God's thought focussed on the cosmos...the difference between God and his Logos appears to be kept to a minimum, perhaps a matter of aspect rather than level... But when the immanent presence of the Logos is stressed...the Logos has to all appearances become a *hypostasis*, a level of God's being given real existence outside God himself.' This retains something of the tensions in Philo's thought; my formulation is designed to do more justice still to Philo. But compare also Winston, *Logos*, pp. 49-50.

5. *Dunn and Philo and the New Testament*

We round off the discussion with a consideration of some of the passages which Dunn lists (pp. 220-28),[23] and where he allows that 'on the face of it there would appear to be little room for dispute regarding our question: Philo quite often speaks of the Logos as though a real being quite distinct from God, who acts as an intermediary between God and the world'. Is Dunn's preferred explanation of this in terms of 'vigorous metaphorical style', or is 'divinely created and effective ideas more real than we' the better characterization for what we find when we look below the surface of Philo's discussion?

At *Rer. Div. Her.* 205, the first of Dunn's passages, Philo writes:

> To his Word, his chief messenger (archangel), highest in age and honour, the Father of all has given the special prerogative, to stand on the border and separate the creature and the Creator. This same Word both pleads with the immortal as suppliant for afflicted mortality and acts as ambassador of the ruler to the subject.

The context in Philo is a discussion of 'dividing'. Philo uses Genesis 15.10 as a springboard for a lengthy disquisition, adducing a variety of other texts of Scripture that involve 'division'. He comes finally to the cloud which divides the Egyptians from the Israelites, but which also suggests Moses (as effective symbol of the Word of God) who 'stood between' (Deut. 5.5), as indeed the cloud also did between God and the people. Taken literally, all the passages that Philo draws on here stress the objectivity of the phenomena experienced. Allegorized they indicate the human experience of being drawn to God by our inspired reflections and of being overwhelmed by their objective cogency, their power, while at the same time they still keep us separate from God as he really is. So, though the reality of God is always other, 'divinely created and effective ideas' seem nearer the mark than 'lively metaphorical style'.

Philo can also talk of the Word as 'interpreter and spokesman [prophet] of God' (*Deus Imm.* 138, the fourth of Dunn's passages). The section begins with Gen. 6.1, 'the earth was corrupt before the Lord, and filled with iniquity', and Philo is drawn to reflect on human experience of being mastered instead by (good) conviction, as objective as the onset of leprosy. This good conviction that we experience as entering

---

23. In this and what follows I retain with Dunn the LCL translation. The first four of his examples are taken from Dey, *Intermediary World.*

us from outside is the divine Word, before whom we passively 'conceive', the matter as little in our own hands as was the inspiration of a prophet in Scripture. The stress is again on the reality of what comes to us in such experience. To suggest that all this was for Philo simply our metaphorical imagining would be to misinterpret what he wrote.

The Word is also 'ruler and steersman of all' (*Cher.* 36, Dunn's fifth example). Philo has been asking what the tale of the cherubim with flaming sword should be taken as signifying. Again, a picture presented in Scripture as objective suggests reflections on experiences that come to us, rather than inventions of our own. A little earlier Philo has recounted some particularly vivid thoughts:

> But there is a higher thought than these. It comes from a voice in my own soul which oftentimes is god-possessed and divines where [what?] it does not know…This voice told me that while God is indeed one, his highest and chief powers are two, even Goodness and Sovereignty. Through his goodness he begat all that is, through his Sovereignty he rules what he has begotten. And in the midst, between the two there is a third which unites them, the Word; for it is through his rational Word that God is both ruler and good (*Cher.* 27-28; cf. *Sacr.* 119).

'Ruler' and 'steersman' are metaphors created by us, though Philo finds them very appropriate. What they refer to, the Word through whom God rules, is a reality given and guaranteed by God.

Dunn quotes further, as his seventh example,

> This hallowed flock [the heavenly bodies] he leads in accordance with right and law, setting over it his true Word and firstborn Son, who shall take upon him its government like some viceroy of a great king (*Agr.* 51).

Noah's work as a planter has suggested other land-workers, among them shepherds and cattlemen; the latter then indicate to Philo our vices, the former the experience of self-control, leading to reason and virtue (e.g. 44). For this shepherding the disciplined regularity of the physical universe is the most impresssive and obvious enacted example, encouraging us to accept God's own shepherding of our souls (53). 'Shepherding' and 'flock' are clearly metaphors. The Word is no more metaphor for Philo than are the sun, moon and planets.

Another sequence chosen by Dunn, his eighth, refers to 'God's first-born, the Word, who holds the eldership among the angels, their ruler, as it were…' (*Conf. Ling.* 146). It comes in a passage where Philo is contrasting man-made polytheism (exemplified by the Tower of Babel) with the objective, given knowledge of (the existence of) the One God, whose acceptance makes us instead 'sons of God'. Especially in the light of the stated contrast we would expect a realistic treatment of that to which our 'knowledge' corresponds. In fact Philo continues, 'If we have not yet become fit to be thought sons of God, yet we may be sons of his invisible image, the most holy Word' (*Conf. Ling.* 147). The Word is the real object of our awareness, really shaping our minds for an awareness of God—and as really reminding us that God himself is beyond our comprehension. Of him, as so often insisted, we can only know that he is.[24]

In these contexts the Word and other 'powers' impress themselves on us as very real (to repeat, 'more real' than we are). In other settings, as we have already seen, Philo insists that God alone exists in the truest sense (or perhaps God's Word does, too, in some strong sense). The scriptural contexts of these latter passages deploy anthropomorphisms which present Philo with an apologetic problem. They lead him to stress the precise opposite, with the help of his tag, 'God is not as human is.' Scripture's vivid 'metaphorical' language makes Philo most aware of its inadequacy. That metaphorical language is a concession to our weakness. Talk of God's Word and God's powers is other than such concessionary metaphor.[25] The conclusions argued by Dunn among others seem now widely off target. The Logos is real because it/he is less

---

24. The relation of Philo's original of the passages from *Quaest. in Gen.* and *Quaest. in Exod.* included by Dunn are too unsure for us to build much on them, and warrant only a brief footnote. *Quaest. in Exod.* 2.13, the Word as judge, mediator, angel (p. 220), is explictly linked to the exigencies of sense-experience in the context, as is the next passage cited, 2.94, on the Word as veil but also as that which enables our seeing. *Quaest. in Gen.* 2.62, the last of Dunn's nine passages (p. 221), expresses very clearly (though some of its language is unparalleled elsewhere in Philo) Philo's conviction that there is available to us a God-given reality, truer to God than anything else, and therefore 'real'—though still not adequate to the truth of the one who is, 'existing in the best and special form': 'the second God who is his Word'. Dunn also chooses (p. 221) from *Sacr.* 119 'It is reason (λόγος, Word) which has taken refuge with God.' But in fact here Philo is talking about reason as it is experienced in ourselves, 'the sovereign part of the soul;' and though that is continuous in some way with divine Reason, the passage is not directly relevant to this discussion.

25. So, too, for example, compare *Deus Imm.* 55 with 51 in context; *Fug.* 164-65 with 162; *Mut. Nom.* 7-10 with 1; *Poster. C.* 14 with 1-9. Cf. also A. Segal, *Two Powers in Heaven* (Leiden: E.J. Brill, 1977), p. 161.

distinct from God than any other reality of which we can conceive. But because our conception of the Logos (itself God-given) does match in some measure (because God-given) the reality of the Logos, the Logos must be conceptually distinguishable from God, for us to be capable of conceiving of him at all. Thus the Word is both distinguishable from God and real, certainly more real than any metaphorical imaginings of our own, for he/it is more real than we are ourselves.

Dunn argues that it is only at the end of the first century CE that the idea of 'pre-existent' divine figures became available (p. 260). But if Philo is taken as a clue to possible early Christian speculation, he must also be allowed to encourage us to suppose that some people at the time, Jews among them, would have been readily convinced of the possibility of a real transcendent figure (or figures) as a link between themselves and God; and so, much readier for a 'pre-existent' Christ than Dunn allows. (At the same time they would most likely be much more agnostic about all theological language than are Dunn and many contemporaries in this ingenuously kataphatic age, with its ready talk of 'knowing God' and of 'God's self-revelation'.)[26]

Whether Paul and the members of his congregations in particular are to be thought likely to have moved in such intellectual circles cannot be argued here. We simply point again to the fact that Philo is widely cited to establish some of the parameters for our understanding of early Christian thinking. He may of course represent only some esoteric Alexandrian Jewish thinking. Yet it is worth noting that Paul does seem to use quite naturally and without explanation some of the common presuppositions of this theology (the 'prepositional metaphysics', the phrase τὰ μὴ ὄντα, the discounting of our present knowledge, along with other items of popular philosophy, Stoic and Cynic.[27]

It seems very important to Dunn to be able to argue that the early Christians did not simply pick up from the culture around them ideas of

---

26. 'Kataphatus' is the contrary of 'apophatic' where apophatic theology emphasizes the incomprehensibility of God (as more than we can get our minds round). On which see Downing, *Has Christianity a Revelation?*; 'Revelation, Disagreement and Obscurity', pp. 219-30; and the final chapter, below.

27. 'Propositional metaphysics': Rom. 11.36; 1 Cor. 8.6; cf. Eph. 4.6; Heb. 2.10; τὰ μὴ ὄντα, Rom. 4.17; 1 Cor 1.28; cf. Heb. 11.3; discounting present knowledge: 1 Cor. 8.1-3; 13.12. See also Malherbe, *Paul and the Popular Philosophers*. Since this was first written I have explored much more popular philosophy in Paul: Downing, *Cynics, Paul and the Pauline Churches*.

transcendent figures linking humanity and God, but developed them for themselves (pp. 258-61). 'Christian faith...may have to be credited with much more or most of the stimulus which resulted in this new break-through in religious thought' (p. 261). A closer study of Philo suggests that there was in some quarters already a body of careful reflection along these lines, whether or not it was known in any form to Paul, or 'John' or the author to Hebrews.[28]

The 'apophatic' tradition of 'negative theology' in Philo, where God is acknowledged as 'incomprehensible' can have an appeal today,[29] whereas speculative metaphysics in Philo may well be for many a foreign country, just as the practice of magic may well be another, distancing us from the first century; save that ancient credulity and ancient scepticism perhaps find more resonances today than may the urbane cerebrations of the great Philo. It is attitudes to magic in the Mediterranean world of late antiquity that we now attempt to discern.

28. Even the extent to which the early Christians were distinctive in addressing prayer to a second transcendent figure, as argued by Hurtado, *One God*, remains debatable. Although his book has the commendation of A. Segal on its cover (first edition), one needs to note Segal's own *Two Powers*, Ch. 6, on 'Mishnaic Prohibitions against Unorthodox Prayer'. I also note in Philo *Somn.* 1.163-64, where Philo clearly takes the LXX εὐχή, εὔχομαι as 'prayer', addressed to the Word; and compare *Abr.* 127, in the light of what precedes it (God accepts approaches to himself made in terms of (mistaken) address to his shadowy Powers; and, with this, *Quaest. in Gen.* 4.8; and, negatively, e.g., *Gig.* 54 (worship truly directed to the Existent is very rare indeed). Williamson, *Philo*, p. 116, notes that at *Somn.* 1.164, Philo seems to address Moses in prayer; but this may rather be rhetorical apostrophe. I would firmly agree with Hurtado, following conversation, that we have no record of Jewish *liturgical* prayer addressed to other than God. The niceties of Philo's philosophical reinterpretations of practice have no direct bearing on that practice itself.

29. See, e.g., J. Derrida, *Sauf le nom* (Paris: Galilée, 1993); and Ch. 13, below.

Chapter 11

MAGIC AND SCEPTICISM IN AND AROUND
THE FIRST CHRISTIAN CENTURY*

We are told on all sides that a belief in magic was widespread in the
early Christian centuries; for while much of the illustrative material
cited—the 'magical papyri'—is dated to the fourth and fifth centuries,
there are frequent references from earlier years to the use of magic as
conventionally defined. Problems of definition are discussed. Borrow-
ing a device from Bertrand Russell, we might explain, 'I serve divine
powers, you try to persuade them, he attempts to manipulate them.'[1] Or
we might say, 'what you see as magical ritual I see as a devout sacra-
ment', and echoes of Protestant–Catholic polemics are noted. But a
polemical use of the terms is not new—some practices categorized as
'magical' were banned under ancient Roman law.[2] And rites that seek
some defined benefit and are new, or imported, or both, may be seen as
magical.[3]

---

*   This piece is also to appear in *Magic and the New Testament World* (ed.
T. Klutz; JSNTSup; Sheffield: Sheffield Academic Press, forthcoming), and appears
here with the kind permission of both the volume and the series editors.

1.   Already in Pliny the Elder, for instance: 'aliquid immensum exspectans ac
dignum deo movendo, immo vero quod numini imperet' ('on the look-out for
something impressive, fit to persuade a God—or, rather, to command one's deity'),
Hist. nat. 28.4.20; cf. J. Thérasse, 'Croyances et crédulité des Romains d'àprès
Pline l'Ancien et les écrivains latins', in J.-B. Caron, M. Fortin, G. Maloney (eds.),
Mélanges d'études anciennes offerts à Maurice Lebel (Québec: Editions du Sphinx,
1980), pp. 283-319 (292 and n. 41), with references to Lucan and Apuleius.

2.   Pliny the Elder, *Hist. nat.* 28.4.18.

3.   Sources consulted: D.E. Aune, 'Magic in Early Christianity', *ANRW* 2.23.2,
pp. 1505-23; and *idem*, 'The Apocalypse of John and Graeco-Roman Regulatory
Magic', *NTS* 33.4 (1987), pp. 481-501; J. H. Elliott, *Social Scientific Criticism of
the New Testament* (London: SPCK, 1995); A. Ernout, 'La magie chez Pline
l'Ancien', in M. Renard and R. Schilling (eds.), *Hommages à Jean Bayet* (Brussels:

An in-depth discussion of 'belief' in magic is harder to come by. In fact I do not think I have met with one. The tacit assumption seems to be, if the practice was as widespread as it seems to have been, people—lots of them, most of them—must have believed it. But the quality of such belief—or of suspension of disbelief—is not assessed. It is not gauged in general, still less in relation to particular kinds of magical practices.

You see, there is a problem. We seem to know of only one person in the ancient Mediterranean world who became seriously wealthy by sell-ing his magical services, and that is the second century Alexander of Abonoteichos, and that only as recounted by Lucian of Samosata (though we have wider evidence of a later cult of Alexander); yet Alexander specialized in just one branch, that of oracular magic. He seems to have had no seriously wealthy competitors, and had been able to corner the top end of the market for quite a while, without any effec-tive competition. Physicians may have regularly included among their remedies what we might designate as 'magic' (or what today's physi-cians might call 'placebos' or 'alternative medicines'), though Lucian, for instance, takes it for granted that a physician would despise any such resort.[4] Some physicians became very wealthy, but specifically as physicians in the guild. Pliny the Elder, who complains bitterly about the wealth of some physicians, nonetheless makes the distinction quite clear.[5] Luke tells us of a magus-chaplain to Sergius Paulus, proconsul

Latomus, 1967), pp. 191-95; E. Ferguson, *Backgrounds of Early Christianity* (Grand Rapids: Eerdmans, 1987; F. Graf, *La magie dans l'antiquité gréco-romaine* (Paris: Les Belles Lettres, 1994); J.M. Hull, *Hellenistic Magic and the Synoptic Tradition* (SBT 2; London: SCM Press, 1974); H.C. Kee, *Medicine, Miracle and Magic in New Testament Times* (SNTSMS, 55; Cambridge: Cambridge University Press, 1986) and *idem*, *The Origins of Christianity: Sources and Documents* (London: SPCK, 1973); R. MacMullen, *Paganism in the Roman Empire* (New Haven: Yale University Press, 1981); S.J. Scherrer, 'Signs and Wonders in the Imperial Cult: A New Look at a Roman Institution in the Light of Revelation 13:13-15', *JBL* 103.4 (1984), pp. 599-610; Thérasse, 'Croyances et crédulité', pp. 283-319; M. Whittaker, *Jews and Christians: Graeco-Roman Views* (CMWJC 6; Cambridge, Cambridge University Press, 1984); B. Wildhaber, *Paganisme populaire et prédication apos-tolique* (Geneva: Labor et Fides, 1987), pp. 17-18, 77, with references to E.R. Dodds, A.D. Nock and F. Cumont.

    4.   Lucian, *The Lover of Lies* (*Philopseudes*) 8.
    5.   Pliny the Elder, *Natural History* lists seven by name, *Hist. nat.* 29.5.7-10; cf. V. Nutton, 'The Perils of Patriotism: Pliny and Roman Medicine', in R. French

of Cyprus, and the destruction of valuable magical texts in Ephesus; as well as a nice little earner in oracular magic in Philippi. But no one seems to have made really large sums of money out of warding off the evil eye,[6] or from love potions, or spells, not so as to have been picked out by contemporaries for admiration or for ridicule. In other words, no one was particularly convincing—which might seem to indicate that not many were in fact totally or even more than marginally convinced.[7] (There would be little point legislating against magical practices if you believed they had reliable and effective power.)

It would presumably go without saying that no one in the ancient world succeeded in transmuting base metal into gold, or in producing palaces and plenty out of thin air. Celsus (mid-second century) compares the feedings and other miracles ascribed to Jesus with:

> The accomplishments of those who are taught by the Egyptians, who for a few obols make known their sacred lore in the middle of the market place and drive demons out of men and blow away diseases and invoke the souls of heros, displaying expensive banquets and dining tables and cakes and dishes which are non-existent, and who make things move as they were alive although they are not really so, but only appear as such in the imagination.[8]

But clearly (as Celsus notes) these hucksters were not in a sellers' market.

There are, of course, two possible explanations. Perhaps there was too much DIY; everyone was at it, granny, grandad, uncle Dionysius, aunty Artemisia, the lot. And if almost anyone could do it, anyone could set up as a professional for those not on the grapevine, and there would be an over-supply. But the conclusion would still seem clear, that none of

---

and F. Greenaway (eds.), *Science in the Early Roman Empire: Pliny the Elder, his Sources and Influence* (London: Croom Helm, 1986), pp. 30-58 (35). Not all physicians became rich; a number did, but only one magician is said to have done so.

6.   On the 'evil eye' see various pieces by J.H. Elliott, 'The Fear of the Leer', *Forum* 4 (1988), pp. 42-71; *idem*, 'Paul, Galatians, and the Evil Eye', *CurTM* 17 (1990), pp. 262-73; *idem*, 'Matthew 20.1-15: A Parable of Invidious Comparison and Evil Eye Accusation', *BTB* 22 (1992), pp. 52-65.

7.   On the low economic status of practitioners see, eg., Philo, *Spec. Leg.* 100-101 (allowing for the intellectual's snobbishness), 'charlatan beggars and parasites and the basest of the female and slave population', Colson and Whittaker (trans.), *Philo* (LCL).

8.   Origen, *Contra Celsum* 1.68; cf., again, Lucian, *Lover of Lies* 15.

this magic was so convincing as to drive out all competitors or render the professionals—or rival professionals—totally redundant.

Let us return to oracular magic. According to Lucian, Alexander did persuade a lot of people, including quite eminent and supposedly educated ones, and that might seem to make this kind of magical operation a distinct case, one where fewer people had the confidence to practise, but where a competent professional could convince (albeit by trickery). It is precisely this practice which attracts most educated discussion— but also most argued disbelief. And Plutarch notes that the traditional sources of oracles are far from flourishing in his day.[9] It does seem that questions of degrees and kinds of conviction warrant some attention.

Pliny the Elder is clearly an important witness. He is totally unpersuaded by astrology, in fact sure that it has been convincingly disproved. He is as dismissive of oracles, and of physicians and any supposed cure other than simple traditional Roman ones. 'Hence the gloomy inscription on monuments, "Killed by the crowd of physicians"'. Of magic he says, 'it is a detestable thing in itself. Frivolous and lying as it is, it still bears, however, some shadow of truth upon it, though reflected in reality by the practice of those who study the secret arts of poisoning, and not by the pursuit of magic.'[10] Yet Howard Kee, who cites that passage, then goes on to note (as do many others),

> if we take Pliny at his word on the matter of his reasons for having written the voluminous *Natural History*, we must assume that in practice his attitude was not so negative towards magic as the above-announced principle would imply...although his compendium includes 'foreign things and even outlandish customs', [he has] 'striven to find views most universally believed'. If we take him at his word, then his inclusion of what might appear to modern—or even ancient—readers to be bizarre remedies, especially those attributed by him to the Magi, was for the purpose of useful instruction, not merely for the titillation of his readers... He remarks concerning the power of rituals and incantations, 'As individuals...all our wisest men reject belief in them, although, as a body the public at all time believes in them unconsciously.'[11]

9. Plutarch, *Moralia: On the Obsolescence of Oracles*, esp. 411E-412B; but also his note of common uncertainties, *The Oracles at Delphi*, 407C, 408D; cf. Cicero, *De divinatione* 1.37, but also Dionysius of Halicarnassus, *Roman Antiquities* 8.37.3.

10. Pliny the Elder, *Hist. nat.* 2.54; 7.178; 29.1-2; citing 29.11 and 30.6, LCL.

11. H.C. Kee, *Medicine, Miracle and Magic*, p. 162, citing Pliny the Elder, *Hist. nat.* 28.1 and 3.

When Pliny writes 'they say' it is simply, opines Kee, a let-out to avoid accepting responsibility for what he is unable to dismiss.

I suggest, rather, it is important to note what Pliny himself says elsewhere:

> Whoever believed in the Ethiopians before actually seeing them? Or what is not deemed miraculous when we first have knowedge of it? How many things are judged impossible before they actually occur? Indeed, the powers and majesty of the nature of the universe at every turn lack credibility if one's mind considers only the parts and not the entirety.[12]

Pliny is heir to (or had adopted) an empiricist tradition that takes experience and reported experience very seriously, at least until some persuasive argument has shown it mistaken, or at least to be without adequate warrant for generalization and practice. It is the attitude expressed by Shakespeare's Hamlet,

> There are more things in heaven and earth, Horatio,
> Than are dreamt of in [y]our philosophy,[13]

a couplet much quoted today in connection with ley-lines and crop circles and the like.

I have myself argued elsewhere for the wider relevance of ancient highbrow debates for our understanding of the attitudes of ordinary people—the highly educated spoke in public, to persuade the public; and at home they were among servants.[14] It is worth now considering in a little detail philosophical dogmatism, skepticism, doubts and certainties, and ways of testing or establishing them.

We commence with oracular magic, the kind of which we have noted that it was possible, in the second century at least, for one man at any rate to gain sufficient credence to become wealthy. Oracles were accepted by middle Platonists such as Plutarch, though he is well aware that many dismiss them, and their validity has to be argued with care. Stoics also accepted them, as entailed by their belief in divine provi-

---

12. Pliny the Elder, *Hist. nat.* 7.6 (Rackham [trans.], LCL); cf. Ernout, 'La magie', pp. 192-93; and Beacon, *Roman Nature*, pp. 9-11, citing *Hist. nat.* 11.6 (Rackham [trans.], LCL) 'the more I observe nature, the less prone I am to consider any statement about her to be impossible.'

13. *Hamlet*, I.v.166.

14. Downing, 'A bas les aristos', pp. 212-30, repr. in Downing, *Doing Things with Words*.

dence. 'They defended nearly every sort of divination.'[15] The foreordained could in principle be foreknown and so foretold by divine beings who had the foreknowledge; although Stoics, too, had to admit that oracles could be and often were mistaken.[16] Epicureans rejected any idea of divine providence or any other form of determinism. All was a matter of chance, the way the atoms fell and randomly swerved. Foreknowledge was therefore impossible.[17] Epicurus was singled out for attack by Alexander, and Epicureans and Christians were to be excluded from Alexander's meetings, as 'atheists', disbelievers in the Apollo who inspired him.[18]

One of the most elaborate arguments against oracles and divination of any kind is preserved for us in the second book of Cicero's *De divinatione*, depending on the thought of the second leader of the 'New Academy', Carneades. His was a critical empiricism, as opposed to that of the Stoics and even to that of Epicurus, and to that we return in a moment. Cicero from Carneades asks, ironically, for differences between philosophical schools to be persuasively settled by divination. He asks, what is the point of foreknowledge if all is predetermined, anyway? He asks, if foretelling is based on determinate causality (as the Stoics averred), what are the actual regular causal links between kinds of augural events and the happenings they point to? and on this basis dissects the very different methods employed—and results forthcoming. He quotes Cato, 'A soothsayer doesn't laugh when he sees another soothsayer.' And he cites the many disasters that were known to have struck people devoutly guided by various foretellings—and the successes of those who deliberately refused to ask for or accept them. And how can horoscopes cope with twins, or with people born at the same time in different parts of the world under different configurations of stars and planets? This latter is presumably the kind of argument whose conclusion we have seen Pliny the Elder applaud. As he says elsewhere, 'Life is full of these prophecies, but they are not worth collecting; more often than not they are false, as we shall now show by example...'[19]

15. Cicero, *De divinatione* 1. 125-28, and 1.6, 10, 82, 110-111.

16. Cicero, *De divinatione* 1.124.

17. Cicero, *De natura deorum* 1.55; Diogenes Laertius 10.76-83; A.A. Long, *Hellenistic Philosophy* (London: Gerald Duckworth, 1974), pp. 44-45.

18. Lucian, *Alexander* 43, 38.

19. Pliny the Elder, *Hist. nat.* 7.178.

I think we may assume that Epicureans would happily deploy some of these arguments from experience. Cynics would also be happy with them. Oenomaus of Gadara wrote his *Imposters Unmasked* against oracles and soothsayers; he says, after finding an oracle he had purchased had been sold to two others and all three recipients had been given different interpretations of it (none of which had worked out). He cites historical episodes where oracles induced war, greed, and lechery.[20] Popular Cynicism opposed any talk of fate, providence or fortune. 'When Diogenes saw interpreters of dreams and diviners and their clients...he thought no animal sillier than humans.' Plutarch has a Cynic (jokingly called Planetiades) raise ethical questions about oracles, in the manner of Oenomaus.[21] Diogenes's treatment of a diviner (*mantes*), as reported in one of the *Cynic Letters*, echoes the logic of the objections attributed to Carneades. ' "Are you a very good diviner or a poor one?" At his answer that he was very good, I brandished my staff. "What, then, am I going to do? Answer! Will I strike you, or not?" He reflected to himself for a moment, and said, "You won't." But strike him I did, with a laugh, while those standing round shouted. I said, "Why did you people cry out? Since he was obviously an inept diviner, he was beaten".'[22] One may also compare Lucian's Demonax: if oracles are true they can't be of any use.[23]

Though it was noted above that Christians and Epicureans were bracketed as opponents for Alexander, I have myself argued (in this volume and in other places) that Christians here as elsewhere themselves were much more likely to have been influenced by popular Cynicism. Among second-century examples cited, Tatian is significant. Repudiating aspects of deliberately offensive Cynicism, his own programme is summarized in very Cynic terms, as is his rejection of Stoic notions of providence and determination from birth; and he pours scorn on pagan

20. Oenomaus of Garada in Eusebius, *Praeparatio evangelii* 5 and 6.

21. Diogenes Laertius 6.24; Plutarch, *Moralia: On the Obsolescence of Oracles*, 413A-D; see, also, Downing, *Cynics and Christian Origins*, pp. 39-42. I note there (n. 60) that Lucian seems to have derived similar arguments from the Cynic Menippus, quite independently of Carneades; a fact noted by D. Amand, *Fatalisme et liberté dans l'antiquité grecque* (Louvain: Bibliothèque de l'Université, 1945), pp. 109-113, though he still thinks Carneades the main source. The origins do not matter for the present argument; their presence in popular Stoicism is what concerns us here.

22. Pseudo-Diogenes 38.2, in Malherbe (ed.), *Cynic Epistles*, p. 161.

23. Lucian, *Demonax* 37; cf. Diogenes Laertius 6.27, 39.

oracles in much the same terms as did the early second century Cynic philosopher Oenomaus—they incite greed, warfare, lechery rather than poverty and self-control, relying as they often did on irrational animals; while all this is pointless if all is fated.[24] Whatever the sources, it is clear that by the second century at least, and most likely from the start, these sceptical attacks on oracular magic were readily available for Christians among others to deploy.

We need now to return to the issue of suspension of judgment. Epicureans were dogmatic common-sense empiricists. They were aware that one's senses could be deceived; but if one had taken due care to check that the atoms thrown off by some object had not been interfered with, then things were as the sounds or sight indicated. Thus, according to Cicero, 'Epicurus considered the sun perhaps a foot in diameter, pronouncing it to be exactly as big as it appears, give or take just a little'.[25] Dreams, visions of the gods, and so forth, are the product of real assemblies of atoms (but not of solid objects like ourselves).[26] This kind of inclusive empiricism must allow for many claimed experiences to be valid until proven not to be; and I would assume that it is along these lines that Pliny the Elder was arguing about our incredulity until we actually encounter what we would automatically doubt. It is experience that tells whether some plant yields health-giving medicine or poison.[27] In other words, Epicurean empiricism encourages an open mind on reported physical results, even where the metaphysical interpretation may well be challenged. Pliny's eclecticism has a perfectly respectable and widely diffused intellectual rationale.

A different kind of suspension of judgment was urged by the founder of the New Academy, Arcesilaus, using the Socratic method of arguing for and against and leaving the issue in the balance.[28] Carneades (to

24. Tatian, *Oration* 9-11 and 19; cf. Downing, *Cynics and Christian Origins*, pp. 187-88, and the whole argument; also *idem, Cynics, Paul and the Pauline Churche*. Stoic providentialism as such is repudiated by the other Apologists: Justin, *Apology* 1.43-44 and 2.7; *Trypho* 102, 141; Theophilus, *Autolycus* 1.14, 2.27; Athenagoras, *Apology* 24; cf. also Hippolytus, *Refutation* 1.19-20 (Epicurus and Pyrrho) and 4.1-27 (astrology unmasked).

25. Cicero, *De finibus* 1.20; *Academica* 2.79-80; Long, *Hellenistic Philosophy*, pp. 21-30.

26. Cicero, *De natura deorum* 1.43-50.

27. Lucretius, *De rerum natura* 6.1225-29; cf. 4.124-25.

28. Cicero, *Academica* 2.99-100; Long, *Hellenistic Philosophy*, pp. 88-94, also discussing Pyrrho and Timon, and the later Sextus Empiricus.

whom we averted earlier), mid-second-century BCE, argued for a more
graduated judgment of probabilities; but there was still no room for the
Stoic conviction that 'the wise man' could be absolutely certain. In the
state of ancient science with its lack of controlled conditions for attempting to falsify claims, still a lot more possibilities must be granted attention. Carneades' 'wise man' 'will make use of whatever probable presentation he encounters, and his whole life-plan will be charted out in
this manner'. He waits to be proved wrong, rather than deciding he
cannot be; and rather than deciding the truth *a priori*.[29]

The Pyrrhonian tradition receives less attention in our period, even
though revived by Aenesideimus, a near contemporary of Cicero's, and
we depend for any account of it largely on the second-century physician
Sextus Empiricus. Pyrrho of Elis is linked in the tradition as received
with the Indian 'naked philosophers' said to have been encountered on
Alexander's expedition (as is the early Cynic Onesicritus). Pyrrho rejects
assent to philosophical dogmatism, but otherwise conforms. Cynics
similarly reject conventional ethical certainties, but also astrological
and other physical speculations.[30]

We need to attempt to discern how far such 'open-mindedness' pre-
vailed in the wider population. Taking it that histories were most often
written for a much wider audience than simply that of other historians,
we may note the frequent tag in Dionysius of Halicarnassus when relating anything that might seem to run counter to common experience, 'let
every listener decide as seems best to him (her)'. This is picked up by
Josephus, when recording such items as the supposed longevity of the
ancients, the crossing of the Red Sea dry-shod, or the cloud of the
divine presence: 'but on these matters let everyone decide as seems best

29. Cicero, *Academica* 2.99, again, and 100-101 (against Anaxagoras, determined that snow, as frozen water, could not look white); cf. *De finibus* 5.42: the
Stoic sage investigates astral phenomena intending to assent, believe, affirm; the
sage of the New Academy 'with the resolve to be afraid of forming rash opinions,
and to deem that it goes well with him if in matters of this kind he has discovered
something that resembles the truth' (Rackham [trans.], *Cicero*, XXI [LCL]).
Whether Cicero is right about Arcesilaus is debated: cf. P. Coussin, 'The Stoicism
of the New Academy', in M. Bunyeat (ed.), *The Sceptical Tradition* (Berkeley:
University of California Press, 1983), pp. 31-63. For my purposes it is sufficient to
note the varieties of scepticism that were current, whatever their precise origins. See
also Long, *Hellenistic Philosophy*, Ch. 3, Scepticism.

30. D. Sedley, 'The Motivations of Greek Scepticism', in M. Bunyeat (ed.), *The
Sceptical Tradition* (Berkeley: University of California Press, 1983), pp. 14-21.

to him (her)'. Lucian of Samosata accepts such a let-out clause as a standard feature in historiography: 'and should any myth come into question, it should be related but not wholly credited: rather, it should be left open for hearers to conjecture about it as they will with you (the author) running no risks, inclining to neither side'.[31]

Despite Pliny's record of popular mistrust of physicians, we find regular references to people using their services with prayer or enchantments simply kept in reserve. In the previous century Cicero had noted, 'When people are sick, we as a general rule do not call in a prophet or a seer, but a physician.'[32] Philo complains (presumably about some fellow Jews),

> They have never had firm faith in God their saviour, so they first flee to the help of things created, to physicians, herbs, drugs, strict rules of diet, and all the other aids that mortals use. And if someone says, 'Flee, you fools, to the one and only physician of soul-sickness and throw away the so-called help of the created and the mutable', they laugh and mock and reply, 'There is tomorrow for all that.'

Despite this, Philo himself can allow that physicians are validated by their patients' experience of them.[33] Plutarch tells us, 'When people with chronic diseases have despaired of ordinary remedies and customary regimens, *then* they turn to expiations and amulets and dreams.'[34]

---

31. Dionysius of Halicarnassus, *Roman Antiquities* 1.48.1; Josephus, *Ant.* 1.108, 2.348, 3.81; Lucian, *How to Write History* 60; cf. Tacitus, *History* 2.1.50, 'While I must hold it inconsistent with the dignity of the work I have undertaken to collect fabulous tales and to delight my hearers with fictitious stories, I cannot, however, dare to deny the truth of common tradition.' He then relates a bird omen. Cf. Ernout, 'La magie', p. 192, citing a similar point from Pliny the Elder, *Hist. nat.* 28.5.29; and note also P. Veyne, *Les grecs, ont-ils cru à leurs mythes?* (Paris: Editions du Seuil, 1983); ET, *Did the Greeks Believe their Myths?* (Chicago: University of Chicago Press, 1988).

32. Cicero, *De divinatione* 2.9.

33. Philo, *Sacr.* 70 (Colson and Whittaker [trans.], *Philo* [LCL]), *Spec. Leg.* 4.153. Philo is fully aware of the sceptic suspension of judgment, for instance on celestial phenomena; one may compare *De congressu* 51 with Cicero, *De finibus* 5.42, quoted above, n. 23.

34. Plutarch, *Moralia: De facie* 920B; cf. Dio Chrysostom, *Discourses* 6.23-24, where 'seers and exorcists' come at the end of the list of therapists, after 'drugs, surgery, cautery'.

Dio Chrysostom marvels at the ready audience for any physician offering to share his latest insights into human anatomy.[35]

There is no indication in all this of any widespread *firm* belief in spells and charms, only some trust in physicians together with some willingness to fall back on magic or prayer. Much as people do today; as Pierre Veyne also notes.[36]

I suggest that accounts that come down to us of agricultural practice and other manual skills are also signficant. There was a traditional and growing understanding of soils, seasons, propagation and other techniques. Though people may well have used prayers and other rituals and charms, Pliny the Elder for instance includes none such in book 14 of his *Natural History*.[37]

I do not think we can tell how far the purveyors of spells, charms, amulets themselves believed in their products, though I think we may assume that some did. On the other hand, I am not aware of accounts of specialists in magic being caught out using other ingredients than those advertised. We do, though, have accounts of deliberate falsification of audio-visual effects.

We have the well-known example of Alexander's canvas snake, Glykon, 'born' from a pre-prepared egg, and provided by horse-hair threads with a moving mouth and tongue, and speech through cranes' wind-pipes, answering sealed requests for oracles read and reclosed with a fresh matrix made from the undisturbed wax.[38] Hippolytus, bishop (or rival bishop) in Rome knew of these and similar tricks (lighting and sound-effects included), one may assume from a published source (he does not claim it as his own private detective work).[39] Fakery of this sort provides part of the plot of Achilles Tatius's popular romance, *Leucippe and Cleitophon* (15-20). The heroine has a bladder full of offal attached to her stomach, allowing her to survive an apparent disembowelling in a cannibalistic rite. Different kinds of fakery figure in

35. Dio Chrysostom, *Discourses* 33.6.

36. Cf. Veyne, *Les grecs*, Ch. 7.

37. If I read him right, Fritz Graf argues that socially disturbing success in farming or elsewhere would be much more readily ascribed to magic than to good practice. I would argue that this is to impose a sociologist's model onto the evidence; Graf, *La magie*, pp. 69, 77-78; but compare Pliny's account of Palaemon, *Hist. nat.* 14.5.49-52, and comments of Beacon, *Roman Nature*, pp. 20-21, 162-67.

38. Lucian, *Alexander* 12, 14, 19-21.

39. Hippolytus, *Refutation of all Heresies* 4.28-42.

Iamblichus, *A Babylonian Tale*, 5-7. Elsewhere, however, there is direct divine intervention.[40]

There are no overt references to these immediate issues in our New Testament canon. There may seem to be implicit allusions to them, nonetheless.

There was an intriguing article some fifteen years ago by S.J. Scherrer, deploying some of the matter in Lucian and Hippolytus just noted, and other similar exposés, to illuminate Revelation 13.13-15. 'The second beast works great signs, even making fire come down from heaven in the sight of men; and by the signs it is allowed to work in the presence of the beast, it deceives those who dwell on earth...and it was allowed to give breath to the image of the beast so that the image of the beast should even speak.' Scherrer argued that the priests of the imperial cult of Rome and Caesar seem to have been using some of the tricks later exposed. 'The technology was apparently available.'[41] As it stands, of course, John the Seer seems to accept the *son et lumière* at face value: onlookers are genuinely deceived.

Luke presents an intriguing puzzle. In many ways, as I hope I have shown elsewhere, his ethos has much in common with Josephus, and with one of the latter's likely models, Dionysius of Halicarnassus.[42] Yet there is no 'let the hearer decide'. In fact Luke, it has been argued by John Hull, comes closest to presenting Jesus and his followers as competitors in the same market as Elymas barJesus and the like, performing what others would interpret as magic, only insisting that it is free, not for sale: we may instance the therapeutic shadows and handkerchiefs in Acts (5.15, 19.12). Furthermore, the matter-of-factness of healings and other miracles are vividly stressed by Luke.[43] Where Mark seems to leave some miracles affirmed (of course) but understated, Luke has, for

40. Philip Alexander, in conversation and by letter, promises sometime to publish a study of a passage in *b. Sanh.* which makes a clear distinction between legerdemain and 'real' magic.

41. Scherrer, 'Signs and Wonders', p. 601.

42. F.G. Downing, 'Redaction Criticism: Josephus' *Antiquities* and the Synoptic Gospels I and II', *JSNT* 8 (1980) pp. 46-55, and 9 (1980), pp. 29-48; repr. in S.E. Porter and C.A. Evans (eds.), *New Testament Interpretation and Methods* (BS, 45; Sheffield: Sheffield Academic Press, 1997), pp. 161-199.

43. Hull, *Hellenistic Magic*, Ch. 6, 'Luke: The Tradition Penetrated by Magic', pp. 87-115.

instances, the voice and the dove at Jesus' baptism as public phenomena, and has Jairus's daughter's spirit return from the dead, not just the girl get up (Lk. 3.22, 8.55).

However, in my own study just referred to it, was pointed out that elaborating the narrative was a part of Josephus' response to likely incredulity among his hearers. If he is going to tell the tale at all, he will make it circumstantially detailed (as does Dionysius, of course). One well-known example from Josephus is the exorcism recounted at *Ant.* 8.46-49, where the departing demon knocks over a cup of water; others would be the plagues of Egypt. It is not just that the Egyptians found the colour of the water turned into blood repugnant (and could not drink it), they tried it and were agonized; the frogs died, even in new-dug wells, and stank out the land; the gnats' bites were resistant to all known lotions and ointments; and so forth.[44] Rather than displaying and expecting among his hearers an unthinking credulity, Luke is more probably responding in this conventional way to contemporary scepticism. You are only likely to feel the need to add corroborative detail if you are aware that you may well otherwise have a bare and unconvincing narrative.[45] Christian miracles are for Luke real, believable, but different in ethos from magic (not least by not being charged for),[46] but also in being part of a theology that can be shown to be eminently respectable by accepted criteria, as I have tried to show elsewhere (and as such as Bruno Wildhaber has argued in other ways).[47]

And so, if Matthew, Luke and John are to include encounters with the risen Jesus, doubts have to be expressed so they may be answered (despite Mark's reticence and Paul's earlier conviction that the risen Lord had to have been changed to a 'spiritual body', 'for flesh and blood cannot inherit the kingdom of God').[48]

Matthew's evaluation of his mages (2.1-12) is widely agreed to be unclear; they may be offering loyal homage, they may be surrendering their wicked crafts. The latter would seem to be Ignatius's view, of

44. Josephus, *Ant.* 2.293-300 (and on to 314); cf. Exod. 7.20-8.18 (and on to 12.30); cf. Downing, 'Redaction Criticism', II, p. 38 and n. 25.

45. With acknowledgment to W.S. Gilbert, *The Mikado*.

46. Wildhaber, *Paganisme populaire*, p. 105 and nn.

47. Downing, 'Ethical Pagan', pp. 544-63; and *idem*, 'Common Ground with Paganism in Luke and in Josephus', *NTS* 28.4 (1982), pp. 546-59; cf. Wildhaber, *Paganisme populaire*, pp. 161-63.

48. Mt. 28.17; Lk. 24.39-43; Jn 20.24-29; Mk 16.1-8; 1 Cor. 15.42-50.

course, perhaps interpreting Matthew's story itself: when 'a star shone forth in the heaven above every other star...every sorcery and every spell was dissolved'.[49] For Ignatius, at least, magic (or, all others' magic) cannot be shown to have been unreal, but now, for Christians at least, it is ineffectual, powerless.

Quite what Paul means by 'signs and wonders' (2 Cor. 12.12, Rom. 15.19) is unclear, but it would seem to include healing miracles (1 Cor. 12.9-10, 28; cf. Gal. 3.5). It is noteworthy that he narrates none of them, nor does he base any important conclusions on them (cf. 1 Cor. 1.22). At most these infrequent references supplement other arguments. The fact that some of the addressees had accepted 'conversion', and their reception of the Holy Spirit, and Paul's own physical endurance, and their (newly) shared beliefs and traditions—all these are much more significant than any signs. It is possible to argue from admitted past experience and new convictions, but not from a promise of miracles to come.

Neither Jesus nor Paul nor their associates had any great impact numerically, despite the reported signs and wonders. Tales of miracles seemed to the evangelists to be worth repeating among the committed, they had little impact outside.

Of course there is nothing really remarkable in this. People back in older Jewish scripture do not *expect* miracles, do not assume that something as good as or better than magic has been promised them. But all I would seek to argue from all the foregoing is that we have no widespread evidence for any widespread *firm* belief in 'magic' or in 'miracle' whichever term is chosen, in the world where the Christian movement began. Recourse to such might be attempted, especially if all else failed (Mk 5.26), you had nothing much to lose. Magic was cheap, miracles could be free. But the level of belief—or suspension of disbelief—seems to have been not much different from what we find today for belief in alternative medicines, belief in ley-lines, belief in visitors from outer space, or belief in the free market economy.[50]

49. Ignatius of Antioch, *Ephesians* 19.3; cf. W.R. Schoedel, *Ignatius* (Hermeneia; Philadelphia: Fortress Press, 1985), p. 93.

50. Thus Thérasse, 'Croyances et crédultié', p. 317, is far too sweeping in his 'les Romains, même cultivés ou haut placés, firent preuve d'une crédulité assez surprenante; rationalisme et scepticisme ne semblent avoir été le fait que d'une minorité de bons esprits, et n'eurent guère de prise sur la masse' ('The Romans, even cultured or eminent ones, demonstrate an astonishing credulity. Rationalism

It was intriguing to read Fritz Graf on magic alongside Pierre Veyne on scepticism. Veyne remarks,

> I know a doctor who is a passionate homeopath but who nevertheless has the wisdom to prescribe antibiotics in serious cases; he reserves homeopathy for mild or hopeless situations. His good faith is whole. I attest to it.[51]

and scepticism seem to occur only among an acute minority, with scarcely any popular effect').

51. Veyne, *Les grecs,* p. 86.

Chapter 12

INTERPRETATION AND THE 'CULTURE GAP'*

Presumably it is not necessary here to offer a potted history of discussions of 'cultural relativity' and supposed 'culture gaps'...we can press the story back through Dennis Nineham (and other contributors to *The Myth of God Incarnate*) to T.S. Kuhn and to suggestions from Alasdair MacIntyre, and to others such as Peter Winch claiming the support of Ludwig Wittgenstein.[1] We can go back beyond them to Rudolph Bultmann,[2] and even further back to Albert Schweitzer ('Jesus as a concrete historical personality remains a stranger to our time')[3] and then behind him to the Enlightenment—or at least to its immediate heirs' assessment of it.

I may well have missed any major theoretical restatement of the idea that has come out in the last twenty years, but my impression is that no one now argues in detail for 'hard gappism'. Joseph Runzo [writing shortly before this piece was put together], for instance, seemed mostly to presuppose the validity of what he termed a 'consistent' position, but

*   Reprinted from *SJT* 40 (1987), pp. 161-71, with kind permission.

1.   D.E. Nineham, *The Use and Abuse of the Bible* (London: Macmillan, 1976); J. Hick (ed.), *The Myth of God Incarnate* (London: SCM Press, 1977); T.S. Kuhn, *The Structure of Scientific Revolutions* (Chicago: University of Chicago Press, 1964); A. MacIntyre, 'God and the Theologians', *Encounter* 120 (1963), pp. 3-10; P. Winch, *The Idea of a Social Science* (London: Routledge, 1958); on Wittgenstein, F.G. Downing, 'Games, Families, the Public and Religion', *Philosophy* 46 (1972), pp. 38-55; and, more recently, e.g., O. Hanfling, *Wittgenstein's Later Philosophy* (Basingstoke: Macmillan, 1989); F. Kerr, *Theology after Wittgenstein* (London, SPCK, 2nd edn, 1997).

2.   As did J. Runzo, in his 'Relativism and Absolutism in Bultmann's Demythologising Hermeneutic', *SJT* 32 (1979), pp. 401-19; referring, e.g., to R. Bultmann, *Jesus Christ and Mythology* (ET; London: SCM Press, 1960).

3.   A. Schweitzer, *The Quest of the Historical Jesus* (ET, London: A. & C. Black, 3rd edn, 1954), p. 399.

argued on from it, rather than establishing it. At other times—as when he commended 'the comparison of one world-view with another, or... the examination of a single idea from the point of view [sic] of different world-views'—he seemed to allow for genuine movement across the borders.[4] If you insist that some other culture is totally inaccessible, you leave yourself with no way to verify or even falsify your assertion, and so for many of your own contemporaries your assertion is itself meaningless. In fact most proponents (like Runzo) instance particular alien facets of a supposedly very foreign culture, and assume that they have understood something of that culture so as to have got their bizarre examples in proper focus. They have already understood, in some measure, this 'soft' gappism. But now it is always open to someone else to ask the proponents (or exponents) to try to understand a little better.

'Soft cultural gappism', 'cultural relativity' proper is, however, no push-over. A genuine understanding of a culture distinguishable from your own—a genuine understanding that can be shown to be such—may be very hard to achieve. (The alternative assumption, that understanding someone else is easy, is only a mirror-image of hard-gappism: still the only sense allowed for is 'my' sense.)[5]

Other people's 'body language' can seem comical—especially to those unaware of their own (which is 'natural'). But it can be learned—and then one's own can be better understood. If someone has grown up lacking any engagement with any overt communal myths at all, it may be very difficult for that person to understand a culture rich in these: difficult, but not impossible (especially if there comes an awareness of one's own society's own implicit myths).

As clearly, if history is limited to the golden oldies of ten years ago, awaking dim memories for our parents (and who cares if the disc jockey

4. J. Runzo, 'Relativism', p. 418. (The present chapter was written, of course, before theologians in droves took to post-modernist versions of relativism. I reproduce this discussion in the conviction that its arguments stand against all proposals for 'culture gaps', though not, of course, against sheer assertion.)

5. I note B. Wilson (ed.), *Rationality* (Oxford: Basil Blackwell, 1970); M. Hollis and S. Lukes (eds.), *Rationality and Relativism* (Oxford: Basil Blackwell, 1982); D. Davidson, *Truth and Interpretation* (New York: Oxford University Press, 1985); J. Skorupski, 'Relativity, Realism and Consensus', *Philosophy* 60 (1985), pp. 341-58; and G. Dawson, 'Perspectivism in the Social Sciences', *Philosophy* 60 (1985), pp. 373-80. Note also an earlier piece of my own, 'Our Access to Other Cultures, Past and Present', *Mod.C.* 21 (1977), pp. 28-42; and J. Barton, 'Cultural Relativism', *Theology* 82 (1979), pp. 103-109.

gets it wrong, anyway?) then engaging with a more distant past may be far from easy. In practice it may be quite difficult, even though the logic of the enquiry is not different from that of 'Who's nicked my bloody *Star*?' One fascination of Henning Graf Reventlow's very thorough study, *The Authority of the Bible and the Rise of the Modern World*,[6] is the strong case he has made for many dominant themes of the Enlightenment being neither brand-new, nor rediscoveries of a lost classical rationalism, but persistent motifs among Christian intellectuals down the ages. There are changes, but there are no gaps other than those of our imaginings or actual ignorance or wilful blindness. If we can take just one valid step back, then at least in theory we can take the next, through the myriad continuities that have made us what we are. No 'age' is other than an arbitrary construct, no culture is a 'totality' relating only inwards. 'Relativity' reaches in all directions, not simply to the interior.

The least useful place to start, it seems to me, is with the technicalities or other specifics of the person or people you hope to understand. It is fun in a way as an English person to chat with a North American about the vocabularies of our respective kinds of English; but when we've swapped 'muffler' with 'silencer' and 'vest' with 'waistcoat', we've really not learned much about each other. It is interesting to do comparative liturgics, and note the different structures of Eucharistic canons; but till you have some indication of how people regard their participation in the rite, you're not a lot forrarder in your comprehension. It is intriguing to hear a sketch of a millennium of Norwegian history; but till you have gathered the range of attitudes among Norwegians to their shared history you are still very much a spectator standing outside and only made aware of just how outside you are.

So it seems to me that the 'background', 'context', 'environment' books for New Testament study do more to prevent understanding than enable it. At best they only prevent their readers from assuming too readily that they do understand; but that gain is bought at a heavy price.[7]

---

6. H. Graf Reventlow, *The Authority of the Bible and the Rise of the Modern World* (ET; London: SCM Press, 1984).

7. Examples of 'background' works include E. Lohse, *The New Testament Environment* (ET; London: SCM Press, 1976; recently re-issued); A.R.C. Leaney, *The Jewish and Christian World 200 BC–AD 200* (Cambridge: Cambridge University Press, 1984); E. Yamauchi, *The World of the First Christians* (London: Lion, 1981); and Ferguson, *Backgrounds of Early Christianity*, best but uneven. For illustrative texts, Kee, *The Origins of Christianity*; D.R. Cartlidge and D.L. Dungan,

You tend to be plunged into a lengthy political history—including the history of theological politics. You are not told whether people in general (and, in this instance, the early Jewish and Gentile Christians) lived that history, or were even aware of it. Failing such information, this diachronic introduction is a distracting waste of time. It means nothing to you, and anything—or nothing—to those whose lived thoughts (or purposeful living) you are trying to get to grips with. In fact, because you are told about it, you assume it must be relevant, even if you can't tell how, and simply have to admit to yourself, you are baffled. Much better is a synchronic analysis of socio-political reality, as I would judge from the reading of those who have been students with me in the past.[8]

But still on that level what we mostly receive is technicalities: the structures of provincial administration, deeds of sale, contracts, wills, formal public notices; leadership in social groups, income levels, relative economic security. There is sometimes a possibility of gleaning more how people actually lived all this, from the way these formal documents are phrased. But it is about as immediate as a textbook on today's British economy, or the flow-chart of a town hall's procedures, or an auctioneer's catalogue. Technicalities alienate. If you want culture-gaps, this is a good way to create them or maintain them.

When it comes to 'religion', then the least promising way to an understanding of the strands of others' lives which we choose to label so is by way of their myths and their rituals. Classically, 'the sun is a white cockatoo' or 'this cucumber is an ox' are either poetically fanciful or funny. We are left trying to imagine using such verbal devices ourselves, and realizing how foolish we would sound—to ourselves. But that is what the books tend to give us: myths, purity laws, technical religious language, rituals as bizarre as cricket or the Miss World contest. If you want a good culture-gap, we can supply them off the peg.

And to demonstrate the depth of the chasm that separates us, we need

Documents for the Study of the Gospels (New York: Collins, 1980); and C.K. Barrett, *The New Testament Background, Selected Documents* (London: SPCK, 1957), the best of these.

8. Much more commendable in aim, works such as Theissen, *Lokalkolorit*; S. Freyne, *Galilee, Jesus and the Gospels* (Dublin: Gill & Macmillan, 1988), and R.A. Horsley, *Galilee: History, Politics, People* (Valley Forge, PA: Trinity Press International, 1995), even while their disagreements show how provisional are any conclusions.

only to drop in a fragment of metaphysical philosophy, a chunk of dessicated gnosticism or an apocalyptic white stone. The long-delayed echo will persuade us finally of the futility of any attempt to cross the yawning gulf.

Where else might we start, should we actually want to make demonstrable contact (given a willingness to essay it, and to try to test the attempt?)

In their collection, *Documents for the Study of the Gospels*, D.R. Cartlidge and D.L. Dungan choose, as examples of Epictetus attempting to 'connect' with his students, two stories. One is of Helvidius Priscus insisting on attending a meeting of the senate against the express wishes of Vespasian: 'You do your task, I'll do mine. Your task will be to execute me, mine will be to die unafraid.' The other story is of an athlete who would die if he did not agree to the amputation of his genitals. He stands firm and dies 'a man'.[9]

This introduction to people's lived attitudes is, I would judge, one step in the right direction. We start to see them as living beings, not abstractions. We can put the first alongside political protesters in the old Soviet Union, Chile, South Africa, Greenham Common. We can put the second alongside the young lad who has lost his legs in a motorcycle crash, or a woman facing mastectomy or hysterectomy: ourselves. Yet the examples chosen are from exceptional and minority areas of life: the personal politics of the Roman aristocrat, the very masculine aesthetics of the gymnasium.

I would rather start from Epictetus elsewhere; perhaps best with Epictetus and young children. 'Who is not tempted by attractive lively children, to join their play and crawl on all fours and talk baby-talk?'[10] 'Don't be a greater coward than the children are. If things don't please them, they say, "I shan't play any more."'[11] 'Whoever', he asks, 'whoever follows your [Epicurean] advice when he sees his child fallen on the ground and crying?'[12]

At one point Epictetus is confronted by a father distraught at the illness of his little girl. He has found her plight so unbearable he has

9. Cartlidge and Dungan, *Documents*, pp. 148-49, citing *Arrian's Discourses of Epictetus*, 1.2.19-20, 25; in W.A. Oldfather (trans.), *Epictetus*, I (LCL; 2 vols.; London: Heinemann; Cambridge, MA, Harvard University Press, 1925); pp. 19-21.
10. Oldfather (trans.), Epictetus, *Dissertations* 2.24.18 (LCL).
11. Oldfather (trans.), Epictetus, *Dissertations* 1.24.20 (LCL).
12. Oldfather (trans.), Epictetus, *Dissertations* 1.23.8 (LCL).

rushed out of the house. Epictetus does not reprimand him for being concerned, but only for being so wrapped up in his own feelings as to be an ineffective parent.[13] In this instance we have a household with a number of servants. Elsewhere Epictetus discusses the reasons why a philosopher concerned with family case-work needs himself to stay celibate. A married philosopher may well have to nurse the baby, get in all the child-care equipment...and later on, get the children ready for school (and make the beds, even).[14]

Having glanced at parental care across apparent social divides, I'd take note of, say, an acid little joke ascribed to Rabbi Gamaliel. On her marriage his daughter asks, 'Father, pray for me'. 'May you never return here again.' When she gives birth to a son she again begs a blessing of him. 'May "woe" never leave your lips.' 'Father, on both happy occasions you've invoked a curse on me.' 'They were both blessings', he replied. 'Living at peace in your home, you will never return here. And as long as your son lives, "woe" will never leave your lips: "woe that he's not eaten up his food", 'woe that he's not had anything to drink", "woe that he's not got off to school"'. There is a strangeness for us, of course, in the daughter's rootedness in her husband's home; but much else is familiar.[15]

Then I would turn to one of Dio of Prusa's little bits of romantic fiction, the idealized countryfolk of Euboea. There a boy and girl have grown up together and have fallen in love, and their parents' consent is really a formality, once the couple seem mature enough. This is much better than conventional match-making among the wealthy, with all the family tensions involved. But I would go in the same discourse to Dio's discernment of the pain of unemployment, and the risks of sexual exploitation of the young and of any woman among the poor. Perhaps a note should be added on objections to town-planning and the cries of the conservationists on behalf of the old smithy (with the threat of auditors being sent in to sort out a prodigal city council).[16]

Then there might be Quintilian on the educational importance of

13. Oldfather (trans.), Epictetus, *Dissertations* 1.11.

14. Epictetus, *Dissertations* 3.22.71-74.

15. H. Freedman (trans.), *Midrash Rabbah: Genesis 26.4*, I (2 vols.; London: Soncino, 1939), pp. 212-13.

16. Dio Chrysostom (of Prusa) *Discourses* 7.64-86; 103-39; 40.6-8. For contemporary romantic fiction, Reardon, *Collected Ancient Greek Novels*; Hock, Chance and Perkins, *Ancient Fiction*.

maintaining children's interest, Cicero on the insatiable curiosity of the young, Philo on what people at lectures are really thinking about—these would start to round out the picture. And there is much else.[17]

It will be clear that I am concentrating on attitudes, rather than on their emotional loading as such, for though emotions are important for a full understanding of another ('I didn't realize it mattered so much to you'), they are much harder to discern on the written page of any age, or from the painting, the statue, the architecture. Concentrating on attitudes we may well, however, pick up something of the emotive force of a passage, which will then be more 'meaning-full' still. (And, yes, of course, we have to ask questions of ideological loading, as of any contemporary, including ourselves.)

It is also the case that I am using 'attitude' somewhat loosely to cover much of what J.L. Austin designated 'performative force', and then (I think, fairly light-heartedly), analysed into 'verdictive', 'exercitive', 'commissive', 'behabitive', and 'expositive' 'illocutionary force' and 'perlocutionary effect'. Most utterances (even 'pure' ejaculations) also have some 'constative' component, to wit, at least some 'factual' implication or presupposition. What I am suggesting is that it is where the illocutionary force is strongest that we do best to start our interpretation. It is here that we are most likely to find common ground. It is here, by the same token, that we find what mattered most to the people we are studying. And from this point we can begin to penetrate the factual and then even the quite technical language they used.[18]

Of course this attempt to understand runs in a circle—or at best a virtuous spiral—and we need at least some factual information (such as whether there is any exclusive child-to-particular-parent relationship in the culture in question, any private space, property, and so on). Only then can the attitudes we discern begin to take on any kind of determinate character. But only if we are able to discern attitudes is anyavailable factual material even interesting. As R. Olmsted wrote not long before this essay took shape, 'All the aspects of a particular

17. F.G. Downing, *Strangely Familiar*.

18. J.L. Austin, *How to Do Things with Words* (Oxford: Clarendon Press, 1962). See also F.G. Downing, 'Meanings', in M. Hooker and C.J. Hickling (eds.), *What about the New Testament* (London: SCM Press, 1975), pp. 127-42. Note also G.D. Chryssides, 'Meaning, Metaphor and Meta-Theology', *SJT* 38 (1985), pp. 145-53 (147): 'intellect...emotions, intentions and decisions—indeed, one might say, one's whole being'.

'swatch' of [a person]'s life provide the context in which their use of a particular expression performs its particular role. It is only by being given a use in our lives that our words acquire the significance they have...Being in a life-context of practices and interests...enables us to refer to the world and understand one another.'[19]

It should be obvious , however, that what I am trying to argue is that this is more than convenient or attractive or interesting for bored or bemused congregations, school-children, undergraduates, or the post-graduate seminar. The pervasive 'attitudinal' element, strand, colour in any communication is an integral aspect, component, factor in 'mean-ing'. If we have not understood people's attitudes in and to what they said and are reported as doing, we certainly have not yet understood. It is this, as I have already suggested, that gets 'cultural relativity' off the ground. So much of our study is abstract, formal, impersonal, that when we have done it, yes, there is a gap, a wide one, between us and what the utterances actually meant. But if we *are* able to start here, or reach here, we may genuinely get understanding under way.

If I have read him right, I am arguing something akin to R.G. Col-lingwood's position, that any worthwhile history must involve 'thinking the characters' thoughts after them'.[20] I would suggest that it is the dif-ficulty of doing this when we plunge into complex theological or philo-sophical (or even social, political and/or economic) cerebrations that has persuaded some into cultural relativism: we would here seem pre-cluded from this essential component of meaningful understanding. It is certainly a difficulty that persuades me that we must put up with com-peting 'understandings', 'interpretations', of the New Testament mate-rial.[22] But I would strongly urge that our best hope lies in approaching these documents through the everyday attitudes and reflections of peo-ple at the time. We approach them, not through their bizarre pharma-copeia (as in Pliny the Elder), but in their attitudes to physicians, drugs

19. R. Olsted, 'Wittgenstein and Christian Truth Claims', *SJT* 33 (1980), pp. 121-32 (130, 129). His reading of Wittgenstein is similar to mine (n. 2, above). The importance and propriety of asking such questions in archaeology (often taken to be purely 'factually descriptive') was strongly argued by J.F. Strange, 'Interpretation in Archaeology', paper delivered at SNTS, Trondheim, 1985.

20. R.G. Collingwood, *The Idea of History* (London: Oxford University Press, 1946).

21. Cf. F.G. Downing, *The Church and Jesus* (SBT, 10; London: SCM Press, 1968); and *idem*, 'The Social Contexts of Jesus the Teacher: Construction or Recon-

and surgery (as in Pliny the Elder, of course, but also in others); not in their Midrashic or allegorizing procedures, but in the attitudes to ordinary life they attempt to articulate.

Following these procedures, we may still find aspects of life in the first century that are strange, alien, hard to comprehend (if no more so than among some of our immediate and contemporary neighbours). But now we shall be able to warrant even our impressions of alienation, rather than simply assert them beyond any meaningful 'falsification'. Once we reach people's attitudes we should be able to check whether they really were 'other', or only seemed so while we remained at the level of abstractions. In practice—for instance, with the material I myself have assembled[22]—I think we are likely to find much more that is strangely familiar. To coin a phrase.

I end with a brief discussion of some further examples from Epictetus. He frequently speaks of Zeus as 'father':

> No human being is an orphan, but all have every and constantly the Father who cares for them. Why, to Odysseus it was no mere story which he had heard, that Zeus is the father of all humans. He always thought of him as his own father, and called him that, and in all that he did, looked on him as as such.[23]

We are often encouraged to interpret this in a very 'formal' and impersonal way. And we must certainly read it in the light of 'a son's profession is to treat everything that is his as belonging to his father, to be obedient to him in all things, never speak ill of him to anyone else, to give way to him in everything, and yield him precedence...'[24] That on its own can seem to take parenthood in Epictetus quite outside the range of our experience. But we need yet further balancing material. Epictetus also says,

> God has not merely given us faculties to enable us to bear all that happens without being crushed, but, as becomes a good king and in very truth a father, he has given them to us free from restraint, compulsion or

---

struction?' *NTS* 33.3 (1987), pp. 439-51; and 'The Jewish Cynic Jesus', in M. Labahn and A. Schmidt (eds.), *The Historical Jesus in New Research* (JSNTSup; Sheffield: Sheffield Academic Press), forthcoming.
22. Downing, *Strangely Familiar*.
23. Oldfather (trans.), Epictetus, *Dissertations* 3.24.16 (LCL).
24. Oldfather (trans.), Epictetus, *Dissertations* 2.10.7 (LCL).

hindrance. He has put the whole matter under our control without reserving to himself even the power to prevent or hinder.[25]

And he insists, 'I am a free man and a friend of God, so as to obey him of my own free will.'[26]

Together with earlier notes from Epictetus on fathering, this makes up a picture that certainly tallies with my own experience of being child and parent. From my early experience, with an emotionally dominant mother and largely absent father, I'm not sure that I would have felt I could understand. But that would have been a barrier of individual psychology, not of socio-cultural context. With our own children I learned —at least, I think I did—to stand back, learned to care with what I at least saw as minimal interference. But then I began to see that this was perhaps how our father treated my sister and my brother and me; and how our mother, with greater emotional needs of her own, struggled to let go without ceasing to care. Epictetus's Father Zeus is concerned and still leaves his children free, caringly. He has enabled their freedom, not simply abandoned them. And the quality of the care is shown in the earlier quotations, on parental concern for children while young.

If that kind of parent could be taken for granted by Epictetus, talking to a range of listeners (recalling that in some examples the father is doing his own shopping and housework, while in others there are a range of slave attendants), then I begin to feel I can make fair sense of it.

And if that kind of parenting makes sense across a wide social range in Epictetus's Rome, then I begin to feel I can understand the kind of parenting presupposed by Paul in Galatians 4, and by Jesus in Luke 15.

I conclude this discussion, then, with a rhetorical challenge. How, in the light of these examples, could a cultural relativist go about showing that Epictetus's attitude to parenting was alien to us? I say it is a rhetorical challenge, because I do not see how such an interpreter could succeed in the demonstration without showing that they understood Epictetus so well as to defeat the relativist argument. But perhaps they would have a sense of 'understand' which I do not understand, and the gap is between them and me, rather than between me and Epictetus; or between me and Paul, or me and Jesus.

25. Oldfather (trans.), Epictetus, *Dissertations* 1.6.40 (LCL).
26. Oldfather (trans.), Epictetus, *Dissertations* 4.3.9 (LCL).

Chapter 13

REFLECTING IN THE FIRST CHRISTIAN CENTURY:
1 CORINTHIANS 13.12*

To achieve a genuine understanding of the New Testament documents
we must gain a genuine and wide understanding of their environment:
with that perhaps most scholars would agree. The issue becomes con-
tentious when we try to decide what counts as relevant environment,
and is still more disputed when some would insist that just such a fuller
awareness of the first-century Mediterranean world must serve primarily to demonstrate the foreignness of the New Testament writings, part
of a culture quite alien, it is said, to our own.

At 1 Cor. 13.12 Paul tells us, 'Now we see only puzzling reflections
in a mirror' (βλέπομεν γὰρ ἄρτι δι᾽ ἐσόπτρου ἐν αἰνίγματι). Most
commentators will tell us that 'of course' first century mirrors were of a
poor quality—and we already feel technologically distanced from Paul.
We may even be referred to Plutarch—who actually says, 'just as a
mirror is useless unless it gives a true reflection...' (so the mirror may
show us quite accurately what is still itself puzzling).[1]

Many commentators go on from here to 'katoptromancy', the use of
mirrors to foresee the future (although the only references to such practice come from the late second century CE and later still). 'Late antiquity' is taken as a monochrome and static whole, despite the many first-
century writers who note changes of all kinds in society, thought and
technology.[2]

* Reprinted from *Exp.T* 95 (1984), pp. 176-77, with kind permission.

1. Plutarch, *Moralia: Coniugalia praecepta* 139F, in F.C. Babbitt (trans.)
Plutarch's Moralia, II (LCL; 16 vols.; London: Heinemann; Cambridge, MA: Harvard University Press), p. 307; cf. Lucian, *De historia scribendi* 50; and Epictetus,
Dissertation 2.14.21 and 3.22.51; correctly noted by G. Kittel, *TWNT/TDNT*, art.
αἴνιγμα.
2. Correctly noted by H. Conzelmann, *1 Corinthians* (Hermeneia; Philadel-

It is, however, worth noting that just fifty or sixty years after Paul, Plutarch could use both ἔσοπτρον and αἴνιγμα of the difficulties involved in comprehending deity, almost as technical terms.[3] There is no suggestion that this is a new coinage. And aspects of this usage then appear in Lucian (a little later) and among the Rabbis (rather later still).[4] It would seem at least possible that Paul is using (also without further explanation) the conventional language of popular pious philosophical agnosticism. It also seems clear that the early Christian fathers (much closer in time to Paul than we are) took it for granted that this is what Paul was doing.[5] Such an understanding may appear as early as Clement of Rome.[6]

'The incomprehensibility' (τὸ ἀκατάληπτον) of God does not appear in Paul; but Philo can elaborate it without apparently finding it necessary to argue for its base;[7] there are signs of it in Cicero,[8] and it seems to stem from a popular understanding of Plato. It could reasonably be taken to lie behind Jn 1.5; and that is clearly what the early fathers took it Paul was alluding to here.[9] What Paul does do elsewhere as here is shy away from claiming to 'know God'. It is much better to talk of

phia: Fortress Press , 1975), pp. 226-28. *Gen. R.* 91.6 has 'He saw him in the glass of vision', but that is late; the only other passage cited seems to be from Philostratus, *Life of Apollonius*, but I have not been able to trace it. On awareness of change among people in the first-century Graeco-Roman world, see Downing, *Strangely Familar*, Index.

3.   Plutarch, especially in *De iside et osiride, Moralia* 382A and 384A, but also elsewhere. Conzelmann, *1 Corinthians*, p. 227, suggests that for Plutarch it is only the inanimate that leaves us with an 'enigma', yet Plutarch is arguing over all just as Paul does, that our entire present knowledge, by whatever means, is all partial; and only 'then' shall we know. Cf. my discussion in *Has Christianity a Revelation*, pp. 68-69.

4.   Lucian, *Parliament of the Gods* 11; from a later date still, *Lev. R.* 1.14.

5.   Downing, *Has Christianity a Revelation*, Ch. 4, pp. 126-55.

6.   *1 Clement* 33.3; 36.2; and Ch. 49.

7.   Philo, *Mut. Nom.* 15; *Poster. C.* 15-16; 169; *Det. Pot. Ins.* 89; *Praem. Poen.* 40; *Somn.* 1.66; *Spec. Leg.* 1.46-47; *Leg. All.* 3.101; etc. Cf. Josephus, *Apion* 2.167 and 224 (on Plato).

8.   Cicero, *Tusculan Disputations* 1.47; cf. Seneca, *Epistulae morales* 102.28-29, 'then shall we know;' and *Nat. quaest.* 7.5.30; 1.5.15, 17; and Lucian, *Parliament* 11, again.

9.   See, as one example, *Jean Chrysostom: Sur l'incompréhensibilité de Dieu*, (trans. R. Flagelière; Sources Chrétiennes; Paris: Editions de Cerf, 1951), already in a tradition.

being known by God (1 Cor. 8.1-3; Gal. 4.9). Only 'then' shall we know as we are known. And that is what writers like John Chrysostom have in mind in talking of the incomprehensibility of God.

Leslie Houlden wrote a few years before [this chapter was written], 'We have no reason to suppose that Paul would have appreciated' a distinction between God and what we say about God; yet that is just the kind of issue that Paul would have seemed to at least some of his contemporaries to have been concerned with at 1 Cor. 13.12.[10]

Seneca and Lucian both use 'looking in a mirror' as a metaphor for contemplating our own impressions of things, or, as we say, 'reflecting'. Philo talks of seeing your origin in yourself 'as in a mirror'. Priests wash in a basin that reflects 'so they may be helped to see themselves reflected by recollecting the mirrors out of which the laver was fashioned, for, if they do this, they will not overlook any ugly thing showing itself in the appearance of the soul'.[11] If, as Paul believes, we are being changed to be like Christ, glorified into his glory as his glory shines on us, reflecting as in a mirror the glory of the Lord (2 Cor. 3.18; 4.6) then 'reflecting' on ourselves we must, it would seem, 'see' at least some puzzling image of him.

It is difficult to find anything in contemporary God-talk that takes us much further than this; in fact there is often rather less sophistication in today's chatter about 'divine self-revelation' than in the first centuries' preference for keeping 'revelation' primarily as a term for '*un*-realized' eschatology, for a hoped-for consummation.[12] We may agree we have to say as much as Paul seems to here, about human and Christian human experience enshrining, we may trust, an awareness (of sorts) of God; but surely we also need to be no less cautious and self-critical.

A fuller awareness of the first-century environment will not always make us feel aliens in a strange landscape. We have to find that out item by item, as I have attempted to show, here and elsewhere. Sometimes— and maybe quite often—we will find ourselves at home with a new and refreshed clarity in our reflections.

10. L. Houlden, 'The Creed of Experience', in J. Hick (ed.), *The Myth of God Incarnate* (London: SCM Press, 1977), pp. 125-32 (129). See, again, Ch. 11, above.

11. Seneca and Lucian as in n. 9; Philo, *Op. Mund.* 76; and *Migr. Abr.* 98, in Colson and Whitaker (trans.), *Philo*, p. 189. Cf. also *Jos.* 87; *Somn.* 2.206; *Fug.* 213; *Dec.* 105; *Vit. Cont.* 78.

12. Downing, *Has Christianity a Revelation*; and 'Revelation, Disagreement and Obscurity' in Colson and Whitaker (trans.), *Philo* (LCL), p. 189.

BIBLIOGRAPHY

Abegg, M.G., Jr, 'Exile and the Dead Sea Scrolls', in Scott (ed.), *Exile*, pp. 111-25.

Abrahams, I., *Studies in Pharisaism and the Gospels* (2 vols.; Cambridge: Cambridge University Press, 1917; repr., New York: Ktav, 1967).

Ackroyd, P.R., *Exile and Restoration* (London: SCM Press, 1968).

Adam, E., 'Historical Crisis and Cosmic Crisis in Mark 13 and in Lucan's *Civil War*', *TynBul* 48 (1997), pp. 329-44.

Alexander, L., ' "Better to Marry than to Burn": St Paul and the Greek Novel', in Hock *et al.* (eds.), *Ancient Fiction*, pp. 235-56.

—'Sisters in Adversity: Retelling Martha's Story', in Brooke (ed.), *Women in the Biblical Tradition*, pp. 167-86.

—'Paul and the Hellenistic Schools: the Evidence of Galen', in Engberg-Pedersen (ed.), *Paul in his Hellenistic Context*, pp. 60-83.

Allison, D.C., *Jesus of Nazareth, Millenarian Prophet* (Minneapolis: Fortress Press, 1998).

Amand, D., *Fatalisme et liberté dans l'antiquité grecque* (Louvain: Bibliothèque de l'Université, 1945).

Anderson, H., *Gospel of Mark* (NCB; London: Oliphants, 1976).

Andria, R.G., 'Diogene Cinico nei Papiri Ercolanesi', *Cronache Ercolanesi* 10 (1980), pp. 129-51.

Aune, D.E., *The Cultic Setting of Realised Eschatology* (Leiden: E.J. Brill, 1972).

—'Magic in Early Christianity', *ANRW* 2.23.2, pp. 1505-23.

—'The Apocalypse of John and Graeco-Roman Regulatory Magic', *NTS* 33.4 (1987), pp. 481-501.

Aune, D.E. (ed.), *Greco-Roman Literature and the New Testament* (SBLSBS, 21; Atlanta: Scholars Press, 1988).

Austin, J.L., *How to Do Things with Words* (Oxford: Clarendon Press, 1962).

Barnard, L.W., 'Justin Martyr's Eschatology', *VC* 19 (1965), pp. 86-98.

Barr, J., *The Semantics of Biblical Language* (London: Oxford University Press, 1961).

Barrett, C.K., *The New Testament Background, Selected Documents* (London: SPCK, 1957).

Barstad, H.M., *The Myth of the Empty Land: A Study in the History and Archaeology of Judah during the 'Exilic' Period* (Symbolae osloenses, 28; Oslo: Scandinavian University Press, 1996).

—'The Strange Fear of the Bible: Some Reflections on the "Bibliophobia" in some Recent Ancient Israelite Historiography', in Grabbe (ed.), *Leading Captivity Captive*, pp. 120-27.

Bartchy, S.S., ΜΑΛΛΟΝ ΧΡΗΣΑΙ: *First-Century Slavery and the Interpretation of First Corinthians 7:21* (SBLDS, 11; Missoula, MT: Scholars Press, 1971).

Bartelink, C.J.M., 'Le thème du monde vieilli', *Orpheus* 4 (1983), pp. 342-54.

Barton, J., 'Cultural Relativism', *Theology* 82 (1979), pp. 103-109.

Basso, K.H., and H.A. Selby (eds.), *Meaning and Anthropology* (Albuquerque: University of New Mexico Press, 1976), pp. 221-37.

Batey, R.A., 'Jesus and the Theatre', *NTS* 30.4 (1984), pp. 563-73.

Bauckham, R.J., *Jude, 2 Peter* (WBC; Waco: Word Books, 1983).

Bauer, W., *Orthodoxy and Heresy in Earliest Christianity* (ET; Philadelphia: Fortress Press, 1971).

Beacon, M., *Roman Nature: The Thoughts of Pliny the Elder* (Oxford: Clarendon Press, 1992).

Beare, F.W., *The Earliest Records of Jesus* (Oxford: Basil Blackwell, 1962).

Bels, J., 'Le thème de la Grande Année d'Héraclite aux Stoïciens', *RPA* 7.2 (1980), pp. 169-83.

Benko, S., *Pagan Rome and the Early Christians* (Bloomington: Indiana University Press, 1984).

Benn, P., 'Forgiveness and Loyalty', *Philosophy* 71.277 (1996), pp. 369-83.

Berger, K., *Formgeschichte des Neuen Testaments* (Heidelberg: Quelle & Meyer, 1984).

Betz, H.D., *Galatians* (Hermeneia; Philadelphia: Fortress Press, 1979).

—'Jesus and the Cynics: Survey and Analysis of a Hypothesis', *JR* 74.4 (1994), pp. 453-75.

Biblia Patristica (4 vols, Paris: Centre National de la Recherche Scientifique, 1975-87).

Bonner, S.F., *Education in Ancient Rome* (London: Methuen, 1977).

Borgen, P., 'Two Philonic Prayers in their Context: An Analysis of *Who is the Heir of Divine Things* (*Her.*) 24-29, and *Against Flaccus* (Flac.) 170-75', *NTS* NS 45.3 (1999), pp. 291-309.

Brakenhielm, C.R., *Forgiveness* (Philadelphia: Fortress Press, 1993).

Branham, R.B., and M.-O. Goulet-Cazé (eds.) *The Cynics* (Berkeley: University of California Press, 1996).

Braun, W., *Feasting and Social Rhetoric in Luke 14* (SNTSMS, 85; Cambridge: Cambridge University Press, 1995).

Bréhier, E., *Les idées philosophiques et religieuses de Philon d'Alexandrie* (Paris: Vrin, 1950).

Broek, R. van den, and M.J. Vermasseren (eds.), *Studies in Gnosticism and Hellenistic Religions Presented to Gilles Quispel* (Leiden: E.J. Brill, 1981).

Baada ,T., and J. Mansfeld (eds.), *Knowledge of God in the Greco-Roman World* (Leiden: E.J. Brill, 1988).

Brooke, G.J. (ed.), *Women in the Biblical Tradition* (Studies in Women and Religion, 31; Lewiston, NY: Edwin Mellen Press, 1992).

Brown, P., *The Body and Society: Men, Women and Sexual Renunciation in Early Christianity* (New York: Columbia University Press, 1988).

Bryan, D.J., *Cosmos, Chaos and the Kosher Mentality* (JSPSup, 12; Sheffield: Sheffield Academic Press, 1995).

Bultmann, R., *Jesus and the Word* (ET; London: Collins, 1958).

—*Jesus Christ and Mythology* (ET; London: SCM Press, 1960).

—*The History of the Synoptic Tradition* (ET; Oxford: Basil Blackwell, 1963).

Bunyeat, M. (ed.), *The Sceptical Tradition* (Berkeley: University of California Press, 1983).

Burkhill, T.A., 'The Syrophoenician Woman: The Congruence of Mark 7 24-31', *ZNW* 57 (1966), pp. 23-37.

—'The Historical Development of the Story of the Syrophoenician Woman (Mark vii:24-31)', *NovT* 9 (1967), pp. 161-71.

Carcopino, J., *Virgile et le mystère de la IVe Eclogue* (Paris: Artisan du Livre, 1930).

Caron, J.-B., M. Fortin and G. Maloney (eds.), *Mélanges d'études anciennes offerts à Maurice Lebel* (Québec: Editions du Sphinx, 1980).

Carrington, P., *According to Mark* (Cambridge: Cambridge University Press, 1960).

Carroll, J.T., 'Luke's Portayal of the Pharisees', *CBQ* 50 (1988), pp. 604-621.

Cartlidge, D.R., and D.L. Dungan, *Documents for the Study of the Gospels* (New York: Collins, 1980).

Casey, M., 'Where Wright is Wrong', *JSNT* 69 (1998), pp. 95-103.

Champlin, E., *Fronto and Antonine Rome* (Cambridge, MA: Harvard University Press, 1980).

Chilton, B., *A Galilaean Rabbi and his Bible* (London: SPCK, 1984).

Chilton, B., and J.I.H. McDonald, *Jesus and the Ethics of the Kingdom* (London: SPCK, 1987).

Chroust, A.-H., 'The "Great Deluge" in Aristotle's On Philosophy', *AC* 43 (1973), pp. 113-22.

Chryssides, G.D., 'Meaning, Metaphor and Meta-Theology', *SJT* 38 (1985), pp. 145-53.

Clay, D., 'Picturing Diogenes', in Branham and Goulet-Cazé (eds.), *The Cynics*, pp. 366-87.

Coate, M.A., *Sin, Guilt and Forgiveness* (London: SPCK, 1994).

Collingwood, R.G., *The Idea of History* (London: Oxford University Press, 1946).

Conzelmann, H., *1 Corinthians* (Hermeneia; Philadelphia: Fortress Press, 1975).

Corley, K.E., *Private Women, Public Meals* (Peabody, MA: Hendrickson, 1993).

Cooper, K., *The Virgin and the Bride: Ideological Womanhood in Late Antiquity* (Cambridge, MA: Harvard University Press, 1996).

Coussin, P., 'The Stoicism of the New Academy', in Bunyeat (ed.), *The Sceptical Tradition*, pp. 31-63.

Cranfield, C.E.B., *The Gospel According to Mark* (Cambridge: Cambridge University Press, 1954).

—*A Critical and Exegetical Commentary on the Epistle to the Romans* (ICC; Edinburgh: T. & T. Clark, 1975).

Creed, J.M., *The Gospel According to St. Luke* (London: Macmillan, 1930).

Cronert, W., *Kolotes und Menedemus* (TU 6; Leipzig: J.C. Heinrichs, 1906).

Crossan, J.D., *In Parables* (San Francisco: Harper & Row, 1973).

—*The Historical Jesus* (San Francisco: HarperSanFrancisco; Edinburgh: T. & T. Clark, 1991).

Cullmann, O., *Christus und die Zeit* (Zollikon-Zürich: Evangelischer Verlag, 1946); ET, *Christ and Time* (London: SCM Press, 1951).

Cumont, F., *Afterlife in Roman Paganism* (New Haven: Yale University Press, 1992).

Daley, B.E., *The Hope of the Early Church* (Cambridge: Cambridge University Press, 1991).

Davidson, D., *Truth and Interpretation* (New York: Oxford University Press, 1985).

Davies, P.R., 'Eschatology at Qumran', *JBL* 104.1 (1985), pp. 39-55.

—*In Search of Ancient Israel* (Sheffield: JSOT Press, 1992).

Dawson, G., 'Perspectivism in the Social Sciences', *Philosophy* 60 (1985), pp. 373-80.

Dermience, A., 'Tradition et rédaction dans la péricope de la Syrophénicienne: Marc 7, 24-30', *RTL* 7 (1977), pp. 15-29.

Derrett, J.D.M., 'Law in the New Testament: The Syrophoenician Woman and the Centurion of Capurnaum', *NovT* 15 (1973), pp. 161-86.

Derrida, J., *Sauf le nom* (Paris: Galilée, 1993).

deSilva, D.A., 'Despising Shame: A Cultural-Anthropological Investigation of the Epistle to the Hebrews', *JBL* 113.3 (1994), pp. 439-61.

—*Despising Shame: Honor Discourse and Community Maintenance in the Epistle to the Hebrew* (SBLDS, 152; Atlanta: Scholars Press, 1995).

—'The Wisdom of Ben Sira: Honor, Shame, and the Maintenance of the Values of a Minority Culture', *CBQ* 58 (1996), pp. 433-35.

Dey, L.K.K., *The Intermediary World and Patterns of Perfection in Philo and Hebrews* (Missoula, MT: Scholars Press, 1975).

Dill, S., *Roman Society from Nero to Marcus Aurelius* (London: Macmillan, 1905; repr., New York: Meridian, 1956).

Dorandi, T., 'Filodemi: Gli stoici', *Cronache ercolanesi* 12 (1982), pp. 91-133.

Dorival, G., 'L'image des Cyniques chez les pères grecs', in Goulet-Cazé and Goulet (eds.), *Le cynisme ancien*, pp. 419-44.

Douglas, M., *Purity and Danger* (London: Routledge & Kegan Paul, 1966).

Downing, F.G., *Has Christianity a Revelation?* (Library of Philosophy and Theology; London: SCM Press, 1964).

—'A bas les aristos: The Relevance of Higher Literature for the Understanding of the Earliest Christian Writings', *NovT* 30.3 (1988), pp. 212-30; repr. in Downing, *Doing Things with Words*, ch. 1.

—*Christ and the Cynics* (JSOT Manuals, 4; Sheffield: JSOT Press, 1988).

—'Common Ground with Paganism in Luke and in Josephus', *NTS* 28 (1982), pp. 546-59.

—'Cosmic Eschatology in the First Century: "Pagan", Jewish and Christian', *AC* 64 (1995), pp. 99-109.

—*Cynics and Christian Origins* (Edinburgh: T. & T. Clark, 1992).

—*Cynics, Paul and the Pauline Churches: Cynics and Christian Origins*, II (London: Routledge, 1998).

—*Doing Things with Words in the First Christian Century* (JSNTSup 200; Sheffield: Sheffield Academic Press, 2000).

—'Ethical Pagan Theism and the Speeches in Acts', *NTS* 27 (1981), pp. 544-63.

—'Games, Families, the Public and Religion', *Philosophy* 46 (1972), pp. 38-55.

—*Jesus and the Threat of Freedom* (London: SCM Press, 1987).

—'The Jewish Cynic Jesus', in Labahn and Schmidt (eds.), *The Historical Jesus in Recent Research.*

—*A Man for Us and a God for Us* (London: Epworth Press, 1968).

—'Meanings', in Hooker and Hickling (eds.), *What about the New Testament?*, pp. 127-42.

—'Our Access to Other Cultures, Past and Present', *Mod.C.* 21 (1977), pp. 28-42.

—'A Paradigm Perplex: Luke, Matthew and Mark', *NTS* 38 (1992), pp. 15-36, repr. in Downing, *Doing Things with Words,* Ch. 9.

—'Pliny's Prosections of Christians: Revelation and 1 Peter', *JSNT* 34 (1988), pp. 105-23; repr. in Porter and Evans (eds.), *The Johannine Writings*, pp. 232-49.

—'Le problème du choix de l'intertexte: Paul, s'oppose-t-il radicalement ou superficiellement à la culture de son temps?', in D. Marguerat and A. Curtis (eds.), *Intertextualités: La Bible en echos* (La Monde de la Bible, 40; Geneva: Lenbar et Fides, 2000), pp. 238-50.

—'The Resurrection of the Dead: Jesus and Philo', *JSNT* 15 (1982), pp. 42-50; repr. in Porter and Evans (eds.), *The Historical Jesus*, pp. 167-75.

—'Revelation, Disagreement and Obscurity', *RelS* 21 (1986), pp. 219-30.

—'The Social Contexts of Jesus the Teacher: Construction or Reconstruction?' *NTS* 33.3 (1987), pp. 439-51.

—'Theophilus' First Reading of Luke–Acts', in Tuckett (ed.), *Luke's Literary Achievement*, pp. 91-109, repr. in Downing, *Doing Things with Words*, ch. 10.

—'Word-Processing in the Ancient World: The Social Production and Performance of Q', *JSNT* 64 (1996), pp. 29-48, repr. in Downing, *Doing Things with Words,* ch. 4.

—'Words as Deeds and Deeds as Words', *BibInt* 3.2 (1995), pp. 129-43, repr. in Downing, *Doing Things with Words*, ch. 2.

—*Strangely Familiar: An Introductory Reader to the First Century, to the Life and Loves, the Hopes and Fears, the Doubts and Certainties, of Pagans, Jews and Christians* (Manchester: Downing, 1985).

—*The Church and Jesus* (SBT, 10; London: SCM Press, 1968).

Drummond, J., *Philo Judaeus* (2 vols.; London: Williams and Norgate, 1886).

Drury, J., *The Parables in the Gospels: History and Allegory* (London: SPCK, 1985).

Dunn, J.D.G., *Unity and Diversity in the New Testament* (London: SCM Press, 1977).

—*Christology in the Making* (London: SCM Press, 1980).

—review of Wright, *The New Testament*, *JTS* NS 46 (1995), pp. 241-43.

—*The Theology of Paul the Apostle* (Grand Rapids: Eerdmans, 1998).

Ebner, M., *Leidenlisten und Apostelbrief* (FB, 66; Würzburg: Echter Verlag, 1991).

Eddy, P.R., 'Jesus as Diogenes? Reflections on the Cynic Jesus Thesis', *JBL* 115.3 (1996), pp. 449-69.

Eisen, U.E., *Amtsträgerinnen in frühen Christentum: Epigraphische und literarische Studien* (Forschungen zur Kirchen- und Dogmengeschichte, 61; Göttingen: Vandenhoeck & Ruprecht, 1996).

Elliott, J.H., 'The Fear of the Leer', *Forum* 4 (1988), pp. 42-71.

—'Paul, Galatians, and the Evil Eye', *CurTM* 17 (1990), pp. 262-73.

—'Matthew 20.1-15: A Parable of Invidious Comparison and Evil Eye Accusation', *BTB* 22 (1992), pp. 52-65.

—*Social Scientific Criticism of the New Testament* (London: SPCK, 1995).

Engberg-Pedersen, T. (ed.), *Paul in his Hellenistic Context* (Minneapolis: Fortress Press, 1995).

Ernout, A., 'La magie chez Pline l'Ancien', in Renard and Schilling (eds.), *Hommages à Jean Bayet*, pp. 191-95.

Esler, P.F., *The First Christians in their Social Worlds: Social-scientific Approaches to New Testament Interpretation* (London: Routledge, 1994).

Esler, P.F. (ed.), *Modelling Early Christianity: Social-scientific Studies of the New Testament in its Context* (London: Routledge, 1995).

—*Galatians* (London: Routledge, 1998).

Evans, C.A., 'Exile and Restoration in the Proclamation of Jesus', in Scott (ed.), *Exile*, pp. 300-305.

Fander, M., *Die Stellung der Frau im Markusevangelium* (Altenberge: Telos, 1989).

Farandos, G.D., *Kosmos und Logos nach Philon von Alexandria* (Elementa, 4; Amsterdam: Rodopi, 1976).

Ferguson, E. (ed.), *Christian Teaching: Studies in Honor of Lemoine G. Lewis* (Abilene: Abilene Christian University Bookstore, 1981).

—*Backgrounds of Early Christianity* (Grand Rapids: Eerdmans, 1987).

Fiedler, P., *Jesus und die Sünder* (BBET, 3; Frankfurt: Peter Lang; Bern: H. Lang, 1985).

Fischel, H.A., 'Studies in Cynicism', in Neusner (ed.), *Religion in Antiquity*, pp. 372-411.

—*Essays in Greco-Roman and Related Talmudic Studies* (New York: Ktav, 1977).

Fitzgerald, J.T. (ed.), *Friendship, Flattery and Frankness of Speech: Studies on Friendship in the New Testmanent Period* (NovT Sup, 82; Leiden: E.J. Brill, 1995).

Fox, R.L., *Pagans and Christians in the Mediterranean World from the Second Century AD to the Conversion of Constantine* (London: Viking, 1986; Harmondsworth: Penguin Books, 1988).

Foucault, M., *Surveiller et punir: La naissance de la prison* (Paris: Gallimard, 1975).

French R., and F. Greenaway (eds.), *Science in the Early Roman Empire: Pliny the Elder, his Sources and Influence* (London: Croom Helm, 1986).

Frend, W.H.C., 'The Persecutions: Some Links between Judaism and the Early Church', *JEH* 9 (1958), pp. 141-58.

—*Martyrdom and Persecution in the Early Church* (Oxford: Basil Blackwell, 1965).

Freyne, S., *Galilee from Alexander the Great to Hadrian 323 B.C.E.-135 C.E.: A Study of Second Temple Judaism* (Studies in Judaism and Christianity in Antiquity, 5; Wilmington, DE: Michael Glazier, 1980).

—*Galilee, Jesus and the Gospels* (Dublin: Gill & MacMillan, 1988).

Fredriksen, P., 'Judaism, the Circumcision of the Gentiles and Apocalyptic Hope', *JTS* NS 42 (1991), pp. 532-64.

Funke, H., 'Antisthenes bei Paulus', *Hermes* 98 (1970), pp. 459-71.

Gafni, I.M., *Land, Centre and Diaspora: Jewish Constructs in Late Antiquity* (JSPSup, 21; Sheffield: Sheffield Academic Press, 1997).

Garbini, G., *History and Ideology in Ancient Israel* (ET: London: SCM Press, 1986).

Garnet, P., 'Some Qumran Exegetical Cruces in the Light of Exilic Soteriology', in E.A. Livingstone (ed.), *Studia Evangelica*, VII (TU 67.3; Berlin: Akademie Verlag, 1982), pp. 201-204.

Geertz, C., ' "From the Native's Point of View": On the Nature of Anthropological Understanding', in Basso and Selby (eds.), *Meaning and Anthropology*, pp. 221-37.

Georgi, D., 'Who is the True Prophet?' in Macrae (ed.), *Christians among Jews and Gentiles*, pp. 100-26.

Glad, C.E., *Paul and Philodemus: Adaptability in Epicurean and Early Christian Psychology* (NovT Sup, 81; Leiden: E.J. Brill, 1996).

—'Frank Speech, Flattery and Friendship in Philodemus', in Fitzgerald (ed.), *Friendship, Flattery and Frankness of Speech*, pp. 21-60.

Glasson, T.F., *Greek Influence in Jewish Eschatology* (London: SPCK, 1961).

Glen, J.S., *The Parables of Conflict in Luke* (Philadelphia: Westminster Press, 1962).

Goldstein, J.A., 'How the Authors of 1 and 2 Maccabees treated the "Messaianic" Prophecies', in Neusner *et al.* (eds.), *Judaisms and their Messiahs*, pp. 69-96.

Goodenough, E.R., *By Light, Light* (New Haven: Yale University Press, 1935).

Goodman, M., review of F.G. Downing, *Jesus and the Threat of Freedom, JJS* 12.1 (1990), p. 127.

Görgemanns, H., and H. Karpp (eds.), *Origines: von den Prinzipen* (Darmstadt: Wissenschaftliche Buchgesellschaft, 1976).

Goulder, M.D., *Luke: A New Paradigm* (2 vols.; JSNTSup, 20; Sheffield: JSOT Press, 1989).

Goulet-Cazé, M.-O., *L'ascèse cynique* (Paris: Vrin, 1986).

—'Le cynisme à l'époque impériale', *ANRW*, II, 36.4 (1990), pp. 2720-2823.

Goulet-Cazé, M.-O., and R. Goulet (eds.), *Le cynisme ancien et ses prolongements* (Paris: Presses Universitaires de France, 1993).

Grabbe, L.L. (ed.), *Can a 'History of Israel' be Written?* (JSOTSup, 245, European Seminar in Historical Methodology, 1; Sheffield: Sheffield Academic Press, 1997).

—*Leading Captivity Captive* (JSOTSup, 278; ESHM, 2; Sheffield: Sheffield Academic Press, 1999).

Graf, F., *La magie dans l'antiquité gréco-romaine* (Paris: Les Belles Lettres, 1994).

Granfield, P., and J.A. Jungmann (eds.), *Kyriakon* (Festschrift Johannes Quasten; Munich: Kösel, 1970).

Grant, R.M., 'Charges of "Immorality" Against Various Religious Groups in Antiquity', in van den Broek and Vermasseren (eds.), *Studies in Gnosticism and Hellenistic Religions*, pp. 161-70.

Green, W.M., 'The Dying World of Lucretius', *AJP* 63 (1942), pp. 51-60.

Hafemann, S.J., 'Paul and the Exile of Israel in Galatians 3-4', in Scott (ed.), *Exile*, pp. 329-71.

Halpern-Amaru, B., 'Exile and Return in *Jubilees*', in Scott (ed.), *Exile*, pp. 127-44.

—'The New Names of Isaiah 62:4: Jeremiah's Reception in the Restoration and the Politics of "Third Isaiah"', *JBL* 117.4 (1998), pp. 623-43.

Hanfling, O., *Wittgenstein's Later Philosophy* (Basingstoke: Macmillan, 1989).

Hanson, P.D., *The Dawn of Apocalyptic* (Philadelphia: Fortress Press, 1979).

R., Harré, *Personal Being* (Cambridge, Cambridge University Press, 1984).

—*Social Being* (Oxford: Basil Blackwell, 2nd edn, 1993).

Harrill, J.A., *The Manumission of Slaves in Early Christianity* (HUT 32; Tübingen: Mohr-Siebeck, 1995).

Harrison, K.C., 'How Honorable! How Shameful! A Cultural Analysis of Matthew's Makarisms and Reproaches', in Matthew and Benjamin (eds.), *Honor and Shame*, pp. 81-111.

Harrisville, R.A., 'The Woman of Canaan: A Chapter in the History of Exegesis', *Int* 20 (1966), pp. 274-87.

Harvey, A.E., *Jesus and the Constraints of History* (London: Gerald Duckworth, 1980).

—review of N.T. Wright, *Jesus and the Victory of God*, *Theology* 100.796 (July/Aug. 1997), p. 296.

Heinrichs, A., 'Pagan Ritual and the Alleged Crimes of Christians', in Cranfield and Jungmann (eds.), *Kyriakon*, pp. 345-51.

Hellholm, D. (ed.), *Apocalypticism in the Mediterranean World and the Near East* (Tübingen: Mohr-Siebeck, 1983).

Hendrickx, H., *The Parables of Jesus* (London: Geoffrey Chapman, 1986).

Herzog, W.R., *Parables as Subversive Speech: Jesus as Pedagogue of the Oppressed* (Louisville, KY: Westminster/John Knox Press, 1994).

Hezser, C., 'Die Verwendung der hellenistichen Gattung Chrie im frühen Christentum und Judentum', *JSJ* 27.4 (1996), pp. 371-439.

Hick, J. (ed.), *The Myth of God Incarnate* (London: SCM Press, 1977).

Hock, R.F., 'Lazarus and Micyllus: Greco-Roman backgrounds to Luke 16:19-31', *JBL* 106 (1987), pp. 447-63.

—*The Social Context of Paul's Ministry* (Philadelphia: Fortress Press, 1980).

Hock, R.F., J.B. Chance and J. Perkins (eds.), *Ancient Fiction and Early Christian Narrative* (Atlanta: Scholars Press, 1998).

Hock, R.F., and E.N. O'Neil, *The Chreia in Ancient Rhetoric*. I. *The Progymnasmata* (SBLTT, 27; Atlanta: Scholars Press, 1986).

Höistad, R., *Cynic Hero and Cynic King* (Uppsala: Lundeqvist, 1948).

Hollis, M., and S. Lukes (eds.), *Rationality and Relativism* (Oxford: Basil Blackwell, 1982).

Hooker, M., and C.J. Hickling (eds.), *What about the New Testament? Essays in Honour of Christopher Evans* (London: SCM Press, 1975).

Horsley, R.A., and J.S. Hanson, *Bandits, Prophets and Messiahs: Popular Movements in the Time of Jesus* (New Voices in Biblical Studies; Minneapolis: Winston, 1985).

—*Galilee: History, Politics, People* (Valley Forge, PA: Trinity Press International, 1995).

Houlden, L., 'The Creed of Experience', in Hick (ed.), *The Myth of God Incarnate*, pp. 125-32.

Hoven, R., *Stoïcisme et stoïciens face au problème de l'au-delà* (Paris: Les Belles Lettres, 1971).

Hull, J.M., *Hellenistic Magic and the Synoptic Tradition* (SBT, 2; London: SCM Press, 1974).

Hurtado, L.W., *One God, One Lord* (Philadelphia: Fortress Press, 1988; 2nd edn, Edinburgh: T. & T. Clark, 1998).

Ito, Akio, 'Romans 2: A Deuteronomic Reading', *JSNT* 59 (1995), pp. 21-37.

Janssen, L.F., ' "Superstitio" and the Persecution of Christians', *VC* 33 (1979), pp. 131-59.

Jeremias, J., *The Parables of Jesus* (ET; London: SCM Press, 1972).

Johnson, L.T., 'The New Testament's Anti-Jewish Slander and the Conventions of Ancient Polemic', *JBL* 108 (1989), pp. 419-41.

Jones, H., *The Epicurean Tradition* (London: Routledge, 1989).

Jones, L.G., *Embodying Forgiveness: A Theological Analysis* (Grand Rapids: Eerdmans, 1998).

Jonge, J.J. de, 'ΒΟΥΤΡΟΣ ΒΟHCEI: The Age of Cronos and the Millennium in Papias of Hierapolis', in Vermasseren (ed.), *Studies in Hellenistic Religion*, pp. 37-49.

Käsemann, E., *Commentary on Romans* (ET; London: SCM Press, 1980).

Kautsky, J.H., *The Politics of Aristocratic Empires* (Chapel Hill: University of North. Carolina Press, 1982).

Kee, H.C., *The Origins of Christianity: Sources and Documents* (London: SPCK, 1973).

—*Medicine, Miracle and Magic in New Testament Times* (SNTSMS, 55; Cambridge: Cambridge University Press, 1986).

Keresztes, P., 'The Emperor Antoninus Pius and the Christians', *JEH* 22 (1971), pp. 1-19.

Kerr, F., *Theology after Wittgenstein* (London, SPCK, 2nd edn, 1997).

Kloppenborg, J.S., and S.G. Wilson (eds.), *Voluntary Associations in the Graeco-Roman World* (London: Routledge, 1996).

Kloppenborg Verbin, J.S., 'A Dog among the Pigeons: The "Cynic Hypothesis" as a Theological Problem', in J. Asgeirsson, K. de Troyer and M.W. Meyer (eds.), *From Quest to Quelle* (Festschrift James M. Robinson; BETL; Leuven: Peeters, 1999).

Knibb, M.A., 'The Exile in the Literature of the Intertestamental Period', *HeyJ* 53.4 (1976), pp. 253-72.

—'Exile in the Damascus Document', *JSOT* 25 (1983), pp. 99-117.

Koester, H., 'Jesus the Victim', *JBL* 111 (1992), pp. 3-15.

Konstans, D., *Sexual Symmetry: Love in the Ancient Novel* (Princeton, NJ: Princeton, University Press, 1994).

Körtner, U.H.J., 'Weltzeit, Weltangst und Weltende. Zum Daseins- und Zeitverständnis der Apokalyptik', *THZ* 45 (1989), pp. 32-42.

Kraabel, A.T., 'Unity and Diversity among Diaspora Synagogues', in Levine (ed.), *The Synagogue*, pp. 49-60.

Kroeber, A., *Anthropology: Race, Language, Culture, Psychology, Prehistory* (New York: Harcourt, Brace & World, rev. edn, 1948).

Krueger, D., 'The Bawdy and Society: The Shamelessness of Diogenes in Roman Imperial Culture', in Branham and Goulet-Cazé (eds.), *The Cynics*, pp. 222-39.

Kuhn, T.S., *The Structure of Scientific Revolutions* (Chicago: University of Chicago Press, 1964).

Labahn, M., and A. Schmidt (eds.), *Jesus, Mark and Q: The Teaching of Jesus and its Earliest Records* (JSNTSup; Sheffield: Sheffield Academic Press, forthcoming).

Lachs, S.T., *A Rabbinic Commentary on the New Testament* (Hoboken: Ktav, 1987).

Lagrange, M.J., *St. Paul: L'épître aux Romains* (Paris: J. Gabalda, 1950).

Lambrecht, J., 'The Groaning of Creation: A Study of Rom. 8.18-30', *Louvain Studies* 15 (1990), pp. 3-18.

Lapidge, M., 'Stoic Cosmology', in Rist (ed.), *The Stoics*, pp. 180-85.

Leaney, A.R.C., *The Jewish and Christian World 200 BC–AD 200* (Cambridge: Cambridge University Press, 1984).

Levinas, E., *Difficult Freedom: Essays on Judaism* (Baltimore: The Johns Hopkins University Press, 1990).

Levine, L.L. (ed.), *The Synagogue in Late Antiquity* (Philadelphia: American Schools of Oriental Research, 1987).

Lohmeyer, E., *Das Evangelium des Markus* (KEK, 1.2; Göttingen: Vandenhoeck & Ruprecht, 10th edn, 1937).

Lohse, E., *The New Testament Environment* (ET; London: SCM Press, 1976).

Long, A.A., *Hellenistic Philosophy* (London: Gerald Duckworth, 1974).

—'The Stoics on World-Conflagration and the Everlasting Recurrence', *SJP* Supp. 23 (1985), pp. 13-17.

Lovejoy, A.O., and G. Boas, *Primitivism and Related Ideas in Antiquity* (Baltimore: The Johns Hopkins University Press, 1935; New York: Octagon, 1965).

MacIntosh, H.R., *The Christian Experience of Forgiveness* (London: Nisbet, 1927).

MacIntyre, A., 'God and the Theologians', *Encounter* 120 (1963), pp. 3-10.

Mack, B.L., *A Myth of Innocence: Mark and Christian Origins* (Philadelphia: Fortress Press, 1988).

Mack, B.L. and V.K. Robbins (eds.), *Patterns of Persuasion in the Gospels* (Sonoma: Polebridge Press, 1989).

MacMullen, R., *Paganism in the Roman Empire* (New Haven: Yale University Press, 1981).

MacMurray, John, *The Form of the Personal* (Gifford Lectures for 1953-54; London: Faber, 1957).

Macrae, G. (ed.), *Christians among Jews and Gentiles* (Philadelphia: Fortress Press, 1986).

Malherbe, A.J., 'The Beasts at Ephesus', *JBL* 87 (1968), pp. 71-80, repr. in *idem*, *Paul and the Popular Philosophers*, pp. 79-89.

—'Justin and Crescens', in Ferguson (ed.), *Christian Teaching*, pp. 312-27.

—*Paul and the Popular Philosophers* (Minneapolis: Fortress Press, 1989).

Malina, B.J., *The New Testament World: Insights from Cultural Anthropology* (Louisville: Westminster/John Knox Press, rev. edn, 1993).

Malina, B.J. and J.H. Neyrey, 'First Century Personality: Dyadic, Not Individualistic', in
Neyrey (ed.), *The Social World of Luke–Acts*, pp. 67-96.

Malina, B.J. and J.H. Neyrey, 'Honor and Shame in Luke–Acts: Pivotal Values of the
Mediterranean World', in Neyrey (ed.), *The Social World of Luke–Acts*, pp. 24-46.

Mansfeld, J., 'Providence and the Destruction of the Universe in Early Stoic Thought', in
Vermasseren (ed.), *Studies in Hellenistic Religion*, pp. 129-88.

Manson, T.W., *The Sayings of Jesus* (London: SCM Press, 1949).

Marr, A., review of *Fasting, Feasting* by Anita Desai, *Guardian Weekly* (London) July 1–
7, 1999, p. 23.

Marrou, H., *A History of Education* (ET; London: Sheed & Ward, 1956).

Marrow, S.B., '*Parrhêsia* and the New Testament', *CBQ* 44 (1982), pp. 431-46.

Marshall, I.H., *The Gospel of Luke* (NIGTC, 3; Exeter: Paternoster Press, 1978).

Martin, D.B., *Slavery as Salvation: The Metaphor of Slavery in Pauline Christianity* (New
Haven: Yale University Press, 1990).

Matthews, V.H., and D.C. Benjamin (eds.), *Honor and Shame in the World of the Bible*
(Semeia, 68; Atlanta: Scholars Press, 1996).

Meigham, R., Letter, *The Guardian* (London), 19 December 1998, p. 24.

Momigliano, A., 'The Origins of Universal History', *ASNS* 3.12.2 (1982), pp. 533-60.

Montefiore, C.G., *The Synoptic Gospels* (2 vols.; London: Macmillan, 1927).

Morrison, D., 'Evidence for Degrees of Being in Aristotle', *CQ* 37 (1987), pp. 382-401.

Mortley, R. and D. Dockrill (eds.), *The Via Negativa Prudentia* Supp. (Auckland, NZ,
1981).

—*From Word to Silence*. I. *The Rise and Fall of the Logos* (Bonn: Peter Hanstein, 1986).

Moule, C.F.D., 'The Influence of Circumstances on the Use of Eschatological Terms', *JTS*
NS 16 (1964), pp. 1-15.

Moxnes, H., 'Honour and Righteousness in Romans', *JSNT* 32 (1988), pp. 61-77.

Neusner, J. (ed.), *Religion in Antiquity: Essays in Memory of Edwin Ramsdell Goodenough*
(Leiden: E.J. Brill, 1968).

Neusner, J., W.S. Green and E. Frerichs (eds.), *Judaisms and their Messiahs at the Turn of
the Christian Era* (Cambridge: Cambridge University Press 1987).

Neyrey, J.H., 'The Form and Background of the Polemic in 2 Peter', *JBL* 99 (1980), pp.
407-31.

Neyrey, J.H. (ed.), *The Social World of Luke–Acts: Models for Interpretation* (Peabody,
MA: Hendrickson, 1991).

—'Dyadism' in Pilch and Malina (eds.), *Biblical Social Values and their Meaning*, pp. 49-
52.

—'Loss of Wealth, Family and Honour', in Esler (eds.), *Modelling Early Christianity*, pp.
139-58.

Nicklesburg, G.W.E., *Jewish Literature between the Bible and the Mishnah* (London: SCM
Press, 1981).

Nineham, D.E., *Saint Mark* (London: Penguin Books, 1963).

—*The Use and Abuse of the Bible* (London: Macmillan, 1976).

Nodet, E., *A Search for the Origins of Judaism from Joshua to the Mishnah* (JSOTSup,
248, Sheffield: Sheffield Academic Press, 1997).

Peristiany, J.G. (ed.), *Honour and Shame: The Values of Mediterranean Society* (London:
Weidenfeld & Nicolson, 1965).

Peristiany, J.C., and J. Pitt-Rivers (eds.), *Honor and Grace in Anthropology* (Cambridge
Studies in Social Anthropology, 76; Cambridge: Cambridge University Press, 1992).

Pesch, R., *Das Markusevangelium*, I (HTK, 2; Freiburg: Herder, 1976).

Plevnik, J., 'Honor/Shame', in Pilch and Malina (eds.), *Biblical Social Values and their Meaning*, pp. 95-104.

Pilch, J.J., and B.J. Malina (eds.), *Biblical Social Values and their Meaning* (Peabody, MA: Hendrickson, 1993).

Pogoloff, S.M., *Logos and Sophia: The Rhetorical Situation of 1 Corinthians* (SBLDS, 134; Atlanta: Scholars Press, 1992).

Porter, S.E., 'Two Myths: Corporate Personality and Language/Mentality Determinism', *SJT* 43 (1990), pp. 289-307.

Porter, S.E., and C.A. Evans (eds.), *The Johannine Writings* (BS, 32; Sheffield: Sheffield Academic Press, 1995).

—*The Historical Jesus* (BS, 33; Sheffield: Sheffield Academic Press, 1995).

Rajak, T., *Josephus: The Historian and his Sources* (London: Gerald Duckworth, 1983).

Reardon, B.P. (ed.), *Collected Ancient Greek Novels* (Berkeley: University of California Press, 1989).

Renard, M., and R. Schilling (eds.), *Hommages à Jean Bayet* (Brussels: Latomus, 1967).

Rengstorf, K., *Das Evangelium nach Lukas* (NTD, 3; Göttingen: Vandenhoeck & Ruprecht, 1962).

Reuss, J., *Matthäus Kommentare aus der Griechen Kirche* (TU; Berlin: Akademie Verlag, 1957).

Reventlow, H. Graf, *The Authority of the Bible and the Rise of the Modern World* (ET; London: SCM Press, 1984).

Rist, J.M., *Epicurus: An Introduction* (Cambridge: Cambridge University Press, 1972).

Rist, J.M. (ed.), *The Stoics* (Berkeley: University of California Press, 1978).

Robbins, V.K., 'The Chreia', in Aune (ed.), *Greco-Roman Literature and the New Testament*, 1988, pp. 1-23.

—*The Tapestry of Early Christian Discourse: Rhetoric, Society and Ideology* (London: Routledge, 1996).

—*Exploring the Texture of Texts* (Valley Forge, PA: Trinity Press International, 1996).

Rohrbaugh, R., 'The Pre-Industrial City in Luke–Acts', in Neyrey (ed.), *Social World of Luke–Acts*, pp. 125-50.

Roloff, J., *Das Kerygma und der irdische Jesus* (Göttingen: Vandenhoeck & Ruprecht, 1974).

Rowland, C., *The Open Heaven* (London: SPCK, 1982).

Runia, D., *Philo of Alexandria and the TIMAEUS of Plato* (Leiden: E.J. Brill, 1986).

—'How to read Philo', *NTT* 40 (1986), pp. 185-98.

—'God and Man in Philo of Alexandria', *JTS* NS 39 (1988), pp. 48-75.

Runzo, J., 'Relativism and Absolutism in Bultmann's Demythologising Hermeneutic', *SJT* 32 (1979), pp. 401-19.

Ryle, G., *The Concept of Mind* (London: Hutchinson, 1949; repr., Harmondsworth: Penguin Books, 1963).

Ste Croix, G.E.M de, *The Crucible of Christianity* (London: Duckworth, 1969).

—*The Class Struggle in the Ancient Greek World from the Archaic Age to the Arab Conquests* (London: Gerald Duckworth; Ithaca, NY: Cornell University Press, 1981).

Sanders, E.P. (ed.), *Jewish and Christian Self-Definition* (London: SCM Press, 1980).

—*Paul, the Law and the Jewish People* (London: SCM Press, 1983).

—*Jesus and Judaism* (London: SCM Press, 1985).

Sanders, J.T., *The Jews in Luke–Acts* (London: SCM Press, 1987).

Sandmel, S., *Philo of Alexandria* (New York: Oxford University Press, 1979).

Scherrer, S.J., 'Signs and Wonders in the Imperial Cult: A New Look at a Roman Institution in the Light of Revelation 13:13-15', *JBL* 103.4 (1984), pp. 599-610.

Schmid, J., *The Gospel According to Mark* (RNT; Cork: Mercer, 1968).

Schnider, F., 'Ausschliessen und ausgeschlossen werden: Beobachtungen zur Struktur des Gleichnisse vom Pharisäer und Zöllner Lk 18, 10-14a', *BZ* 24 (1980), pp. 42-56.

Schoedel, W.R., *Ignatius* (Hermeneia; Philadelphia: Fortress Press, 1985).

Schottroff, L., 'Die Erzählung vom Pharisäer und Zöllner als Beispiel für die theologische Kunst des Überredens', in H. Betz and L. Schottroff (eds.), *Neues Testament und christliche Existenz* (Festschrift H. Braun; Tübingen: Mohr-Siebeck, 1973), pp. 439-61.

Schüssler Fiorenza, E., *In Memory of Her* (London: SCM Press, 1983).

Schweitzer, A., *The Quest of the Historical Jesus* (ET; London: A. & C. Black, 3rd edn, 1954).

Schweizer, E., *The Good News According to Mark* (London: SPCK, 1967).

Scott, B.B., *Hear Then the Parable* (Minneapolis: Fortress Press, 1989).

Scott, J.M., 'Paul's Use of Deuteronomic Tradition', *JBL* 112.4 (1993), pp. 645-65.

—'Exile and the Self-understanding of Diaspora Jews in the Greco-Roman Period', in J.M. Scott (ed.), *Exile*, pp. 178-218.

Scott, J.M. (ed.), *Exile: Old Testament, Jewish and Christian Conceptions* (Leiden: E.J. Brill, 1997).

Searle, J.R., *Speech Acts: An Essay in the Philosophy of Language* (Cambridge: Cambridge University Press, 1969).

Sedley, D., 'The Motivations of Greek Scepticism', in Bunyeat (ed.), *The Sceptical Tradition*, pp. 14-21.

Seeley, D., 'Jesus and the Cynics: A Response to Hans Dieter Betz', *JHC* 3.2 (1996), pp. 284-90.

—'Jesus and the Cynics Revisited', *JBL* 116.4 (1997), pp. 704-12.

Segal, A., *Two Powers in Heaven* (Leiden: E.J. Brill, 1977).

Segal, C., *Lucretius on Death and Anxiety* (New Jersey: Princeton University Press, 1990).

Sera, G. Roca, *Censorinus: Le jour natal* (Paris: Vrin, 1980).

Sherwin-White, A.N., *The Letters of Pliny* (Oxford: Clarendon Press, 1966).

Skorupski, J., 'Relativity, Realism and Consensus', *Philosophy* 60 (1985), pp. 341-58.

Smedes, L.B., *Forgive and Forget: Healing the Hurts We Don't Deserve* (New York: Harper & Row, 1984).

Smith, M.F., 'Thirteen New Fragments of Diogenes of Oenoanda', *Ergänzungbände zu den Tituli Asiae Minoris* 6 (1974), pp. 21-27.

Smith-Christopher, D.L., 'Reassessing the Historical and Sociological Impact of the Babylonian Exile (597/587–539 BCE)', in Scott (ed.), *Exile*, pp. 17-21.

Solmsen, F., 'Epicurus on the Growth and Decline of the Cosmos', *AJP* 74 (1953), pp. 34-51.

—*Aristotle's System of the Physical World* (Cornell Studies in Classical Philology; Cornell: Cornell University Press, 1960).

Steck, O.H., *Israel und das gewaltsame Geschick der Propheten: Untersuchungen zur Überlieferung des deuteronomistischen Geschichtsbildes im Alten Testament, Spätjudentum und Urchristentum* (WMANT, 23; Neukirchen-Vluyn: Neukirchener Verlag, 1967).

—'Das Problem theologischer Strömungen in nachexilischer Zeit', *EvT* 28 (1968), pp. 445-58.

Stendahl, K., *Paul among Jews and Gentiles and other Essays* (Philadelphia: Fortress Press, 1976).

Stock, A., 'Jesus and the Lady from Tyre: Encounter in the Border District', *Emmanuel* 93 (1987), pp. 336-39.

Streeter, B.H., *The Four Gospels: A Study in Origins* (London: Macmillan, 1924).

Sugirtharajah, R.S., 'The Syropoenician Woman', *Exp.Tim* 98 (1986), pp. 13-15.

Swete, H.B., *The Gospel According to St. Mark* (London: Macmillan , 3rd edn, 1953).

Swinburne, R., *Responsibility and Atonement* (Oxford: Clarendon Press, 1989).

Tajfel, H. (ed.), *Social Identity and Intergroup Relations* (Cambridge: Cambridge University Press, 1982).

Talmon, S., 'Waiting for the Messiah: The Spiritual World of the Qumran Covenanters', in Neusner *et al* (eds.), *Judaisms*, pp. 111-37.

Taylor, C., *Sources of the Self: The Making of Modern Identity* (Cambridge: Cambridge University Press, 1989).

Taylor, V., *The Gospel According to St. Mark* (London: Macmillan, 1953).

Thackeray, W.M., *The Virginians* (Collins Library of Classics; London: Collins, n.d. [1859]).

Thérasse, J., 'Croyances et crédulité des Romains d'àprès Pline l'Ancien et les écrivains latins', in Caron *et al.* (eds.), *Mélanges d'études anciennes,* pp. 283-319.

Theissen, G., *Miracle Stories of the Early Christian Tradition* (ET; Edinburgh: T. & T. Clark, 1983).

—*Lokalkolorit und Zeitgeschichte in den Evangelien* (NTOA, 8; Göttingen: Vandenhoeck & Ruprecht, 1989).

Thompson, T.L., 'The Exile in History and Myth: A Response to Hans Barstad', in Grabbe (ed.), *Leading Captivity Captive*, pp. 101-18.

Tilborg, S. van, *Imaginative Love in John* (BIS, 2; Leiden: E.J. Brill, 1993).

Tuckett, C.M., 'A Cynic Q?' *Bib.* 70.2 (1989), pp. 349-76.

Tuckett, C.M. (ed.), *Luke's Literary Achievement* (JSNTSup, 116; Sheffield: Sheffield Academic Press, 1995).

Unnik, W.C. van, *Das Selbstverständnis der jüdischen Diaspora in der hellenistisch-römischen Zeit* (AGJU; Leiden: E.J. Brill, 1993).

Vaage, L., 'The Ethos and Ethics of an Itinerant Intelligence' (PhD thesis, Claremont Graduate School, California, 1987).

VanderKam, J.C., *Textual and Historical Studies in the Book of Jubilees* (Harvard Semitic Monograph, 14; Missoula, MT: Scholars Press, 1977).

Vermassaren, H.J. (ed.), *Studies in Hellenistic Religion* (Leiden: E.J. Brill, 1979).

Vermes, G., *Jesus the Jew* (London: Collins, 1973).

Veyne, P., 'The Roman Empire', in *idem* (ed.), *A History of Private Life.* I. *From Pagan Rome to Byzantium* (Cambridge, MA: Belknapp/Harvard University Press, 1987), pp. 37-45.

—*Les grecs, ont-ils cru à leurs mythes?* (Paris: Editions du Seuil, 1983); ET, *Did the Greeks Believe their Myths?* (Chicago: University of Chicago Press, 1988).

Vidal-Naquet, P., 'Plato's Myth of the Statesman, the Ambiguities of the Golden Age and of History', *JHS* 98 (1978), pp. 132-41.

Visgotsky, B.L., 'Overturning the lamp', *JJS* 28 (1987), pp. 72-80.

Vollenweider, S., *Freiheit als neue Schöpfung* (Göttingen: Vandenhoeck & Ruprecht, 1989).

Waerden, B.L. van der, 'The Great Year in Greek, Persian and Hindu Astronomy', *AHES* 18 (1977/78), pp. 359-83.

Walsh, J.W., 'On Christian Atheism', *VC* 45 (1991), pp. 255-77.

Weber, H.-R., *The Child and the Church* (Geneva: WCC, 1978).

Wellhausen, J., *Das Evangelium Marci* (Berlin: Georg Reimer, 1903).

Werner, M., *Die Entstehung des christlichen Dogmas* (Bern: Peter Lang, 1941); ET, *The Formation of Christian Dogma* (London: A. & C. Black, 1957).

Whittaker, J., 'Christian Morality in the Roman Empire', *VC* 33 (1979), pp. 209-25.

Whittaker, M., *Jews and Christians: Graeco-Roman Views* (CCWJC, 6; Cambridge: Cambridge University Press, 1984).

Wilckens, U., *Der brief an die Römer* (EKKNT, 6.2; Zürich: Benziger Verlag, 1980).

Wildhaber, B., *Paganisme populaire et prédication apostolique* (Geneva: Labor et Fides, 1987).

Wilken, R.L., 'Towards a Social Interpretation of Early Christian Apologetics', *CH* 39 (1970), pp. 437-58.

—'The Christians as the Romans and Greeks Saw Them', in Sanders (ed.), *Jewish and Christian Self-Definition*, pp. 100-25.

—*The Christians as the Romans Saw Them* (New Haven: Yale University Press, 1984).

Williamson, R., *Jews in the Hellenistic World: Philo* (Cambridge, Cambridge University Press, 1989).

Wilson, B. (ed.), *Rationality* (Oxford: Basil Blackwell, 1970).

Winch, P., *The Idea of a Social Science* (London: Routledge, 1958).

Winston, D., *Logos and Mystical Theology in Philo of Alexandria* (Cincinnati: Hebrew Union College Press, 1985).

Witherington, B., *Jesus the Sage: The Pilgrimage of Wisdom* (Minneapolis: Fortress Press, 1994).

Wolfson, H.A., *Philo: Foundations of Religious Thought in Judaism, Christianity and Islam*, I (2 vols.; Cambridge, MA: Harvard University Press, 1947).

Wright, N.T., *The New Testament and the People of God* (London: SPCK, 1992).

—*Jesus and the Victory of God* (London: SPCK, 1996).

Yamauchi, E., *The World of the First Christians* (London: Lion, 1981).

Zeller, E., *Die Philosophie der Griechen*, III.1 (Leipzig: Reisland, 1923).

INDEXES

INDEX OF REFERENCES

OLD TESTAMENT

CLASSICAL AUTHORS

Dermience, A. 102
Derrett, J.D.M. 102
Derrida, J. 207
deSilva, D.A. 20, 21, 23, 26, 29, 31-33, 36
Dey, L.K.K. 190, 194, 201, 203
Dill, S. 56
Dodds, E.R. 209
Dorandi, T. 138
Dorival, G. 132, 142, 146, 183
Douglas, M. 110
Downing, F.G. 14-18, 22, 26, 27, 36, 39, 41, 47, 48, 50, 66, 73, 79, 80, 83, 113, 114, 115, 119, 122-24, 126-30, 132, 133, 139, 143, 144, 146, 174, 183, 186, 206, 212, 215, 219, 220, 223, 229-31, 234, 235
Drake, K. 78
Drummond, J. 189, 190
Drury, J. 91
Dungan, D.L. 225, 227
Dunn, J.D.G. 70, 74, 142, 148, 170, 188, 189, 193, 198, 203-206

Ebner, M. 123, 124
Eddy, P.R. 122-27, 129, 130, 132, 133
Eisen, U.E. 25
Elliott, J.H. 208, 210
Ellis, E.E. 78
Engberg-Pedersen. T. 36
Ernout, A. 208, 212, 217
Esler, P.F. 20, 22, 24, 29, 43, 45, 46
Evans, C.A. 155, 163, 164, 166

Fander, M. 102, 105, 106
Farandos, G.D. 190
Feldman, L.H. 161
Ferguson, E. 209, 225
Festugière, A.-J. 179
Feuillet, A. 78
Fiedler, P. 91, 93
Fischel, H.A. 129
Foucault, M. 74, 75
Fox, R.L. 172
Fredriksen, P. 185
Frend, W.H.C. 136, 143-45
Freyne, S. 38, 92, 226
Funke, H. 128

Gafni, I.M. 154, 160
Garbini, G. 151
Garnet, P. 159

Geertz, C. 45, 57
Georgi, D. 170, 179, 184
Giannantoni, G. 128
Gilbert, W.S. 220
Glad, C.E. 59
Glasson, T.F. 170, 183, 186
Glen, J.S. 99
Goldstein, J.A. 149
Goodenough, E.R. 189, 193, 196
Goodman, M. 132
Görgemanns, H. 202
Goulder, M.D. 79, 91, 98, 99
Goulet-Caz,, M.-O. 85, 113, 118, 123, 125, 138, 140, 146
Grabbe, L.L. 151, 152
Graf, F. 209, 218, 222
Grant, R.M. 136, 141
Green, W.M. 174

Hafemann, S.J. 166
Halpern-Amaru, B. 154, 158, 159
Hampton, J. 69, 72, 75
Hanfling, O. 223
Hanson, J.S. 38, 164
Hanson, P.D. 153
Harré, R. 45-47, 52, 57, 60
Harrill, J.A. 38
Harrison, K.C. 40
Harrisville, R.A. 102
Harvey, A.E. 149
Heinrichs, A. 136, 141, 143
Hellholm, D. 170
Hendrickx, H. 78, 80, 91, 99
Herzfeld, M. 23
Herzog, W.R. 66, 79
Hezser, C. 129
Hicks, R.D. 137
Hock, R.F. 53, 104, 123, 124, 129, 141, 228
Hoïstad, R. 138, 139
Hollis, M. 224
Horsley, R.A. 38, 164, 226
Houlden, L. 235
Hoven, R. 173
Hull, J.M. 209, 219
Hurtado, L.W. 189, 190, 207

Ito, A. 167

Janssen, L.F. 142
Jeremias, J. 87, 93, 95
Johnson, L.T. 140

Russell, B. 208
Ryle, G. 61

Sanders, E.P. 63, 70, 91, 95
Sanders, J.T. 91
Sandmel, S. 189
Scherrer, S.J. 209, 219
Schilling, E. 169
Schilling, R. 173
Schlatter, A. 78
Schmid, J. 102, 110-12, 114
Schneider, J. 21
Schnider, F. 80, 83, 91, 99
Schoedel, W.R. 221
Schottroff, L. 79, 82-84, 90, 91, 94, 96,
    98
Schüssler Fiorenza, E. 102, 106, 112
Schwabl, H. 182, 184
Schweitzer, A. 223
Schweizer, E. 103, 109
Scott, B.B. 66, 78, 85, 91, 92, 95, 97,
    100, 129
Scott, J.M. 159, 160, 162-64, 167
Searle, J.R. 105
Sedlcy, D. 216
Seeley, D. 122, 131
Segal, A. 205, 207
Segal, C. 174
Shogren, G.S. 62, 65, 70
Simon, M. 175
Skorupski, J. 224
Smedes, L.B. 64
Smith, M.F. 183
Smith-Christopher, D.L. 151
Solmsen, F. 174
Ste Croix, G.E.M. de 38
Steck, O.H. 167
Stein, R.S. 78
Stendahl, K. 60
Stock, A. 103
Streeter, B.H. 103
Sugirtharajah, R.S. 103
Swete, H.B. 103, 110
Swinburne, R. 77

Tajfel, H. 45
Talmon, S. 149

Taylor, C. 46, 57, 58, 60
Taylor, V. 103, 109, 111, 112, 114
Thackeray, W.M. 64
Theissen, G. 103, 105, 108, 110-12, 115,
    226
Thérasse, J. 208, 209, 221
Thompson, T.L. 152
Tiede, D.L. 78
Tilborg, S. van 53
Tuckett, C.M. 122

Unnik, W.C. van 160, 162

Vaage, L. 122, 183
VanderKam, J.C. 156-58, 160
Vermes, G. 92, 114
Veyne, P. 55, 217, 218, 222
Via, D.O. 78
Vidal-Naquet, P. 182
Visgotsky, B.L. 143
Vollenweider, S. 123

Waerden, B.L. van der 184
Walsh, J.W. 141
Walzer, R. 145
Weber, H.-R. 48
Wellhausen, J. 103, 108-10
Werner, M. 142, 171, 185
Whittaker, J. 134
Whittaker, M. 209
Wilckens, U. 181
Wildhaber, B. 209, 220
Wilken, R.N. 78, 136, 137, 141, 142, 145
Wilkin, R.L. 134, 136
Williamson, R. 190, 207
Wilson, B. 224
Wilson, S.G. 142
Winch, P. 223
Winston, D. 190, 199, 200, 202
Wintermute, O.S. 158
Witherington, B. 122, 130, 132
Wolfson, H.A. 190, 193, 196
Wright, N.T. 148, 149, 166-68, 187

Yamauchi, E. 225

Zeller, E. 173

INDEX OF SUBJECTS